WHY FRANCE FELL

WHY
FRANCE
FELL

The Defeat of the French Army in 1940

BY GUY CHAPMAN

HOLT, RINEHART AND WINSTON
NEW YORK   CHICAGO   SAN FRANCISCO

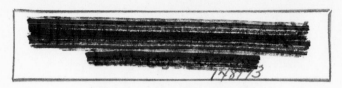

LIBRARY OF CONGRESS CATALOG CARD NUMBER: 69-10229

FIRST PUBLISHED IN THE UNITED STATES, FEBRUARY 1969

SBN: 03-072490-2

PRINTED IN THE UNITED STATES OF AMERICA

CONTENTS

MAPS

PREFACE

THE following pages are concerned with the defeat of the French Army in 1940. They are not concerned with the armies of the Netherlands, Belgium, or the British Commonwealth. These of course appear, but only in their relation to the French forces.

On 25 June 1940, the French Army (with the exception of a few divisions facing the Italians) had been to all military purposes annihilated, reduced to three dislocated fragments. This wholesale destruction, which involved also the Allied armies, had been accomplished in slightly over six weeks. It is the purpose of the following pages to try to determine the reasons for this *chambardement*. At the time the British, whose army had left the field, were inclined to attribute the defeat to the French moral corruption, the British themselves being naturally untainted. Frenchmen, among them Daladier, said that the infantry soldiers were not those of 1914. All this of course was nonsense. The reasons for the defeat were deeper rooted and more complex than these simple critics knew.

Once, after 1918, answering a somewhat fatuous questioner who asked who had won the battle of the Marne, Marshal Joffre replied that he did not know, but that, had the battle been lost, the commander responsible for the disaster would have been called Joffre. All over the world there are statues of men who have been hailed as victors in this, that, or the other war, and no doubt, overwhelmed with the adulation, each has come to believe it. Like the general invented by Mr Dooley, he says, at least to himself: 'Obsarve my supayrior jaynius, I meant it to come so.' Much praise has rightly been showered on Generals Guderian and Rommel for their startling successes in these weeks. Both had taken swift advantage of chances that were offered them. But why were they offered such advantages, not only once but again and again ? No one had foreseen such a cataclysm.

The answer is not simple. Of the defeat of 1870, the Germans said that the French armies were dedicated to defeat. The same might be said of those of 1940, since the seeds of defeat were sown even in the hour of victory in 1918. Though, in 1940, personalities play a large part in the drama, they were under the influence of much that had happened during the previous twenty years. I have tried to follow out the various clues that run to the final calamity. '*Le dernier acte est sanglant.*'

The elucidation is in three parts. The first covers the years 1919–39, and deals with the influences which hampered the reconstruction of the French Army and led to numerous errors. The second deals with the *drôle de guerre* between September 1939 and May 1940. The third and longest narrates the fighting, between 10 May and 25 June, of the

French armies. It concentrates on the soldiers, and the details of the battles, first up to the end of the evacuation from Dunkirk, then on the fighting from the opening of the second stage of the German attack, *Fall Rot*, to the last days.

I have omitted as far as is possible the repeated, acrimonious and futile wrangles of politicians and generals that accompanied the gradual destruction of the armies. After 18 May the defeat of the Allies was not to be conjured, and the conversations of Reynaud with Churchill, with the two-minded French cabinet, with an importunate de Gaulle and a Pétain over-persuaded of his capabilities, with the deceived and outraged Weygand, are of less moment than the words of the chorus that accompany the slaying of Agamemnon.

Much of what happened has been overlaid by the personal narratives of the politicians and the political soldiery. Most of them are devoted to denigrating those with whom they disagreed. Some years ago, the military historian, Captain E. W. Sheppard, wrote that there is a tendency among students of the history of war towards sweeping generalizations, and to showing generals either as superhuman geniuses or congenital idiots. 'The latter genus is really an uncommon one . . . and behind even what seems to our eyes the most foolish of operations, there may usually be discovered some plausible and often quite sensible motive, if we will investigate the matter diligently enough.' Too much malice has been shown against some generals, too much flattery to others. I hope to have corrected the balance.

But for the episode of the garrisons of the Maginot Line forts, I have not carried the narrative beyond 25 June. I have therefore not dealt with the exchanges between General Weygand and General Noguès on the question of North Africa. They are primarily political.

And I have eschewed speculation as to what might have happened if . . .

> *Hélas! La Palice est mort,*
> *Il est mort devant Pavie.*
> *Hélas! s'il n'était pas mort,*
> *Il serait encore en vie.*

Theseus Never excuse; for when the players are all dead, then need none be blamed.

A Midsummer Night's Dream

PART ONE

The Withered Laurels

1 THE QUAVERING HANDS

THE defeat of France in 1940 began twenty years earlier, in the years immediately following the First World War. In 1919 the French were battered, worn, plundered and frustrated. A million and a half Frenchmen had been killed. Another 300,000 were permanently disabled. As in every belligerent country, the educated classes had suffered proportionately worst, while the peasantry, that is to say the most unchanged, the most backward element, had suffered proportionately least. Ten departments had been fought over. In these, many towns and villages were in ruins. Mines had been sabotaged; factories plundered of machinery, where it had not been destroyed. A strip of land not less than twenty-five miles wide, some of the most productive arable in France, had been torn, flayed and devastated from Houplines to the Swiss frontier. Animals had been killed or driven off. With the signature of the Treaty of Versailles in June 1919, the nation could turn to reconstruction. But with reservations. At the Paris Conference, the intention of the French delegation had been to obtain reparation in the present and security in the future. To meet the second demand, Germany, under Articles 42, 43 and 44 of the treaty, was largely disarmed, her land forces reduced to a small long-service professional army without armour or heavy weapons, while the east bank of the Rhine, to a depth of fifty kilometres, was to be permanently demilitarized. On the eastern frontier of Germany, the succession states, Poland and Czechoslovakia, had as big a stake as France in German military impotence. So too had Belgium. Finally, Lorraine had been recovered, together with Alsace and its nationally indeterminate and indigestible natives. As compensation for the flooding and looting of the Pas-de-Calais coal-mines, the French were granted the right to reparation from the Saar coal-field for fifteen years, during which the territory was to be administered under the League of Nations: at the end of the period a plebiscite was to be held to decide whether the Saar should be annexed to France in perpetuity or returned to Germany.

The pledge for the fulfilment of the treaty obligations was the occupation of the left bank of the Rhine by the Allies, together with three bridgeheads across the river, held by the French with headquarters in Mainz, the Americans with headquarters at Koblenz and by the British with theirs at Cologne. The Belgians did not cross the river.

The problem of French (and Belgian) security roused fierce controversy within military circles. From November 1918 Foch had urged on the Allies that the only line defensible by the comparatively weak populations of France and Belgium was that of the Rhine along its 600 miles from Rotterdam to Basle. The same thesis was held by Clemenceau up to the date when he secured from Lloyd George and a reluctant President Wilson the promise of an Anglo-American guarantee to come to the aid of France should the Germans infringe Articles 42-4 of the Treaty by moving troops into the demilitarized zone. To this Foch retorted that it was far from certain that the guarantee would be ratified by the American Senate, and that for his part the bone was preferable to the reflection. In any case there was no certainty that help from either ally would arrive in time.

Emmanuel Berl said of the Tiger: 'From the moment he felt a resistance, he scented treachery.' Thereafter he and Foch were not on speaking terms. Yet as Poincaré said at the reception of the Marshal at the Academy in February 1920: 'It was not your task to make peace. Nevertheless, yours was the right to say what, according to you, should be for the better prevention of war. . . . Let us hope that the world will never have to repent that it was not wholly inspired by your opinions.' As indeed happened. The American Senate rejected the treaty, and an Anglo-French attempt at a compromise blew up over French distrust of Briand. To the relief of the British, it was assumed that everything could be left to the scarcely fledged League of Nations.

On the other hand, Clemenceau had succeeded in imposing Foch as Commander-in-Chief of the Allied Forces in Germany, and later as overseer of the compliance of the German government with the disarmament clauses of the treaty.

This solution of the problem was only temporary. For the permanent security of France, there must be reconstruction of the defences and reorganization of the army. Clemenceau's personal military assistant, General Mordacq, had given much thought during 1919 to the future, and particularly to the structure of the Army Council (*Conseil Supérieur de la Guerre*) on the resumption of peace.

In 1917 (law of 17 April), it had been laid down that divisional generals should be retired at sixty-two and brigadier-generals at fifty-eight, and Clemenceau had used his authority to retire officers at even earlier ages, in spite of the protests of both Foch and Pétain. All these emergency decrees and regulations were due to vanish as soon as the treaty was ratified. Hence, in the latter half of 1919, the definition of the army system became urgent. But whereas Clemenceau, with Mordacq, had in mind an army of young, prescient and energetic soldiers—they seriously considered an organization similar to the British system of linked battalions at home and overseas, to replace the soul-destroying system of routine duties in small provincial garrison towns—Pétain and his entourage had other views. The proposal they put forward, says Mordacq, 'staggered me. It was neither more nor less than the monopoly of the rue St Dominique by the Vice-President [Pétain] of the Army Council.'* The Minister of War would become a cipher and the staff

---

* The Ministry of War is at 3 rue St Dominique, Paris 7. The Minister of War is *ex officio* the President of the Army Council. The Vice-President was

and the directorates would fall into the hands of the senior professional. Clemenceau, old anti-militarist radical, would have none of this, but, involved as he was in many more urgent matters, he lent only half an ear to Mordacq, no doubt expecting to deal with the matter when he succeeded Poincaré at the Élysée Palace.

He was not elected, and a few days after Deschanel's assumption of office, the decrees on the organization of the Army Council appeared. These killed Mordacq's sensible and forward-looking schemes. He and Clemenceau had looked to the creation of a small body, with perhaps the three marshals, Joffre, Foch and Pétain, alternating as chairmen with merely advisory roles, and seven or eight youngish generals, of whom half would return to commands each year. The decree of 23 January 1919 created a body consisting of the Marshals of France as life members, shortly to be joined by Fayolle, Franchet d'Esperey and Lyautey, generals of high reputation retained beyond the age-limit, and ten (later twelve) divisional generals, including the Chief of the General Staff. All had a right to vote. These would be appointed by decree at the beginning of each year. They were to be selected from men who had commanded an army corps during at least a year and were considered capable of commanding an army or an army group on mobilization. The future Commander-in-Chief designate would be Vice-President and also inspector of troops, services and schools, and he would appoint the other inspectors. The Vice-President would be Pétain.

'It was,' wrote Mordacq, 'the complete negation of every lesson of the war. It became a true Aulic Council of which the membership would be increased each month and end in reaching a figure so high that one could no longer make oneself heard.'

It did indeed reach a point at which the Minister of War gave up consulting it except as a formality. Inside the War Office the old anarchy prevailed and each directorate became a law to itself. 'Since 1920, ministers come and go, but the anarchy remains and the *new army* still awaits its charter. . . . On it [the Army Council] were to be seen far too many men who had been *limogés* and symbolized too much the ideas of the pre-war army. . . . In any case, it is a verifiable fact that many too many of the newly appointed members were far from possessing the confidence of military circles.'[1]

Further, there was a return to the practice of the years before Joffre. In 1911, the offices of Vice-President of the Army Council and Chief of the General Staff had been united in the person of the man who later became Commander-in-Chief. In 1920, Pétain, as Vice-President and Inspector-General of the Army, refused the appointment of Chief of the General Staff. Foch sent his right-hand man, General Maxime Weygand, to ask him not to divide the offices, which would mean a disastrous division of authority. Pétain replied disdainfully: 'Do you

---

also Inspector-General of the Army and Commander-in-Chief designate in the event of war.

seriously think that I would wait on the minister every day when he signs his letters ?'

Mordacq's animadversions against the new council had some justification. Of the fourteen members of 1920, five were Marshals of France. Foch and Joffre were both seventy, Fayolle was sixty-seven, Pétain sixty-five and Franchet d'Esperey sixty-four. Of the other nine, the youngest was fifty-four. None could be described as innovators. The Chief of Staff was General E. A. L. Buat, who in spite of political hostility—he had been *chef de cabinet* to Millerand in 1914–15—had made a highly successful career: after commanding an army, he had been appointed Major-Général, Chief of Staff to Pétain and was, it is said, the organizer of the counter-attacks of July 1918, which had begun the German rout. His influence on Pétain was one of pressure, and it is probable that the cynical, cautious, now ageing military dandy, who had always recognized that soldiering is a dangerous trade—*le feu tue*— valued a subordinate who drove him.

But Buat died comparatively young—he was fifty-three—in December 1923. In his place Pétain appointed General Marie-Eugène Debeney, now fifty-nine, as Chief of the General Staff. Debeney's career had differed little from that of the normal successful soldier who had not served in the colonies and had never put a foot wrong—*chasseur-à-pied* subaltern, staff captain in a good army corps, orderly officer to General Hagron (who in 1907 resigned from the Vice-Presidency of the Army Council when the government gave way over the Two Year Service law and left the Commander-in-Chief without an adequate army to meet war), professor at the Staff College, assistant and then chief of staff to an army in 1914, then to an army group, followed by command of a division in May 1915; a corps in the following April, an army in December, Major-Général to Pétain after the Chemin-des-Dames disaster of May 1917, and finally in December command of the First Army next on the right of the British until the end of the war. With the British his reputation was one of soundness over-tempered with caution. In the reorganization of 1920 he had been appointed Commandant of the École Supérieure de Guerre and of the Centre des Hautes Études Militaires, the super-staff college invented just before the war by Foch as a finishing-school for the brightest regimental officers, colonels and lieutenant-colonels, to learn the esoteric side of war. Perhaps in consequence of a bad digestion, which condemned him to a permanent diet of pasta and toast, he was a born pessimist.[2] His army-group commander in 1918, Fayolle, thought him crabbed, grumpy, tortuous and a complicator. General Serrigny* said that, in 1917, Debeney allowed himself such intemperate language to visiting politicians that more than once Pétain was asked for his head.

---

* Of General Bernard Serrigny, who was his personal assistant for nearly three years, Pétain said: 'He was my imagination.'

[2]

In 1914, the structure of the French Army had been based on the army-corps formation of two active infantry divisions, together with corps troops, infantry, cavalry and artillery. The infantry amounted to 28,000, with 120 75-mm. field guns. The twenty-one corps were numbered I-XVIII, XX, XXI and Colonial, with forty-six infantry divisions. In addition, there were ·two North African (Algerian and Tunisian) divisions, nominally of XIX Corps, whose headquarters remained in Algiers, a Moroccan division, twenty-five French reserve divisions, twelve territorial divisions, and a number of unincorporated brigades and regiments. It moved either by rail or on foot. It was clumsy and slow.

By the end of 1918, the structure had been transformed. This had begun during the first half of 1915, largely due to the heavy casualties, but the transformation was not completed until a few months before the armistice. By this time, the original distinction between active and reserve divisions and units had disappeared, and the territorial divisions had been disbanded. The corps was no longer a permanent formation, though a few still had nominally their original two divisions. Corps troops had disappeared. The active infantry division, which in 1914 had two brigades each of two regiments of three battalions, was now reduced to three infantry regiments with nine battalions in place of twelve. In 1914, divisional infantry numbered 12,000; in 1918, it was closer to 5,000. Though it still had three groups of three four-gun batteries of 75-mm., the former corps artillery was now withdrawn into the General Artillery Reserve. The original sixty-two artillery regiments had become 148, the 3,400 field guns of 1914 were now 6,200, and the 230 heavy pieces had increased to 6,800. There were also 2,200 trench-mortars. The cavalry divisions had been reduced from ten to six, and six *cuirassier* regiments had been converted to infantry. Finally, there had appeared the *artillerie d'assaut*, otherwise *chars d'assaut*, *anglice*, 'tanks'.

In 1914, excluding the territorial divisions, a few of which had indeed been occasionally employed in battle, there were rather more than a million infantrymen. By August 1918, this figure had been reduced by half. In August 1914 there had been seventy-two infantry divisions; in August 1918 there were 103 with another ten in Italy or Macedonia. The independent infantry division was the standard formation.

These reductions made the French Army far more flexible. The small division, now about the size of a 1914 brigade, but with the fire power (due to the provision of the *fusil-mitrailleuse*, the light machine-gun, and the light mortar) of a division, could be moved and administered far more easily than the 1914 brigade.

All this, equipment and much more, was now obviously extravagant *vis-à-vis* a Germany reduced to naval and military powerlessness with a long-service army of 100,000 soldiers of all ranks, a prohibition on the possession and manufacture of heavy guns, tanks and military aircraft, a demilitarized zone, and allies of France on its eastern frontier. Demobilization was carried out, and the Army of Occupation formed largely of professional soldiers and the new classes of conscripts of 1919 and 1920.*

As early as 1920, Pétain had spoken publicly of the probability of one-year service. In the meantime, from April 1923, the period was reduced to eighteen months. In all arms many regiments were not only disbanded but abolished, and the whole system of the past profoundly modified. The former 173 infantry regiments were reduced to sixty-five, though all except one of the thirty-one *chasseurs* (*à-pied* or *alpins*) were retained, and the four zouave regiments increased to six. All the reserve regiments were abolished. In future, on mobilization, reservists were to report not to regimental depots but to their mobilization centre, from which new units would emerge. To compensate for the disappearance of 113 infantry regiments, there were now thirteen machine-gun battalions. Further, the number of North African regiments of enlisted natives of Morocco, Algeria and Tunisia was greatly increased, as were those of Senegal and other imperial domains.† A number of these regiments of extra-European origin were to be stationed in France.

---

* The Rhine Army was six divisions strong, some 97,000. Behind it six more divisions occupied the former frontier districts and the recovered departments, with headquarters in Metz, Besançon and Strasbourg.

† Zouaves were based on Algeria and Tunisia, but were white conscripts in contrast to the *tirailleurs* from North Africa, who were enlisted professional native soldiers with a white cadre.

2 THE RETURN TO THE MIDDLE AGES

THE failure to extract the expected reparations from Germany, and the occupation of the Ruhr in 1923, followed by the collapse of the mark, prefaced the Dawes agreement on reparations and the Locarno treaties. The French financial difficulties of 1926 ended in the return of Poincaré to power with what amounted to a government based on the centre groups in the Chamber. This, with a devalued but stable franc, produced three years of political neutrality during which the systematization of the French defence was undertaken.

The intense natural pacifism of the French people was reinforced by the experience of 1914–18 and materialized in the 'pacification' (*apaisement*) policies of Briand.* Controversies and myths about the conduct of the war continued to mature and fester in people's minds. These had begun almost before the victorious armies had occupied the Rhine bridgeheads, and continued through a number of years. There were considered attacks on the École Supérieure de Guerre. On the incitation of a right-wing deputy, a parliamentary committee inquired into the evacuation of the Briey iron-ore basin in 1914, which gave every senior officer with a grievance the opportunity to vent it in public.† There were quarrels between Mangin and Painlevé over the Chemin-des-Dames battle of 1917. There were the grievances of General Sarrail, the pet of the Radicals. There was bitter criticism of Joffre for the failure of the attacks at Charleroi, in the Ardennes and in Alsace in August 1914.

All these somewhat facile examinations of unsuccessful combats, coupled with the desire to unmask *responsibles* or find scapegoats, encouraged the belief that in battle the offensive was bad in itself, instead of establishing the reality, that the armies had been badly trained and badly engaged. With this was coupled another belief that in the course of four years of war, the French front, in spite of deep withdrawals, had never been broken. This was elevated to the position of a dogma, the creed of the 'inviolable front'.[1] The obvious breaks of 1918, from which the allied divisions escaped only owing to the inability of the enemy to follow up fast enough, were ignored.

In October 1921, a committee headed by Marshal Pétain published provisional regulations for the tactical handling of formations (*grandes unités*), which were based on a small brochure (known to the army as the

---

* The dangerous English habit of adapting French words and falsifying their meaning is exemplified by translating *apaisement* as *appeasement*.

† It was only the fiftieth witness, the Secretary-General of the Comité des Forges, who reduced the question to sensible proportions by revealing that the Briey ores, though plentiful, were not very important since they were unsuited to either gun founding or shell manufacture.

bouquin rouge) issued under Pétain's auspices after the mutinies of 1917. The committee was composed of senior officers, among whom were several cavalrymen. There was no officer from the tank corps and none from the air force, which at this date was still a branch of the army. The main point of the *bouquin rouge* was the suppression of the thesis which had appeared in the 1913 field service regulations that the offensive alone produced decisive results. This omission was repeated in the new edition. The references to armoured vehicles laid down that they were 'intended to augment the offensive power of the infantry'.

This leaning towards the defensive acquired a further respectability in that Germany could take no hostile steps against France and that any hint of a change in this situation could be met with full diplomatic pressure before it became dangerous.*

[2]

The laws for the reconstruction of the army went through a long period of gestation. The first draft, submitted to the Army Council in 1924, was rejected. While it reduced the length of national service to twelve months, it failed to make re-enlistment sufficiently attractive and soldiers tended to disappear into civil life the moment they were trained. The next draft was influenced by the Locarno agreements. Further, the committee was faced by the knowledge that owing to the fall in the birth-rate during the war—in 1917, the crude rate had dropped to seven per thousand—the call-up between 1935 and 1939 would be enormously reduced. In addition there were the inevitable doctrinal and electoral considerations: a general election was due to take place in 1928. As finally passed,† the three Bills reflected the pre-occupations of the politicians rather than those of the soldiers. The immediate post-war reduction in the number of units became a permanent structure. The new army was to consist of the metropolitan army, the overseas army (both white and coloured) and a white and coloured force stationed in France and North Africa. There would be a

---

* It is to be noted that throughout the last years of the war, certainly from the appointment of Pétain to command of the French armies in May 1917, there was professional jealousy and rivalry between Pétain and Foch which became more acute after Foch had overtaken Pétain by becoming commander-in-chief of the allied forces in March 1918. Much of this is to be read in Marshal Fayolle's *Cahiers secrets*, in which he set down his criticisms of the over-offensive activity of Foch, with its unnecessary casualties and the lethargic cautiousness of Pétain, who could finish off nothing. This rivalry naturally permeated the staffs of both generals. Up to the death of Foch, and indeed up to that of Joffre eighteen months later, that is in the first post-war decade, the subterranean hostility continued. This is reflected in the appointment of Weygand, first as Foch's representative in Poland, followed by the command in Syria and on his return to France to the Centre des Hautes Études Militaires, and by the seconding of Gamelin, Joffre's former personal assistant, to Brazil, and then to the command of troops in the Levant until 1930.

† 13 July 1927; 28 and 31 March 1929.

long service cadre of professional soldiers of 106,000, with a body of non-combatant 'duty-men', or *agents militaires*.

The great change from 1914 was the incorporation of 94,000 North African enlisted regulars, Algerians, Tunisians, Moroccans, and 84,000 from the other colonies, from West Africa (Senegal), Madgascar (Malgaches) and Indo-China, who were to make up for the war-loss of a million and a half. The bulk of the army would still be the conscripts, at this date 240,000; the length of service was to be twelve months, beginning with the call-up of 1929.

In 1928 there was created an Air Ministry which grouped all the air services hitherto under the ministers of Commerce, War and Marine. The minister was Laurent-Eynac, who had already held the under-secretaryship for Air. As in Great Britain, the new Air Force was now divorced from the Army, and far more interested in the technical problems of their arm than in its ultimate employment in war.

This year, 1928, was also that of the 'Kellogg Pact' outlawing war, by some considered the high point of security diplomacy, but one in which no experienced diplomat could place the smallest faith.

Army reorganization was carried through by Paul Painlevé, the mathematician, who, in spite of being Minister of War, was a pacifist as well as an extremely muddle-headed socialist, 'the most inconsistent of men'. Between Painlevé the pacifist and Pétain the sceptic, the army that emerged from the debates of 1927–8 was a mere simulacrum of an army, intended only for defence. The German army, the only possible aggressor, was at this date non-existent as an attacking force. Should, however, a German government ever begin rearmament and occupy the demilitarized zones and the Saar, the only way that this menace could be removed would be by an invasion of German territory. And for this the new French Army was neither trained nor equipped. In 1929, to meet the possible threat of a once again hostile Germany, Painlevé, this White Knight, conceived the fortification which was to be known as the Maginot Line.

Shortly after the armistice of 1918, an army committee had been set up to consider the defence works of the recovered departments. This committee had both Joffre and Pétain as members. Joffre had commended large fortified areas, Pétain the continuous line. The committee members had supported Pétain, and Joffre had resigned. Later, Pétain changed his mind and was ready to fall in with Painlevé's plans. Hence, in 1929, with the approach of the date for the final evacuation of the Rhineland (30 June 1930), the proposal to fortify the French frontier towards Germany was adopted, with the purpose of providing serious outposts against the myth originally conceived by the Quai d'Orsay in 1912, the *attaque brusquée*, in which by pressing a button the Kaiser could dispatch army corps over the frontier.

In the further belief that such defences would economize in men, the Chamber and Senate agreed to the expenditure of large sums of money, four billion francs, on permanent fortifications. In the first place, the *Comité d'organisation de la Région fortifiée* (the C.O.R.F.) prepared two groups of fortifications, one to the east, called the Région de la Lauter, running from the Rhine where it touches Haguenau Forest to a point a little west of the garrison town of Bitche; the other from Faulquemont, north-east of Metz, to north of Thionville on the high ground of the right bank of the Moselle, the Région de Metz. On the Rhine itself, from Lauterbourg to the south-eastern corner of the Hardt Forest, was to run a double line of casemates commanding the river. Finally, a strong group of casemates was planned to be built on a line facing the Belgian frontier from the Forêt de Raismes to the Forêt de Mormal.

The two Alsace sectors consisted of elaborate clusters of fortress constructions of all sizes, deep in the ground, joined by tunnels with their own store-rooms, engine-rooms, living quarters, etc., armed with guns and machine-guns of all calibres in concealed emplacements which rose and sank as required. The garrisons were teams specially trained to handle unconventional weapons. In front lay deep fields of heavy rails, strongly wired. This complex was named the Maginot Line, after the deputy for the Meuse, who as a sergeant had distinguished himself during the war and been severely wounded. The line looked formidable, but it was observed that while it appeared invincible from the front, the rear was unprotected.

In 1930, Maginot, who had been appointed Minister of War in Tardieu's government, had the Metz line prolonged to cover Thionville and the iron-fields. It was to have included the frontier iron town of Longwy, but Pétain, arguing that the position would be jeopardized by dead ground across the frontier, had the line brought back to Longuyon.* He also refused to cover the great industrial triangle Lille-Roubaix-Tourcoing. In 1932, Weygand, and with him General Gamelin, proposed a bridge-head at Montmédy and a much enlarged fortified region, Forêt de Mormal–Maubeuge–Forêt de Raismes, to cover Valenciennes and other localities in the north, including Dunkirk. This was advocated in the belief that a lightning attack on Belgium and Holland would succeed with such rapidity as to prevent the French from coming to the rescue. Pétain opposed the proposal, and forced a split in the Army Council, which convinced the government that the Army did not know its own mind. At a later meeting, Pétain's mouth-piece, Debeney, insisted that to protect the Nord department the French would have to advance into Belgium.

---

* In 1932, the northern line was stopped at the Escaut on Pétain's order. In the following year, the Montmédy bridge-head beyond Longuyon was created. In 1935, the modernization of the old frontier fortress of Maubeuge was undertaken, but this was not completed in 1939.

3 THE BAULKING OF WEYGAND

ALTHOUGH the German government subscribed to the Treaty of Versailles, at no time did the shadow German General Staff (its existence was forbidden by the treaty) accept the military terms as other than temporary. The restricted long-term professional army was conceived by von Seeckt as a cadre, a skeleton to be covered with flesh: '*Nicht ein Soldatenheer, aber ein Führerheer.*' Of this professional army more than half were officers and non-commissioned officers. That disarmament was less than half-hearted had been patent without the Control Commission's report, a veritable indictment, of February 1925. Nevertheless, the optimistic sentimentalists, Briand and Austen Chamberlain, had allowed themselves to be persuaded, as indeed they were anxious to be, by the German Chancellor Stresemann, with the consequence that the evacuation of the first occupied zone, that of Cologne, was begun in December 1925 and the end of the Military Control Commission followed in January 1927. In the following year, agreement was reached to open negotiations for an earlier evacuation of the Rhineland and a final reparations settlement. From these emerged the Young Plan, followed by the withdrawal of the last French troops in 1930. In 1928 the National Socialist Party of Adolf Hitler, with twelve deputies in the Reichstag, had not been regarded as a politically serious entity. Nor was it even in 1930, when the Nazi contingent of 107 cut a minor figure against the massed forces of the Left and Centre parties.

The Versailles Treaty, although looking forward to general disarmament, contained no concession to German rearmament, nor did any subsequent negotiation between the Allied and German governments. On the other hand, the treaty contained no provision for Allied action in case of German rearmament, while the gradual whittling down of reparations under the pressure of economic collapse and general unemployment, and the final abrogation of the Young Plan at Lausanne in July 1932, deprived the Allies of an instrument for exacting an agreement as to sanctions in the event of infringement of Articles 42–4 of the treaty. In consequence, the German government was virtually uncontrollable.

In Geneva, the Disarmament Conference dragged on without tangible result, the Germans asking that Allied armaments be reduced to their level and the French pointing out that there was no such obligation on the Allied signatories to the treaty. British public opinion, as voiced by the British press, was unsympathetic to both legal interpretations and to delay. The in-and-out running of the negotiators has little interest. The end lies in the German political background. Stresemann had died in 1929. Brüning was dismissed by Hindenburg in 1932. Governments by von Papen and General Schleicher made way for the appointment of Hitler in January 1933. By this time, it had long been obvious that no agreement on disarmament was possible between the French and German governments, whoever headed the latter. It was well known that Germany was secretly rearming as far as possible and that the training of personnel for the forbidden air force was in progress. Fruitless argument went on until, in October 1933, Germany resigned from the League of Nations.

[2]

With the passage of the laws bringing the refounded French Army into existence, Debeney, now approaching sixty-five, prepared to retire at the beginning of 1930. In the spring of 1929, his obvious successor was General Maxime Weygand, now sixty-one and still commandant of the Centre des Hautes Études Militaires. His nomination by Pétain, at the age of seventy-four still Vice-President of the Army Council and Commander-in-Chief in case of war, would no doubt have been unopposed but for the opposition of the Minister of War in Poincaré's government, Painlevé. He rejected the proposal, apparently on the grounds that Weygand was a believing and practising Catholic, who, Clemenceau had once jestingly said, would bring down the Republic. Moreover he had been military adviser to Pilsudski in 1920 when the Russian invasion was stemmed at the gates of Warsaw, a fact which stuck in Painlevé's socialist throat.* Painlevé's candidate, whoever he may have been, was obnoxious to Pétain, who would have him as his major-general on an outbreak of hostilities.

Poincaré, a sick man, resigned in July 1929, and withdrew from politics. Briand stepped into his shoes with the same cabinet. He was defeated in October, to be succeeded by André Tardieu, who appointed Maginot to the Ministry of War in place of Painlevé, who as leader of the Independent Socialists still remained an influential deputy. Negotiations between Pétain and the interested politicians eventually, in January 1930, brought about Weygand's appointment as Chief of the General Staff, simultaneously with that of General Maurice Gamelin as senior sub-chief, on the condition that Pétain remained Inspector-General and Vice-President of the Army Council. There appears to have been no reason for the objection to Weygand other than Painlevé's fanaticism. Weygand was naturally chagrined by this obvious and

---

* Flaubert, in his *Sottisier*, mocks the famous Bishop of Orléans, Dupanloup, for writing that the study of mathematics often led to the most terrifying emotional outbursts. Dupanloup is certainly justified in Painlevé, eminent mathematician. Having lived as a young man in the shadow of the Dreyfus case, he had become so bemused that he found it impossible to believe that an army officer could be a practising Catholic and a good republican, and conceived that every senior professional soldier, especially if he had a particle to his name, must be a reactionary burning to restore the monarchy.

groundless distrust, particularly since it forced on him as his closest colleague an officer whom he scarcely knew except by reputation, and who had been overseas during almost the whole of the last ten years. And Gamelin, who had only recently been given command of XX Corps at Nancy, the plum command with two crack infantry divisions, was no less annoyed. He protested vigorously at his transfer to the rue St Dominique, but, according to his own account of his interview with Pétain, he was told that his transfer was at the demand of the President of the Council, Tardieu. In any case, Pétain added, he was necessary, since Weygand had never served on the staff in peace-time and did not know the ropes: '*il ne connaît pas la maison*'.[1]

Weygand's reputation has suffered from the defeat of 1940, for which he cannot be held responsible, and from his connexion at that date with Pétain. Astier de la Vigerie has very sensibly said that Pétain became like the cat that is blamed for every household accident, and Weygand is linked with him in the memoirs of prominent politicians and others, from Reynaud's manifold apologia, from the interested criticisms of de Gaulle and from the interested efforts of the parliamentary 'Commission on the Events from 1933 to 1945',[2] sweating to justify the actions of their friends of Senate and Chamber over a number of years and condemn their rivals. Yet, in view of the abuse showered on him, Weygand's memoirs are remarkable for their restraint.

His assumption of office as Chief of the General Staff followed closely on the beginnings of the Maginot Line. His first examination of the army of 1930 revealed that, though Debeney's work had been laborious, it had shown few results, only a number of unfinished undertakings jostling each other. There was little accurate information about the planning of equipment or the numbers on mobilization. The 1927 programme, due for completion in 1935, could not be finished before 1943. The modernization of weapons had scarcely begun. The army would find itself in woeful inferiority to an up-to-date aggressor. It needed anti-aircraft and anti-tank guns, a light howitzer, field guns of increased range, signal material of modern design.

The root cause of the delays, as Mordacq had foretold, was lack of authority at the top, due to the division between the Minister, the Army Council and the General Staff. The divorce of the vice-presidency of the Army Council from the Staff gave the former the responsibility and the latter the power. In 1912, the effects of such a divorce had been clearly understood, and had led to the offices being united in Joffre.

Though Weygand was not a reactionary, as a cavalryman he had a deeper interest in his own arm. He was not hostile to mechanization, but he had only gone part of the way. He recognized the increase in speed, but not all its implications. As Commandant of the Centre des Hautes Études Militaires, he had welcomed lectures on armoured warfare by General Doumenc, an enthusiastic advocate of the tank, but that was all. His programme of 4 July 1930 was limited to the motorization of five infantry divisions and the transformation of one cavalry division to a *division légère mécanisée*, i.e. a light armoured division, coupled with the motorization of one brigade in each of the five cavalry divisions. At the same time he asked the automobile manufacturers, Renault and Citroën, to plan and construct embryos of what would become the reconnaissance cars of 1939.

At the time of his arrival at the rue St Dominique, all weapon manufacture was controlled by the artillery directorate at the War Ministry, a body jealous of its prerogatives.[3] The growing complexity and specialization led to constant delays and obstruction. Weygand set up a new secretariat, a technical cabinet responsible directly to the Chief of Staff under Colonel, as he then was, Bloch (later Bloch-Dassault, a son of the aeroplane constructor) to advise him on inventions. Bloch was also to head a second secretariat to (another innovation) the consultative committee on armament, on which sat the directors of arms, the inspectors-general, the Secretary-General (Army finance) and ultimately the director of armament manufacture. This partly remedied the anarchy then reigning. During the period 1931–4, much preliminary work was sorted out and either accepted or rejected. 'Unhappily, war is not carried on by prototypes.' Unhappily, too, the technical cabinet with responsibility to the Chief of Staff alone was not liked, and in due course was metamorphosed into a third sub-chief of staff and given two other bureaux to administer. 'In point of fact,' said General Bloch-Dassault to the Commission on Events, 'it was a veto on my devoting myself to armament, while giving to the research and construction services the impression that nothing of the muddles of the past had been changed.'[4]

[3]

At the end of 1930, Pétain, now seventy-five, at long last retired, surrendering the vice-presidency of the Army Council. Weygand, being C.G.S. and the next in the hierarchy, was promoted in his place in January 1931. Painlevé's injunction on Weygand's tenure of both offices still stood—Painlevé was now influencing to no better effect the Air Ministry, whenever he got the opportunity—and Weygand became Vice-President of the Army Council and Inspector-General of the army, while Gamelin assumed the office of Chief of Staff.

During 1931, with Maginot at the rue St Dominique, matters went with tolerable smoothness. Germany was having its own troubles. Although clandestine armament was going on, with the connivance of all parties in the Reichstag except the Communists, it was not thought to be serious. The obvious enemy of German governments, as of most French, was Russia. In France the successors of Poincaré continued a chequered course, but the general slump brought with it severe financial distress. For the next five years, the Finance Ministers, the Treasury and the Banque de France practised deflation of brutal weight. All government expenditure was cut and naturally the heaviest pressure was on the defence services, particularly in view of the sessions of the dis-armament conference at Geneva.

The French Army suffered in 1931, even if Maginot was able to prevent the deepest cuts. But Maginot died in January 1932, and in May, the general election once more produced a majority for a Left coalition. From June 1932 to February 1934 the governments were all Socialist-Radical with first Paul-Boncour as Minister of War, and from December, Édouard Daladier. With these Weygand's troubles began in earnest. He himself says that as Vice-President of the Army Council, he had responsibility but no power. Though Commander-in-Chief designate for War, in time of peace he was unable to address directly commanders of regions or army corps. All he could do, as Inspector-General, was to report to the Minister, who in turn would issue his orders through the Chief of Staff, who was not under the orders of the Vice-President but, like him, directly under the Minister. Weygand could only hope for the unanimous support of the Army Council, which might possibly bring pressure to bear on the army committees in Chamber and Senate. Thus, particularly over eighteen months, the army suffered cut after cut, while six successive ministries fell, the last (Daladier's second) in February 1934 in a crisis of confidence arising out of the irrelevant Stavisky affair. By now the external situation had been transformed.

[4]

The appointment of Hitler as Chancellor of the Reich in January 1933 was the first serious warning. The revelation in the spring of 1934 of the scale of German rearmament was the second. After the turn of the year, warning succeeded warning until 7 March 1936, when they became serious menaces. From the beginning Weygand had been uneasy, but could not make ministers share his view. He felt himself impotent and he was not helped by Gamelin.

Whether or not 1934 is the decisive year, it is from that summer and autumn that to many people, particularly in the Succession States, it appeared inevitable that there must be either resistance or capitulation to the demands of the Third Reich. That the Hitler following would not shrink from violence was made clear by the slaughter of 30 June and the murder of Chancellor Dollfuss in August, while the rejection of Barthou's attempt to negotiate a parallel to the Locarno treaties in eastern Europe appeared yet another manifestation of German bad faith.

This was the last year of Weygand's vice-presidency. In his eyes the omens were formidably unfavourable. Pétain had become Minister of

War in Doumergue's government. Unfamiliar with politics, he accepted, in the sphere of finance, the pressure of the Finance Minister. Weygand submitted a report which he had drawn up in January. In the last paragraph he drew attention to the decline in North African enlistments and the indiscipline of the North African troops stationed in France. He underlined the lack of training of the home army due to the one-year term of service. He repeated his warnings of the previous year against the reduction of units to cadre and the reduction even of cadres. At the same time he drew Gamelin's attention to the shifting of effectives away from the active mobile units towards the Maginot Line garrisons and the consequent decline of the field troops in the three main frontier regions, VI, VII and XX: Metz, Besançon and Nancy. Only five of the twenty divisions regarded as the essential defensive cadre were at strength, while of the covering force on mobilization, eight out of twenty-one formations were North African. Gamelin replied that it was due to lack of funds, and forwarded the letter to Pétain. And that was all.

In March, Pétain told the army committee of the Senate that it was unnecessary to extend the Maginot Line, since with a few destructions the Ardennes would be impenetrable, while to defend the northern frontier, 'one must go into Belgium'.*

[5]

After the defeat, it was said that Parliament was responsible for reducing the army's demands. This was denied. Politicians claimed that they had always granted what was asked. Yes, replied the soldiers, but the cuts were made by the Ministry of Finance before the requests were produced in the Chamber. 'That is all very well,' retorted the Finance Ministry, 'but you failed to confess that you rarely used what you did get, and great sums with which you were credited were carried over from year to year. What is more, you never had a coherent plan. The directorates asked for credits for equipment of which the employment had not been fully thought out and for operations which had not been completely planned.'

Weygand had tried to amend this situation by his technical cabinet, but Daladier created on top of it yet another Directorate of Army Manufacture, which traversed the other War Ministry directorates.

The cause of all these conflicts is to be traced to the absence of any military doctrine. The excision of the offensive from the regulations had destroyed the faculty of initiative. Nothing was left except the passive defensive, which naturally implied that the initiative was left to the enemy and that no action could be taken until he had disclosed his intentions. Only when the enemy had been brought to a halt would the moment for the counter-offensive appear. Thus the army was without

---

* Belgium was still allied to France.

direction, and without direction was unable to explain its needs to the parliamentary committees.

This indefiniteness could only leave the directorates at sixes and sevens and exacerbate the normal friction between offices working to the same end on different lines.

4 THE SURRENDER OF THE RHINELAND OUTWORK

THE murder of Barthou at the side of King Alexander of Yugoslavia at Marseille in October 1934 shook the ageing and tired Doumergue, already soured by the attacks and jeers of the Left. He resigned in November after the resignation of Herriot and three of the Radicals from the ministry. Invited by Flandin to join the new cabinet, Pétain refused. At this date Weygand was looking forward to his own retirement in the following January. Asked by Pétain to recommend a War Minister, he suggested General Georges, a member of the Army Council, who in 1918 had been on Foch's staff, in 1926 Chief of Staff to Pétain during the Riff campaign, then *chef de cabinet* to Maginot, and in 1931 had commanded XIX (North African) Corps. The suggestion was not adopted, and when Flandin asked for a War Minister, Pétain suggested the Chief of Staff, Gamelin. Gamelin had other ambitions. At this date, he was sixty-two. He was well aware of the uncertainty of political life, whereas as Chief of Staff he would be pretty sure of holding his appointment for another three years, when, at sixty-five, he would normally retire. And if he was also appointed Vice-President of the Army Council—and thus Commander-in-Chief should war break out— he would be retained until the age of sixty-eight. He declined Pétain's invitation. The ministry was filled by General Maurin, a retired gunner, who was on the point of going blind.

Weygand, with perhaps some justice, had no liking for Gamelin. Gamelin, who had been put in as first sub-Chief of Staff to act as a make-weight against the distrusted Weygand, had moved up when Weygand became Vice-President of the Army Council in 1931. In his memoirs Weygand makes no bones about his opinion that Gamelin did not further the army's interests.[1] He admits that the separation of the offices of Chief of Staff and Vice-President made the Chief of Staff's position difficult, and that Gamelin 'being the sole judge of his duty, might think that he had not the right to combat the minister's opinions: that was one of the vices of our double-headed army.'[1] Yet three years of collaboration had not brought us together: our temperaments and characters differed too much. A reserve, turning to distrust of my immediate collaborator, from whom I never felt any warmth, any spontaneous gesture, made the work of the last two years of command all the more irksome as my differences with the minister became more complicated.' On 20 January 1935 Weygand bade his successor good-bye. Said Gamelin, 'I am not an administrator but a strategist.' '*Évidemment,*' comments Weygand dryly.[2]

Maurice Gamelin had deservedly a high reputation. The legend that it was he who won the battle of the Marne in 1914 is of course exaggerated; but in fact the then Major Gamelin had been the earliest to grasp the significance of von Kluck's swing south-eastward on 4 September and had had the courage, in opposition to the two chiefs of staff, to press Joffre to act immediately instead of delaying for another two days.[3] Thereafter his career was made and his promotion to each new rank was usually at least twelve months ahead of his coevals. He had been careful. He had made no enemies, he had never gone up on a forlorn hope. He made no fusses. If the minister objected, he tried to find a way round, and if that was blocked, he gave way. He claimed to stay aloof from politics, yet knew all the politicians. In trouble he was always preparing to resign and then allowing himself to be persuaded to withdraw his resignation. He was a complete contrast to the abrupt and forthright Weygand, and ministers naturally preferred his subservience. Moreover, never having shown any signs of political bias, he was trusted not to assassinate the Republic. In consequence he was allowed now to combine the two posts of Vice-President of the Army Council and Chief of the General Staff, thus ending the dichotomy deplored by Foch and Weygand. Small, plump, slightly puffy, with his hair tinted, he might, but for the uniform, be an abbé, a fashionable abbé, really a *préfet diplomate*. 'He's like a silk shirt,' said Bonhomme, Pétain's A.D.C., 'the more you rub him, the suppler he becomes.'[4]

[2]

The early months of Gamelin's tenure were agitated by a number and variety of incidents which cumulatively amounted to the revelation that French influence in Europe was not as dominant as it had appeared at the beginning of 1934. In January, Flandin's Foreign Minister, Laval, visited Rome and in conversation with Mussolini indicated that the French would not hinder Italian pressure on another member of the League of Nations, Abyssinia. A week later the Saar voted overwhelmingly for its reincorporation in the Reich, which was approved by the Council of the League on the 17th. On 11 March, the Germans by the mouth of Goering announced the creation of a German Air Force, the first scratch on the veneer of friendliness with France.

In 1934, Weygand had demonstrated that the reductions of various units to cadre in the interests of economy had brought the number of divisions required for *couverture* during mobilization below the safety point, that many units were under even peace-time strength and that the natives of North Africa were no longer enlisting in their previous numbers. It was known that the Germans had perhaps 300,000 trained soldiers and the skeleton of twenty-one divisions. Gamelin was, of course, well aware that in twelve months' time, in 1936, the first of the 'hollow years', there would be a serious deficiency in the French call-up and that, for another four years, this would amount on the annual average to 120,000, or half the number laid down under the law of 1927. On 15 March, the Chamber passed a law extending the length of service from one to two years, beginning with the October call-up. Hitler immediately riposted by proclaiming the re-establishment of universal service and the organization of a new German army of twelve army corps and thirty-six divisions.

This defiance of the western powers raised no flicker of agitation in the mind of the new Vice-President of the Army Council. André François-Poncet, the French ambassador to Germany, when visiting Paris, made his usual call on the Chief of the General Staff. Gamelin's brow was unclouded: he had already remarked that they would see how long it would take the Germans to catch up with the twenty milliards the French had put into armaments. When François-Poncet spoke of the German intention of equipping 300 divisions, Gamelin answered that they would not have the necessary cadres, particularly non-commissioned officers. 'I objected,' said the ambassador, 'that all Germans were born such.'[5] The general retorted that it needed years, perhaps generations, to organize a competent body of N.C.O.s. According to the ambassador, Gamelin always replied in this manner when challenged. 'Aircraft do not decide the outcome of a battle.' 'Armoured divisions are too heavy and cumbersome; they may penetrate our lines, but the lips of the gash will close up behind them and we shall crush them with our reserves.'

'From these conversations,' François-Poncet told the Commission on Events, 'I used to come away very sensible of the perfect courtesy of the general and the kindly patience with which he listened to me, but also convinced that he was blind to reality.'

In April, an Anglo-French-Italian conference took place at Stresa and ended in one of those unreal joint declarations reaffirming the obligations of the three states under the Treaty of Locarno and the indispensability of Austrian independence. The delegates passed over in silence the unconcealed dispatch of Italian troops to Eritrea on the Abyssinian frontier. A few weeks later, on 2 May, Laval reluctantly signed a pact with the U.S.S.R., a Locarno pact similar to the pacts with Poland and Czechoslovakia. A fortnight later, when he visited Moscow, Stalin declared that he welcomed an intensification of French defensive measures. It was both a warning to Germany and a call to order of the French Communist party to abandon their opposition to the lengthened military service and to rearmament.

In June, the Germans announced yet one more infringement of treaties, that they had already constructed a fleet of submarines, and offered to negotiate a treaty of limitation with the British government. The British Foreign Secretary, Simon, submitted to the humiliation and accepted terms which he was well aware would not be respected.

The fall of Flandin at the end of May, and the failure of Bouisson to win a vote of confidence, prepared the return of a Laval administration on 7 June.

During the rest of the year, the British and French governments found themselves gradually involved in the Abyssinian crisis during which both governments tried to conceal their firm determination to do nothing obnoxious to the Italians, with the consequence that both Laval and the British Foreign Secretary, Hoare, were exposed as humbugs. Laval was forced to resign, in January 1936. He was succeeded by Albert Sarraut, who was meant to do no more than hold the fort until the general election, due in April-May, was over. His Foreign Minister was Flandin. The rumpus in both France and England over Abyssinia had been enough to show Hitler that Mussolini had been able to defy a negative Anglo-French combination plus the League of Nations. From now he began the seduction of the Duce. In January, Mussolini admitted to the German ambassador in Rome that he would abandon his quasi-protection of Austria.

The Rhineland, from which the French troops had been withdrawn in 1930, was still subject to the military terms of the Locarno and Versailles treaties. That the Germans were preparing the demilitarized zone for military occupation had long been known. The French consul-general in Cologne, Dobler, had been established in that city for the purpose of political observation of the demilitarized region. Since 1933 there had been clandestine and camouflaged preparations for reoccupation, which increased month by month as the Germans grew bolder. After Hitler's declaration of rearmament on 17 March 1935, troops had been sent in by night to occupy the police barracks while at the same time landing-grounds for aircraft had been made ready. Dobler warned the Quai d'Orsay on a number of occasions of what was happening. On discovering some of the German entries, he forced the authorities to withdraw their agents. He interviewed Laval, when the latter passed through Cologne on his way back from Moscow in May 1935, and was snubbed. Later the Quai d'Orsay told him that this was none of his business.

The decay of the previous fifteen years was now painfully clear. Before the end of the year Gamelin was quite certain that the Germans intended to occupy the Rhineland at some not too far distant date. And from the hour of taking office at the Quai d'Orsay in January, Flandin, too, foresaw the imminent reoccupation. He asked the cabinet whether this move should be resisted, and on receiving their assent called a meeting in late February of the three ministers concerned, Maurin (War), Piétri (Marine) and Déat (Air). It was entirely inconclusive. Maurin said that the troops under arms were so few that they could be employed only for strictly defensive action; for any offensive operation reservists must be called up, including the frontiersmen of all classes: for the situation described by the Foreign Minister no preparations had been made. Piétri for the Marine declared that blockade was the only action and that it must be with the British Navy, while Déat said that all the French Air Force could do would be to bomb, an act of war and one liable to injure the civil population. In his memoirs Gamelin much approves Maurin's answer, but at no point in them does he show that he had ever brought this argument forward. Thus no decision as to action had been taken when, on the morning of 7 March, German troops marched into the Rhenish cities amid the frantic cheering of the population.

The German stroke threw the French cabinet and the defence staffs into confusion. Léger, the permanent secretary-general of the Quai d'Orsay, wanted immediate action. He asked the British and the Belgians. The latter were very naturally scared to death and were ready to accept the *fait accompli*. The British were not allies, though bound by the Treaty of Locarno, and were cool to positive action. At a cabinet meeting[6] on the next day, Flandin offered the ministers a series of alternatives from mobilization and invasion of the Rhineland to diplomatic protests with recourse to the League of Nations, but recommended none. 'In his cold and unemotional voice, he limited himself to "Such are the alternatives open to us. The cabinet will select".' Maurin, 'in a strangled voice', said that mobilization and entry into the Rhineland meant risks, and that the actual state of the French Army did not allow them to run risks. Déat and Piétri were equally reserved. Only Sarraut, Guernut, Delbos and Mandel favoured strong action. Sarraut had rashly broadcast that France would not tolerate that Strasbourg should lie under the threat of German guns. But he did not try to force Flandin. According to Flandin, both London and Brussels were reticent. He and Paul-Boncour hastened to London, where among other disappointments they found that the British could provide no more than two infantry divisions. By the morning of 9 March, what enthusiasm for action there had been was dissipated. Gamelin had summoned the Army Council, the members of which had been given no orders and little information. 'From the moment he began to speak, it became evident that General Gamelin was about to expound a decision already reached and that he was, admittedly without much enthusiasm, about to justify it. Which explains the confused and difficult turn his monologue took towards his quickly disappointed and disheartened subordinates.'[7] He made it clear that positive action would require improvisation, by taking troops from the covering force, a course which would be full of risk, and that to undertake serious operations, having regard to all future possibilities, required mobilization. Mobilization was only to be thought of for war. General Albord adds that the only value of this meeting had been to demonstrate to all 'our impotence, for want of an appropriate instrument, the huge gaps in our army and what is worse, the disarray, the hesitation and indeed the pusillanimity which had flowered during the recent critical hours'.[8]

In his memoirs,[9] Gamelin is profuse with explanation as to why no action was taken at this point. He quotes Maurin's note of 11 March that the Germans had nearly 300,000 men but does not disclose that half of these were S.A. men and another 30,000 were Labour Corps, and that the Germans who marched in were four token forces. He says that this was more than twice the French troops available. Elsewhere he points out that even if the Germans withdrew their detachments, they would try again, and that similar action would be needed. What he fails to explain is why he had made no preparations to meet an approaching challenge of which both the Foreign Office and the War Ministry, as well presumably as the Air Ministry, were well aware.

In his evidence before the Commission on Events, Sarraut quotes from an unnamed journalist, who wrote: 'One can be certain that to excuse each of the mistakes with which he is charged, Gamelin will always find a scapegoat. He will persuade no one.'[10]

For the rest, the matter was brought to the League of Nations, which rebuked the German government. And that was all, except that Hitler was fortified in his belief that the French were either unable or unwilling to defend themselves, let alone be drawn into a war on behalf of an ally. In France, most public opinion approved the mild action of the government. It was feared that the '*bellicistes*', a newly invented word, the warmongers, would involve the country in war.

Later, of course, no words would be too contemptuous for the cowardice of the Sarraut government.

[3]

The failure to act in March 1936 was to have consequences far graver than the immediate problem of the loss of a no-man's-land beyond Rhine and Sarre. The Italian dictator, already enlightened by his immunity during the Abyssinian War, readily abandoned the cause of Austrian independence in return for the goodwill of the German Führer over the Mediterranean. The outbreak of the Spanish Civil War in July added another unpleasant ingredient to the witches' cauldron of international enmities. In 1937, the intervention of Italian 'volunteers' in Spain on behalf of Franco and the brutal bombing of small towns such as Guernica by German-manned German aircraft added anxiety about the Pyrenees to the concern for the French eastern frontiers, while the occupation of Minorca by the Italians raised the spectre of threatened communications with French North African ports.

[4]

The combination of external rebuffs and defeats, coupled with the effects of the harsh deflationary policies of Laval and his Finance Minister, Marcel Regnier, had heated popular feeling to a state in which almost any régime, even a serious Left government, was preferable. The elections of 26 April and 3 May 1936 were held against a background of industrial strikes and the occupation of certain key factories by the employees. A combination of Socialist-Radicals, Socialists, Independent Socialists and Communists in a 'Popular Front' led to the return of a Chamber in which for the first time the Socialists, led by Léon Blum, became the biggest group. The Communists, with seventy-two seats, tripled their number of deputies. The shift of power, apparent rather than real, led to the implementation of various items of the Popular Front programme which affected the army and its preparation for war.

[5]

The military reoccupation of the Rhineland had not brought the German forces in close proximity to the French defences alone. It had taken them up to the Belgian-Luxembourg frontier. Facing the Reich, the French had some, if frail, security, with 150 kilometres of Rhine, and another 150 from Lauterbourg to the Moselle at Apach, partly covered by the Maginot Line fortress sectors, while the country from Wissembourg to Rohrbach was thickly wooded and largely roadless. From Apach north-west, the French frontier was shielded by the Grand Duchy of Luxembourg and by Belgium. The Grand Duchy was strictly neutral and demilitarized under the treaty of 1867,[11] the padlock, it had been called, to French security, a padlock which could easily be forced, though it was difficult country to cross from east to west.

With Belgium there had been a defensive military pact since 1920, but not a strict alliance. In 1936, the kingdom was plagued by a revival of the eternal Flemish-Walloon quarrel, to which had now been added the unrest of the sub-Fascist Rexist movement of Léon Degrelle. The King, Leopold III, had succeeded his father, Albert I, only in 1934. He had seen the grip of Hitler's National-Socialist movement on Germany and the failure of the Powers to coerce Italy in the matter of Abyssinia. He had seen the impotence or unwillingness of the members of the League of Nations to take material measures against the flouting of the Locarno Treaty by the reoccupation of the Rhineland. He had been disturbed by the ratification of the Franco-Russian pact in March and alarmed by the victory of the Front Populaire at the elections and by the proceedings of the Blum government. There had been the Italian-German agreement of 11 July, a rapprochement between the Third Reich and Fascist Italy which boded no good. And on 18 July had come the invasion of Spain by the rebel general Franco, which provoked in France only embarrassed shuffling in the face of the threat to her southern frontier. From the king's point of view, his country might be involved in a German-French quarrel in which Belgium had no interest. At a cabinet meeting on 14 October, he announced that, while still ready to observe her obligations under the Covenant of the League, Belgium would withdraw from all pacts, declare her permanent neutrality and look to her own defences. At the same time he expressed the government's intentions to reorganize the Belgian Army.

The Belgian decision raised yet another problem for the French general staff. In 1934, when the Maginot Line was nearing completion,

Pétain, then Minister of War, had told the Senate Army Committee[12] that with a few impeding destructions, the Ardennes could be made impenetrable, and should invaders come through, they would be dealt with in detail as they emerged. Further to protect the northern industrial network from Valenciennes to Lille, it would be necessary to go forward into Belgium.

The situation created by Leopold's declaration was disturbing. Belgian fortifications were known to be weak and the army underequipped and not highly trained. In 1932, Tardieu had offered the Belgian government a loan to help them to improve their frontier forts and strengthen the defences of their canal and river lines, but nothing had come of the proposal. At the end of 1936, the Foreign Minister, van Zeeland, told Blum that if the pact with France had been continued, the Belgian Parliament would have refused the government credits for re-armament. Now that the alliance was dead, the Belgians would be able to repair their defences. 'Thus you will have Belgian fortifications which today don't exist, and a Belgian army, at this moment also nonexistent, while on the other hand you will have nearly another two hundred kilometres to defend.' Blum recognized with pain that here was yet another symptom of the progressive dismantling of French defences, 'not only materially, but politically'.[13] Whereas formerly Belgium and France had a joint interest and could consult, in future the French must rely on an unknown plan of defence by an army of which they could know little. The problem of security had become more complex. (The guarantee of Belgian neutrality given by France and Great Britain at Geneva on 24 April next year was rather a warning to Germany than an effective instrument.)

Moreover, the Maginot defences, which blocked some of the classical invasion gateways to France, the Moselle valley between the Hunsrück and the Eifel and the roads which converge on the Sarre valley, sharpened the expectation that the enemy would make his major thrust across the Low Countries. It was now incumbent on the French to prepare to come to the aid of the Belgians with all speed if the Germans attacked. There were two possibilities. The first that the Germans would repeat their invasion of 1914 and send their divisions south of the Limburg appendix of Holland. This by narrowing the gateway would cause some delay in the approach march. The more probable alternative was an extension of their right flank to include Holland in their plan.

The Belgians were, of course, perfectly alive to the fact that the Germans, if they wished to defeat France, must invade Belgium and that the French would hurry to their assistance if the Germans crossed the border. They could not and would not discuss the matter with the French, since, if known, it would give Hitler justification for action. So they said nothing. On the other hand, for the French now arose the problem of arriving in time to prevent the Belgian Army from being driven out of their defences before the French army could organize a line. And the matter was further complicated by the possibility of a simultaneous invasion of Holland. But the Belgians and Dutch were not on good terms, and between the military staffs of the two countries there were no conversations between October 1936 and September 1939.

5 ARMS FOR DEFEAT

IN 1945 much criticism was levelled at the failure of the French to prepare for war, in particular to the slowness in developing the armoured fighting vehicle (A.F.V.). As usual in such cases, there is a plethora of memoralists to claim that if only their advice had been taken, the catastrophe of 1940 would not have befallen the country. The assertions are exaggerated. Since the armoured fighting vehicle was a conspicuous element in the following years, it is well to remember that, as all who fought in France between 1916 and 1918 learned, the tank was not an infallible answer to the infantryman's prayer and not all that was later claimed for it. There had, of course, been the great spectacular surprises of Cambrai, Soissons and Amiens in 1917 and 1918; but there had also been a number of failures which were naturally not accorded the same publicity. The tank was not a panacea. There were plenty of soldiers who had seen these instruments fail to do their stuff: there were also plenty who had been in successful fights without the aid of armour. It is to be noted that the two most conspicuous French advocates, Charles de Gaulle and Paul Reynaud, had never seen a tank in battle since neither had been in France during the years 1917–18.

The French A.F.V. had been the brain-child of General Estienne whose memorial stands high above the Mediterranean in Cimiez. Estienne, a senior gunner officer, had imagined the tank* earlier than the British inventors, but was slower in getting his ideas accepted. It was not until 1917 that his first machines, a 13-ton Schneider and a 23-ton St Chamond, described by General Fuller as 'kitchen ranges', appeared. (The caustic English general in his autobiography speaks of Estienne as 'an amusing little dud'.) These tanks were unsatisfactory and were discarded. In the end, the French fought during the last months of the war with the Renault F.T. of 6–7 tons, which ran at 5 m.p.h. and was armed with either a machine-gun or a not very powerful 3·7-mm. gun. In 1919, there were about 3,000 of these, which were employed as the accompaniment of the infantry.

In the post-war French army, Estienne, who was a friend of Pétain, was appointed inspector-general of A.F.V. He had already imagined battles between armoured forces on a gigantic scale and in 1921 produced a monster of 70 tons, capable of 8 m.p.h., armed with a 75-mm. gun and four machine-guns, and manned by a crew of twelve. Six of

---

* Estienne considered the word 'tank' an outrage on the successor of the Roman chariot. He eventually accepted that the French versions should be called *chars*. There would be *chars de combat* and *chars d'accompagnement*. They were also called *blindés* by the infantry.

these were built, and at the end of the 1920s were used for training drivers. But they had no successors.

Estienne, however, developed other plans. He invited a number of automobile and engineering firms to produce a model tank to his specifications. In 1924, four of these were tested at the Rueil arsenal. Each had faults and all suffered from damaged track plates. In 1925, Estienne asked them to try again, incorporating new details. From these eventually emerged the inventor's masterpiece, the B.1, later B.1 *bis*. Three prototypes were ordered in March 1927 and were delivered in August 1934. There had, of course, been trials all through the seven years, and progress was often interrupted for modifications, all of which added to the cost. Before the first were delivered, it was found satisfactory enough to order seven more, which were handed over to the *Chars de Combat* brigade between December 1935 and May 1936, that is, in the period of crisis.

During these years, the question of their employment had been bedevilled by the controversies about disarmament. Since the tank had been designated an offensive weapon, which was denied to the Germans, was it just that the pacific and legalistic French should not only retain their armour but develop it? And anyhow, for an army existing on much reduced budgets, the A.F.V. seemed an extravagance, extremely costly, far more than the horse, as a certain General Rampont expounded in the *Revue des Deux Mondes*.

[2]

Léon Blum's government came to power on a programme based on the slogans of the Popular Front, like all popular programmes a mass of grievances of which the chief two were unemployment and warmongering, the enemies being the Banque de France and *les deux cents familles*, and the armaments kings, *les marchands de canons*. It was incumbent on the new government to satisfy its supporters. And Blum was in fact lucky to have arrived at the moment when the external threat appeared for the first time since 1914. He was thus enabled to secure government control of the Banque de France, to nationalize a number of arms factories and to persuade Chamber and Senate, both the least *belliciste* of bodies, to sanction the grant of fourteen milliard francs for rearmament projects. At the same time he was able to placate the more extreme of his followers by decreeing the forty-hour week. The last, though at times criticized for hindering rearmament, was of little importance, since at the date of its introduction, weekly hours in a large section of industry were as low as thirty-two, in some twenty-four and even twenty-two. It was hoped that by setting forty hours as the normal week, a part of the unemployed would be reabsorbed, though in fact the real tonic was the fourteen milliards.

[3]

As in countries other than France, the armament industry had naturally declined with the end of the war. The great providers, Schneider and the rest, suffered. They let their plant run down, their machinery decay. Even the failure of the disarmament conference had done nothing to stimulate them. Only a few South American governments occasionally ordered a battery, and were charged exceptional prices. Most of the new European governments contented themselves with bargains from the scrap merchants. Hitler should therefore have appeared as a fairy god-mother to the *marchands des canons*. And, of course, as in all fairy-tales, the recipients of the fairy's benefits were quite unprepared for them.

The commonplace that France before 1945 was in the main an agri-cultural country underlines the antithesis that its industry was largely concerned with consumption goods, as were its export trades. During the boom years of 1926-9, it was these that flourished. In 1921, a parlia-mentary committee on French industry reported that the country had almost no machine tools. 'No country can be a Great Power unless (among other things) it is an arsenal—that is, equipped with a reason-ably complete outfit of weapons of modern warfare. A native machine-tool industry is an essential requirement of an arsenal.'[1] This France did not have in 1936. When money was allotted by the government with an unprecedented generosity, it was discovered that a great number of manufacturers whose tenders were solicited were in no condition to fill the orders at even reasonable speed. 'French industry is characterized by the very weak importance of the average firm, the multiplicity of articles produced, the excessive number of types and models, the insufficient output from such methods of work, the age of the machinery and tools.'[2] The manufacture of shells for the celebrated 75-mm. gun had been stopped since 1920, and except at Le Creusot the manufacture of steel for guns had ceased. In 1930, at Schneider's artillery foundry at Le Havre ('whose clientele for the most part were foreigners'), there was no central workshop or magazine. 'The tooling is old, the machines for the most part out of date—there are some even from before 1870—and the overall good performance is due solely to the professional quality of the foremen and the skill of the workmen. When taken over by the State, the expert report showed that 80 per cent of the machinery was decayed. The Manurhin cartridge works, transferred on purchase by the State from Mulhouse to Le Mans, had no drawing office, no workshop for precision instruments, no central shop for repair of machines.'[3] At Hotchkiss of Levallois, also taken over in 1936, except for some Ameri-can milling machines nearly everything had been bought from bankrupt firms and the like, and many machines were from before 1914. There was absolutely no possibility of large-scale production; they were incap-able of producing with regularity. Articles coming from the machine had to be completed by hand. At the State factory at Chatellerault, ten expert hands could complete fifty weapons a day, while at Hotchkiss it needed 200 fitters working with hand-files, much as Chatellerault had been doing about 1890.*

In the machine-tool industry in 1934-5, the average age of machine-tools was twenty years, compared with seven in Germany and three in America. Of 555,000 machines in France, only 20,000 were less than ten years old, while 25,000 were more than fifty. The industry had only 10,000 employees against 20,000 in Switzerland, 70,000 in Germany and 100,000 in the U.S.A.

[4]

That production was slow was due not only to the obsolescence of machinery and the deficiencies of labour. At least part of the delays was due to the soldiers themselves, at all levels. In the last months of his inspectorship, Weygand had at last screwed, through Pétain, a grant of four milliard francs out of the Ministry of Finance, but to be spread over four years. The first *tranche* was a mere 800 million francs, which fell to Gamelin on his succession to Weygand in 1935. But the two Ministers of War during the next seventeen months were General Maurin, a gunner, and Fabry, a retired colonel, both traditionalists. The money went to guns. Ministers, however, are temporary. Daladier returned to the Ministry of War in June 1936 and remained there until 1940. There were more persistent hindrances further down the scale. More than one of the engineer officers in the Directorate of Arms Manufacture complained that the soldiers never knew what they wanted, or only discovered it when the article in question was partly made, because they had not thought out how the piece in question should be used. This becomes transparent in the post-war evidence regarding armoured divisions and armour generally. General Devaux, who served on the staff of the 3rd Armoured Division, said that up to the formation of these divisions (i.e. two to three months before the German attack), all training had been as accompaniment to infantry. There was no agreed doctrine as to their employment as independent formations. He shows that of the first three armoured divisions (4th Armoured, though powerful, was a scratch formation), each had a different theory. And it was generally agreed among the officers that their divisions had too few infantry.

---

* An acquaintance, a member of the Chamber Air Committee, told me that in 1938 he had been through all the German and French aircraft factories. Practically all the French planes were hand-built, perfection was sought. In the war, the French air staff had a shock when they discovered the Messerschmidt to be a very rough practical machine. Also in 1938, in French factories there was much sabotage, not from political motives; materials were stolen in large quantities from which workmen made household gadgets for themselves or for sale. The same observer said that after seeing the German fitters working with power tools it was painful to see the Frenchmen slowly putting in screws by human power.

[5]

The Air Ministry held itself as aloof from the Ministry of War as the British Air Ministry from the British Army. There appears indeed to have been even less co-operation on the part of the French 'Army of the Air', and its representatives in the Chamber were fiercely jealous of its independence.

Up to the early 1930s, the French had believed with some justice that they had the strongest air force in Europe. In 1933, General Denain, Chief of the Air Staff, at last perceived that his force was out of date. No plan of attack or defence had been drawn up since 1918. Denain sought a revival, and when he became Air Minister in Doumergue's government in February 1934, he persuaded the Chamber and Senate to accept a scheme, Plan I, which he had drawn up in the previous year, for re-equipment. Contracts were drawn up and work begun. Denain had felt the urgency, but he had not plumbed the incapacity of the manufacturers. Engine manufacture was to all intents monopolized by two firms, Gnôme-et-Rhône and Hispano-Suiza. The former, according to Guy la Chambre, Minister of Air from January 1938, was, though unreliable, fairly well-equipped; the latter, though reliable, was comparatively small. But the major obstacle was French traditionalism, which meant that the work was carried out carefully and slowly by skilled workmen, almost craftsmen. Driven by his anxiety to get new planes, Denain squandered his credits by using the existing firms rather than put money into machinery. He did not acquire the tools for the creation of matrices, and so, when in 1938 the first machines of Plan I came from the factories, they were already obsolete. Of the 1,375 planes effective in January 1938, only 130 were from orders given after those of Plan I of 1934, and some came from as far back as 1928. 'We were at exactly the same point as in 1934.'[4]

In the Blum government, the Minister of Air was Pierre Cot, who, although alert to the necessity for an efficient air force, was (one presumes from his evidence to the Commission on Events) largely ignorant about air warfare. Finding that there were no new prototypes and realizing the urgency, he merely added half as many again to the original scheme. Then, finding that there was still a deficiency, he added two more plans, both of which were still-born owing to lack of finance, factories and workmen. Furthermore, the planes were far too complicated. The Lioré 45, which by mid-June 1940 was the most important of the French bombers, needed between 40,000 and 50,000 man-hours to construct.

It was not until January 1938, when Guy la Chambre took over, that the necessary revolution could begin. A new plan, No. V, was rapidly drawn up. It looked forward to 1,081 fighters, 876 bombers of all kinds, though no dive-bomber, 636 reconnaissance and observation planes. It needed three years to carry out. It was complicated by the fact that there was no prototype of a contemporary bomber. The industry had not been improved. Factories had to be enlarged or built and equipped with modern machinery. Furthermore, it had long been recognized that the aircraft industry clustered round the suburbs of Paris was vulnerable. Geographical decentralization had been begun, but there had been no urgency.

Money had to be supplied for all this. Three hundred million francs to Gnôme-et-Rhône at Le Mans, thirty million to Hispano-Suiza at Tarbes, thirty-one million to Talbot for tools, twenty million to Salmson, twenty million to Panhard: factories had to be built at St Étienne, Venissieux, Bordeaux, Pau. All over the country new workshops had to be constructed for frames, for engines, for landing gear, electrical equipment, propellers. Repair shops had to be created for each speciality. It was only too clear, however hard they worked, that the French Air Force might not be ready in time. At the height of the Munich crisis, on 26 September, Vuillemin, Chief of Air Staff, reported to the minister that he could put 250 fighters in the air and 320 bombers. He could expect 120 British bombers at the end of a week and another 120 in twenty-five days. He expected 40 per cent casualties in the first month and 64 per cent by the end of the second. La Chambre had already arranged for the purchase of 100 Curtis fighters from America (later doubled) and some bombers. But these could not be expected before July 1939, and in fact they were not delivered until 1 September.[5]

[6]

Similar difficulties lay in the way of the creation of armoured divisions. Up to the early 1930s, the only tank other than the embryo B.1 and the obsolete F.T. was a machine known as D.1, of 11 tons, with 30-mm. armour, a 47-mm. gun and a machine-gun in the turret and another machine-gun in the body. One hundred and sixty of these had been built before May 1935. This gave way to a second version, the D.2, with heavier armour and a more powerful engine, of which one battalion appeared in 1937. A second, which appeared in June 1940, was still incomplete.

In addition to these, Weygand initiated a Hotchkiss (H.35, later H.39) for the cavalry, a light tank (12 tons), with one machine-gun and one 25-mm. (later 37-mm.) gun, of which 200 were ordered in the autumn of 1935. At the same time he had asked Renault to devise an infantry tank, which appeared as the R.35 in the spring of that year, when 300 were ordered. Finally there appeared the Somua, a speculative enterprise created by the Société d'Outillage Mécanique et d'Usinage d'Artillerie of St Ouen, a Schneider subsidiary, which was adopted by the cavalry. It weighed 20 tons and had a 47-mm. gun and a machine-gun. Both Hotchkiss and Somua according to General Martel were under-engined and slow.

As for the B.1, it was a magnificent machine, heavily armoured (60 mm.) with a 350 h.p. engine capable of doing 40 m.p.h. It had a

machine-gun and a 75-mm. gun in the body, and a machine-gun and a
47-mm. gun in the turret. It had a crew of five. It was, according to
Guderian, the best tank in the field. He personally fired German and
French anti-tank guns at one; the shells bounced off. Unfortunately
there were disadvantages. It was in fact too elaborate, as General Martel
alleged,* with a very delicate steering system, and, which was worse, it
was unsuited to mass production. Also it was very expensive: a million
and a half francs compared with 250,000 francs for a Renault. Further,
in order to give it more power, the technical experts provided the B.1
with two smaller engines, which naturally occupied more space and
consumed more fuel. As a result the effective radius (in time) fell from
8 hours to 5–5½ hours, with serious consequences in battle. The B.1,
however, became the main combat tank of the French Armoured
Division when this was formed.

As with the aeroplane, the production of armoured machines was
delayed by the discovery of faults, failures and changes imposed by
various authorities in the course of manufacture. In 1932, Weygand
constituted a 'détachement mécanique de combat' with the existing modern
machines, i.e. three B.1 and forty-five D.1. The trial was a hopeless
failure: according to Dufieux, the Inspector-General, this was because
the purpose of its employment had not been defined.

In 1936 economy forbade the carrying out of large-scale manœuvres:
so too in 1937. On 1 January of that year, the armour with the tank
brigades were 380 Renault, some without machine-guns, some without
turrets. There were 159 D.1, already condemned as obsolete (but they
were used in the dark days of 1940). There were forty-five D.2, but they
were all back in the workshops for modification. And there were twenty-
four B.1, of which only fifteen had its 75-mm. gun. However, there did
take place a preliminary exercise in April, on Gamelin's instruction, a
scheme laid on by General Delestraint, the foremost armour expert of
high rank. It was carried out at Sissonne and whatever else was learned
from it, it was made clear that the Renault was quite unsuited to inclusion in an armoured division.

After 1940, General Dufieux was abused for having, it was alleged,
opposed the creation of armoured divisions. Dufieux defended himself,
pointing out that, at the conclusion of the Delestraint exercise, he had
proposed that the credits earmarked for the Renault should be cancelled
and the money put to the manufacture of B.1. A month later, trials at the
Bourges arsenal demonstrated that the armour of the Renault could not
resist either the 25-mm. or 37-mm. anti-tank guns. Dufieux, having
reported this to the War Ministry, was given a flea in his ear by Daladier, who said that the exposure of defects would shake the morale of
the troops, and he had no intention of changing the programme of
manufacture. Dufieux should be more discreet.[6]

---

* Details of the French A.F.V. will be found in Appendix A.

[7]

As if there were not difficulties enough within the army, there was the trouble caused by the armament firms. Some, remembering the legislation of 1918 which had restricted their profits, were now reluctant to accept contracts. There were controversies with the Finance Ministry about amortization of new machinery. There was the hostility of Brandt, the manufacturer of mortars and also of shells, who opposed with great violence the nationalization of his works. There was the senior Schneider, who, when the government took over the plant at Le Havre, removed from that part of the works all the foremen and fitters. At their Satory works a wall was built to isolate the State-acquired part of the works. On the other hand, Louis Renault gave every assistance to the tank arsenal at Issy-les-Moulineaux.

Other industrialists were no more helpful, and enlisted the deputies and senators on the various committees to prevent injury to what they conceived their interests, of course identifying these with the national interest. The Chamber Air Committee was critical of purchases in America, and M. Paul-Louis Weiler of Gnôme-et-Rhône did his utmost to stop the purchase of Curtis fighters.[7] He had less success than the builders of lorries, who prevented the importation of American trucks. The water transport interests on the Loire were also able to short-circuit a grant to the Minister of Public Works for the building of a petrol pipeline from St Nazaire to Gien.

[8]

In 1934 appeared a small book, *Vers l'armée de métier*, by Lieutenant-Colonel Charles de Gaulle. This officer, who had served in the 33rd Infantry, Pétain's regiment, had been twice wounded in the early part of the war and on 3 March 1916 had been wounded again and captured at Douaumont. He had made two or three unsuccessful attempts to escape, but he did not return to France until he was repatriated after the armistice. He had served for a short time on Pétain's staff. At the École Supérieure de Guerre he had criticized the course and at the end been given a poor mark until the Marshal intervened and caused it to be raised to second class. In 1928–9 he commanded the 19th Chasseurs-à-Pied. After one or two staff missions, he was promoted to Lieutenant-Colonel and appointed to the secretariat of the Council of National Defence. In 1932 he had published a very small volume of essays from the days when he was at the École de Guerre with the title *Le Fil de l'épée*, 'The Sword-Edge', dedicated to the Marshal. Like other officers of his generation (he was now forty-three) he disliked the age and viewed the future with misgiving. Like others, he thought the French Army out of date. In 1934 the armoured fighting vehicle was still, for the army, a *char d'accompagnement* and not a *char de bataille*. Though Estienne had produced his B.1 and General Doumenc at the C.H.E.M. under Weygand had each year lectured on the possibilities of armoured formations, tank fighting was still limited to the talk of a few specialists.

Vers l'armée de métier cannot be regarded as a classic of armoured warfare. It was written in a high, mighty and noble style; it was intensely patriotic; it appealed to all the most nationalistic emotions of Frenchmen; it saluted the most eminent soldiers of French history; it echoed all the most august trumpetings of national heroes; it quoted all the most elegantly phrased commonplaces of chivalrous literature. It warned its readers that there could be no safety except behind a professional army. This might be thought a slight on the 106,000 professional soldiers of the law of 1928. It was in fact a call to initiate an armoured corps. What the author proposed was perhaps a trifle fanciful. 'A strongly armoured brigade, rolling across fields at the pace of a galloping horse, armed with a hundred and fifty field guns, four hundred of a slightly lesser calibre, six hundred machine-guns, crossing ten-foot-wide ditches, smashing trees of forty years growth, breaking down walls a foot thick, crushing all wire, grills, palisades. . . .' The colonel's fancy was exuberant. True he had never seen a tank in action, having been fast in a prisoner-of-war camp before the appearance of the first armour, and indeed had not thought out most of the material problems, as would appear when he was called on to halt the German armour in 1940. So far as he considered air co-operation, he confined it to producing smoke cover.

No one on the Army Council seems to have shown more than a casual interest in the book. With its commendation of a specialized standing army it was peculiarly calculated to raise the hair and fury of every historically minded democrat, particularly of Léon Blum. Loustaunau-Lacau records a conversation with '*le grand Charles*', which may be of 1933, in which the latter declared that he needed to link up with a rising politician, a prospective minister, and become his technical adviser.[8] It was none the less injudicious of the author to bring his thesis to the notice of Paul Reynaud, who based the whole of a long speech on 15 March 1935 on de Gaulle's theme.[9]

Undoubtedly de Gaulle was ill-regarded after this date and his future jeopardized. He was driven to apply to Reynaud for protection, since his career was threatened.[10] In the post-1918 army nonconformity was not tolerated, and the Historical Section of the Ministry of War was conformity itself. Officers were permitted to write, but the permission was hedged about. Studies relating to 1914–18 could be published only if authorized by the cabinet of the Minister of War. The numerous studies all tended to demonstrate the superiority of the French command. Marshal Juin has written that 'in the twenty years that separated the two wars, the imagination was curbed in an army which occupied itself in going over and over again the methods and processes born of a long and costly experience which had procured victory and in which blind faith survived'.[11]

There is about the French General Staff a natural and somewhat engaging simple vanity deriving from the fact that the French have some claim to be the earliest professional army in modern Europe. 'No war,' it was said in the eighteenth century, 'can take place in Europe without the French.' The tenants of No. 3 rue St Dominique and 4 bis boulevard des Invalides were the spiritual and intellectual heirs of Turenne, Louvois, Vauban and Inspector-General Martinet, and the Marne was as deserved a battle-honour as Austerlitz. They felt no need to look outside the *maison* for intelligence or inspiration. They had accepted but not welcomed the armoured fighting vehicle. The training establishments, St Cyr, the Polytechnique, Saumur, the École Supérieure de Guerre, the Centre des Hautes Études Militaires, considered it in no way revolutionary or necessary, and continued to treat it as an outsider as well as a parvenu.*

In this they were to some extent persuaded by the euphoric politicians after the Locarno treaties, and by the dominating influence of Pétain and Painlevé. The *char* being an aggressive weapon, forbidden to the German Army, it would be treachery to the spirit of Locarno to encourage it. And since apart from General Estienne, who retired in 1930 and died in 1935, there were no highly placed senior officers from the *chars*, the extension of the corps beyond prototypes was bound to be slow.

The defensive ethos was part and parcel of the memories of 1914–18. The beliefs of 1914, the war of movement and manœuvre were out. All tactics were prudent, methodical and slow. The 1936 field service regulations for divisions, *Instruction sur l'emploi tactique des grandes unités*, drafted by a committee of eleven generals, counter-signed by War Minister Daladier, emphasized the continuity of the battle-line and the axiom that no offensive action should be undertaken without a strong preponderance of artillery. The Armoured Fighting Vehicle (A.F.V.) was still regarded as an adjunct to the infantry attack. The committee incidentally propounded the thesis that the anti-tank gun was to the tank what the machine-gun had been to the infantryman in 1914–18. The battlefield was conceived as a *corps-à-corps* struggle, a wrestling bout rather than a boxing match. The flexibility begun in 1914–18 with the reduced division of all arms was not enlarged. In each division there was now an infantry commander and an artillery commander whose actions were to be co-ordinated at divisional headquarters. This made for rigidity and delay. General Héring, commander of the crack XX Corps, who preached on the theme of tactical groups of

---

* It is always to be remembered that before 1914, when commanding the infantry school, General Sarrail told the students that the machine-gun was obsolescent, that Marshal Foch stigmatized the aeroplane as '*zéro*', that the *pantalon rouge* was retained in order to allow the French artillery observers to see their own infantry, and that the War Office expected only three battles in each of which 300 rounds per gun would be enough and was flabbergasted when, at the end of the Marne, there were only forty per gun.

all arms within the division for a war of movement, was regarded as heretical and his suggestions suppressed by the editor of the *Revue militaire*. A British officer who attended a course for divisional and regimental commanders at the Centre des Hautes Études, shortly before the war, reported that 75 per cent of the time was devoted to defence, and the main study the consideration of a kind of enlarged Schlieffen plan, the holding of a German movement which had crossed the Seine west of Paris. It was estimated that six days were needed to bring up the necessary reserves, and when he suggested that they should use their tanks he was told there was only one battalion of cruisers available. The main theme was artillery, which nothing could replace; this was stressed by both Gamelin and Georges. There was no tank officer among the instructors. There was no sense of the time element in war, which was presented as a series of mathematical problems, rules for frontages, numbers, weight of fire. The defence was ingrained and initiative deprecated. His fellow students complained bitterly about the shortage of equipment, the money for which had gone into the Maginot Line. There was no co-operation with the Air Force, which was also starved of money, and there was little trust in it.[12]

6 THE BETRAYAL OF AN ALLY

NINETEEN-THIRTY-EIGHT, the year of the Austrian *Anschluss* and of the Munich capitulation, is the one in which the French people at last woke up to the inexorable German pressure, and to the fact that, whether they liked it or not, the period of French influence in Europe was almost, if not already, over; even the state of equilibrium was no longer certain. The situation was made all the more difficult in that part of the nation remained impenitently Left, while another part regarded Hitler as the friend and shield of European civilization against the barbarian Russians and considered the Popular Front governments as warmongers.

In January, the Ministry of National Defence, which had existed in an imprecise way since 1936, was converted into a responsible body with the Minister of War, Daladier, presiding over the three service ministers and Gamelin as Chief of Staff, for the purpose of co-ordinating their duties and actions. As in its parallel in Great Britain, each member looked on himself as the defender of the prerogatives of his own service. Co-ordination, as later appeared, only becomes real in the face of extreme mutual danger. In France, as Daladier and Gamelin recognized, what they had was at best no more than a starting-point; any step beyond that would be and was combated by the members of services committees in Chamber and Senate.

The seizure of Austria had been foreseen. Gamelin says that he warned Daladier that this would uncover the southern frontier of Czechoslovakia as far as the Austrian-Hungarian border and render worthless all the Czech expenditure on their northern frontier facing Germany. Except for the temporary stoppage of leave for the frontier troops, the French command did nothing. The Quai d'Orsay consulted the British Foreign Office, which deprecated any comminatory move in Berlin.

From mid-March, the menace to Prague increased week after week, and the Sudeten Germans, supported by a virulent German press, began to make demands impossible to accept. The Chautemps cabinet had fallen on the day before the entry into Austria. It was replaced by a Blum government which lasted scarcely four weeks. On 10 April, Édouard Daladier, Minister of War since June 1936, formed his fourth government. Within a fortnight he asked Gamelin to detail how France could aid Czechoslovakia, 'it being understood that mobilization is only the first act.'

The alliance between France and Czechoslovakia went back to 25 January 1924. It contained a secret annexe of the same date that the two staffs should collaborate in the preparation of plans to deal with any aggression by a common enemy. But there had never been a further consultation. In 1924 the territory containing Bohemia-Moravia-Slovakia, which had been created as an economic rather than a political unit, had been very weak, and the French had therefore lent the Czechs a professional military staff to organize their defences. The Czechs had done little until the advent of Hitler in 1933. During the next five years they transformed their northern and western borderlands—those facing Germany—into defences stronger than the Maginot Line, and built up a modern army of seventeen divisions, well armed from the great Skoda arsenal with some 500 tanks and a force of fighter aircraft: a young army, but tough and well trained.

The Prague government, and indeed the Paris government, accepted the fact that the two countries were allied. Gamelin's reply to Daladier's question, however, drew attention to the fact that there was no military convention nor had the two staffs consulted. All the French could do would be to move by stages to full mobilization, at the conclusion of which the French land and air armies would be able to act offensively. But the real material help to the Czechs should and could come far more adequately and speedily from Yugoslavia and Romania, partners in the Little Entente, and from Russia and Poland (though Gamelin should have known the Polish hatred for the Czechs), and even from the British Empire than from France. He neglected to remind Daladier—perhaps he thought it unnecessary—that the French had maintained General Faucher and a military mission in Prague ever since 1919.

General Faucher had not been consulted. General Faucher was in fact a nuisance. He liked the Czechs and he thought highly of their small army. He was shocked by the indecision of the French government. He was also furious at the misrepresentation of the Czechs in the French official military journal, *Bulletin des armées étrangères*, and elsewhere. His protests brought about the cessation of the articles, but the contributor, obviously from the Deuxième Bureau, was never unmasked. To Gamelin, Faucher insisted that the thirty divisions which the Czechs could put in the field when fully mobilized could hold up the Germans for a fairly long time, and that though they were short of bombing planes, they had 1,500 fighters.*

In March, a British inquiry as to what the French government could do to help their allies in Czechoslovakia had led to the calling of the Defence Committee, at which Daladier said that the French could mobilize enough to hold a certain number of German divisions on the French frontier. On this Gamelin commented that they could attack, but it would require considerable time to make any impression. Daladier

---

* It is to be noted that the Commissioners on Events who heard Faucher on 20 July 1948 did not like his evidence. Several members tried to upset it but failed. They thanked him coldly and did not avail themselves of his offer to appear again. The desertion of the Czechs had been too base to be recalled without pain and resentment.

said that, to maintain her position in Europe, France must support the Czech government, but added 'provided that it did not show itself uncompromising'. At one moment during the crisis in August, he consented to the recall of the recently liberated class to the fortified sectors, the retention of the class holding these, and the calling up of various other reservists including anti-aircraft gunners, some 700,000 in all.[*]

In July, the Germans, once more defying the Versailles treaty, sent a large body of civilian workers into the Saar territory to fortify their frontier opposite the Maginot Line. The fortifications, chiefly concrete blocks, ran from south of Pirmasens and Zweibrucken (Deux Ponts), and included Saarbrucken on the frontier. Thereafter they followed the German side of the Sarre as far as its junction with the Moselle south of Trèves. The main work was completed at the end of November, but the line, to be called Siegfried, was in fact far from complete.

On 26 September, in full crisis, Chamberlain asked Gamelin, who had come to London, to explain to him what the French Army hoped to do. Gamelin gave the British Prime Minister a somewhat highly coloured description of the French military situation: five million armed men, a hundred divisions (to begin with), a system of fortifications which guaranteed complete liberty of manœuvre. Admittedly the French Air Force was inferior to the German, but adequate for short-range work. On the other hand, the German High Command was fully aware of its own dangers. German fortifications were not finished. There was a shortage of officers and N.C.O.s and the reserves were not trained. There was a great shortage of raw materials, especially petrol. Against Italy, 'we shall take the offensive as soon as winter is over. The Czechs have thirty divisions against the German forty and if they stand on the Moravian border, they can hold out.'[1]

All this may have reflected what Gamelin believed, but in view of 1939, it looks as if it was for the record. In point of fact, at the best the French could mobilize at this date sixty-eight infantry divisions facing Germany, plus three cavalry and two light armoured divisions and the equivalent of the infantry of eleven divisions in fortress positions, but wholly immobile. There was no armoured division, but there were two battalions of heavy (B.1) tanks, sixty-six machines. Apart from these there were 800 Renault infantry tanks and 400 Hotchkiss with the cavalry.

Gradually it became clear that Great Britain, on whom the French leaned, was going to find a method of squaring the circle, of satisfying Hitler's appetite and the British Parliament's tender conscience. Daladier trailed along to Munich behind Neville Chamberlain. And Czechoslovakia was shorn, disarmed and handed over to Germany, while the rash and greedy Poles grabbed as much as they could.

---

[*] The retained classes were held until after the Munich settlement and then released. They were called up again in the following March.

Gamelin's conscience was not wholly clear.

Throughout the crisis the negotiators had (quite dishonestly) talked as if the Sudeten problem was a local quarrel in which the Czechs were being foolishly, unnecessarily and rashly obstinate: when the difficulty had been removed, everything would be as before. It was not until March 1939 that this illusion was blown away. Gamelin had pointed out to Daladier and the Foreign Minister, Bonnet, that the frontier zones handed over contained the defences of the country and that, when they had gone, the Czech Army would be impotent. In other words, France would lose an ally. Throughout the critical period of August and September he had acted with cool efficiency. At the end of August he had suggested to Daladier the precaution of calling up certain reserves, particularly of the fortified regions, and also some of the 'formation' units. On 12 September, Daladier called in Gamelin and Georges. To his question of what could be done to help the Czechs, Gamelin read a long survey which amounted to a proposal to attack in the Saar, to mount a battle which 'initially will be a modern version of the battle of the Somme', words nicely calculated to discourage a Minister of War who had himself experienced battle.[2] Georges let fall a caution against hope of a quick decision.

All this was highly Gamelinesque. He envisaged a number of hypothetical situations which did not arise. It was like so much of *Servir*, words. What Gamelin does not disclose in his memoirs is that at no point did he press for action or show the advantages of fighting in 1938 before the Germans had trained their new formations. In fact he was the smoothly efficient public servant—'a mere spirit of persuasion, only professing to persuade'. According to Baudouin, Daladier in April 1940 told Weygand: 'When you speak, something stays, while with Gamelin it's all sand that runs through one's fingers.'[3] One thing is certain. Gamelin never took up a position, never insisted. He resigned, or at least pretended to resign, a couple of times and allowed himself to be persuaded to withdraw his resignation. But he never stood firm over any principle.

It should be said that, in the autumn of 1938, the French Air Force was in no state to meet the German. Vuillemin, Chief of Air Staff, was scared out of his wits.[4] But Gamelin never speaks of this. Possibly he was sure that no one was going to fight 'for a people of whom we have scarcely heard'.

There is no indication that the French military authorities made any official comment on the Munich negotiations. French action was restricted to the mobilization of 700,000, and Gamelin gives no hint of plans other than waiting and seeing. There were no preparations for active assistance to their staunchest allies. Nor does he appear to have modified French plans as a result of losing the best-equipped and best-trained army in eastern Europe. Much more stress was laid on the inability of the Czechs to hold the Germans than on the existence of thirty infantry divisions and a number of A.F.V. (Armoured Fighting Vehicles)—the Czech tanks were in some respects better than the German.* The Polish Army was no substitute. Though Poland had a much larger population, its army was far less up to date than the Czech: it had about 750 light tanks and a number of infantry and cavalry divisions. But there were no fortifications.

[2]

When Potiemkin, ex-ambassador and assistant commissar in the Russian Foreign Office, saw the French ambassador, Coulondre, after the announcement of the Munich settlement, he said: 'What *have* you done, my poor friend, what *have* you done? I see no other solution for us than a fourth partition of Poland.'[5]

---

* The heavy tanks of three German Panzer Divisions, 6th, 7th and 8th, which crossed the Meuse in May 1940, were of Czech design from the Skoda works.

7 ON THE BRINK

As Gamelin says, the great part of French opinion was wholly at sea. The felicitations to Daladier after Munich demonstrated that the public had no understanding of the situation, that Great Britain was unprepared for a war on the Continent (it was already involved in Palestine), that France had betrayed a faithful ally in eastern Europe and that all she had left was Poland, the government of which leant rather towards Germany than to France and detested and feared the Russians, on whom the maintenance of peace depended. And at least half the French electorate shrank from an alliance with the government of the U.S.S.R., as did the President of the Republic, Albert Lebrun, who said that the 'only consequence of a pact with the Russians would be to inoculate France with the Bolshevik virus'.[1]

[2]

There remained the alliance with Poland. This was based on the two treaties of February 1921: a political treaty dated the 19th, which required the two governments to concert in the event of unprovoked aggression by Germany, and was supplemented by a military convention of the 21st, binding the parties to efficacious and immediate aid. Both countries were also pledged to act should the League of Nations decide to apply Article 16 of the League Covenant—in the circumstances of 1938-9 an unlikely occurrence. On the other hand, the League was involved, in that the so-called 'free' city of Danzig at the mouth of the Vistula was a mandated league entity with a league commissioner, a city inhabited by Germans for six centuries, surrounded on all land sides by the 'Polish Corridor', through which the Germans had transit rights to East Prussia. The situation offered an array of juridical conundrums to be exploited by a Hitler. Of this the Poles were aware. In October 1938, Ribbentrop warned the Polish ambassador in Berlin that the time had come to settle the Danzig question.

The French ambassador to Poland, Léon Noel, had been transferred from Prague to Warsaw in 1935. Having seen the Czechs deserted by the French during the Munich crisis, he thought it advisable to re-examine the Franco-Polish treaties of 1921 in order to consider how tightly the French were bound, especially since already the phrase 'Die for Danzig?' had been coined by an alert political journalist, Marcel Déat, once Minister of Air. Noel says that his conscience urged him to try to prevent the Quai d'Orsay allowing yet another ally to believe up to the last minute that France would keep her promise when she had no real intention of doing so. On reading the texts, he saw that their application was automatic and immediate; the French would be involved in war before the possibility of diplomatic intervention. Moreover, he was conscious that while Hitler had publicly recognized Poland's right to access to the sea (and the Poles had built the new port, Gdynia), he had at no time accepted the continued existence of the Polish Corridor.

Alarmed by what he had read, Noel spent a fortnight in Paris in November. He saw Weygand and Gamelin privately (the former had kept many of his old Polish contacts) and asked them whether, in view of what he had read, the terms of the treaties should not be revised. Both men considered that French interests and the state of their forces required the amendment of the military convention to more prudent and limited engagements. Noel therefore consulted Bonnet, the Minister of Foreign Affairs. With some difficulty he brought that serpentine politician round to admitting his point of view. Daladier, whom he tried to see, evaded a meeting. He returned to Warsaw to await instructions to open negotiations with the Poles. Nothing happened.[2]

[3]

The service chiefs, aware of the deficiencies in their armoury, though how comprehensive their awareness cannot be guessed, succeeded in securing credits for 1939 double those of 1938. Production was slow. To stimulate rearmament, Daladier obtained full powers from Parliament on 4 October. Paul Reynaud, who took over the Ministry of Finance on 1 November, on 12 November spoke on the radio about the state of the French budget and declared that an increase of more than 30 per cent in production was needed: more hours should therefore be worked. The Confédération Générale du Travail responded with a call for a general strike, which was a complete fiasco. Nevertheless, to satisfy the army and air force needs, it is probable that little short of putting the country's industry on a war footing would have been successful. So drastic a policy was unthinkable to the ministries. As Raoul Dautry, later Minister of Armaments, told the Commission on Events: 'Not a soldier really understood the size of the industrial problem the country would have to solve at the threat of war.'[3] In the last months of 1938, the paramount need was to gain time and to use it. The Franco-German declaration signed in Paris on 6 December was not the closure of an unpleasant episode, but a pause which, with luck and dexterous negotiation, might hold long enough to repair the neglect of the past.

The reality, the shortness of time, was not recognized. On 2 December, a meeting of the Army Council, with Gamelin in the chair, was held to discuss 'the composition of an armoured division and the creation of formations of this type'. (It had held one almost exactly a year earlier, quite fruitless.) The discussion was vague and ran away in the sands of minor detail; no one expected the materialization of such a body before the autumn of 1940. The minutes of the meeting[4] reveal no anxiety, no sense of urgency among the members. Whereas diplomats passing through Paris either on leave or between assignments showed their apprehension of coming events, the soldiers appeared confident that there was no cause for alarm. Robert Coulondre, in Paris in October 1938, on transfer from Moscow to Berlin, was assured by Gamelin and others that all was well. 'How could I imagine that a commander so master of himself [as Gamelin] was so little master of his armies and that the keep at Vincennes was an ivory tower.'[5] At the back of their confidence lay the dogma that when it came war must be long, and therefore one could take one's time over preparation.

[4]

While the co-ordination of the national defence had been agreed a necessity, and formal steps taken towards it by setting up a secretariat and the passage of various enactments, there was in reality only a masquerade of central control. The natural jealousy between services had not been dissipated. Admiral Darlan kept the navy to himself and did not trespass on the other two services. The air force had its champions in Chamber and Senate who suspiciously watched all proposals which might impinge on the autonomy of the air staff. Neither Daladier, chairman of the National Defence Council, nor Gamelin, Chief of Staff, exercised the slightest influence on either Darlan or Vuillemin. Neither indeed tried. Early in 1939 Gamelin suggested the conversion of the council into an authoritative body. While not refusing, Daladier temporized so effectively that there was no change. His reasons were not clearly expressed, but from what Gamelin says it is to be surmised that the President believed that this would place General Georges in a key position. Should the Defence Council become a reality, Georges, now assistant to Gamelin, would become Chief of the General Staff when Gamelin became Chief of Staff to the Defence Council. And Daladier was unwilling to have as C.G.S. a man he regarded as too friendly with his political enemies.

Alphonse-Joseph Georges came from the Isère. In 1914, when reaching forty, he was commanding an infantry battalion. Later he was attached to Sarrail's staff in Salonika. He appears to have had trouble with that difficult personality and to have been brought back to France to be placed on the staff of Foch. In 1926, he was Chief of Staff to Pétain during the Riff campaign. In 1931, he was *chef de cabinet* to Maginot. After Maginot's death, he became commander of the XIX Corps at Algiers. He was Weygand's candidate for Vice-President of the Army Council in succession to himself. In October 1934 he had been escorting Alexander of Yugoslavia and Barthou at Marseille when king and minister were murdered. Georges himself was severely wounded. In spite of a slow recovery, he was appointed *major-général des armées désigné* in case of war, when in 1935 Gamelin was promoted to Vice-President of the Army Council, of which Georges had been a member since 1934. This was a newly created title, in that the holder was not on the War Ministry staff, but on the Army Council. He was thus freed from administrative duties. A big square man, almost clean-shaven, with a firm chin, he gave the impression of strength and sincerity, but his wounds had damaged him more than he himself was aware. Major-General E. L. Spears, who had served with the French as liaison officer during 1914–18, thought highly of him. It is possible that he criticized too freely, which caused the suspicious Daladier to accuse him of intrigue. It is to be noted that Georges was due to retire in 1940, about the same time as Gamelin, which would clear the board for a Daladier nominee to the command of the army. But should war break out in 1939, Gamelin would command in all theatres and Georges would become commander of the army on the north-east front, i.e. from Switzerland to Dunkirk.

[5]

On 15 March, Hitler—to whom the Slovak leader, Father Tiso, had appealed when the central government in Prague dismissed his government—declared the 'protection' of Slovakia and occupied Prague. This unilateral action swept away the shoddy façade of the Munich agreement, and demonstrated to all that the Third Reich would not hesitate to break every contractual obligation at will. On 18 March, protests from Paris and London were rejected. Nevertheless Bonnet, the Foreign Minister, let it be known that the guarantees undertaken by France could not be expected to apply to a state which collapsed from within, and Neville Chamberlain told a local party meeting that the British Government no longer acknowledged the Munich agreement.

On 21 March, however, the Polish ambassador in Berlin protested over the German protectorate of Slovakia, which, though this does not appear in Lipski's report to Warsaw, menaced the southern frontier of Poland. Ribbentrop retorted that the Poles were showing hostility to Germany and that they had made no move towards freeing Danzig from the League of Nations.[6] These suggestions of Ribbentrop's were rejected two days later by Beck. Thereafter rumour and counter-rumour on both sides inflamed the controversy.

Up to now, both British and French Foreign Offices had wrongly believed that Romania was Hitler's next intended victim. It was not for another week that Poland appeared to stand in the greater peril. On 31 March, after consultation between the two governments, Chamberlain declared the intention of the British government to support the Polish government in resisting aggression. The French, of course, were already bound by the treaties of 1921, which had not been modified as desired by Léon Noel.

On 27 March, a French military mission came to London and was brought to the War Office by the military attaché, General Lelong. Colonel, later General, Noiret and Colonel Aymé from Gamelin's staff talked with Major-General Kennedy, Deputy-Director of Military Operations, Group-Captain Slessor of the Air Force and Captain

Danckwerts from the Admiralty. The French delegates appear to have known nothing about the size or state of the British land forces and were not a little horrified to learn how little their future allies were capable of providing in the way of support for the British government's declarations. They gave an approximation of the strength of the French forces, but disclosed nothing of their own plans. Possibly due to reports of the French dismay, possibly due to the discovery that the anti-aircraft defences of London were negligible, possibly, again, under pressure from the Foreign Secretary, Lord Halifax, on the evening of the 28th Chamberlain announced and repeated in the Commons on the following day that there would be an immediate addition of 40,000 to the Territorial Army followed by a doubling of the whole force, making a total of 340,000. On the 31st, he told the House that the French and British governments had informed the Polish government that, in the event of any threat to Polish independence, they would lend the Polish government all the support in their power.

This was all very fine, but though the British had been slightly worried by the indifferent state of British armaments since the abandon-ment of the 'Ten-Year Rule', there had been little material remedy. There was an air force, with the bombers of which they were ready to support the French, but the Air Staff had shown no interest in co-operation with the ground forces. It was also very short of fighters. The army had men for five infantry divisions but could arm only two. Hore-Belisha had been transferred to the War Office by Chamberlain in May 1937 with instructions to make 'drastic changes' in the army organization, but a number of his new appointments were mistaken and were resented. In the War Office and the commands, the 'cavalry spirit' survived, while some of the best brains in service were kept in positions where they were powerless to make reforms. Lord Gort, the Chief of the Imperial General Staff, in spite of many soldierly virtues, which would be seen fifteen months later, was not an organizer. 'If,' wrote Major-General Kennedy, 'General Dill had been appointed in Novem-ber 1937, it is fairly certain that neither Ironside nor Gort would have been in key positions at the outbreak of war.'[7]

[6]

There was the complication of Italy. Gamelin's opposite number, Marshal Badoglio, was not *bien vu* by Mussolini, but the choice of King Victor Emmanuel. He in no way shared the Fascist dictator's lust for acquisition and was content with the formal Franco-Italian relations at such points as the Savoys, Nice, Corsica and the Italian settlers in Tunisia. On the other hand, he favoured Italian interests in the Balkans and the Danube basin. During the period of German pressure on Austria after the murder of Chancellor Dollfuss in July 1934, he had prepared for Italian intervention. During 1935, as an outcome of the Laval-Mussolini talks, there had been a number of confidential but inconclusive talks between the French and Italian army and air force staffs. All this was blown away when Abyssinia was annexed, especially when the Italians added claims to Djibouti and French Somaliland. Relations became still more embittered with the intervention in Spain on behalf of General Franco. After the unmasking of French indecision and nullity during the Czech crisis of 1938, Mussolini's menacing speeches became more insolent, and the Italians began to build up the forces in Tripolitania. In April, on Good Friday, Mussolini sent troops into Albania and annexed it. It was followed by the grandiosely named 'Pact of Steel' with Hitler. The pact added to French embarrassment, requiring increased vigilance on the African shipping routes to Nice and Marseille and the maintenance of French troops in abnormal strength in the Niessel Line between Tunisia and Tripolitania.

[7]

It was clear that whatever political equilibrium survived in Europe was now rocking. On 25 April, Chamberlain introduced a Military Service Bill, in other words conscription, a measure which, while it was approved in principle by the armed services, had the disadvantage of hampering and delaying the reorganization of the army already in hand, since it filled new formations with scarcely trained officers and N.C.O.s; 'lance-bombardiers became lance-sergeants', as a military critic has written.

Chamberlain and Halifax had believed that the adoption of conscription by Great Britain would act as a deterrent on Hitler. Its effect was clean contrary. The German dictator merely concluded that to achieve his purposes he must not delay. On 28 April, the German government transmitted a memorandum to the British government terminating the naval agreement of 18 June 1935, and on the same day a memorandum was handed to the Polish government denouncing the Polish-German non-aggression declaration of January 1934 on the ground that Poland and Great Britain were obviously concerting the encirclement of Germany. The crisis began to develop at an unexpected pace.

[8]

In 1936, when visiting Warsaw, Gamelin had warned the Polish command that they would have to prepare for a long resistance against invasion, since the French Army would have trouble in attacking Germany on the narrow front available between Luxemburg and Switzerland and that progress towards Mainz must inevitably be slow. He suggested that the Poles should fortify their frontiers. They replied that these were far too extensive for any reasonable system. He told them that they were planning to meet the enemy much too far forward. Also he considered that they should co-operate with Czechoslovakia. The Inspector-General of the Polish Army, General Smigly-Rydz, replied that nothing would induce them to approach the Czechs any more than they would the Russians. Polish unwillingness to remedy their vulnerability made Gamelin cautious. Plans of co-operation remained imprecise, but the French government agreed to a loan, a heavy loan, two million francs for rearmament, it seems, with no strings attached. This did not prove as satisfactory as had been hoped. However, in June 1938, that is just before the Munich crisis, further conversations appear to have led the French to promise an immediate offensive between the Hardt and the Moselle. But the behaviour of the Polish government during the Czech crisis of September and their seizure of the border area of Teschen with a population of nearly a quarter of a million, considerably chilled French sympathy with the Warsaw government, in particular with the Foreign Minister, Colonel Josef Beck, and that cultivated soldier Smigly-Rydz, who had sworn to Gamelin that the Poles would not seize Teschen.

The spring crisis of 1939 arrived before Bonnet had taken any step towards the modification of the terms of the Polish alliance. But the opening of military conversations with the British led to a beginning of serious consultations with the Poles. In May, the Polish Minister of War, General Kasprzycki, came to Paris and discussed with Gamelin, Admiral Darlan, Generals Vuillemin, Georges and others plans to be put into operation if, as was now seen to be almost inevitable, the conflict with Germany led to war. In the curiously involved exchanges, as narrated by Gamelin,[8] the French general was obviously reluctant to promise too much. But Vuillemin for the French Air Force was far less restrained and undertook to dispatch five groups of Amiot 143 bombers, sixty machines, to Poland on the outbreak of hostilities provided the Poles would provide air-fields. Gamelin contented himself with saying that the French would gain touch with the Siegfried Line in order to hold the maximum number of German divisions. Georges, on the other hand, 'in the obvious desire, like Vuillemin, not to discourage our allies', foreshadowed a serious attack on the Siegfried Line about the seventeenth day from the opening of hostilities. Gamelin says that he reiterated his early warnings to the Poles, warnings which had become all the weightier with the disappearance of Czechoslovakia and the envelopment of the Polish southern frontier. At the conclusion of the conversations, however, he was relieved to discover that whatever he signed would be subject to a political agreement, at the moment being discussed by Bonnet and the Polish ambassador, Lukaciewicz. In the event, the political instrument was not signed until 4 September, when Poland was already invaded. By that time Gamelin had substituted for the military agreement a far less positive directive as to the initial operations between Rhine and Moselle.

[9]

Both French and British Foreign Offices remained under a number of illusions of which one of the chief was that the Russians would realize that they were the ultimate prey of the Germans, and that therefore it was to their interest to help in the defence of Poland. And though well aware that the Poles detested the Russians, the western powers believed that the Poles would see that the Russian army could give much more powerful aid than the French and British armies could provide, and that it was in their interest to invite the Russians to come. Both suppositions were wrong, as the ambassadors to these countries knew. Noel said that Daladier's cabinet and the French general staff were inexcusable if they seriously believed in the possibility of Polish-Russian agreement. Nevertheless, early in August the French and British governments sent a joint mission of generals, admirals and air-marshals with the appropriate assistants to Moscow. Whether from consciousness that the mission was futile or from sheer indifference, their organizers sent them slowly by sea. It took them a week to reach their destination. General Doumenc, who headed the mission, was instructed to be as non-committal as possible, which was fatuous, since the French were bound to the Poles by their alliance, and the British were as closely clipped by Chamberlain's guarantee of April. The mission was deprived of any possibility of manœuvre. From the beginning the Russian chief representative, Marshal Voroshilov, was stiff. Doumenc's statements of what the French could and would do were, to say the least, vague, exaggerated and unconvincing. For example, that the Maginot Line stretched from the Swiss frontier to the sea, that the French could move fifteen divisions by motor transport, etc. Voroshilov told them bluntly that the Russians would expect an immediate opening to them of naval bases in Estonia and Latvia and areas for ground troops round Lvov and Wilno. 'It was perfectly well known in Moscow—and much better than Paris wanted to hear—that the consent of Poland would never be obtained and that neither France nor Great Britain would ever force it from her.'[9] From 17 August, negotiations were suspended in order to allow this vital question to be put to the Poles. In the interval, the German Foreign Minister, Ribbentrop, whose officials were already discussing the terms of a commercial treaty with Moscow, suggested to the Russian Foreign Minister Molotov a more extensive political treaty. On 21 August he came to Moscow by air, where a Russo-German mutual non-aggression treaty was signed. Its second article declared that should either country be the object of an act by a third party, the other signatory would lend no aid to the assailant. That took care of Poland. The conclusion of the agreement was made public on the 23rd, and on this day Hitler set down dawn on the 26th for the invasion of Poland.

The delegation of the western powers saw Voroshilov for the last time on the 25th, when he said to them that during the whole period of their conversations the Polish press and people had continued to proclaim that they wanted no Soviet help. 'Were we to have to conquer Poland in order to offer them our help? The position is impossible.'[10]

Before the news of the Russo-German treaty had reached Paris, at a meeting on the 23 August of the Council of National Defence, the three

service chiefs, Gamelin, Darlan and Vuillemin, had said in answer to
Daladier's question that they were ready.[11] Precautionary measures had
been ordered on the 21st, when all men on leave were recalled and units
in camp sent back to their barracks. On the 22nd the first stages of
French frontier protection were begun on the German, Italian and
Tripolitanian frontiers. The Italian embassy in Paris was assured that
these measures were purely precautionary and had no hostile intention.
Thereafter the full machinery of French mobilization was put into
operation. The frontiersmen joined the permanent frontier garrisons;
the *couverture* reserve, seven active divisions, began to move. By the
evening of the 25th nearly two million men were under arms. On 1 September, general mobilization was decreed to begin on the following day.
In 1938, the reservists had marched up with a certain confident determination: '*il faut en finir*'. The same phrase was to be heard in 1939, but
the tone was one of exasperated resignation.

[10]

For some time the Germans had been gradually and scarcely perceptibly
mobilizing, and were continuing to do so during August. On the 21st
four divisions were on the Polish frontier. The Poles began to mobilize
on 23 August, and on the next day called up three classes of reservists.
On the 25th Italy began its call-up. On the 28th King Leopold of
Belgium offered his good offices to France, Italy, Germany, Poland and
Great Britain. None accepted.

During these weeks, Hitler pursued his hitherto successful tactics of
cajolement and menace. On 29 August, German forces occupied
Slovakia, confirming Polish fears. Late in the evening of 31 August the
Germans presented imperative demands on Poland regarding Danzig
and the Corridor in such a manner that the terms could not even be
accepted within the time-limit, and at 5.30, on 1 September, German
infantry and tanks entered Poland and their air forces began the ruthless
bombing of Polish towns. French and British demands for withdrawal
were rejected. Once again, as at Munich, Mussolini made proposals for
a four-power conference. They were ignored. At 11 a.m. on 3 September a state of war existed between Great Britain and Germany and at
5.30 p.m. between France and Germany.*

---

* Mussolini had already told Hitler that the Italian Army was as yet insuffi-
ciently equipped to allow him to declare war on France. On 1 September Hitler
replied that he would not need Italian military support.

PART TWO

Drôle de Guerre

THE LOSS OF A SECOND ALLY

SINCE it was generally accepted that the French intentions were to defend, the earliest engagements could be only on French soil and the inhabitants of Alsace and Lorraine would be on or near the battle-fields, not only in danger but worse, a nuisance to the combatants. Up to the German reoccupation of the demilitarized zone, it had seemed that there would be plenty of time for the evacuation of the frontier departments on the declaration of war, although, with the withdrawal of the Army of the Rhine in 1930, the French authorities had begun to worry about the threat of bombing in the urban areas. As early as February 1930, instructions for dealing with such an emergency were issued and further more elaborate orders followed at intervals. In June 1935, regulations for the evacuation of the frontier and near-frontier departments from the Nord down to Alpes-Maritimes and the Var came out, with allocation of the centres to which the evacuated should go. In July 1938, between the occupation of Austria and the Munich crisis, further instructions for the withdrawal of all civilians from the combat zone were circulated, with considerable detail as to the disposal of live-stock and the lifting at the appropriate dates of cereals, beets, potatoes, grapes, etc. There were further notes on the problems of hands for factories engaged in the production of weapons and explosives, as well as food supplies for the troops, particularly to replace men who had been called up to the armed forces. There was the problem of bringing additional workers to areas where plans for military needs were being increased. And there were not only these problems, involving the movement of an enormous part of the population, but the problem of transporting the administrative paraphernalia: for example, the depart-ment of the Ardennes required a convoy big enough to remove 114 metric tons of documents relating to the taxpayers and their taxes to a place of safety.

All this was further complicated by the need to maintain secrecy in the area to be cleared, which meant that much would have to be impro-vised at the last moment. The *maire* of Nouvion-sur-Meuse reported that there was only one town councillor who would not be called up, to arrange and supervise the removal of 1,600 children.

There were also the problems attendant on the fitting of urban populations into rural reception areas. The Paris officials attempted to equalize numbers, causing immense confusion on the railways. When the time came, the big colonies of Bretons and Auvergnats in Paris found themselves dispersed in regions far from those they had come from. Another plan distributed the evacuees according to their professions and offices. Hence the Foreign Office was eventually transferred to Langeais, the Ministry of Finance to Chinon, the Cour de Cassation to Angers and the Chamber of Deputies settled very easily and appropriately in the theatre at Tours.

[2]

From the end of August a double movement ebbed and flowed along the frontier from Givet to Basle, of civilians moving to provinces far from the battle-zone, and of troops and reinforcements for the Maginot Line garrisons moving up. The frontier area along the Rhine was emptied to a depth of five kilometres from the river. In forty-eight hours, with the aid of one regional regiment, 250,000 Strasbourgeois were dispatched to the south, and the great bridge to Kehl was empty of traffic; at each end bored soldiers watched the flood on which no barges slid by. Yet the bridges, though empty, were not destroyed, and the great Kembs power station, which supplied light and power to both sides of the river, continued to work.

In the no-man's-land along the Lauter, the Blies, the Sarre north of the Maginot *ouvrages*, *maires* and town councillors hurried on the removal of women and children from farms and villages, sometimes with their goods, often with no more than they could carry. Longwy, facing the Luxembourg frontier, the iron and steel town, threaded with rails between the works and the slag heaps, with its old Vauban fortress with galleries driven deep into the rock, continued to work day and night, but the women and children were gone; their place was taken by splendid Moroccan and Algerian spahis in their red cloaks with their little Arab horses.

On 7 September the 2nd Dismounted Dragoons (*Les Dragons de Condé*) passed through the Maginot Line east of Thionville.

We had heard nothing about the evacuation. To ask our way, we halted late that night at the first village we came to, Monneren, and knocked at doors. No answer. We peeped through a shutter; there was a table laid and a lighted lamp. We tapped at the window. Not a soul came. We opened the stable door, and were nearly knocked down by the beasts that plunged out, dying of thirst, lowing and bellowing. It might have been a scene from Dante. And next morning, the sight was even more heart-breaking. The geraniums in the windows invited you to come in—you expected to find someone. Nothing; just the tick-tock of the clock counting the minutes of this nightmare, the cats begging to be stroked, the dogs rubbing against our legs. Across the fields, the goats and cows, with swollen udders at the point of bursting, the pigs rooting in the potato fields to find something to eat. The church even had been hurriedly abandoned by the curé. The Lamp of the Holy Sacrament was still alight and the chairs in the chancel showed that a wedding had just been celebrated. . . . This morning our division had its baptism of fire.[1]

During these days, the fortress regiments had been filling up with their local reserves and tripling their numbers, while the cavalry masked the concentration of the Third, Fourth and Fifth Armies, the three parts of the Second Army Group (AG Two) commanded by General Prételat, who this year reached the age of retirement but was maintained. AG Two covered the front from Longuyon to the Rhine between Strasbourg and Sélestat and included the Maginot Line. On the left, General Condé's Third Army occupied the stretch from Longuyon to Faulquemont and protected the Briey iron-field and the industrial areas of Metz and Thionville. Next came Requin's Fourth Army, which held the deep re-entrant to the Sarre at Sarreguemines and then swung eastward to its junction with the Fifth Army (General Bourret). The Fifth Army spanned the largely unfortified Vosges and then swung southeastward with the fortified Haguenau sector down to the Rhine at Rhinau.

As to the Siegfried Line, the French had only sketchy information. Parts of it were visible to travellers on the Saarbrucken to Saarburg rail, but no one was sure whether it was as flimsy as it appeared, or whether, as some said, it had been very skilfully sited and had great depth.

Gamelin's engagement to the Poles concerning the French Army's action on the declaration of war was based on the presumption that the Polish forces could withstand German attacks for some months, and, if the invasion came after the beginning of the winter's snow, until the spring. The French armies would thus be able to mobilize and concentrate without haste. 'I shall shelter under the Siegfried Line,' Gamelin had told Smigly-Rydz, 'and wait.'[2]

As early as 24 August, General Georges had warned Prételat to push the Fourth Army across the Sarre and the Blies, to secure positions from which to attack the enemy defences round Saarbrucken, and push on further east towards Zweibrucken, and on 4 September he appeared at the headquarters of AG Two at Nancy with messages from Gamelin to hasten the attack. This was far from easy. The motorized infantry divisions from the centre were still *en route* and many of the infantry units in front of the Maginot defences were still at their peace-time strength. Writing of the forward movements of the Fifth Army, General Bourret said: 'I used divisions which had not yet received their Echelon B, that is, they had only two regiments of two battalions of two companies of two platoons and two groups of artillery with two batteries with two guns and no ammunition column.'[3] Further, Vuillemin said that he could not assure air protection until the air force concentration was complete.[4]

Nevertheless, in spite of these troubles, the Fourth Army began to move forward on the night of 8th/9th, when *'La Division de Fer'*, the 11th Division from Nancy, crossed the Blies and the Sarre on both sides of Sarreguemines in the dark, and advanced nine kilometres to a point from which they could look down on Saarbrucken. At the same time, a cavalry regiment, and Algerians from the 4th North African Division, occupied part of the Warndt Forest, and to the east General Dassault's

V Corps moved into the Ohrenthal salient. Much further west, near the point on the Moselle where the frontiers of France, Germany and Luxembourg meet, there was a swift and fierce reaction to a French snatch of some hills, which was followed by heavy fighting for another ten days before the objective was secured.

At the end of the first two days' fighting, the French had advanced along the whole of a forty-kilometre front, but they had not reached the Siegfried Line. The fighting had been stiff and the casualties, though not heavy, were disturbing, since many of them came from an un-suspected defensive weapon, the land-mine, used against both soldiers and A.F.V. As yet the French soldier did not know how to deal with these.[5]

Prételat prepared to continue the attacks, though he had little con-fidence in the newly formed divisions which were to reinforce his armies. But on the 11th, G.Q.G.N.E. stopped the attacks. It was abundantly clear that the Poles were not halting the German advance, and further attacks in Lorraine would involve profitless losses. The divisions facing the Sarre were ordered to consolidate their positions.

[3]

On 9 September the Polish military attaché in Paris began to ask ques-tions about the promised French aid. Had the French Air Force yet begun to attack the German Air Force in Germany ? What was happen-ing to the general attack ? A few days later, there were further questions about the sixty Amiot 143 which had not reached the Poles. They were unlikely to do so, since the airfields were already in German hands, but the five squadrons had not even started. Gamelin tried to hustle Georges and Prételat, but they were not going to jeopardize their troops at bidding.

The Polish Army was rapidly crushed. The German Air Force began raiding in great strength, relative to that of the Poles on 1 September. Attacks by ground forces began at the same time, from East Prussia at Mlawa and from the Gleiwitz–High Tatra angle towards Czestochowa. On both sides there were the usual unverifiable enumeration of victories and denials of losses. In order to prevent a charge of aggression the Poles had mobilized late. Even so, their forces were smaller and less well equipped than the German. At the most they had fewer than fifty infantry divisions, and their thirteen cavalry brigades might as well have not existed. Bromberg was lost on 5 September, Cracow on the 6th. On the 7th, the Germans were only thirty miles from Warsaw. On the same day invasion began from eastern Slovakia towards Lvov. By the 13th Warsaw was surrounded; western Poland was wholly conquered, and already the Germans were able to transfer divisions to the west.

By 14 September German headquarters had already seen the end of the Poles, and some eighteen divisions seem to have left Poland for the west.

From 12 September, Gamelin dropped the idea of a French offensive. Nothing could be done for the Poles. On the 17th the troops of the Workers' and Peasants' Red Army crossed the frontier, marched rapidly into Poland, and reported the jubilation with which they were received. On the 28th Warsaw and Modlin surrendered. On the 21st, Gamelin renounced his intention of advancing up to the Sarre, let alone to the Siegfried Line. French Intelligence calculated that within a week the Germans would be able to attack, and that the Third, Fourth and Fifth Armies had better withdraw from their most forward points. The French had previously lost the Czechs, a competent ally with thirty well-equipped divisions; they had now lost a brave but vain ally with forty ill-found divisions. There remained a single ally, with four divisions. There was little to be done, in fact nothing except to wait. The *drôle de guerre* was beginning. '*Je serai avare du sang,*' General Gamelin told an interviewer.

Early in October there began the reconstitution and consolidation of the front, the withdrawal of the motorized divisions and the beginning of the training of all active and 'A' formations in the wasteland between the Maginot Line and the River Sarre. The front lines were thinned out to about half strength. The weather broke and the rivers rose. On 16 October the enemy attacked the outposts on the Sarre and the Blies and at Niedergailbach. The weak frontline garrisons, thrown back to the rivers, had great trouble in escaping, as most of the bridges had been swept away. But the positions were held on the Sarre and the Blies, where they would remain through the winter with little change.

2 ILLUSIONS AND DISILLUSION

O N the whole, mobilization had been carried out expeditiously and efficiently. There had been no sabotage, no indiscipline; even Thorez had gone quietly. The whole exercise had been infinitely more supple than in 1914. In that year the quantity of cars and trucks had been negligible. In 1939, there were 139,000 at the disposal of the forces and nearly 9,000 trains against less than 5,000 twenty-five years earlier.[1]

It was not so in other spheres. If the active regiments were reasonably equipped, the newly formed 'A' divisions were without many necessities, while most of the requisitioned elements, especially transport, were defective. The army had only 30,000 trucks and the balance was made up by civilian machines. Many of the 270,000 taken were in lamentable condition: 40,000 went through the workshops in the next few months. A corps reconnaissance group states that one squadron had cars and motor-cycles of twenty-four manufactures and forty-two types: and of its 125 men, forty-five had never used a motor-cycle.[2] A reserve artillery regiment's historian wrote that 'our transport requisitioned from round Paris beggared description, not to speak of the farm tractors which had not been repaired for twenty years. We piled them with our 75s (Model 1897, unimproved!) on our trucks. . . .'[3] In October, Third Army headquarters reported a shortage of 130,000 pairs of boots, and the commander of the 42nd Active Division of Metz claimed that a quarter of his infantry was marching barefoot owing to the rottenness of the socks.[4] 'The armament of my corps reconnaissance group,' wrote General de la Laurencie, 'was defective equally in quantity and quality. An appreciable number of the 25-mm. guns had to be replaced by 37-mm. drill-purpose pieces, very worn and for the most part without sights. A third of the machine-guns and light machine-guns were at the end of their life. The rifle-grenade cups could not be used on the 1936 rifle with which the units were armed. There were only eleven of the side-cars on the establishment. They were made up with well-worn motor-cycles of nineteen different makes.'[5] Such complaints fill several pages in most unit and formation histories.

This was not all. Whereas much of the rearmament programme of 1936 had been fulfilled, it was becoming clear that in some directions needs had been underestimated. Six thousand 25-mm. anti-tank guns had been authorized. At the outbreak of war only 4,000 had been delivered. On 10 May 1940 the whole 6,000 had been distributed; even so the deficiency of anti-tank guns yawned. It is probable that not a single one of the 'B' infantry divisions had a full complement, and this applies equally to the 47-mm., of which the official table says 25 per cent above the figure asked for was delivered. At the height of the last struggle in Alsace in June 1940, General Bourret[6] could only equip the 62nd Division with 25-mm. guns to defend the Vosges passes by taking them from the fortress troops in the Maginot Line. Four months after the outbreak of war, the anti-tank team of the 159th Alpine Regiment (Active) was still kicking its heels at the mobilization centre waiting for its guns: 'We shall probably end like that, the 25-mm. section that went through the war without a gun. Don't worry.'[7]

As the call-up became more comprehensive, many more gaps in equipment than had been expected appeared. It was found impossible to equip every soldier with personal weapons. So arms were withdrawn from the type of warrior believed to be safe from close contact with the enemy—with unimagined results. In the Ninth Army, signal units had only 15 per cent of their weapons, labour units did not have rifles.[8] A number of shortages, of course, were due to bad store-keeping. These faults would no doubt have been remedied but for the suddenness of the defeat. The British, whose shortcomings were equally glaring, had the advantage of an island citadel which allowed them to borrow time.

Further, in the early months, the anti-aircraft batteries had only out-of-date guns with muzzle velocity, rate of fire and ceiling of an earlier epoch, for use against aircraft flying at 200 k.p.h.

For reasons which still remain unintelligible, but which appear in fact due to the dislike of surrendering any fragment of power, Daladier had on more than one occasion refused to appoint a Minister of Armaments before war was declared. It was only on 13 September that he summoned Raoul Dautry,* deservedly one of the most acclaimed civil engineers in France, who for months had been denouncing the lack of preparedness for war, the lack of understanding on the part of the Ministers of Public Works, the lack of workshops, of machine tools and other equipment. 'Not one soldier had really understood the immensity of the industrial problems which the country would have to solve when war came, a magnitude which a Millerand, an Albert Thomas, a Pain-levé, a Loucheur, had once been able to measure.'[9] Dautry at once confirmed what he had already surmised, that the War Ministry 'suffered at least as much as the majority of the civilian administrations . . . from bureaucratic habits, conformity, abuse of the regulations and confusion of responsibilities'. The Labour Minister, Pomaret, whose duty it was to produce workers for the armament factories, not only had neither the means nor the technical capacity to enlist them, but resented the fact that Dautry, by the strength of his personality, was able to win the collaboration of masters, workmen and trades-union officials. Working day and night untiringly for the next eight months, Dautry did all that was

---

* Raoul Dautry (1880–1951), Engineer-in-Chief Nord Railway, 1914–18; Reconstructor of the Devastated Regions, 1918; Director-General French State Railways, 1928–37; Director-General of the French State Railway System (S.N.C.F.) from 1936, maire of Loumarie, Vaucluse, where he died.

humanly possible to repair the years of neglect, to destroy vested interests, to inspire physicists and chemists, masters and workmen. He even spent a night in the Admiralty in London at the side of Winston Churchill, arranging for the reciprocal manufacture of parts of tanks. 'All my difficulties were as nothing beside the uncertainty of obtaining the men from the army. . . . The battle for labour with G.Q.G. and the Army Staff was perpetual. . . . Though I understood their preoccupations I never stopped repeating that to my mind it was better to have forty well-armed divisions than seventy-five less well-equipped.'[10]

During the months of the *drôle de guerre* the selfish interests survived. 'At the Ripault powder works several county councillors from Tours brought along the *préfet* to ask for the demobilization of some farmers. In their presence two conscripts loudly demanded their own release. One was a pianist, the other a singer. It seemed that it was to the country's interest that they should be exempted to go and play at café concerts to raise the morale of the nation.' The deputies were no better. In February and March 1940, there were harsh interpellations in the Chamber on behalf of the return to civil life of agricultural workers, including oyster breeders. To one deputy, who said that the Minister of Armaments knew nothing about the sowing seasons, Dautry snapped back: 'But he knows what is the season for shells.'[11]

'*Drôle de guerre !*' 'More than once I was convinced that too often the conscripts were badly looked after and that in spite of my objurgations and orders many managers remained wholly indifferent to the conditions of life and labour of their men. . . . After six months of war there were still managers—otherwise perfectly competent—who had not yet grasped their elementary duty! At the time I thought I was being hard on these military and civilian controllers. Alas, I had always only too good reasons to be so in the powder works and arsenals, in the war workshops of Renault, Berliet and the rest. . . .'[12]

Dautry's error, like that of many others, was to believe Gamelin's often repeated line that the war would be long. How was he to know that Gamelin's conception of war had not changed since 1918 and that the laurels of that year had had no seeds. Even as late as 18 May 1940 he was dispatching a dozen of his best engineers to New York to contract for every kind of weapon. On 14 May Lieutenant-Colonel Raguet, his liaison officer with Gamelin, pointed to the map and said: 'Everything is going as the Commander-in-Chief predicted. Two or three years ago he told us during a war-game: "I shall deliver my armoured counter-attack in this quadrilateral and I shall win."'[13]

Nor were the civilian evacuees any more cheerful than the conscripts, though the civil authorities had shown greater awareness of realities and more acuteness in dealing with them. The emptying of Strasbourg and the transfer of its population out of the war zone within twenty-four hours had been masterly. The villages within five kilometres of the Rhine had been dealt with equally speedily, as had the re-entrant of the

Maginot Line. But the cleanly urbanized and industrial citizens of these Alsatian and Lorraine towns found the peasants of Périgord and Quercy, whither they were transplanted, far from congenial, and the villages insanitary and wretched, while those on whom they were billeted looked on them as *bouches inutiles* spending their days coffee-housing from village to village.[14]

Yet there was little evidence of anti-war discontent, just dull acceptance of the inevitable. The Russo-German treaty had shocked most Frenchmen and the proscription of the Communist party was regarded as necessary. The Communist leaders were in disarray after the Russian *volte-face*, especially as nearly a third of the Communist deputies had resigned from the party, many even before the outbreak of war. Thorez, called up to the army, was successfully spirited away to Russia before the end of September, to be followed by Marty and Cachin, while Duclos crossed the frontier. Florimonde Bonté attempted to keep the party alive under the name of Peasants and Workers but had no success.

It is said that much anti-war propaganda was carried out by Communists in the army, but it is difficult to trace. In any case there was plenty of natural discontent untinged with politics. Only one division is spoken of as politically influenced, the 71st, a 'B' division, chiefly because it was recruited in Paris, and even this is by no means certain. Sabotage in factories of war equipment is spoken of, but vaguely. Rossi quotes only one case, of three youths and a much older brother, who were tried at Bordeaux in May. Two were shot and two given long terms of *travaux forcés*. This seems an isolated case.

3 DEFICIENCIES AND DEFECTS

THE army* that was eventually concentrated on the north-eastern front in September consisted of thirty-nine first-line infantry divisions, nine 'B' divisions, three cavalry, and a number of unincorporated machine-gun regiments and battalions, and a quantity of artillery regiments. There were two light-armoured divisions and a number of independent tank battalions, some still in the process of formation, but as yet no armoured division. The seven fortress regiments were rapidly expanded to forty.†

The first-line infantry divisions comprised seven motorized and ten normal active divisions, three North African‡ and three colonial.§ Then came sixteen 'A' formation divisions of men roughly between the ages of twenty-four and thirty-two, who had done their service. These formation divisions received on mobilization a proportion of serving officers and other ranks from active regiments. The North African divisions were Algerians, Tunisian and more recently Moroccan, who were brought to France after the final 'pacification' of the Riff in 1934. In these all the officers except nine were white, and about 15 per cent of the other ranks. All were enlisted and not conscripts.

The 'B' infantry divisions, of which the numbers were those between 51 and 71, were made up of men over thirty-two and were on a lower establishment than the first-line divisions. At best they had no more

---

* A skeleton Order of Battle as at 10 May 1940 is printed at p. 339.

† The fortress regiments, though static, were drawn from the same age-groups as the other first-line units. The garrisons of the Maginot *ouvrages* were technicians trained to handle the equipment peculiar to these forts.

‡ North African divisions, except the Moroccan Division, consisted of one Zouave regiment and two Tirailleur (either Algérien, Tunisien or Moroccan) regiments. The Zouaves are white conscripts, the others enlisted. There were four divisions on 3 September, the 1st North African with the Sixth Army on the Italian front, the 2nd, 3rd and 4th in Lorraine. To these were gradually added the 82nd and 87th brought from Africa, and the newly recruited 5th and 6th. The 7th was not formed until the middle of May at Valdahon camp near Besançon.

§ The colonial regiments formally were white volunteers stationed at the naval stations Brest, Rochefort, Toulon, etc., for service overseas. (These were the equivalent of 'linked' regiments in the colonies.) When constituted, the divisions were expanded by the introduction of colonial natives, 'Senegalese', though these seem to have included natives from Madagascar and Indo-China. During the winter, the Senegalese were transferred to the south of France, to be brought back with the spring. In September 1939, there were four colonial divisions, of which three were in the north, the 2nd being retained with the Sixth Army in Alpes-Maritimes. The 3rd Colonial Division remained a white division throughout, all the others getting two regiments of Senegalese *tirailleurs*. The 5th, 6th and 7th Colonial Divisions were constituted during the autumn.

than three serving officers, one of whom would be the divisional commander and the others probably the infantry and artillery commanders.
Eventually there were sixteen of these on the north-eastern front. Most
of them were used to garrison the defences between and forward of the
Maginot *ouvrages*. They were terribly short of every kind of equipment.

In September, the cavalry was still cavalry, in that each of the three
divisions had two horsed brigades of two regiments, but these were
strengthened by the addition of one armoured-car regiment (*auto-
mitrailleuse*) and one battalion of dismounted dragoons (*dragons portés*)
with an artillery regiment of one group of 75s and one of 105s. These
three cavalry divisions were broken up during the winter and early
spring and converted to five 'Light Cavalry Divisions', consisting of one
horsed brigade and one mechanized. The sixth horsed brigade, the 1st,
became an independent formation without artillery. During the spring
three independent cavalry brigades of Spahi, either Algerian or Moroccan, were brought from Africa.

As yet there were only two armoured divisions, both light, *Divisions
légères mécanisées*, derived from Weygand's initiative of 1930, conceived
as the modern version of a cavalry division. A third division was constituted in the spring. When active operations were about to start, the
2nd and 3rd divisions were formed into the 'Cavalry Corps', though
there was not a horse with them, under General Prioux. These
divisions consisted of a 'combat brigade' of Hotchkiss and Somua
tanks, and an 'observation brigade' (*brigade de découverte*) of armoured
cars, motor-cyclists, and a regiment of three battalions of motorized
dragoons.

Apart from the organic divisional artillery, there was a large array of
guns of every kind from the new anti-tank 25-mm. and 47-mm. up to
the 320-mm. railway guns. The post-1918 version of the famous '75'
had been modified, together with its ammunition, and its range had
been increased from 5,000 to 9,000 metres. There were also new larger
guns, a 105 gun-howitzer for the divisional artillery. But in the reserves
there were still a number of, to say the least, obsolescent pieces, 75s
carried on lorries unconverted from the first model of 1897. And there
were more than a thousand 105-mm. of 1915, which General Bourret of
the Fifth Army avers were useless. There were above 3,000 155s of
various types and even some large trench mortars. The weakest section
was undoubtedly the anti-aircraft. Much of it bore no relation to the
increase in speed and height since 1918, and there was little of serious
value at the outbreak of war.

In January it was at last considered that the production of the B.1 *bis*
heavy tank had reached the point at which it was possible to constitute
two armoured divisions (*divisions cuirassées*—D.C.R.). A third was con-
templated and eventually begun on 20 March. All three were stationed
on the great Châlons-sur-Marne military area, the Salisbury Plain of the

French Army. Each division had a combat brigade of two battalions each of 31 B, and two of Hotchkiss, each of forty-two tanks. To this was added one battalion of *chasseurs-à-pied* in armoured carriers, an artillery regiment (two groups each of twelve short 105-mm.) and a battery of 47-mm. anti-tank guns. There were engineers, signal companies including radio. Each division should have had an air reconnaissance squadron, but not one appeared. Also the commanders had expected a third artillery group and two battalions of dismounted dragoons.[1]

Beyond these, there were sixteen battalions of Renault 35, two of F.C.M. light tanks, one of Hotchkiss, attached to armies in varying numbers, *chars d'accompagnement* for the infantry. Each battalion numbered forty-five machines. There were also six battalions of the 1918 Renault F.T., quite useless. There were sixty-three of these to each battalion. And finally there were Estienne's six 70-ton C somewhere near Metz.

In addition to the above, there were mobilized a great number of units of all kinds. There were two regiments of the Foreign Legion and also units from '*les joyeux*'—penal battalions. There were regiments and battalions of Foreign Volunteers, exiles and expatriates from Germany, Austria, Russia and the Balkans. There were battalions of African Light Infantry. There were Chasseurs Pyrénéens. There were companies of the Garde Républicaine Mobile and the gendarmerie. There were many Poles. The 1st Polish Division took over part of the Sarre sector in the spring; the 2nd, ill-armed but brave, was to fight round Belfort in June; a third division was training in Brittany. There were two Czech legions. And all over the country were regional regiments, labour regiments and so forth.

[2]

On the south-eastern frontier facing the Italians was the Sixth Army of General Besson, which was presently to be entitled the Army of the Alps. It was made up of two army corps, XIV of Lyon and XV of Marseille. These corps consisted of Alpine troops, either normal three-battalion infantry regiments, or demi-brigades of *chasseurs-alpins*, each consisting of three independent battalions. On mobilization the three active divisions were amalgamated with two 'A' formation divisions, producing five formations numbered 27, 28, 29, 30, and 31 Alpine, which were a third larger than the divisions on the north-eastern front.

The defences facing Italy had been constructed during Weygand's period by the garrisons and were, from the mountainous nature of the country, pretty formidable to assault from the east. They consisted of three 'fortified' sectors: Alpes-Maritimes, Dauphiné and Savoie, with, to the north facing Switzerland, a 'defensive' sector, Rhône. The XV Corps sector, the more vulnerable owing to coast-line, had four divisions, 29, 30, and 31, with the 2nd Colonial, and in reserve the 65th

Alpine, a 'B' formation. The northern, being more easily defensible, had 27th and 28th divisions with, in support, the 64th and 66th.

As it gradually became clear that Mussolini had no intention of attacking until such time as the Germans had broken the French armies in the north, Gamelin in October began to transfer the active divisions to the northern front, where in turn they did periods in the Maginot outpost lines, while some were left with XXIII Corps in reserve round Dijon to be used either on the Alpine or the Vosges front as circumstances required. General Besson, who had commanded the southern front, was given command at Dôle of a new Army Group, AG Three, consisting of this reserve corps and the Eighth Army and the XLV Corps, holding the Rhine from Sélestat to Pontarlier on the Swiss frontier.

The defences against an Italian invasion were thus, from the end of November, entrusted to no more than one Colonial division, the 2nd, and three 'B' Alpine divisions plus seven fortress demi-brigades. This tiny army was strengthened by an outpost line in the high Alps of ski-observers (*éclaireurs*); these belonged to all Alpine units and had been left behind when the active divisions went north.

[3]

The British Expeditionary Force had developed better than had seemed possible at the first contact between staffs in March. By reducing the size of the infantry division, and by other means of a similar nature, the British were able to produce four instead of two divisions and to ship them to France within a comparatively short time. In September two army corps were concentrated between Amiens, St Pol and Vimy, and in October took over the Lille defensive sector along the Belgian frontier from Maulde to Armentières from the French 51st Division. British headquarters were eventually situated at Arras. On its left, as far as the sea at Bray, was General Fagalde's XVI Corps, to be absorbed into General Giraud's Seventh Army. It is to be noted that the British, the pioneers of the armoured fighting vehicle, were unable to produce an armoured division. Apart from two tank battalions, in all a hundred infantry tanks, British armour consisted of light (4/5-ton) tanks, qualified by General Brooke as 'ridiculous'.

A fifth division (the 5th) landed at the end of December and was followed by five territorial divisions (48, 50, 51, 42 and 44) between January and April. Three other divisions without artillery (12, 23 and 46) were also added during the last month.

[4]

The potentiality of the French Air Force is almost impossible to estimate. The Commission on Events called no service witness from that arm, but it heard the evidence of two Air Ministers, Pierre Cot (1933-4 and the second half of 1937) and Guy la Chambre (1938-9). Cot was garrulous and uninformative, la Chambre devastatingly critical. It is clear from this that the Chiefs of Air Staff were not competent enough to be able to stand up to politician ministers such as Cot, and, when they had their own man (Denain) in office, he was unintelligent.

When M. Robert Coulondre, as already related, came to Paris in the autumn of 1938 between *postes*, from Moscow to Berlin, he lunched with General Georges and Air Force General Mouchard. Coulondre asked the latter whether it was true that the air force had no bombers. Mouchard replied that it was so, in accordance with the international agreements which banned the bombing of non-military objects, although there were excellent fighters. 'I am aghast,' said Coulondre to Georges. 'I am as surprised as you are,' replied Georges.[2] Prételat says that the lamentable state of the air force was familiar to the members of the Army Council, but—'on every occasion during a skeleton exercise when I wanted to give the quantity and type of aircraft needed for the success of the operation, all I got from General Gamelin was, "This question does not concern us. There is an air force." It was his way of dodging a discussion which would have obliged him to agree that we were unprepared to carry on a war with an adversary who, unlike him, did not propose to fight according to the tactical methods of 1918.'[3]

It is now seen that before the outbreak of war in 1939, neither the British nor the French air staff had given thought to the matter of war. To be sure, they had prepared for fighting, but that is not the same thing. Neither air force was prepared for or had given serious thought to co-operation with the ground troops, and, by 1939, the soldiers had little respect for air force plans, which seem to be confined to bombing factories in Germany and employing their fighters against similar enemy bombing attacks.

At the outbreak of war the British sent over to France two air groups under the command of Air Marshal A. S. Barratt. The first, the Air Component (two bomber-reconnaissance squadrons, two fighter squadrons, six army co-operation squadrons) took over airfields between Seclin, south of Lille and Péronne, while the Advance Air Striking Force (A.A.S.F.) were stretched out east of Reims on a series of airfields between Aisne and Marne, from which they hoped to bomb Germany. In the early days, there were insufficient aerodromes to accommodate the whole British air group. Until they had built these, some planes had to be returned to England.

The French Air Force was in three zones: North, East and South. The northern and strongest was stationed west of a line from Calais through Aire–Cambrai–Laon to Vitry-le-François. The eastern zone had a line of fields from Anglure near the junction of Seine and Aube, through Toul to near Rambervillers. The southern zone was widely scattered between Lyon, Tours and Bordeaux.

The British had two fine fighters in the Hurricane and the Spitfire, but their bombers, Blenheims and Battles, were unsuited to daylight bombing.

Owing to Denain's over-hasty policy, the French aircraft proved to be a very mixed lot, as a table of 1 February 1940 shows:[4]

	Total	First Line	First Line Modern
Fighters	2,671	614	523
Bombers	873	170	37
Reconnaissance and Observation	1,318	363	118
	4,862	1,147	678

Of the fighters, by far the largest number were the Morane 406. Guy la Chambre says that it had been in existence since before the war; it had gone through its trials, the engines were run in. It gave no trouble and though, compared with the Spitfire or the Me 109E, it was under-armed and slow, it was handy enough to give a trained pilot plenty of confidence. But the other types introduced during the war were always breaking down. Moreover (he cites the Lioré 45 bomber), while the test-pilots at Villacoublay, like the famous *cadre noir* of the Saumur cavalry school, were so skilled that they could do anything, the Air Force pilots with comparatively short training were always smashing the landing gear.[5]

From the point of view of the ground forces, the worst deficiency was the absence of a good reconnaissance and observation plane, a machine which could fly slowly enough for photography and observation and, if attacked, could accelerate quickly enough to escape. Work on such a plane had been in progress when Vuillemin, at last aware of the need for army co-operation, ordered the directorate to stop[6] and instead produce the inadequate Mureaux 117. These, and elderly Potez 25 and 39, were given to the army corps. The Potez could not be sent beyond the gun-line without being shot down while the Bloch 131 could not be used during the day at all. Prételat ordered the Potez, too, to be grounded after a heavy loss of pilots. The Mureaux, he said, was 'just acceptable', but had to be used in pairs and anyhow could not cross the enemy line.[7] In the Ninth Army, there were twenty-six Morane fighters and some thirty old Potez for observation, 'doomed to a quick end'.

Even worse was the organization which forced on the army a circuit-ous system of communication with the air force. Last of all, there was a deficiency of airfields.

As with the British there were no dive-bombers. Daladier said that he had asked Vuillemin about bombing bridges and had been told that this was mere aerobatics. 'All the same,' Daladier rejoined, 'the Germans do it.' He also said that he spoke more than once about the Lioré-Nieuport of French invention, which he saw at an air exhibition. Asked whether experiments had been made with it, Vuillemin replied: 'We've studied it, but it is of no interest for land operations. It might do for the Navy. . . .' 'Has the Navy ordered some?' 'Yes, about fifty.'[8]

4 FORECASTS AND PLANS

THE Belgian government was naturally acutely aware of the country's peril between Germany and France. The Low Countries have not been called the cockpit of Europe for nothing, and experience had taught the Belgians that they lay across one of the historical gateways to France. Belgian independence had been guaranteed by the Powers in 1838, and the Belgians had seen the value of that guarantee in 1914. The country was not big enough or strong enough to avoid being used and fought over in a Franco-German quarrel, all the more so since the Maginot Line would induce the Germans to turn against the weaker Belgian defences.

Like other states, Belgian politics were divided between Left and Right, between National-Socialism (i.e. Rexism) and Communism. The Belgian government knew, however, that it had far less to fear from the French than from the Germans of the Third Reich. Hence, at the beginning of French mobilization, the Belgian government began slowly to put the country on a war footing. On 26 August the six active divisions and a division of Chasseurs Ardennais were mobilized, with frontier troops, the cavalry corps and the fortress garrisons. Two days later, two more divisions and three further regiments of Chasseurs Ardennais were called up. After this, between 1 September and 7 November, the first reserve was mobilized, the active divisions expanded to twelve, and the second reserve divisions called up. The Belgian Army amounted to twenty infantry divisions and two cavalry. The Belgian Air Force possessed 200 planes, but of these only twenty-four British Hurricanes and twenty-four Fairey Battle light bombers were modern.

[2]

The country which would be the battlefield lies roughly in three parts. To the south of the line of the Sambre-Meuse, the Ardennes appear difficult ground for movement or battle, hilly, boggy and wooded with few roads. The independent Grand Duchy of Luxembourg, between Belgium, France and Germany, forms part of the Ardennes. From Givet southward the Meuse flows in French territory. At its junction with the Sambre lay Namur with its ring of forts. Liège, also within a ring of forts, lay forty miles to the east-north-east on the Meuse, which here bends northwards and enters Holland at Maastricht. Between Liège and Maastricht, the river-crossing was guarded by the huge modern fort of Eben-Emael. To a superficial glance, north Belgium was protected by what is called the Limburg appendix of Holland. From Maastricht westward the Albert Canal crosses the flat country to Antwerp, itself in a ring of forts, standing at the point where the Scheldt (otherwise Escaut) swells out into the great shipping basin.

It will be seen that, should the Meuse north of Liège be overcome, the smaller river and canal lines would be the only serious obstacle to the conquest of central Belgium. South of the Liège–Namur line, the rough and comparatively empty Ardennes could, even if not defended, be used to delay an invading army. The Belgian defence scheme laid down three lines. The outermost, which ran along the various canals between Meuse and Scheldt and down the German-Luxembourg border, was to be occupied by frontier troops for the purposes of demolishing bridges, mining cross-roads, etc. Behind this, the line of resistance was marked by Antwerp and its forts, the Albert Canal to the Meuse above Maastricht, Liège, and Namur. Behind this again lay the reserve position, the K–W (Koningsbooikt–Wavre) line running from Antwerp to Louvain and continued through Wavre to Namur. This wedge could be prolonged, facing south, to Charleroi. Outside this area, the Ardennes south of the Meuse was to be occupied, or, better, patrolled in the country between Luxembourg and the French frontier by the K. Group (of General Keyaerts), made up of the 1st Chasseur Ardennais Division, motorized or cyclist infantry without artillery, and further north, facing the German frontier, the 1st Cavalry Division. The line of the Meuse between Huy and Namur was guarded by the 2nd Chasseur Ardennais Division.

Knowledge of the intention of the Belgians to resist and their plans was a *sine qua non* of the French defence. Almost immediately after the declaration of war, at the end of September, tentative interchanges were begun through the French embassy in Brussels and between the French and Belgian military staffs. According to Gamelin,[1] the Belgians wanted French support, if they were attacked, on the Antwerp–Liège front. Gamelin replied that with the agreement and assistance of the British, a force could be sent forward to the line of the Meuse between Givet and Namur and prolonged northward to the Dyle River and along this to Antwerp. But this would be done only on condition that, first, the Belgian Army remained mobilized in sufficient strength to resist a surprise attack, secondly, that a defensive line should be organized for occupation by British and French from Givet through Namur to Louvain. Lastly, that the Belgian forward troops on the Albert Canal and the German and Luxembourg frontiers should provide a covering force for the concentration of the arriving divisions. These provisions were agreed to by the Commander-in-Chief of the Belgian Army, otherwise King Leopold III.

Through the autumn, Gamelin and his staff, Georges and his, Billotte and the staff of AG One, Blanchard (First Army), Lord Gort and the others, studied the situation. There appeared three alternatives, the first, like the tribe of Assher, being to 'abide in their breaches', in other words, to hold the French northern frontier from Givet through

Trelon to Maubeuge, some of which had been partly fortified, and thence onward to the sea, leaving the Belgians to defend themselves unaided. The second alternative was to move forward to the line of the Scheldt, linking at Tournai with the Belgians, who would hold to the river mouth. The third was to advance to the K–W line from Louvain to Namur, the northern section of which, from Wavre, would be on the River Dyle, and at the same time to occupy the Meuse up-river to the point between Dinant and Givet where the French defences began. A fourth suggestion, that the Franco-English force should attempt to reinforce the Albert Canal defences, was immediately discarded as impossible.

The advantage of the Dyle over the Scheldt line was its relative short-ness and greater defensive depth. Its disadvantage lay in its distance from the French frontier (sixty miles); it would realize the worst French nightmare, the risk of an encounter battle on an unprepared line—there was no naturally strong line between Wavre and Namur—with tired troops and supplies lost or late in arriving. Blanchard, for the First Army, said it could not be done; it would require eight days to reach the line and prepare it against assault. General Prioux of the Cavalry Corps was dubious; so too was Billotte of AG One, while Georges was far from eager.

On 9 November Gamelin confided his latest conception to General Ironside, the British Chief of Imperial General Staff, and Lord Gort. It came out of a request from the Belgians to move eastward to a much more forward line (Ironside had voiced his dislike of the Scheldt plan). Georges had already discussed it with Gort. By this time the earlier anxiety which the French had expressed ever since March, as to the need to provide *un temps utile* in which to organize new positions much further forward, had disappeared, though Gamelin offered no new arguments. General Kennedy, Deputy Director of Military Operations at the War Office, who since March had been involved in the planning, says he was horrified that Ironside, Gort and Air Vice-Marshal Newall all accepted this 'happy-go-lucky plan' in spite of the fact that Ironside had more than once decried the fragility of the French positions. 'We [of the War Office] did our level best to shoot this ill-founded optimistic plan into splinters—without success.' Word of their objections reached Gamelin's ears. He complained to Ironside of the fact that his plan was criticized by English junior officers. And Ironside sympathized.[2]

Like the realists in London, the corps commanders in France were considerably alarmed by Gamelin's easy optimism and filled with dismay at the way the blustering Ironside, having talked freely of the inability of the French to put up a serious fight, capitulated as soon as he was faced by French complaints.

Still pondering the map, Gamelin saw that the Germans might easily go further and add the weak unarmed and practically indefensible Holland to their objectives, which would both facilitate their advance into Belgium and put them in a splendid situation opposite Great Britain. Holland in German hands would jeopardize the whole of the British east coast shipping and open the way for invasion. The preservation of Holland now became a necessity for all, including the uncooperative Belgians. And if the Germans ignored Belgium and attacked Holland alone? Then, said Gamelin, the French must invade Belgium. And the strategist envisaged an addendum to the entry into Belgium: the dispatch of an expedition to form a link between the left of the Belgian Army round Antwerp and the right of the Dutch north of Breda, plus the occupation of islands in the mouth of the Scheldt, Walcheren and Sud Beverland. When worked out, it became clear that the essential of this scheme was speed.

But speed was also the vital element in the Dyle scheme, which required two of the three light armoured divisions and four of the seven motorized infantry divisions. Beyond these, there were only three motorized infantry divisions and one light armoured. The 1st Light Armoured and the 9th and 25th Motorized Divisions were the more mobile part of the Seventh Army and the best. The Seventh was the reserve army in the hands of G.Q.G.F.T., i.e. Gamelin, not Georges, and was now established round Reims. Its commander was General Giraud, who, according to Gamelin,[3] 'appeared to us the most brilliant of our leaders', but to the British commander of II Corps, General Brooke, seemed a Don Quixote who 'would have ridden gallantly at any windmill regardless of consequences but who inspired one with little confidence when operating on one's left flank'.[4]

[3]

By the beginning of October, the Germans had already brought a number of the divisions engaged in Poland to the west and in position opposite both Dutch and Belgian frontiers. On the Sarre front, General Georges had already countermanded offensive operations, and the forward posts had been withdrawn to an intermediate line of observation Launstroff–Berus–Cadenbronn–Ohrenthal. One corps and three motorized divisions had been brought into G.Q.G. reserve. At the end of the first week of October there were signs of an impending attack, which opened on the night 16th/17th. A severe storm had carried away almost all the bridges over the Sarre and the Blies. There was heavy fighting at the junction of the two rivers, in which the 11th Division succeeded in stopping the enemy for a couple of days before being brought back to the main line. Thereafter the battle died down and the divisions of Army Group Two 'went into winter quarters' for the next six bitter months.

In the belief that the Allies would occupy Belgium and Holland, Hitler had already decided to forestall them by annexing both the Low Countries and northern France, in order to secure enough space from which to launch a sea and air attack on Great Britain. This was to take place as soon as possible after the end of October. He was opposed by the Army Staff, which claimed not to be ready. He insisted, and eventually the two Army Groups B (von Bock) and A (von Rundstedt) were put on four days' notice. However, the weather worsened. It was not until January, after eight weeks of repeated orders and counter-orders, that a promising weather forecast for the middle of the month allowed the date of the preliminary movements to be confirmed.

At the end of October or beginning of November, the Germans approached the Dutch with a request to be allowed to occupy certain strategic points within their frontiers. The Dutch refused. This approach became known to the Belgians, whose fears had not been allayed by German protestations of friendship. Their alarm was sharpened by the stream of rumours which flooded in from all neutral countries including Italy, whence Leopold's sister, the Princess of Piedmont, passed on information of Mussolini's projects, whispered by Ciano. There were two rumour crises in November and these were repeated just before Christmas.

The British, far from happy at Gamelin's proposed advance into Belgium, urged that it should not go too far. At a meeting of the two staffs on 16 November it was agreed to limit the choice of their plans to two: Escaut (Scheldt) and Dyle. On 17 November the Supreme War Council confirmed that if Belgium were invaded every effort should be made by the total forces, French, British and Belgian, to meet and hold the German attack as far east as possible and in any case on the Dyle Line. This needed considerable change in the former plans. As has been seen, to reach the Dyle meant a race across a hundred kilometres, or sixty miles, along roads, with every probability of heavy air attack. The advance guard and reconnaissance would be carried out by the cavalry corps and the motorized brigades of the cavalry divisions in daylight, and their main bodies would follow by night. On the second night the motorized infantry divisions would follow. In the meantime the cavalry, having secured the Dyle Line, would have pushed on to meet the enemy. After the second night, the other non-motorized divisions would follow by road or rail.

The scheme was accepted by General Billotte for Army Group One, but the First Army Commander, General Blanchard, objected that it was impossible for his army to get into position to fight on the Dyle before J/8 (J being zero), and that the time-table was far too tight. The troops could reach the Dyle Line only if there were no obstacles. And no one knew what defences the Belgians had prepared. 'It is absolutely indispensable from the moment of the beginning of the operation that we should be completely certain of not meeting the enemy in less than eight days. Otherwise it becomes an encounter battle engaged in the worst conditions.'[5]

The orders had been issued by G.Q.G.N.E. on 17 November. On the 23rd, Gamelin called a conference of army commanders at Arras from

which Georges* was omitted. At this he broached a further plan to
extend the French advance north of Antwerp to Breda to link up with
the Dutch, and sent his hearers away to consider the proposal. Their
comments came in a week later. They all said the scheme was impossible
without prior understanding between the Belgian and Dutch commands.
The Dutch asked the Belgians to prepare a flank guard to their southern
Peel defence line. The Belgians declined: moreover they ignored the
suggestions and preparations of the French.

In the meantime, Gamelin had directed Giraud of the Seventh Army
to work out the Breda plan. On 3 December Giraud asked for five
divisions for the first line, including one light armoured and two
motorized, but he added that unless the Dutch and Belgian cavalry
could hold well forward, there would be no stopping the Germans once
they were across the Zuid Willems canal (Bois-le-Duc to Roermond),
and the French would be forestalled. Also Seventh Army supplies must
be sent by sea, since Giraud's land communications would cross those
of the Belgian defences. This should be arranged beforehand. His report
was forwarded through Georges, who added that the whole scheme was
dominated by the question of the means available. Anyhow, a German
move might be no more than a feint to draw the French northward.

On 10 January, a German plane, of which the pilot had lost his way in
the fog hanging over the Low Countries, crash-landed near Mechelen.
His passenger, before he was arrested, tried to burn his papers but was
only partly successful. Enough survived to betray that they were orders
to the German 22nd Airborne Division for an air attack across the
Meuse. Copies of the remnants were passed on to the French and the
Dutch on the next day.

There were no firm agreements between the Belgians and any other
government, French, British or Dutch, as to what was to be done in the
event of an attack. The Belgian military attaché in Paris, Colonel
Delvoie, had never succeeded in getting anything concrete out of Gamelin as to where the Anglo-French forces would be after forty-eight hours
or four days. The Belgian command gave no orders to the frontier posts
to remove the barriers on the roads out of France. This was a matter for
the government, not the soldiers. However, on the afternoon of 14
January, Gamelin informed Daladier and Georges that AG One should
be ordered to close the divisions ear-marked for Belgium up to the
frontier. The same evening it was reported that a French cavalry column
had entered Luxembourg. But on the next day it was agreed that a movement into Belgium would be a grave error. Military history was full of
traps to mislead and the captured documents might be an attempt to
distract the defence from the area of the real assault. Some local commanders in Hainaut had in fact hurriedly removed the frontier barriers,

---

* Gamelin's reasons for keeping Georges away were obviously to prevent
adverse criticism.

though they had replaced them before the line had been crossed. Thus the immediate scare died down in Brussels, Paris and London.[6]

The incident had not been faked—the officer with the orders for the 22nd Airborne had disobeyed a standing injunction against travelling by air. The German troops had already begun to move towards their starting-points. The report of the capture caused the immediate postponement of the operation. The orders had been for an attack on Holland by both air and sea, coupled with an air-drop across the Meuse between Annevoie and Dinant and the build-up of a main bridge-head at Yvoir. There were two consequences of the exposure. First, the plans were now changed as regards the main thrust of attack, the *Schwerpunkt*. Secondly, the length of time between start and assault was curtailed. On the immediate scheme, the attacking divisions had needed eight days to reach the Meuse, a period which made surprise impossible. In future, instead of four days' warning, the divisions would be given twenty-four hours, and on '*Tag A*' the troops on the frontiers would clear away the barricades and take the first objective, while the main bodies and the armour came forward with a rush from behind.

The fact that the German armies had approached closer during November and January seems to have been seen by the French Intelligence, but its significance was not interpreted.

The intention of the original plan (known as *Fall Gelb*) had been to seize as much of Holland, Belgium and northern France as was needed as a base for air and sea attacks on England. At the end of October this plan was discarded in favour of another version, in which the main assault would be north and south of Liège by the Army Group of von Bock, while von Rundstedt's Army Group A would cover von Bock's left flank, and Army Group C would make feint attacks on the Maginot Line. Both these plans were criticized by von Rundstedt, who began to advocate a much more thorough operation intended to cut off the left wing of the enemy north of the Somme and drive it back against the coast. About the same time (early November), Hitler conceived the idea of attacking through Sedan. During the next months, December, January and February, additions of weight to the German left flank continued, though not preponderantly. Even after the January postponement the idea of the attack remained as it had been in November. Von Rundstedt and his chief of staff von Manstein continued to press their views. During February, von Manstein had the opportunity of explaining directly to Hitler von Rundstedt's and his view, which fitted in easily with a plan Hitler had been unsuccessfully pondering. In consequence, the main weight of the attack was shifted further south. Army Group B would be reduced to two armies, the Sixth and Eighteenth, with three armoured divisions. Army Group A would have three armies, Fourth, Twelfth and Sixteenth plus the Kleist group of three armoured corps (seven Panzer divisions) and a corps of three motorized infantry divisions. Von Bock would attack Holland and Belgium north of the Liège-Namur line, von Rundstedt from this boundary as far as the Luxembourg–French–German junction. Beyond this, von Leeb, commanding Army Group C, would do no more than demonstrate until the time was ripe to demolish the Maginot and cross the Rhine.[7]

All this, of course, was and remained hidden from the French. That there might be an alternative to a classical attack appears never to have crossed Gamelin's mind.

In February, discouraged by the apparent Belgian indifference, the Dutch drew back their troops to the north of the Waal–Meuse area, thereby widening the distance between their forces and their neighbour's.

On 12 March Gamelin insisted that the plan for the advance of the Seventh Army into Holland should be confirmed, since the occupation of the Scheldt estuary and Antwerp would make it possible to cover and extend the advance of the B.E.F. and the First Army beyond the Dyle up to the Albert Canal and the Meuse east of Namur. He held stubbornly to his project in spite of the protests of Giraud and the warnings of Georges.

The Instruction was finally registered and communicated to the lower formations on 20 March. Even so, both Georges and Giraud remained severely critical of the dispatch of the Seventh Army north of the Scheldt and into Holland, thus risking committing a major part of the French reserves to an eccentric deployment on what might be merely a diversion. In spite of the now added doubts of Billotte, Gamelin continued obdurate. He rejected all proposals to reduce the scope of the move, and on 16 April confirmed the instruction of 20 March. The German invasion of Denmark and Norway on 9 April had encouraged him to believe that a large part of the German Air Force had been transferred from the French front.

[4]

It had not occurred to the French Intelligence chiefs that the Germans might change their plans, let alone switch the weight of their attack from right to left, seeing that the country north of Namur was the weakest point of the defences. For the rest, the French staff believed with Pétain that the Germans, looking at the ground between the Schnee Eifel and the Mons–Maubeuge–Avesnes line, would conclude that it was unsuited to rapid movement and at most should simply be masked. They had therefore contented themselves with comparatively minor defences. Three bridgeheads had been built east of the Meuse at Mézières. Maubeuge, an old fortress about to be dismantled, had instead been modernized and a belt of blockhouses added. Other small fortifications of an inexpensive nature had been built by the troops. The area roughly between the River Aisne and the Sambre was thus regarded without anxiety. From August 1939, when it was first designated, up to 15 October, the first six weeks after mobilization, the area and its garrison was no more than the Ardennes Army Detachment, dependent on the grace and favour of General Huntziger's Second Army. It had no organic services, though it had a staff and troops. On 15 October it was renamed the Ninth Army, with headquarters at Vervins, under the command of General André Corap, most of whose career had been in North Africa.

Up to the November alert, the rôle of the Ninth Army had been purely defensive along the Meuse from the Bar to Givet, thence along the Belgian frontier to the Maubeuge defences. With the Dyle Line conception, its role became more closely involved with the First Army on its left. While the First Army hastened towards the Dyle, the Ninth would have to advance to occupy the Meuse from Givet to Namur. This would require, first, a dash across Belgium from near Hirson through a stretch of country ill served by road and rail, and secondly, screening the occupation of the Meuse as far east as possible. For this screen, it was allotted two of the reconstructed Cavalry divisions, 1st and 4th. Their role was to hasten eastward with their mechanized units and the reconnaissance groups of the infantry divisions, first to assure the line of the Meuse and then to continue further east, join the presumed covering forces of the Belgian Army and delay the Germans for a matter of five days. During this time, the infantry divisions of the II and XI Corps would have taken up their positions on the left bank of the Meuse as far north as the Namur southern forts. II Corps consisted of only one division, the 5th Motorized, but as yet it was at the disposal of the Ninth Army only after it had been released by G.Q.G.N.E. XI Corps, which would come in south of II Corps, had the 18th and 22nd Divisions ('A' type). One regiment of the 22nd was already in position on the Meuse in the French town of Givet. The right corps of the army was XLI Corps, a static formation already occupying the Meuse from Givet to Flize. This was a new formation. In touch with 22nd Division it had the 61st (B) Division on the river from Vireux to the 'Dames de Meuse', and on the right of the 61st the 102nd Fortress Division with two demi-brigades of colonial machine-gunners, the 42nd (Malgaches) and 52nd (Indo-Chinese). Its other unit was the 148th, an active Fortress regiment. There were two divisions in Army reserve: the 4th North African, a very fine fighting formation, and the 53rd (B), a good Norman division, which also was at the disposal of G.Q.G.N.E.

General Corap was acutely conscious of the weakness of the position he was to occupy and of the state of the troops. Certainly he did what he could to build up the defences on the Belgian frontier, Rocroi–Hirson–Inor–Trelon, but the hard winter hindered progress. Work could only be resumed in April. In this month, Gamelin at last came to look round. Corap failed to interest the strategist in his woes, and later it was intimated from Vincennes that he would be wise not to complain.

But the tasks of the Ninth Army were complex and difficult. There was no knowledge of what the Belgians were doing to fortify the Meuse from Givet to Namur and none as to the Belgian dispositions facing the German and Luxembourg frontiers. The army commander was well aware that much of XLI Corps defences were incomplete. Apart from the old fort of Ayvelles south of Charleville-Mézières, there were three solid casemates at Villers-Semeuse, Flize, and behind the fort. But the bridgeheads at Mézières had not yet been completed, and though the other defences from Nouzonville to Vireux along the winding river, with dense rough woods coming down to the water, were not easy to attack, they were also far from easy to defend. In early May, the defences at Givet and Vireux had only been sketched, while those at Monthermé were still being worked on. There was no depth to the position and the stop-line was no more than a trace. And there were other deficiencies. Distances were too great for radio communication to be effective and the telephone cables were not buried. Two divisions were without their 25-mm. anti-tank guns. For anti-aircraft defence, only the 5th Division had guns. The army had practically none. In March, in reply to a question as to their needs, they reported that a minimum of forty-five 25-mm. batteries was needed. They were allowed three.

The river, at least from the point by Charleville-Mézières where it begins to cut its way northward between the limestone cliffs, offers an illusion of being both hard to cross and indefensible. Much has been canalized and most of the towns had wharves for loading and off-loading from the *péniches*. The flow was not strong in the French section and the depth some six to seven feet, but in May 1940 it was below normal. Still, it gave an illusion of security. On 7 March 1934 Pétain had said to the Senate army committee: 'On leaving Montmédy, we come to the Ardennes forests. If certain preparations are made, these are impenetrable. Consequently we regard this as a zone for demolitions. . . . This sector is not dangerous.'[8] To the planners of the 3rd Bureau, the river was a remarkably fine tank trap.

The right army of Army Group One, the Second, commanded by General Huntziger, a popular senior colonial general, held from the junction of the Bar and the Meuse, just east of where the river swings northwards into the Ardennes. The position, at right-angles to that of the Ninth Army, faces the Belgian frontier concealed in a dark mass of woodland a few kilometres to the north. The line of defences kept behind the Meuse, until beyond Sedan, and then followed the Chiers eastward. A bridgehead covered Montmédy. The army's right was at Longuyon, where the Third Army of AG Two took over and the Maginot Line proper began. The Second Army had two corps: on the left, X Corps, with the 55th Division (B) and the 3rd North African. On the right came XVIII Corps, with the 1st Colonial Division and the 41st (A). Like Ninth Army, it had two of the reformed cavalry divisions, the 5th and 2nd, and also the 1st Cavalry Brigade. The whole line was more or less fortified. These were in four sectors: from the left, Sedan, Mouzon, Montmédy and Marville, each garrisoned by a fortress regiment. Within the Montmédy bridgehead stood the isolated *ouvrage* of La Ferté.

Alone of Army Group One, the Second Army's role was completely static, except that, as soon as the German attack was known, the cavalry divisions would be sent forward to engage and delay the invader. Throughout the winter, attempts had been made to strengthen the defences but the delays had been serious. Autumn rains had been followed by snow and ice. The cold froze the rivers and prevented water transport, while the roads became impassable. Materials did not arrive. Though work could be resumed in April, many of the manufactured additions to the concrete structures did not arrive. Steel doors, shutters and loopholes were not to be had. The camouflage was not completed and the casemates were obvious from the air.

The role of the Third Army beyond the Second was purely defensive in the Maginot fortifications and outposts. But Longwy, on (it might be said, in) the Luxembourg frontier, and the iron workings could not be abandoned before an attack. The Third Army was therefore ordered to send forward its cavalry, 3rd Cavalry Division and the 1st Spahi Brigade, to meet the invaders beyond the frontier as far east as the Moselle.

On the left of the Ninth Army, General Blanchard's First Army would be preceded by the Cavalry Corps of General Prioux, the 2nd and 3rd Light Armoured Divisions. These would cross the Dyle Line and find touch with the Belgians between Tirlemont, Hannut and Huy, it being hoped that the Belgians would be holding on their frontier, or at the worst making a slow retreat. Twenty-four hours behind the main body of the cavalry, the motorized divisions of V, IV and III Corps would race forward to the Dyle Line, that is, the railway from Namur to past Gembloux and Ernage and then the Dyle to Wavre. The three normal divisions of these corps would follow a day later by road or rail.

On the left of the III Corps, I Corps of the B.E.F. and the 3rd Division of the II Corps would extend the First Army line from Wavre to Louvain, where it would join the Belgians. These too would be preceded by a screen of light armour.

It was feared that the movement of all these divisions would offer tempting targets to the German Air Force and bring down on them severe retribution. For this reason all the non-motorized bodies were instructed to move only at night. But with every new day of 1940 the hours of darkness were shrinking. By the beginning of May, eight hours could be expected at most and there might well be delays in occupying the forward positions.

5 THE ELEVENTH HOUR

A CERTAIN amount of hostility, of jealousy, of envy, and of downright distrust is discernible in the relations between Gamelin and his immediate subordinates; or is it Gamelin's fancy? In his prolix defence of his actions,[1] he hints at intrigues against him by the friends of Pétain and, less forthrightly, by those of Weygand and Georges ('*on ne peut aujourd'hui en douter*') without offering serious evidence.[2]

It would be surprising if there were not jealousy. After all, Gamelin had secured the prize, even more, had doubled it, in being both Vice-President of the Army Council and Chief of Staff, with thus an extension of three years to his career and the probability of remaining there until the end of the war. Daladier, he tells us, repeatedly refused to allow him to resign or to promote Georges in his place. Daladier himself says nothing of this. On the outbreak of war Gamelin, who mentions his projects for rejuvenating the staff, had recalled to activity a number of recently retired officers who had passed the age-limit for their rank—Dufieux (his nearest rival) to anti-aircraft command, Héring to the military governorship of Paris, Bineau to be Major-Général to Georges, as well as a number of others to the command of military regions.

Not without justice, he felt that, although the Franco-German struggle round the debatable land was the primary theatre, a quantity of other matters in other areas were perpetually impinging on the main one and that, as Chief of Staff of the Council of National Defence, he should remove himself from the north-eastern theatre, so that he could take a less localized view of the whole war: Finland, Russia, Spain, Italy, Romania, Scandinavia. He decided to have Georges made commander-in-chief of the north-east and relieve him of his share of the responsibility for other problems. To implement this, he removed from La Ferté those officers whom he considered would be of use to him at Vincennes and set up, at Montry, half-way between Paris and La Ferté, a hyphen-G.Q.G.N.E. with General Doumenc as Major-Général and chief of staff to each or either commander. At the same time, he transferred General Bineau from La Ferté to the staff of Marshal Pétain. A number of people protested that the new scheme would lead to confusion, but Gamelin refused to listen. This ramshackle structure began its activities in mid-January.

Up to now, Vincennes had had a small staff, while the four bureaux were at La Ferté. In January, Gamelin had the staff of the 2nd Bureau (Intelligence), with the exception of the greater part of the officers dealing specifically with German military questions, transferred to Vincennes. At the same time, he set up at Montry the whole of the 4th Bureau, handling transport and supply under Doumenc, responsible to both headquarters. The 3rd Bureau (Operations) remained at La Ferté. As Georges said, with all the goodwill in the world between officers who had worked together for some time, delays were unavoidable. During the periods of great activity, the head of the 4th Bureau had to come repeatedly to La Ferté, a distance of twenty miles, and, after 10 May, the difficulties became mischievous: fleeting and interrupted communications were quite incompatible with the conduct of a battle. This undoubtedly affected the subordinate staffs. The responsibility for the change, whether Daladier's, as alleged by Gamelin, or Gamelin's, as alleged by Daladier, cannot be verified.[3]

The change took place officially on 16 January, that is, in the middle of the alert caused by the capture of the German aeroplane at Mechelen.

[2]

In their trading for Russian neutrality, the Germans, to clinch the bargain, were forced to allow their new friends the acquisition of spheres of influence on the Baltic. Estonia, Latvia and Lithuania all submitted to what was virtually abandonment of sovereignty, coupled with occupation by Russian troops, between the last week in September and the first fortnight of October. The fourth state, Finland, refused to surrender to all the Russian demands, on which the U.S.S.R. government broke off negotiations, denounced their treaty of non-aggression and attacked. The Finns resisted and with some success held the enemy off for some months, which persuaded a number of French and British that the time had come to make peace with Germany and for all to join together in an anti-communist crusade. At the same time, with a view to stopping the shipment of iron-ore from Sweden through the Norwegian port of Narvik, it was thought in London that there would be advantages in sending a small expedition to Finland—according to General Brooke, just one more example of the common British folly of dispersal. All this came to nothing, owing to the Finnish capitulation on 12 March. But in the French Chamber, deputies from both right and left attacked Daladier for the general purposelessness of French military activity. During this debate Daladier revealed that the Allied Supreme War Council had on 5 February offered to send troops to Finland and that some 50,000 had been equipped and shipping prepared in the case of acceptance. In the Senate, three days later, after a discussion of the terms of the Russo-Finnish treaty, he received a vote of confidence, but there were sixty abstentions. Then after a debate in secret committee of the Chamber, which went on through the 19th until 4 a.m. on the 20th, a motion from one of the Strasbourg members, Louis Marin, for a more energetic conduct of the war was opposed by a motion of confidence. The latter was carried by 239 votes to one, but 300 deputies abstained. Of these, 144 were Socialist, the strongest group in the Chamber. Daladier resigned. Invited by President Lebrun to try again, he refused. The President then asked Paul Reynaud, the Finance Minister, who accepted. Critics of the new President of the Council said that his cabinet was a weak team, but in fact, apart from the now excluded Bonnet, it was very much the same as Daladier's. Eleven of the seventeen ministers reappeared and the only surprising change was the substitution of Laurent-Eynac for Guy la Chambre at the Air Ministry. Camille Chautemps was appointed Vice-President.

Daladier refused to join the new government in any office other than the Ministry of Defence, and Reynaud submitted. This was an error, indeed a fault and a complete misunderstanding of the causes of Daladier's defeat. It had been on this very ministry's failures that the majority of the Chamber had deserted him. Reynaud would have done better to drop him at this point: instead, he listened to Herriot and weakly allowed his predecessor to remain in occupation of the place in which he had earned the mistrust of all. No doubt Herriot made it clear that he could not count on the support of the Socialist-Radicals without Daladier at the Defence Ministry. In the event, Reynaud soon discovered that he had deprived himself of that full control of policy indispensable to the head of the government. And Daladier, furious that his own blundering had lost him the leading part, used his own position to ignore his chief.

Reynaud's acceptance of office may itself have been a serious error, though his motives were no doubt thoroughly respectable. He had many virtues—intelligence, industry, courage and candour—though in the world of politics the last is possibly not a virtue. But he lacked authority, the authority of a Clemenceau, even of a Briand or a Ribot. He had never had a party behind him and he had no party now. He had resigned from the Alliance Démocratique in 1938, and to many of its members he was anathema. The Right and the Right-Centre disliked his introduction of three members of the Socialist party into his cabinet. And he could by no means be sure of the support of the Socialist-Radicals. His ministerial declaration contained nothing of novel interest, and in the division on the vote of confidence his absolute majority was no more than one, there having been 110 abstentions. The future of the government was obviously precarious. He could count on the Socialists and probably on the various Independent Socialists, but on very little else. But there was really no alternative leader: no other ministers, ex-ministers or *ministrables*, however competent, determined and loyal, were of the stuff to make political leaders in time of war.

From the beginning he wished to create an inner war cabinet of himself, Chautemps and seven ministers. He proposed Colonel de Gaulle as secretary. De Gaulle, knowing that his appointment would be vetoed by Daladier, declined the invitation, and on the advice of Wilfrid Baumgarten, Governor of the Banque de France, Reynaud appointed Paul Baudouin, Director-General of the Banque d'Indo-Chine, to the post.

On 27 March, with the Ministers of Marine (Campinchi) and Air

(Laurent-Eynac), Reynaud flew to London and on the following day signed a Franco-British declaration embodying a mutual undertaking neither to negotiate nor to conclude an armistice or treaty of peace without common consent. Reynaud also agreed to the laying of mines in Norwegian territorial waters by the British Navy. The end of the Russo-Finnish war put an end to the project of a Franco-British expedition to Finland, which would of itself have furnished a pretext for the occupation of Narvik and the cutting of the iron-ore route. However, on 8 April, a combined British and French naval force mined the Norwegian waters. Neither country knew that the Germans had made full preparations for a descent on Denmark and Norway and that this was already on the move.*

[3]

It had been a bad winter, so bad as to make it extremely difficult for work to be done on the defences. The conditions under which the infantry existed were deplorable. There were, of course, all kinds of attempts to lighten their misery, much the same as had been done in the winters of 1916 and 1917. There was sickness, there was discontent, above all when skilled workers were withdrawn from the army to work in Dautry's arms factories. Moreover there was discontent among the civilians, who now saw no possible end to the war. Morale was deteriorating and this was apparent to the army chiefs. Everyone had expected a violent German attack in October and thereafter, and in spite of two alerts, nothing happened. Would the army be able to hold against an assault whenever it came, or would it fold up out of apathy?

This was the kind of problem which worried Gamelin. Already it was being suggested by Admiral Darlan that the blockade should be reinforced, a move which should incite the Germans to attack Belgium and Holland. Gamelin submitted a note to Daladier on 16 March to the effect that such an attack was desirable *à bref délai* ('in a short time'). Gamelin explains that he in no way envisaged an immediate attack, certainly not before the four French armoured divisions and the two

---

* With the rape of Denmark and Holland this book is not concerned. But one aspect of the French response had repercussions. Six regiments or demi-brigades of *chasseurs* were withdrawn from the five Alpine divisions in March to form the expeditionary force for Finland. When this was cancelled, they were earmarked for Norway. Only two reached that country. The 5th landed at Namsos and returned to France on 4 June. The 27th landed at Narvik where it was joined by a demi-brigade of the *Légion étrangère* with which it returned to Brest in mid-June (cf. p. 307). The 2nd and 24th embarked but got no further than the Clyde, whence they returned to France early in June. These two with the 5th demi-brigade became the 40th Division (cf. p. 243). The 26th became part of the new 44th Division. The two regiments, 140 and 141, formed the 3rd Light Division, which did not leave Brest (cf. pp. 188 and 340).

promised by the British for the end of 1940 were ready. This note was seen by Reynaud when he took office a few days later. Hence he was all the more shocked when, on 9 April, he found that the Allies were unprepared to meet the surprise attack on Denmark and Norway, although the British were slowly evolving an expedition. Gamelin's abandonment of control to the British, which he enunciated this same morning ('Study in London has ended in the drafting of a plan. Its execution has been placed in the hands of the British Admiralty. I have not to intervene'), infuriated Reynaud. He burst out to Baudouin: 'He's a *préfet*, he's a bishop, but he's absolutely not a commander. This can't go on!'

He was even more appalled by Gamelin's proposition that the German occupation of Oslo, Trondheim and Narvik should be countered by a French occupation of Belgium.

At a meeting of the war cabinet on 12 April, Gamelin was present and was cross-examined. The official minute reveals little of the temper of the meeting, but Dautry told the Commission on Events that Gamelin, 'usually so disciplined, so master of himself, was insolent to the President of the Council and in an openly mutinous state. . . . As I told Campinchi, if I had been the President, I'd have had him arrested.'[4] And to Baudouin, after the meeting, he said: 'Keep the President up to his intention of ridding us of Gamelin. That general has no willpower and is incapable of giving an order. It's obvious he's terrified of responsibility. He has handed over the Norwegian business to the English simply to be able to wash his hands of it if it goes wrong.'

Gamelin tells us that (once more) he handed his resignation to Daladier, who refused it, saying that though he too wanted to resign, 'he had no right to do it at this time'.

In spite of the negative results of the war-cabinet meeting of 12 April, Reynaud was determined to eliminate Gamelin. And, if necessary, Daladier's disappearance would precede it. According to Baudouin, Reynaud said that to do it, he must have President Lebrun's support, also that of the President of the Senate, Jeanneney, and of Léon Blum. On 27 April Reynaud flew with Daladier to London for a meeting of the Supreme War Council. During his absence, Baudouin approached President Lebrun. Lebrun was completely in the dark as to there being any doubts of 'our Gamelin' and reluctant to take sides between Reynaud and Daladier; in short, as powerless as a used postage stamp. On the other hand, Jeanneney was already angry with Daladier, whom he considered responsible for the general slackness. 'He has lulled them all to sleep. He has done nothing. The awakening will be frightful.' But if Daladier resisted? A cabinet crisis would follow and he might again become President of the Council. And that would be catastrophe.

That night, Reynaud, back from London, downcast at the British decision to withdraw from the Norwegian campaign, complained that the Chamberlain government was without energy and without real leaders. 'They are all old men who daren't take a risk!' And in France?

'Daladier agreed that Gamelin was far from a *foudre de guerre*, but said: "We can't swap horses in mid-stream." '

Next morning Reynaud was down with influenza. Thus it was not until 9 May that he was able to open his case against Gamelin before the war cabinet. Eager as always to protect the general, Daladier complained that Gamelin was not present to refute the accusations. As for the failure in Norway, the British Navy was responsible. He refused to accept Reynaud's criticisms.

Under the decrees of 7 September 1938 relating to the Council of National Defence, the command of the army derived from the Minister of Defence and not from the President of the Council. The only means open to Reynaud to carry out his proposal was by himself assuming the Ministry of Defence. To do this, since Daladier had no intention of resigning, the whole Council of Ministers must resign and a new one be constituted. Reynaud therefore told his cabinet: 'Faced by so serious an opposition, I consider that the cabinet has resigned. I shall inform the President of the Republic of this. He asked me this morning that, in the event of its resignation, the matter should not be made known until the new cabinet has been constituted. In the circumstances, I ask all my colleagues to look on this as confidential.'

Although the normal party negotiations went on during afternoon and evening, no result had been reached before midnight. At 5.30 a.m. on the following morning German forces crossed the Dutch, Belgian and Luxembourg frontiers. For the moment the Germans had saved General Gamelin.*

---

* At ten minutes past eleven on the previous evening (8 May,) a vote in the House of Commons in London had put an end to the equivocations of the past seven years. On the evening of the 10th, Winston Churchill became responsible for the conduct of British policy.

PART THREE

The Disaster

The warning

IN September, after the declaration of war, M. Tarbe de Saint-
Hardouin, Councillor to the French Embassy in Berlin, returned
with the embassy staff to Paris, but had immediately been attached to
the French legation in Luxembourg, nominally as councillor, in fact to
act as an intelligence outpost in the capital of this internationally
guaranteed Grand Duchy. From Luxembourg city he was in touch, on
the one side with the French Second and Third Armies, on the other
with a network of observers looking across the Moselle and the Sure
into Germany. Since the Luxembourg railway system was managed by
the French, a warning system had been established whereby the Luxembourg gendarmerie could telephone simultaneously to Luxembourg city
and to the French Intelligence station at Longwy.

It was also the French councillor's business to keep an eye on the
German fifth column and the Belgian Rexists, who were known to be
active in this undefended neutral state.

On the night of 9/10 May the fifth column rose in the streets of Luxembourg and other towns, and occupied various public buildings, but not, it
seems, the radio station in the capital. This was about 1.30 a.m. Tarbe
de Saint-Hardouin had time to speak to the duty-officer at the Quai
d'Orsay, Seydoux, who at once passed the alarm on to the War Office.

[2]

The surprise

Late in the evening of Friday, 9 May, from the Dutch frontier to
Luxemburg, outposts facing Germany became aware of a vast murmur-
ing on the German side as of the gathering of a host. Some reports
suggested that this was merely a night exercise, but in addition to the
mutter of thousands of men, there was the hum of engines. The same
noises were reported by the Dutch. At Belgian headquarters about nine
in the evening a cipher message from the Belgian military attaché
in Berlin was received, but owing to faulty transmission it was not
deciphered until nearly half-past ten. It was to the effect that the
German attack would be loosed on the following day. A second message,
decoded about 11.30, repeated the first message more emphatically, and
Belgian headquarters at once issued warning orders, including the recall
of men on leave. At 4.30, German parachute and airborne troops began
to land near The Hague and Leyden in the Netherlands and in Belgium
near the bridges over the Meuse between Roermond and Liège. Some of
the bridges already mined were blown, but unhappily two vital ones,
Vroenhoven and Veldwezelt west of Maastricht, were captured before

the demolition squads could act.* At the same time a number of German gliders were landed on the great fort of Eben-Emael, opposite the junction of the Meuse and the Albert Canal, and from the roof the assault parties were able to paralyse the garrison. The Belgian counter-attacks failed, and although the Dutch successfully blew the bridges in the town of Maastricht (General Halder, Chief of Staff of the German Army, ruefully noted that the Trojan horse had failed), the German ground troops, riflemen of the 4th Panzer Division, crossed the river in rubber boats.

[3]

Into the trap

The message from Luxembourg was passed to Gamelin about 2 in the morning. No warning appears to have been passed on to the troops, but bombing by German aircraft of railway junctions and airfields soon after dawn was sufficient to rouse most of the armies. Dunkirk and Calais were bombed soon after 5, and the railways at Laon, Nancy, Toul, Gondrecourt, Sézanne, Villers-Cotterets and Abbeville were all attacked. At Vincennes, Gamelin, wakened by his *chef de cabinet* as soon as the early messages were confirmed, telephoned to General Georges at La Ferté. 'Is it the Dyle scheme?' asked Georges, to which Gamelin replied: 'The Belgians have called to us. What else can we do?' This conversation appears to have taken place about 6.30. Twenty minutes later, Billotte, from Army One headquarters at Folembray, ordered the Seventh Army to move across Belgium into Holland and get in touch with the Dutch at Breda. At the same time, he ordered the Second, Ninth, and First Armies and the B.E.F. to move in accordance with their respective parts of the Dyle Plan.

In view of all the preliminary discussions, especially those on the narrowness of time, the delay in warning subordinate formations, followed by precipitate orders, has not been explained. Gamelin appears to have been told of the Luxembourg alert before 2 a.m. After that there was renewed silence for some two hours before further alarms from Luxembourg through the Foreign Office came in. Few units seem to have received the preliminary warnings. On the other hand, the Air Force seems to have had some sort of alert on the previous evening, which was passed on to the 2nd and 3rd Light Armoured Divisions of the cavalry corps. The 2nd were ready and moved at 4.30 a.m. On the other hand, Second Army headquarters had attended a theatrical performance at Vouziers and did not return to Senuc until one in the morning. Nevertheless its cavalry divisions were roused early.

The Commander-in-Chief 'showed no emotion, no internal disturbance', when he eventually appeared. He remained optimistic. He was

---

* The German detachments wore Belgian uniforms. The bridge at Briegden was also lost but destroyed on the following day in a Belgian counter-attack.

seen at Vincennes striding up and down the corridor, humming to himself with a 'complacent and martial air'. Paul Reynaud at once saw that the resignation of the government must be cancelled and that he must retain the Commander-in-Chief in whom he had no faith. He telephoned Gamelin and exchanged patriotic sentences with the general.

[4]

The Seventh Army in the Netherlands

Even had the French been warned two days beforehand that the Germans would attack the Netherlands and Belgium on 10 May, it is improbable that they could in any way have coped with the situation north of the Scheldt estuary that morning. The surprise of the Dutch—'surprise' in that the character of the attack by air had not been conjectured—was all the more shattering in that the German Minister to The Hague sought an interview with the Dutch Foreign Minister two hours *after* the German bombers had begun to attack the Dutch aerodromes.

The bombing of the airfields round The Hague and Rotterdam was supplemented by the landing of parachutists and glider-borne infantry north of the Meuse on the edge of Rotterdam, at Dordrecht and near Moerdijk, and on the great bridge that spans the Holland Deep and connects Holland proper to Zeeland. At the same time, von Kuechler's Eighteenth Army attacked across the frontier. The Northern Korps (X), with two infantry and one cavalry division, swept across the country up to the Zuyder Zee, where it fought a number of inconclusive engagements with Dutch units until the capitulation of 14th. The Left Korps (XXVI), of two reserve divisions, Hubicki's 9th Panzer Division and part of the S.S. Adolf Hitler Division, came over the Meuse and later the Waal, and broke through the Peel Line. Behind these came XXIX Korps with two more divisions. Then the German armour divided, one part moving on Moerdijk, the other on Tilburg.

Even if the Belgians in the Antwerp *enceinte* and along the Albert Canal had wished to help their Dutch neighbours, they could do no more than hold their defences. This morning, they blew the bridges on the Turnhout canal, between that town to the junction with the Bocholt Canal, and occupied the line with detachments from their own 18th Division.

The main condition of the execution of Gamelin's 'Breda' concept was speed. It was seven hours after the first bombs fell at The Hague when leading detachments of the reconnaissance group of the 25th Motorized Division crossed the Belgian frontier at Oostcapelle and made for Antwerp, a distance of more than 150 kilometres. It is perhaps typical of all that followed that on this morning of 10 May the boat-bridge over the Escaut, by which the French leading detachments should cross, was closed to traffic. The groups had to shift into Antwerp and cross by the tunnel beneath the river. The last section was not through until midnight. There were still fifty kilometres to Breda.

Otherwise the French moves went as expected. On the left, the 68th

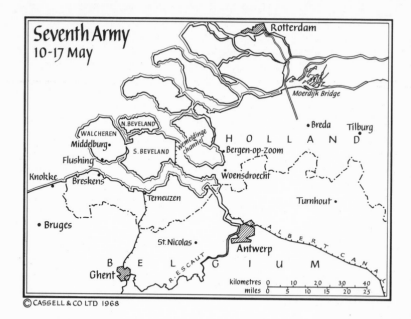

Seventh Army
10-17 May

© CASSELL & CO LTD 1968

Division from General Fagalde's XVI Corps occupied the coast as far as
Knokke on the shoulder of the Scheldt mouth, while the 60th (General
Deslaurens) marched towards the estuary. A detachment of recon-
naissance groups of the 4th, 9th and 21st Divisions under General
Beauchesne, lent by the 1st Light Armoured, raced forward and
occupied the three Dutch ports on the south side of the estuary,
Walsoorden, Terneuzen and Breskens, and then, late in the afternoon,
got themselves transported by the local ferry service to Walcheren.
From here they hastened eastward to try to join the Dutch infantry at
Woensdrecht on the mainland. Behind them, leading companies of the
224th Infantry Regiment (68th Division) had been dispatched by sea
from Dunkirk to Flushing, together with an artillery group. Orders to
its commander, General Durand, were to cross the isthmus to the island
of South Beveland and secure the channel across the neck of the second
isthmus, which connects the peninsula with the mainland south of
Bergen-op-Zoom. This he failed to do. The 224th waited on Walcheren
and suffered casualties from dive-bombers, while the small ships supply-
ing the garrison and guarding the coast had much ado to survive.

To the east, the advance guards of General Sciard's I Corps and the
armoured cars of the 6th Cuirassiers from the 1st Light Armoured
Division crossed the Antwerp canal shortly before dark and threw
patrols out to Driessen, Tilburg, and Breda.

On the next day, the 11th, the remainder of the reconnaissance brigade of the 1st Light Armoured, the rest of the 6th Cuirassiers and the 4th Dragoons, were sent up with the Hotchkiss regiment (the 4th Cuirassiers) to reinforce the Belgian 18th Division facing east. Of the 25th Motorized, two battalions, one from the 38th and one from the 121st, were dispatched to reinforce the outpost-line round Breda. The battalion of the 38th Division got to the town, but the other was caught in transit by dive-bombers, lost a number of trucks, including three quarters of its signal equipment, and had 200 casualties. Breda was occupied and a defence line established on the Marck river. In the evening the advance units of the 9th Motorized, which had followed up behind the armour, came in on the upper Marck. Meanwhile, General Beauchesne's detachment occupied Bergen-op-Zoom.

On the morning of the 12th, General Sciard ordered Beauchesne to capture the key-point, Moerdijk bridge, on which an unsuccessful attempt had already been made by some of the 6th Cuirassiers. This second attempt failed and the attackers fell back on a line north of the Breda–Bergen road.

Though the Dutch in Rotterdam were still fighting fiercely and hanging on to the Vestings Holland position, from the south end of the Zuyder Zee, the Germans were through the Peel line, and Hubicki's armour was driving back the French and Belgian troops.

On the 13th, the overall failure of Gamelin's scheme was patent. General Billotte, who on the previous day had been entrusted with the co-ordination of the operations of the Belgian Army, the B.E.F. and Army Group One, began the regrouping of forces in his charge. He warned General Giraud that the Seventh Army would be needed further south and that he should prepare to transfer some of his divisions. The main body of the 9th Motorized Division was kept south of Antwerp. The 38th Infantry Regiment in and round Breda began its withdrawal, but one battalion and the reconnaissance group were surrounded and, the next day, their ammunition exhausted, they surrendered. At the same time the reconnaissance group of the 4th Division fell back into Bergen-op-Zoom.

The next morning, the 14th, the German High Command, impatient at Dutch obstinacy, finished off this, to them, minor obstacle by permitting the bombing of Rotterdam, which forced the capitulation.

At the same time, a body of the 9th Panzer drove down on the battalions of the 25th Motorized retreating from Breda, and having surrounded Bergen-op-Zoom, where they captured the remains of the 4th Division Reconnaissance Group, drove the 92nd Infantry Regiment past Woensdrecht, thus opening the road along the isthmus to South Beveland and Walcheren. General Fagalde hastily brought up the 21st Division to occupy the southern shore of the Scheldt estuary between Walsoorden and Antwerp.

Towards midday, General Giraud was told to bring the whole of the Seventh Army south of Antwerp and to prepare a move of the 9th

Motorized and the 4th Division on the 16th, to be followed by that of the 1st Light Armoured. So, during the 15th, the units of these three divisions were slowly withdrawn into the Antwerp entrenched camp.

[5]

The end at Walcheren

The failure of the commander of the Walcheren expedition to employ the 224th Infantry Regiment in protecting the road from Flushing through South Beveland to Woensdrecht and Bergen-op-Zoom, and particularly in not securing the line of the Wemeldinge channel between South Beveland and the isthmus eastward, caused considerable anxiety, in view of the pressure on the troops fighting on the mainland. On the 13th, General Deslaurens had been ordered to send a regiment from his 60th Division over the estuary to hold the Wemeldinge channel. On the night of the 13th/14th and on the following day, the 271st Infantry Regiment, with some armoured cars and a few engineers, was carried over in the Dutch ferry-boats with the loss of only one small vessel. In view of the importance of the task, General Deslaurens took command in person. He found installed at Wemeldinge a Dutch regiment which, after welcoming the French, learned by radio of their army's capitulation. It became sensibly less enthusiastic to defend the isthmus *sans esprit de recul*, and during the evening it disappeared.

The occupation of Woensdrecht by the Germans on the 14th opened the way to an attack on Wemeldinge. Supported by the French submarine chasers, the French infantry held on to the channel during the night of the 14th/15th, and next morning began to extract from the north side of the peninsula as much shipping as they could. During the afternoon the Germans attacked with partial success. But the channel, with its high levees and dead ground, was indefensible. So, when on the morning of the 16th, after a fierce air and ground bombardment they attacked in force, General Deslaurens ordered the retreat to Walcheren. Before this could be accomplished, the 271st Infantry Regiment was overrun. Only some 300 got back to Flushing. The French navy did its best both by sea and air. Walcheren was defended through the day, but on the afternoon of the 17th the Germans cut across the neck and thrust rapidly against Flushing, which was now burning. A number of soldiers from the 224th and 271st were shipped back to Breskens on Dutch boats, but the captains refused to return to Walcheren. The French naval commander, Admiral Platon, sent every available submarine-chaser from Dunkirk and himself came to Flushing to supervise the destruction of all stores which could not be removed. General Deslaurens, rifle in hand, was killed a few hundred yards from the quay. Before midnight it was all over. The 60th Division had lost almost the whole of the 271st and its divisional commander; the 68th division two battalions and one artillery group, three batteries with all their guns.

On the morning of the 18th, the Seventh Army had been dissolved.

The Belgian defences

THE Belgian defences were based on three fortified zones: Antwerp, Liège, Namur, with the line of the Meuse. The main defensive line ran from the defended city of Antwerp, occupied by three infantry divisions, along the Albert Canal, west of Maastricht, to the junction with the Meuse down to Eben-Emael. The line then entered the girdle of the Liège forts and thereafter turned westward along the Meuse to Namur. The intention was to abandon the defence of the Ardennes south of the Liège–Namur line, in the well-grounded expectation that, in their own interests, the French would occupy the line of the Meuse from the frontier at Givet as far as Namur. The bulk of the Belgian Army, eighteen infantry divisions, would be north of the Sambre. The Ardennes behind the German and Luxembourg frontiers would be patrolled by the 2nd Cavalry Division and the 1st Chasseurs Ardennais, who, on the German invasion, had orders to execute demolitions and do what they could to delay the enemy, but on no account to get involved in serious combat. They were to withdraw northward into the main Belgian position.

It was recognized that, in spite of local strong-points and fortified areas, the Meuse Line presented a vulnerable salient. Also it was a considerable distance from the French frontier posts. Hence the French decision to go no further than the Dyle Line, that is, the second Belgian line known as KW (Koningsbooikt–Wavre), which ran from Antwerp through Lierre, across the Demer, and joined the Dyle at Wijmael. From Wijmael it followed the railway to Namur and included the towns of Louvain and Wavre. From Louvain southwards, this was the line that the B.E.F. and the French First Army were to occupy while the French Ninth Army would cover the Meuse from south of Namur, the Namur forts being occupied by Belgian garrisons.

The Belgian Air Force was far from adequate. The planes of its eighteen squadrons were out of date; most had an air-speed no better than 225–250 k.p.h. Attempts to buy in England and France had been unsuccessful. In the end, the British sold them twenty-four Hurricanes and twenty-four Fairey Battles, the latter already obsolescent. The total force amounted to about 200. This was soon reduced. Early on 10 May, the aerodromes at Schaffen and Neerhespen suffered severe casualties, followed by equally destructive attacks at Brusthem, Zoute and Nivelles. Most of the Belgian planes were destroyed in the next few days.

[2]

The French Cavalry Corps, the 2nd Light Armoured Division, an active division (General Bougrain) and the 3rd, newly formed from reserve troops (General Langlois) in early May, both lay south and west of the Forêt de Mormal. In the Dyle plan, they were both to move with the utmost speed to the line Tirlemont–Hannut–Huy with the purpose of preventing attempts of the enemy to cross the Meuse between Huy and Namur and of holding the Germans advancing north of Liège until, at worst, J/5, 14 May, but, if possible, until J/8, the period considered irreducible by General Blanchard of the First Army. After this, the two divisions were to fall back slowly along the axis Tongres–Gembloux. General Prioux, the corps commander, from the outset pretty dubious, had been told by Billotte in February to push out beyond the Hannut–Huy line in support of the Belgians. This seemed to Prioux even more risky.

On the afternoon 9 May, both divisions had received warnings of an impending attack and both prepared to move at short notice. They were roused at four next morning and half an hour later were ordered to move. They set off on this sunny morning, between 8 and 9, on half a dozen secondary roads, much more easily than they had expected. By evening the armoured cars of the 12th Cuirassiers were beyond the Petite-Gette, approaching Hasselt and Tongres, while, south of Liège, the 8th Cuirassiers were on the Ourthe, from Comblain-au-Pont to Durbuy, in touch with the advanced parties of the 4th Cavalry division of the Ninth Army.

[3]

In front of the Dyle Line

The loss of the two bridges at Maastricht, coupled with the neutralization of Eben-Emael (the fortress surrendered to the invaders on the 11th), compromised the whole Belgian defence. The centre, held by the 7th Belgian Division, was deeply bitten into early on the 10th. In the late afternoon, Hoeppner's XVI Korps (3rd and 4th Panzer Divisions) was through Maastricht and over the Vroenhoven bridge. The Belgians, seeing that a break-in here would lead to the rolling up of the Albert Canal line, manned the Cortessem switch 15 kilometres to the west and tried to organize an intermediate position Bilzen–Tongres–Glons. At the same time they hurriedly brought up cavalry units from south of Liège. The 4th Panzer brushed aside the scrambling squadrons. By noon on the 11th, the tanks were at Tongres, by 6 at Waremme.

The French light armour reached the Gette–Mehaigne line during the night of the 10th/11th and made uncertain touch with the retreating Belgian cavalry. In front, the 12th Cuirassiers met German patrols towards Tongres. The 8th, with the reconnaissance groups of V Corps and the 5th North African Division attached, occupied the line of the

Mehaigne down to Huy and the Meuse through Ardenne to Namur. By the morning of the 11th, the combat brigades of the Cavalry Corps had occupied the Petite-Gette and the Tirlemont–Huy road. There had been scattered bombing and on all sides villagers and farmers were on the move. The Belgian Cavalry Corps was now back on the Grande Gette from Tirlemont northward to Halen, while beyond Diest the Belgian 14th Division, which had suffered severely, kept a precarious hold on Lummen. Further north the infantry were withdrawing towards the KW line.

On this morning, the 11th, General Prioux, from his headquarters at Aische, 20 kilometres north of Namur, saw all his forebodings confirmed. General Langlois of the 3rd Light Armoured expected to be attacked on his main position during the day. Prioux telephoned Blanchard that the Dyle plan must be abandoned at once and the Escaut scheme substituted. Everywhere there was confusion. The Belgians were falling back as fast as they could, and the French cavalry would be unable to defend their line against the German armour long enough to allow the First Army infantry to establish themselves. Blanchard, as pessimistic as Prioux, passed this view of the situation to Billotte with the addition of his own warning. Communicating these alarms to Georges, Billotte objected that with the advanced elements of French and British divisions already on the Dyle Line and the main bodies in motion, a change of plans could only be disastrous. Later in the day, after visiting Prioux, he accepted that the Tirlemont–Huy line might be evacuated on J/5 (14th) instead of J/6, and that, should the Cavalry Corps be in serious peril, it might withdraw behind the line of the Cointet wire obstacle, roughly the line Andenne–Perwez–Longueville. Consequently, the period for the establishment of the First Army divisions and the B.E.F. on the Dyle–Gembloux position must be reduced.

Except for their reconnaissance groups, which had been sent forward to strengthen the Cavalry Corps, III, IV and V Corps had spent 10 May in preparing to move as soon as the roads were clear. The approach of the infantry began on J/2, the 11th. Only one division in each corps was motorized, the 1st in III Corps, the 15th in IV, and the 12th in V. The other three divisions, the 2nd North African, Moroccan, and the 5th North African, were all normal active divisions. They were supposed to move on foot. The suddenness and rapidity of the German entry into Belgium threw such intentions into confusion. Transport had to be improvised immediately. *Débrouille-toi* was the order. Some regiments were able to borrow the motor transport from the linked division; others only in part. Some moved by train, but many units at the tail had to move not only, as had been laid down, by march-route, but were told to double the length of the march each day. The manning of the Dyle became far more of a gamble than anyone cared to think.

Of III Corps, the 1st Division was in position on J/4 (13th), but of

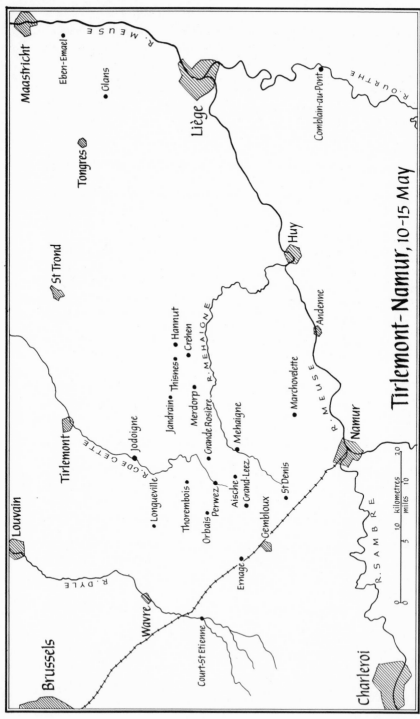

Tirlemont–Namur, 10–15 May

© CASSELL & CO LTD 1968

the 2nd North African only the infantry had arrived. Of IV Corps (General Aymes), General Juin's 15th Motorized arrived early and was able to lay a minefield on its front. Its transport was lent to the Moroccans. Even so IV Corps could not complete its move until the morning of the 14th and only part of the mines could be used. The advance of V Corps (General René Altmayer) went in similar fashion, but it had farther to go, in that the destination of its most forward battalion was to go to the north-east of Namur, where it became mixed with the 2nd Chasseurs Ardennais. Its rear units marched for three days before being taken up, and were scarcely settled in by the morning of the 15th, J/6!

[4]

Having failed to destroy the Maastricht bridges from the ground, the Belgians had tried on the 10th to bomb them. Of the nine planes engaged, seven were shot down. The Germans rushed up their anti-aircraft guns, which they thought more reliable than fighter planes. On Saturday, the 11th, a dozen French bombers attacked the same targets and failed. They were lucky; only one plane was hit. On Whit Sunday, the British No. 12 Squadron sent in five Fairey Battles. All the planes were lost, though one pilot nursed his injured machine back into the British lines. Part of the Veldwezelt bridge was damaged.

In the meantime, the Germans had firm control of the Meuse above Maastricht. Eben-Emael, impotent to fight back, surrendered at noon on the 11th. The field troops defending Liège were withdrawn and brought back to the KW line. The Liège forts, isolated and with no hope of relief, fought on, another week, another fortnight. Fort Pepinster capitulated only after the armistice with Belgium; the garrison was allowed to march out with the honours of war.

By midday on 11 May, Hoeppner's XVI Panzer Korps was well into Belgium. The Belgians abandoned the Cortessem switch, and the divisions of II Corps on the Albert Canal also began to fall back to the KW line. The Germans pressed on. On the 12th they were in St Trond and came on to Hannut, held by a battalion of the 11th Dismounted Dragoons and a Somua squadron of the 2nd Cuirassiers. Soon there was an attack on Thismes and Crehen, near the junction with the 2nd Light Armoured. Crehen was held all day with much desperate fighting. The Hotchkiss tanks, with their obsolete 37-mm. guns, were at a serious disadvantage. The Dragoon battalion was destroyed and what remained of the Hotchkiss squadron—less than half—came away by night.

The 2nd Light Armoured had a day of comparative ease, dealing with small infiltrations. This was J/3 (12th), and the question still remained with no sure answer: could the cavalry hold on until J/6?

At 5.30 in the morning on the next day (the 13th), General Bougrain sent a detachment of Somua to try to restore the position between Crehen and Merdorp a few kilometres west of Thismes. At Crehen it ran into a cluster of anti-tank guns, and the village remained in enemy hands. During the day there was persistent testing of the French defences all along the Mehaigne by enemy armour. The weak spot was the point of junction with the 3rd Light Armoured. Pressure was increasing all along the corps front. To the north, the 12th Cuirassiers were driven back on Jodeigne. A strong enemy attack on the Merdorp–Jandrain line isolated a battalion of the 11th Dismounted Dragoons. Ordered to retire to Jauche, it found the way blocked by a group of German tanks. The dragoons were eventually captured, but the Hotch-kiss squadron forced a passage westward. Of its twenty-one machines, only seven, all riddled with bullets, got back. Of three Somua squadrons engaged in the same area, twenty-five out of sixty were lost, and fifty of 170 troopers. In severe fighting at Marilles, another Dragoon battalion was saved by the intervention of nine Hotchkiss, of which only three returned, and only one of these undamaged. General Langlois's head-quarters at Huppaye was threatened and he was forced to withdraw.

At 6 in the evening, General Prioux, fearing that the centre of the Cavalry Corps might be pierced by the influx of an irresistible body of tanks, ordered both his divisions to retire to the Cointet line, eleven or so kilometres to the rear. The retreat of the 3rd Armoured was covered by the reconnaissance group of the 15th Motorized at Grande-Rosière. But the 2nd Light Armoured, by now closely engaged, could not retire until dusk, when it reached the line Marchovelette–Perwez. The last units to retire were the 54th and 56th Motor Machine-Gun Regiments, which throughout the day had defended Huy.

On this day, the British cavalry screen between the French and the Belgians came back in conformity with the neighbouring units. The Belgians, who had been attacked on the Tirlemont–Diest road, had withdrawn during the afternoon. By dawn on the 14th, except for the 8th Division in the Namur *enceinte*, all Belgian divisions were in and behind the KW line. In five days they had lost their 7th and half their 14th Divisions, while the 2nd, 3rd and 4th had all had substantial casualties.

On the morning of Monday the 13th, J/4, the three corps of the First Army were only partly established on the Namur–Wavre line. In front, the two light armoured divisions were behind the Cointet obstacle, such as it was, the 2nd between Marchovelette and Aische, the 3rd from Orbais to Longueville with the 4th Reconnaissance Group between them. The 2nd, with its headquarters at St Denis, was only a few thousand yards in front of the 12th Division line. The casualties of the 1st Dismounted Dragoons had been heavy, and the two machine-gun battalions had been transferred to V Corps. The enemy pressure did not relax. They crossed the Cointet Line, drove the dragoons out of Aische, surrounded Grand-Leez, forced the armoured cars of the 8th Cuirassiers back on Meux, and reached divisional headquarters. Soon after midday the division was withdrawn behind the line of V Corps, to which the armoured brigade was attached. The 3rd Light Armoured suffered much the same experience. Preceded by heavy artillery fire and dive-bombing, the Germans came over the Cointet Line, took Perwez, pushed the 4th Reconnaissance Group out of Thorembais, and though temporarily held up by the armoured brigade at Orbais, swung south-ward towards Gembloux and attacked the Moroccans in Ernage.

By 2 in the afternoon, General Prioux judged that the Cavalry Corps could no longer do any work of value and ordered the withdrawal behind the main line. The combat brigade of the 3rd Light Armoured was left in reserve to III Corps. In four days the division had lost two thirds of its Hotchkiss, ninety-eight out of 147, and a third of the Somua, twenty-nine out of eighty-seven.

The withdrawal of the 3rd Light Armoured in full combat had un-fortunate consequences. The German tanks following up were mistaken by the Moroccans for French machines and were thus able to break in to Ernage unresisted. As soon as the defence recognized their error, they counter-attacked and drove the enemy out. Further attacks during the day were defeated, though not without difficulty.

[5]

The Dyle Line

The corps and divisional commanders of the First Army were far from satisfied with the Dyle position. This had been identified with the main road from Wavre to Namur. On reconnoitring his sector on 11 May, General de la Laurencie complained that the III Corps line was much exposed and that the Cointet obstacle was full of gaps. He was allowed to draw his position back to the line of the river from Wavre to Court–St Étienne, and then back along the railway to the road, where it joined IV Corps a little north of Ernage. General Aymes of IV Corps, with the Moroccan division on the left, and the 15th Motorized on the right, also found his line along the railway extremely vulnerable, especially to armour, except at the cuttings. The corps had been provided with mines—it seems to have been the only one—but the Moroccans had not arrived in time to use more than half.

The key to the position was Ernage, which lay in a salient in front of the railway. Two battalions of Renault tanks had been attached to the Corps; one was placed behind each division. The defence of the railway was continued by the 12th Motorized of V Corps and, on the right, the 5th North African. The latter had moved almost entirely on foot. Some units had not reached Charleroi until the 13th, let alone the Dyle Line. On the afternoon of this day, the 14th Zouaves were hurried forward by lorry, and early on the morning of the 14th (J/5) were thrust into what proved to be the southern extremity of the Perwez–Namur line, the point from which the 2nd Light Armoured was about to retreat. With no clear orders, the regiment found itself in an unfortified position, the only solid entity in a fluid mass of retreating French and Belgians 'with-out equipment, without transport, sometimes without weapons'.

During the 14th, vague rumours had begun to circulate that all was not well to the south. The names 'Sedan' and 'Dinant' were ominously muttered. General Altmayer became apprehensive about his right flank, which should be in touch with II Corps south of the Sambre. V Corps was responsible for the river, but had no troops on the south bank. Early on 15 May, he ordered Lieutenant-Colonel Marioge, commanding the 6th Tirailleurs Marocains, to cross the Sambre with his regiment, strengthened by a detachment from the 95th Reconnaissance Group of the 5th North African, and a company of tanks, and with his left on the Meuse, to move southward to the level of St Heribert fort, the most southern of the Namur forts, and get into touch with Ninth Army. The detachment crossed the river at dawn and pushed back some parties of lightly armed Germans. In due course Marioge found some of the 8th Infantry Regiment (5th Division) near Dave. Having reported back to V Corps Headquarters, he was once again sent over the river with a single battalion of his Moroccans, the motor-cycle squadron of the Reconnaissance Group, and a company of Renault tanks, with orders to maintain the link with II Corps. Behind him the bridges over the Sambre were blown.

During this day, the Belgian 8th Division left the Namur defences, now partly covered by the 5th North African. This was the last Belgian division outside the KW line. The abandoned fortress troops, like those of Liège, continued to defend themselves and the forts.

The race for the Meuse

THE left formations of the Ninth Army, II and XI Corps, were to move into Belgium and occupy and consolidate the line of the Meuse from Givet to the Namur forts. The river lies some sixty kilometres from the French frontier between Maubeuge and Trelon. Except for the highway from Philippeville to Dinant, most of the roads are secondary and worse. On 10 May, the Ninth Army sent forward the mechanized brigades of its two cavalry divisions, the 4th on the left, the 1st on the right with the motorized parts of the divisional reconnaissance groups. These had two tasks, first to secure the line of the river, and having done this to hasten further east, join the Belgian frontier forces, and as far as possible delay the German advance guards long enough to allow the infantry divisions to reach and occupy the left bank of the Meuse. On the right of the 1st Cavalry, the 3rd Spahis (the 2nd Moroccan and 2nd Algerian Regiments), a horsed brigade without artillery, were to cross the Meuse at Mézières and form the link between the Ninth Army cavalry and that of the Second Army.

On the morning of 10 May, the start went smoothly. 'The weather was so splendid that you could easily take this to be a magnificent military parade such as one had never seen.' Across the frontier in the bigger country towns French flags and garlands were hung in windows. 'Women stood with their arms full of flowers and their aprons bulging with packets of cigarettes, sweets and chocolates. . . .'[1] The Meuse was crossed soon after midday. Army Group One's orders had laid down: 'As soon as the river is strongly held, the cavalry divisions will be sent forward as quickly as possible to find touch with the enemy.' General Corap proposed to delay the further advance until the Meuse Line had been properly organized for defence. He was overruled by General Billotte. The cavalry set out again during the afternoon. Across the river the villagers showed less enthusiasm. 'The streets of Ciney,' says a subaltern of the 4th Cavalry, 'were still and silent, the shutters were closed and the rare spectator showed no visible interest as we passed. . . . The atmosphere was indifferent, even hostile. . . . The further we went and the more our company split up, the emptier and deader became the countryside. As we neared Pessoux we found great herds of cattle in the meadows, abandoned some days earlier, bellowing mournfully, tortured by thirst and in agony from their swollen udders.'[2] Marche was reached in the evening and patrols sent out to the line of the Ourthe. But no enemy was met and what Belgian cavalry was found was moving northward. On the right of the 4th, the 1st Cavalry were on the line of the Lhomme.

Behind the screen, the leading detachments of the infantry divisions had been on their way since midday, by motor transport. The main bodies set out on foot during the evening. The 5th Motorized of II Corps had no trouble. The advanced guard reached the Meuse about midnight, and the main bodies of the units were installed by nightfall on the 11th. The left of the division was inside the ring of the Namur forts between St Heribert and Dave. Two of the regiments manned the river banks; the third, the 39th Infantry Regiment, was kept back in Ninth Army reserve. The divisional artillery was also in position.

It was far otherwise with the 18th Division, which was to hold from south of Anhée (opposite the island of Houx) to Hastière, some fifteen kilometres from Dinant. The leading battalions, one from 66th and two from 77th, were to occupy sixteen kilometres of the winding river. Until the arrival of their horse-drawn batteries, their only support was one regiment of 75s, the 308th from G.Q.G. reserve. The rest of the division was to move by march-route through the next seventy-two hours. To strengthen the left of the 66th, one battalion of the 39th was attached. Ninth Army had obtained some further motor transport for battalions of the advance guard.

The other division of XI Corps, the 22nd, had two battalions of the 19th Regiment (the third was in corps reserve) occupying Givet, the old fortress that lies in the point of the narrow French salient running into Belgian territory on the Meuse. On receipt of the warning order, these battalions were to extend their occupation of the river as far as the Hastière loop, where they were to find touch with the 18th Division advance guards. The other two regiments, the 62nd and 119th, were a long way further south-west, round Rumigny and Liart. Their mission was to send their advance detachments to points on the Meuse between Vireux-Molhain and Givet. But on this morning of 10 May, the infantry of the divisions had gone out on exercise before the arrival of the order to move. In consequence, the advance guards were not in position on the Meuse until twenty-four to thirty-six hours late. Moreover, the divisional anti-tank gun teams were doing their firing practice on the ranges at Sissonne and did not rejoin.[3]

Already what was to prove a major impediment to the defence, columns of fleeing civilians, had begun to appear with their barrows and prams.

[2]

The armoured cars and the motorized dragoons of the two cavalry divisions pushed on during the night. By early morning they were on or east of the line of the Ourthe and the Lhomme. The horsed brigades reached and crossed the Meuse during the morning. During the afternoon German reconnoitring parties began to appear. As yet the French had no idea that they were about to meet a force of considerably greater strength than General Corap's.

The advance into Belgium south of the Liège–Namur line was being made by von Kluge's Fourth Army of three korps (V, VIII, and II), strengthened by General Hoth's XV Panzer Korps of two armoured divisions: on the right, von Hartlieb's 5th, on the left Rommel's 7th. Rommel's division had come across northern Luxembourg, which was undefended. It had run into part of the 3rd Chasseurs Ardennais at Montleban, had wiped it out and reached Chabreleix on the 10th. The leading parties crossed the Ourthe on the morning of the 11th, and there were a few indecisive skirmishes with the French cavalry. In the middle of the morning, Rommel was warned not to pass Marche, a few kilometres beyond the Ourthe, in order to let the French involve themselves more deeply east of the Meuse. On Rommel's right, the 5th Panzer had been delayed by demolitions on the Salm and by some of the Belgian 2nd Cavalry Division, but the advance guard under Colonel Werner drew level with that of the 7th Panzer, and during the day made its first contact with the French, a demolition party of the 4th Cavalry Division engaged in blowing the bridge at Hotton.

On the morning of the 12th, hearing that the cavalry of Second Army was retreating, Ninth Army ordered its own to fall back over the Meuse. The 1st Cavalry crossed at Dinant and Hastière during the afternoon, the 4th further north at dusk. Both destroyed a number of bridges and mined crossroads. The 4th went into II Corps reserve near Fosse, the 1st behind the 18th Division at Flavion.

The injunction on the XV Panzer crossing the Marche–Liège road was raised on the 12th. The 7th Panzer advanced in two parallel columns to the Meuse at Dinant and Houx. The main body of the 5th Panzer was still some distance behind. Colonel Werner's detachment was temporarily transferred to Rommel, and came to Yvoir.

About 4.30 in the afternoon, the German armoured cars appeared opposite the 18th Division. The French sappers blew the bridges at Dinant and the railway bridge at Anseremme. Some two hours later, further down the river at Yvoir in II Corps area, the colonel of the 129th Infantry Regiment, who had crossed to inspect the arrangements for the destruction of the bridge, was surprised by the arrival of two enemy armoured cars. He was able to signal to the sappers on the west bank before he was killed. The bridge went up with one of the German cars. All the other bridges prepared for destruction were made temporarily more or less unusable during the evening. Perhaps owing to shortage of explosives, the preparations had not been thorough enough. In a number of cases, no more than a single span was broken.[4] Another matter of some consequence was that the Belgians had not brought all the boats and barges over to the left bank, nor, in spite of knowing that the French would occupy the Meuse from Givet to Namur, had they taken any steps either to prepare defences for the river or to tell the French anything about it. Nor do the French seem to have made any serious attempt to inform themselves.

[3]

When it was seen that the rear battalions of the 18th Division, moving on foot, would be late in reinforcing the advance guards, Ninth Army headquarters sent one battalion of the 39th Regiment from Army Reserve to fill the gap between the right of the 129th and the left of the 66th, facing the village of Houx. At Houx the left bank is flat, open and dominated by the right. In consequence, the battalion of the 39th took up its position on the wooded slopes of the hills about a kilometre from the stream.

The commander of the 5th Panzer advance guard, Werner, had orders to cross north of Houx. He tried at Yvoir where the bridge had been blown, and failed. He then came by night to Houx, passed over his motor-cyclists and proceeded to attack north-westward the flank of the 129th. The commander of the 129th reported to 5th Division Head-quarters that he was being attacked and that there seemed to be no French troops on his right. A small counter-attack was quickly organized, a battalion of the 14th Dragoons, but it was too late. The Germans were firmly established and were pushing past Anhée towards Haut-le-Wastia. By morning they had reached Senenne château and were approaching Point 190. The reconnaissance group of the 5th Division was able temporarily to block the way, but the reserve battalion of the 129th sent up from Bioul was harassed by German aircraft and needed nine hours to reach Haut-le-Wastia.

At the same time as the Werner group, or a little earlier, the northern of Rommel's two advance guards under Colonel Fürst found that the lock and weir at Houx island were unguarded. They came over in the early morning of the 13th and by 5 a.m. were up the hills on either side of Grange farm. The mist cleared about 7. The 18th Division artillery opened fire, which temporarily stopped the reinforcement of the 7th Panzer intruders. The 66th, having had their left turned, were staunchly defending a line through the farm Hontoir, facing the Surinvaux and Grange woods. On their right, the 77th could still see but not command the Meuse: its right was near Rostenne.

The southern of the two advance guards of the 7th Panzer under Colonel von Bismarck had had considerable difficulties in attempting to secure a bridgehead near Dinant, where the bridge had been broken. Early in the morning of the 13th, covered by the mist, elements of the division had crossed in rubber boats between Leffe and Bouvignes. Hidden in the bushes on the left bank,* French defenders successfully

---

* The left bank of the Meuse, here some 100 yards wide, rises several hundred feet above the river. At Bouvignes, the rise is steep and abrupt. The French gunners could not see to shell the river from Dinant northwards. Hence, when the banks at Bouvignes had been cleared of French infantry by the guns of the heavy tanks brought down by Rommel the German heavy bridge could be built and the crossing eased for armour.

impeded the crossing until Rommel brought up several heavy tanks and moved them up and down, giving covering fire. This enabled reinforcements of riflemen to cross with their anti-tank guns and begin to build up a bridgehead towards Chestruvin. During the next night, the 13/14th, a ferry service was improvised and some armour brought over.

Although the German crossing at Houx had been known at 5th Division Headquarters at Neffe about 1 a.m., the information was slow to reach Ninth Army at Vervins. Early in the morning of the 13th, General Billotte called at Corap's headquarters at Vervins on his way to Second Army, and spoke of his anxiety about General Huntziger's troops, who it was said had shown something like panic on the 12th. But an hour or so later, Ninth Army Headquarters was staggered by the news that the Meuse had been crossed at Houx and a counter-attack of the 129th broken up by bombers.

At the end of the night of the 12/13th, the main bodies of the 18th Division began to arrive, the first batteries and the third battalions of infantry. General Duffet was told to attack during the afternoon with another battalion of the 39th, from Army Reserve, supported by a squadron of Hotchkiss. Although the German riflemen were being reinforced, their situation was not yet secure. Colonel Fürst told Rommel that he expected a counter-attack and needed the support of armour. His alarm was unnecessary. The counter-attack was timed for 6.30 p.m. At this hour, the commander of the 39th telephoned to the 5th Division that he was not ready. At 7.45, he again asked for a postponement. The Hotchkiss groups arrived and went forward to a point over the Meuse between Anhée and Yvoir, clearing the ground, and taking a handful of prisoners; but without infantry the ground could not be held. The tanks came back.[5]

[4]

In reserve to XI Corps, the 4th North African Division had been working during the spring on the defences on the frontier between Trelon and the Forêt de St Michel. On 10 May, the casemates behind the tank trap had not been completed. The division was ordered to move on foot to Florennes, north-east of Philippeville. They abandoned their works, locked the doors and left the keys with the local village authorities, and set out. They had with them three days' rations, which was lucky, since on the 10th German bombers dropped a packet on the transport which was loading supplies at Hirson railhead, and repeated the raid on the 11th. Hirson ceased to supply. However, Cerfontaine, west of Philippeville, had been designated as Ninth Army railhead on the move into Belgium. This, too, now received the attentions of the German bombers, as did other goodsyards. The bulk of the ammunition sent forward by Ninth Army was in two large dumps inside Belgium. Both were destroyed. From the 13th, no more rations or ammunition could be drawn by the forward troops.[6]

Sedan

VARIOUS hours have been given for the first warning that active operations had begun, some as early as 4 in the morning on the 10th. The elaborate schedule of warning orders seems, however, to have been jettisoned. Many units received nothing earlier than the third, the order to move. On the French Third Army front east of Longuyon to the Moselle, the Germans had forestalled them. Belgian Rexists and Luxembourg Nazis opened the way for the German troops, some of whom seem to have crossed the Moselle soon after midnight. When they set out in the early morning, the Third Army screen, the 3rd Cavalry Division of General Petiet, the 1st Spahi Brigade and the recce groups of XXIV Corps, ran into the enemy within half an hour of crossing the Luxembourg frontier and found themselves strenuously engaged with the flank-guards of Guderian's XIX Panzer Korps and glider-borne infantry, which had been put down north of Esch-sur-Alzette on the frontier. The Spahis were met almost immediately they emerged from Longwy, and found themselves subjected to attacks from civilians shooting from houses.

On the left of XXIV Corps, the 2nd and 5th Cavalry Divisions (Generals Berniquet and Chanoine) were able to penetrate further into Belgium, and touch was found with the Belgian general Keyaerts, who commanded the frontier troops. At this southern end of Belgium, the 1st Chasseurs Ardennais division was responsible for the area between the French frontier south of Arlon up to St Vith. As early as 1937, the Belgian staff had come to the conclusion that they could do nothing to stop the enemy and that the troops here should be withdrawn behind the Sambre, but they gave no serious thought to what they might do. On the 10th, the Chasseurs Ardennais 'imperturbably' went on with their demolitions, notwithstanding the fact that they were impeding the movements of the French cavalry. There was some minor scrapping round Martelange on the Luxembourg frontier with elements of Kirschner's 1st Panzer Division, and a fight at Chabreleix, but, says a cynical historian, 'the Belgian Army . . . successfully accomplished a real *tour de force* in not allowing itself to be compromised and having had no casualties whatever, at least among the units initially east of the Meuse'.[1] The Germans found that the demolitions offered no serious impediment to movement.

In consequence, the French cavalry met their enemy on 10 May far

---

* The narrative of the débâcle of the remainder of the Ninth Army, the right wing with XLI Corps, is more involved with the Second Army than with the Ninth and is therefore dealt with here.

earlier than they had expected, and already in full *élan* of anticipated victory. The French reached the Marche–Neufchâteau–Virton railway line. In the evening, the 3rd Spahi Brigade arrived from Ninth Army at Libin, both horses and men exhausted. At 5 p.m. Schaal's 10th Panzer Division drove the left of the 2nd Cavalry Division back to Jamoigne, close to the frontier. Touch with the 5th Cavalry was lost—the country is thickly wooded—and the 1st Cavalry Brigade was sent up to fill the gap.

At dawn on the 11th, the 5th Cavalry, of which the right was open for a matter of ten kilometres, was driven out of Neufchâteau and Libramont by a fast-moving attack by the 2nd and 1st Panzer. It lost a third of its motorized dragoons and a battery of 105-mm., while two squadrons of the 12th Chasseurs were missing. The French fell back and tried to take up a new line on the Semoy, to which a battalion of the 295th Infantry Regiment of 55th Division, and further east, one of the 12th Zouaves from the 3rd North African were dispatched. The Germans followed up rapidly. They were stopped at Bouillon and Rochehaut, but crossed on a partly destroyed bridge five miles up the river. At the same time they captured the ford at Mouzaive on the boundary with the Ninth Army, which for some unknown reason the 3rd Spahis had neglected to guard. The 2nd Cavalry, less hard pressed, found its right flank uncovered by the retreat of XXIV Corps reconnaissance groups, themselves struggling to keep in touch with the Third Army cavalry fighting desperately in front and east of Longwy. There had been little bombing on the 10th, but on the 11th there were a number of Stuka attacks on villages near the line of resistance.

[2]

The civilian population was already moving. The Grand Duchess of Luxembourg headed a cortège of ducal cars which crossed the frontier at Hussigny early in the morning, on her way to Dunkirk and London. Burgomasters sent parties of their villagers into France. Some, however, had not appreciated what was afoot. General Huntziger asked the *maire* of Bouillon on the Semoy, where the commander of the 5th Cavalry had set up his headquarters, whether one of the local hotels could be used for the wounded. 'Of course not, General,' replied the burgomaster; 'this is a summer resort, our hotels are reserved for tourists. Do you really think there is any danger?'[2]

On the French side of the frontier there were no such illusions. Villages east of the Meuse, such as Laifour, were cleared and the inhabitants dispatched by train. On the night of 10 May, the *maire* of Sedan received from the *préfet* of the Meuse the order to evacuate the town, and at 4 next morning the civilian population gathered at the rallyingpoints and entrained. It was to be expected that the Germans would drop a bomb on the line. And they did, in front of the last train, forcing the luckless fugitives to continue their exodus on foot. The hospitals at

Sedan-Monthermé,
13-17 May

Rocroi •

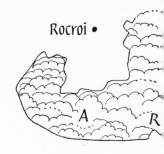

A   R

• Aubenton

•Rumigny

•Lépron

Marlemont •

• Signy-L'Abbaye

•Rocquigny

Hocm

Launois •

• Novion-Porcien

Château Porcien

R. AISNE

| 0 | | | | 10 | kilometr |
| 0 | | | 5 | | miles |

Rethel refused to take the invalids of Sedan until President Lebrun himself intervened. The evacuations were complicated by the panic flight of Belgians, which in turn spurred hitherto equable French citizens to take to the roads.[3]

[3]

As soon as the direction of the German attacks was known, General Huntziger became apprehensive of the weakness of his left flank, in particular the Sedan sector held by the 55th Division of X Corps. On the 10th he ordered his reserve, the 71st Division, of which two regiments were working in the back areas of the army and the third near the junction of the Bar and the Meuse, to move into X Corps area. The X Corps commander, General Grandsard, received no notice of this until late on the night 11th/12th. At this time of night it was out of the question to put this reinforcement into the line—darkness was no more than six hours. In consequence the two incoming regiments did not take over the Douzy sector (Pont-Maugis to Remilly) until the night 12th/13th, when the German XIX Panzer Korps was already in contact with the French line. The 205th Infantry Regiment, the third regiment of the 71st, from Donchéry, was put into corps reserve.

On Whit Sunday (J/3), the Second Army covering force was already beginning to shrink and crumble. Indeed it is difficult to see what the French could have done in the tulgy and unkempt woods of the Ardennes threaded by deep and winding streams against persistent and thrusting patrols with motor-cycles and armoured cars. The failure of the 3rd Spahis in leaving the Mouzaive ford undefended appeared in the context a major error, but it is unlikely that they could have secured the crossing for long. At 8 in the morning, the 5th Cavalry, with both its flanks turned, withdrew to *maisons fortes* over the frontier, but, harried by the 1st Panzer, they were unable to take up the line. By midday they were back at St Mengès, not more than three kilometres from Sedan. The unhappy 295th Infantry Regiment, which had been ordered to support the cavalry on the Semoy, had not been transported forward as ordered but made to march; it was now ordered back. Roughly hunted by the German armoured cars, the infantry was split up and driven into the woods. The battalion commander was killed and only 300 much shaken men got back to the French lines, cursing the cavalry for deserting them. The 1st Cavalry Brigade and the 12th Zouaves, which had been sent up from the 3rd North African, fell back behind the Chiers, whither the 2nd Cavalry Division followed them during the night.

This morning there appears to have been considerable alarm at Second Army Headquarters. About 9, Colonel Lacaille, the Chief of Staff, rang up Ninth Army and reported that a heavy tank attack had chased the 5th Cavalry back to the Meuse, a statement not yet true, and that the 47-mm. anti-tank gun, reputed to be the best in Europe, could not penetrate the enemy tanks. During the afternoon, Huntziger, still worried by the rapid retreat of the cavalry, told Lacaille to ask G.Q.G.N.E. at La Ferté to let him have another division to replace the 71st. Lacaille's report of the situation to General Roton, the *Aide-major-général*, is described as alarming. General Georges was at the moment at Belgian headquarters. Roton consulted Doumenc at Montry. They decided to dispatch the 3rd Armoured Division from Moivre and the 3rd Motorized from the Bar-le-Duc–Vitry-le-François region, to Stonne on the high ground behind X Corps, and the 14th Division (General de Lattre de Tassigny) from Lunéville to Novion-Porcien, to be able to support either the right of Ninth Army or the left of Second. At the same time the 1st Colonial Division, in reserve near Stenay, thirty-five kilometres south of Sedan, was given to Second Army, and General Flavigny, whose XXI Corps staff was also in reserve near Reims, was told to report to Huntziger.

Two hours after his alarmist report, Colonel Lacaille told G.Q.G.N.E. that the situation of Second Army was normal and that there was no urgency for the dispatch of the 3rd Motorized. But La Ferté was not reassured. No change was made in the movement orders. Further, Ninth Army was told to destroy the six railway bridges over the Meuse, which G.Q.G.N.E. had ordered to be left intact. Before dark, the right bank of the Meuse on both sides of Sedan had been evacuated and the bridges were with some trouble blown. Night had fallen before the first enemy patrols appeared near the Givonne ravine north-east of the town.[4]

During the night (12th/13th), the 71st Division, which had been moving since the 10th, came into the middle of X Corps line between the 55th and the 3rd North African divisions, the Douzy sector. The relief had been slow, and the units of the troops which had been relieved had not been accommodated in their new positions by daylight. That an attack was about to take place was apparent, but its form was not. During the night French reconnaissance aircraft had seen and reported that, south of the Namur–Liège line of the Meuse, all the main roads through the Ardennes were crowded with columns of motor-vehicles moving with all their lights blazing, particularly thick on the Bastogne–Sedan axis. This, however, found no space in the morning intelligence summary of the Second Army.[5]

[4]

The Meuse, most meandering of rivers, flows north-westward until it reaches Sedan, and runs through the south-western edge of the town. It then turns abruptly north as far as the village of St Mengès, when it again curves westward for about a kilometre before turning southward to resume its flow westward at Frénois. At Glaire, at the corner of Sedan, this peninsula is cut off by a canal from Glaire to Frénois. Thereafter the river proceeds westward to Flize and Nouvion, past which it resumes its northward course into the Ardennes. Between Sedan and Flize, the river lies in a wide shallow valley. On the south side rises a moderately steep hill, at the top of which stands the Bois de Marfée and la Boulotte. From here the King of Prussia, Moltke, Bismarck and the minor princes of Germany had watched the crash of the Second Empire on 2 September 1870. To the north of the river, a plain rises gently until it disappears behind the wall of trees of the great Ardennes forest. The town of Sedan itself lay outside the French position, but the suburb of Torcy was within it. About a kilometre west of Frénois, north of the river, is the village of Donchéry, and a further two kilometres on is the junction of the Meuse with the Bar River and the Canal des Ardennes, which joins the Meuse to the Aisne.

To the south of Sedan, the defence line lay along the Meuse through Wadelincourt to Aillicourt, where the line turned east behind the tributary Chiers to the Mouzon sector, held by the 3rd North African Division.

The defences of X Corps consisted of a fortified line of various casemates and outworks, which had been built during the autumn and winter. Every obstacle, including the more than usually severe cold, had delayed the completion. Fifty-four constructions had been completed as to the concrete, but the doors and the steel plates for the embrasures had not arrived.[6] The front line of the Sedan sector was covered by anti-tank obstacles, but there were none for the stop-line between one and two kilometres from the front.

With the entrance of the 71st Division, the X Corps position was divided into three divisional sectors, Carignan (3rd North African): Douzy (71st) on both sides of the Meuse, Sedan (55th). In addition, there were two regiments of Fortress infantry (136th and 147th) and the 11th machine-gun battalion. In support there were the three divisional artillery regiments (three groups of 75s each, two of heavies) and various fortress batteries. Finally, the corps heavy artillery, two groups of 105-mm., two of 155, eight batteries in all.

The morning of 13 May was fine and sunny, but for some hours after daybreak river mist hung over the valley. During the night the rumble of engines had been heard across the Chiers, but not west of Sedan. Nothing indicated an immediate attack. The French expected a slow build-up of assault troops over some days. From daylight, the enemy began to come down from the woods, and about 7 in the morning the movement was general. The whole sector from the Bar to Carignan woke up. From 7 o'clock, German infantry and vehicles began to come down from the woods through St Mengès towards Floing, towards the Givonne ravine, towards Sedan, Balan, and Bazeilles. From midday the movement extended further west towards Donchéry. During the morning, the X and XVIII Corps heavies shelled points of passage, cross-roads and the approaches, but economically. Already a shortage of ammunition began to be felt. By 3 in the afternoon corps heavies were down to half a unit and the corps ammunition column had only enough transport for two fifths of a unit. On the previous day, General Grand-sard had asked Second Army to send up enough ammunition to the batteries against the expectation of a major battle. Not much arrived.*[7]

The dominant feature of the morning was the increased activity of the German Air Force, which attacked all the rear approaches as far back as advance corps headquarters at La Berlière. Divisions complained to corps and corps spoke to army. All Grandsard got from Huntziger was: 'They have got to have their baptism of fire.' There was heavy bombing of Hannogne, Flize, the Bar bridges, Torcy. Sedan was in flames. The signal centre at Raucourt, near the headquarters of the 71st Division, was temporarily knocked out. Up to 2 p.m. the enemy had shown no evidence of preparing an assault, although their numbers were visibly increasing. Grandsard felt that the combination of bombing with the closing-up of German infantry towards the river indicated the approach of an assault. 'The whole corps front was threatened, the threat being stronger and more immediate between Donchéry and Wadelincourt.' Although he still believed that any attack would be destroyed, he ordered the 213th Regiment from corps reserves to move into a position he had selected earlier in the spring as a likely jumping-off line for a counter-attack, from Chéhéry to Bulson-Raucourt. At the same time, he summoned the 4th and 7th Battalions of light tanks (F.C.M.) to close up. The 4th was behind the 71st Division, the 7th some twenty kilometres distant at Les Alleux, west of the Bar. His other reserve, the 205th Infantry Regiment, he left near La Besace.

An hour later, between 3 and 4 p.m., the infantry holding the river-line were suddenly smitten by German aircraft. Whereas in the morning the attacks had been short, carried out by two or three dive-bombers with light bombs, the afternoon attack was massive and almost con-tinuous. Three groups appeared simultaneously between Donchéry and Wadelincourt. Two of these consisted of a number of dive-bombers, one group of which bombed and machine-gunned the French trenches and pill-boxes, while above them circled the second similar group, waiting to take over when the first had expended its bombs. Above these again flew a fighter escort. General Guderian says that twelve squadrons

---

* Ammunition at the guns was limited to $1\frac{1}{2}$ units above those carried which amounts to about $2\frac{1}{2}$–3 units in all. (The only exception was for the fortress artil-lery, which was allowed 5 units.) Units of fire varied with the calibre and type of gun.

Gun	At battery	With Ammunition Column (per gun)
75-mm. horsed	277	200
75-mm. tractor	333	200
105-mm.	110	100
155-mm. short	58	75

A forward 155-mm. battery at Torcy fired on 11th 210 rounds. On 12th two batteries here fired some 600 shells between 4 a.m. and midnight.

were employed, apart from fighters. 'On the front Donchéry–Glaire–Wadelincourt, completely covered by smoke for fifty minutes, there were three dive-bombers permanently in action'.[8] Besides the immediate attack, other small groups attended to the anti-aircraft batteries, forcing them to cease fire and move.

While this bombardment was in progress, the German infantry, the 1st Rifle Regiment of 1st Panzer Division, commanded by Colonel Balck, and the independent Gross-Deutschland regiment attached to the XIX Panzer Korps, began crossing the Meuse on rubber boats and rafts under the shelter of the cloud of smoke and dust from the bombing. They were also covered by a fierce bombardment from four brigades of 105-mm. guns. Most of the French infantry had taken refuge from the air attack in the concrete shelters, which, in most cases unfinished, offered scant protection. The men were stunned, shocked and deafened and most of their weapons were clogged with dust.[9] Through this turmoil of swirling dust and smoke, the German infantry suddenly appeared and rushed the front line before the shaken infantry could recover. Gaulier-Villette went at 4, followed by Torcy. The great blockhouse at Bellevue, at the point where the Meuse curves westward, which covered the river-line to Donchéry with a 75-mm. gun, was taken from the rear. The strong-points at Wadelincourt and Frénois had also gone. At 5.50 another irruption—from Donchéry—carried the attackers towards the Croix-Piot, on the hill. An hour and a half later the French were still holding at Pont-Maugis up the river, and at the western end of the sector Villers-sur-Bar, but Balck's infantry were already crossing the stop-line, which was not fortified, and mounting to the Bois de Marfée (supported, it was said, with tanks: there were no tanks) and la Boulotte.

Shortly before 6, the officer in command of the B Group of X Corps heavies round Bulson telephoned to the corps artillery commander that a violent fight was going on less than half a mile from his battle-post and asked whether he should withdraw, adding that it was German machine-gun fire, and that he was about to be surrounded. He was told that in the circumstances he might retire. He then appears to have ordered the commanders of all ten of the batteries under his command to abandon their guns.

Almost simultaneously, General Lafontaine, commander of the 55th Division at Fond Dagot, a mile maybe south of Bulson, was surprised by the appearance outside his headquarters of a crowd of fugitives, infantry and gunners from the Frénois sub-sector. Stopped by the General and his staff, they claimed to be retiring in obedience to orders. It gradually became apparent that most of them were battery drivers and infantry details. They said that German tanks were moving up from the river. Among them were men from the 295th Infantry Regiment and the 147th Fortress Regiment, the garrison of the defences at Frénois. Confirmation, as always, was slow to arrive; the story might be true, especially as observation-posts looking east across the river could see heavy traffic coming down from the hills. There was in fact no valid reason for this mass movement, but it could not be arrested. Everywhere the roads were covered by artillery teams, ration and ammunition wagons, infantry weapon carriers, fatigue parties, horses and motors. What was worse, many of the groups were headed by officers, and, worse still, their guns had been abandoned.

The two reserve regiments, the 213th and 205th, were given to General Lafontaine for an immediate counter-attack, and to these were added the two battalions of tanks, 4th and 7th.

It might still have been possible to mount a successful counter-attack, provided it was carried out before dark, within, that is, the next two or three hours. For this it was vital that orders should be given with speed and clarity. There were still important supports; the field batteries of the 55th divisional artillery had not been affected by the panic and were still in position. But unfortunately the main telephone centre at Raucourt had again been destroyed, and General Lafontaine, after consulting the corps commander, had moved his headquarters to Chémery where there was no telephone. By now all roads were thronged with bewildered and panic-stricken civilians and army details, many with horses. Staff officers trying to disentangle the situation and build up defences were losing precious time moving from place to place, often abandoning their cars in despair. The war diary of the 7th Battalion says that their tanks took more than five hours to cover the five kilometres from Chémery to Tannay.[10] General Lafontaine's counter-attack was postponed until morning.

[5]

To those who now know what was going to happen in the next three days, the situation of X Corps at 6 in the evening of 13 May can be seen to be irremediable unless immediate measures were undertaken. To the commander of X Corps and his staff, it was thought difficult, but possible to master. They had of course no inkling of the intentions of the commander facing them. What then seemed most probable was an attempt to outflank the Maginot Line and roll up Army Group Two. There was no reason as yet to take matters *au tragique*. Just at this time, General Grandsard was fortified by the arrival at his headquarters of the officer commanding the armour of the Second Army, who announced the approach of the French 3rd Armoured Division. He was succeeded by the commander of the 3rd Motorized Division, General Bertin-Boussus, whose leading regiments were even now on the rear position between the Bar and Stonne.

The Germans were in no confusion. By 11 that night, Cheveuges and the Bois de Marfée were in their hands, and Balck's riflemen were moving on Chéhéry and Bulson, while a battalion of the Gross-Deutschland was clearing the area between Wadelincourt and the Ennemane. By midnight, the XIX Korps engineers had completed a bridge at Gaulier and before dawn German tanks were moving up from the south bank of the Meuse.

The French counter-attack by the 213rd Infantry Regiment and a company of the 7th Tank Battalion started at 7 on the morning of the 14th. The left reached Connage on the Bar but an hour later ran into the armour of the 1st Panzer Division. By 9.40 it was all over. Only four of the fifteen French light tanks remained, and of the 55th Division only the detachment of the 331st Infantry Regiment on the Bar still held with a few batteries of 75s. The survivors fell back to the wood at Mont Dieu. At the same time, the 10th Panzer Division had crossed the Meuse above Sedan and driven back the forward elements of the 71st Division. The 205th Infantry Regiment and the 4th Tank battalion, confused by contradictory messages, do not seem to have started before receiving an order to halt. The 205th therefore retreated to the northern edge of the Bois de Raucourt, where it remained all day, and the tank battalion, not having been engaged, dropped back to Sommauthe. The 71st Division had not been attacked, but its commander, General Baudet, seems to have lost his head. Having put two battalions of the 120th Infantry Regiment from reserve on the Ennemane stream between Remilly and Raucourt, he retired from his headquarters to a point on the level of Stonne.[11] The troops, bewildered and without orders, a prey to rumour of disaster, drifted back. By evening, except for the two battalions of the 205th Infantry Regiment north of the Bois de Raucourt, the 71st Division west of the Meuse had to all intents disappeared. General Grandsard was now completely out of touch with the 3rd North African across the Meuse. General Huntziger therefore transferred this division to XVIII Corps and ordered the withdrawal of its units on the line of the Chiers to the switch-line running from the La Ferté outwork to Inor on the Meuse, a line which had been spit-locked but not dug. At the same time he ordered part of the 1st Colonial Division and the 2nd Cavalry to occupy the vacancy caused by the volatization of the 71st.

By midday on the 14th, German infantry and armour were approaching the high ground near Stonne, which dominates the country to the south and at the same time protects the Meuse crossings. Guderian now executed the master-stroke. After consulting von Wietersheim of the XIV Motorized Korps,* he ordered the 1st and 2nd Panzer Divisions (the latter was not yet over the Meuse) to wheel westward across the Bar and handed over to von Wietersheim the 10th Panzer division and the Gross-Deutschland regiment to cover his southern flank and communications. The moves were completed early in the afternoon. The 2nd Panzer crossed the Meuse, captured Villers-sur-Bar and went over the river and the canal both here and at Pont-à-Bar. At neither place, nor at St Aignan, Omicourt or Malmy, had the bridges been blown. Nor

---

* 2nd, 13th and 29th Motorized Divisions.

had they been prepared for destruction; some say from lack of foresight, others from lack of explosives. The 1st Panzer crossed at Omicourt and Malmy and moved westward on both sides of Vendresse. The 2nd Panzer also divided. The last detachments of the 55th Division were disposed of. Dom-le-Mesnil was taken and the garrison (148th Fortress) driven back on Flize. Sapogne went, but at nightfall Hannogne was still holding out.

5 THE MEUSE; MONTHERMÉ,
13–15 May

Monthermé, 10–15 May

WHILE the left of the Ninth Army and X Corps of the Second Army were already involved with Kluge's Fourth Army from the 11th onward, the right-hand corps of the Ninth Army between them was left in comparative peace. General Libaud's XLI Corps had its whole length on the Meuse from Vireux (where the left of the 61st Division was in touch with the 22nd) past Fumay to Anchamps; here the defence was taken up by the 102nd Fortress Division of General Portzert as far as Flize. It was left in peace largely because the absence of good roads through Luxembourg and southern Belgium limited the advance of several armoured corps. While Hoth's XV Panzer and Guderian's XIX Panzer could move on roughly parallel lines (and even in Hoth's corps the 5th Panzer had to follow on the heels of Rommel's 7th), Reinhardt's XLI Panzer Korps had to delay its moves until Guderian's divisions had wheeled southward. It therefore started from an area east of the other divisions. Even so it was necessary for the two divisions to move in column with Kuntzer's 8th Panzer Division, preceding Kempff's 6th, through the night of 10th/11th.

South of Vireux the Meuse passes through the most tortuous miles of its course, between steep hills covered with thick woods and tangled scrub, which dominate the stream. Along it lie villages and small towns, Laifour, Fumay, Revin, Monthermé, Château-Regnault, Nouzonville, Charleville-Mézières, beyond which the valley opens out. Both east and west of the river lie great stretches of forest. The approach to the river is difficult from either side, difficult both to attack and defend.

Of the two divisions of XLI Corps, the left, the 61st, was a B division from Brittany and Poitou, commanded by General Vauthier. It held as far as Anchamps, a little down-stream from Monthermé. From Anchamps to below Nouzonville was the 42nd Demi-Brigade Colonial Machine-Gunners of the 102nd Fortress Division, of whom half were French and half from Madagascar (Malgaches). On their right, the 52nd Colonial Machine-Gunners, half French and half Indo-Chinese, held the bridge-heads in front of Charleville.* Last, from the end of the Charleville sector to Pont-à-Bar, the river was defended by the 148th Fortress Infantry Regiment, a very good regiment with an unusual proportion of active soldiers.

At Ninth Army Headquarters, it had been thought that whatever

---

* These demi-brigades had each only two battalions. The 102nd Division had the 3rd Battalion Machine-Gunners attached from General Reserve.

attack was made on XLI Corps, it would be directed against Charle-ville-Mézières. There had therefore been organized three bridge-heads east of the river, Montcy, St Laurent and Lumes. Otherwise the most vulnerable point was the junction with the Second Army. By stressing the poverty of the means at his disposal, General Corap had persuaded Army Group One to give him the 53rd (a B division from Normandy) to be ready to support the right of the Ninth Army position, and he had it stationed in the region of Novion-Porcien, some thirty kilometres to the south-west of Flize. On 10 May, one of its regiments, the 208th, was engaged in firing practice at Sissonne, another sixty kilometres to the west.

None of the Ninth Army's prognostics was correct. General Rein-hardt set up his headquarters at Bièvre, directly east of Revin, and directed his leading division to Hargnies, north-east of Fumay, in front of which there was a choice of objectives.

[2]

On the morning of 11 May, the French railways had removed the civilians from Laifour and Monthermé, but during the afternoon German bombers began to harass other villages in the neighbourhood already full of refugees. On 12 May, after the last train had gone, General Portzert ordered the bridges to be destroyed and the barges to be brought to the left bank and sunk. Unfortunately the railway bridge at Château-Regnault was only damaged and a number of barges were left afloat.

It was not until the morning of the 13th that the point of the attack was clarified by a heavy bombing assault on the front held by the 42nd Malgache Demi-Brigade. It began at daylight and continued for five hours. During the morning, observers on the high ground west of the Meuse, in the 61st Division area, saw through the gaps in the trees along the Hargnies-Monthermé road, a long procession of vehicles moving southwards, guns, cars, lorries, side-cars. Unhappily for the artillery of the 61st, the range was too great for effective action, while behind the 42nd Demi-Brigade there were only five guns and these of old models. The Germans came on in almost complete immunity.

Monthermé lies in a buckle of the river at its junction with the Semoy, at the end of a peninsula along which runs a stony spine falling away to the river. It is about seven kilometres all round and perhaps one across. The defence of the position was entrusted to the second battalion of the demi-brigade, a unit of three machine-gun companies, Nos. 4, 5 and 6. No. 5 held the river bank all round; No. 4 spanned the neck of the peninsula, while No. 6 covered Château-Regnault, which is to the south and behind the battalion's line. Various block-houses looked down from the flanks of the spine across the river and also guarded the roads. Two kilometres behind the junction with the mainland lay the reserve posi-tion, the stop-line with a barbed-wire curtain, held by a few sections.

Behind again at some distance were a few companies, one from the 42nd, one from the 52nd, and one from the 3rd Machine-Gun Battalion. All these were armed with heavy weapons fixed in position.

Except for the air bombardment, the German attack at Monthermé was on a minor scale. By the skilful employment of assault guns mounted on tank bodies, the posts on the French side were easily reduced. Gaps appeared in the barrage on the river. Rafts and rubber boats were brought to the water by the attacking groups, and though some were sunk, a number crossed. The crews landed and made for the crest of the spine. Having occupied the block-houses here, they were able to take the rest of the defenders at the water-level in reverse. The conquest of the peninsula was finished in an hour. But No. 4 Company, at the exit from the peninsula, still held. A bitter fight followed; a break-out was followed by a counter-attack. The Germans paused.

During the night, General Libaud sent up the reserve of the 61st Division, two battalions of the 248th Infantry Regiment which established themselves, one in close support of the line of resistance, the other 1,500 metres further west.

About 7.30 on the morning of the 14th, the attacks were resumed. Three times the German infantry broke through and three times they were thrown back. The few reserves available were called up, a section of the 3rd Machine-Gunners and two sections from the first battalion of the 42nd, and between 4 and 5 p.m. a half-company from the rear battalion of the 248th. Casualties were heavy and the men exhausted. Many officers and N.C.O.s were killed or wounded and the units badly mixed. Finally, between 7 and 8, the German bombers returned and shattered the resistance. Attacked for the fourth time, the centre of the 4th Malgache company was broken into. Men began to drift back. But the enemy did not follow up. The commander of the rear battalion of the 248th rallied his men and the support line was re-established. But the situation was worse than precarious. At dusk watchers down the river had seen tanks moving out of Monthermé village, and from the right the 1st Battalion of the 42nd saw signs of an attack beginning up the river at Joigny. The commander of the demi-brigade decided to withdraw to the stop-line, but in the confusion, aggravated by the ceaseless artillery fire on the approaches, the reorganization could not be carried out. At 3 in the morning of the 15th, the bombardment began again, to be further weighted by air bombing. At 4 a.m. the German infantry began to advance, and soon after 7 the tanks moved up. Having no anti-tank guns, the 2nd Battalion of the 248th retreated to Sécheval. At 9.15 the headquarters of the demi-brigade was surrounded and its commander and the battalion commander were taken prisoner.

At General Reinhardt's command-post, the Germans showed the commander of the 42nd a map of his line on a 1/50,000 scale with every detail of the defences marked. They assured him that only three infantry battalions had been deployed at Monthermé.

6 G.Q.G. ACTION, *13 May*

INFORMATION of what was happening in the forefront of the battle was slow to reach G.Q.G.N.E. General Georges's first anxiety was whether the advancing Allied forces were moving eastward fast enough, and in the afternoon of the 11th he urged the importance of delaying the German advance guards by 'massive bomber action on bridges, etc., and columns on the march', as well as *'coups d'arrêt brutaux'* by the Cavalry Corps, already hotly engaged with the German armour. Already on the morning of the 10th, the 1st Armoured Division of General Bruneau, stationed at Suippes, had been ordered to move on the following day by road, the tracked elements by rail, to the First Army near Charleroi. On the 11th, few orders of moment were given. It was not until the 12th that the shadow of catastrophe began to fall over La Ferté. Gamelin at Vincennes at last realized that if he was to co-ordinate the whole military side of the war from Beirut to The Hague, he must divest himself of some part of his functions and pass them to a subordinate. He had already arranged that Georges should be his delegate *vis-à-vis* the B.E.F. and that his command should also include the Seventh Army on the extreme left. Now, with the inclusion of the Belgians and the Dutch, the North-Eastern Command had become far too extensive. On 12 May, therefore, Georges flew to Casteau in Belgium and arranged with King Leopold that General Billotte should co-ordinate the operations of Army Group One, the B.E.F., the Belgian forces and the Seventh Army.

On this afternoon of the 12th, while Georges was absent, General Lacaille, Chief of Staff, Second Army, reported on the telephone to General Roton, the Aide-major-général at La Ferté, that the Second Army cavalry had suffered heavy losses: so had X Corps, which had been driven back on to the line of resistance. Impressed by Lacaille's story, Roton passed the information on to Doumenc, the Major-Général (at Montry), and with his agreement at once began to order divisions from the general reserve to the junction of the Ninth and Second Armies. The 3rd Motorized was therefore told to move at once by road from Bar-le-Duc to Buzancy, some fifteen kilometres north of Second Army Headquarters at Senuc, and be ready to go into action on the high ground behind X Corps on the morning of the 14th. At the same time, the 3rd Armoured Division at Moivre in the Châlons-sur-Marne training area was ordered to constitute two groups, each of one B.1 and one Hotchkiss battalion, one for the Second, one for the Ninth Army. Then, after a series of orders and counter-orders, it was given verbal instructions to move as a single body, immediately, by road to Le

Chesne on the Ardennes Canal to be in position at 6 a.m. on the 14th
and come under the orders of Second Army. General Flavigny, commander of XXI Corps, in reserve with a staff and corps troops west
of Reims, had already been told to report to General Huntziger. On
arrival he was given command of the two divisions, and with them the
remains of the 5th Cavalry and the 1st Cavalry Brigade under General
Chanoine. Finally, the 14th Division, which had already that morning
been ordered to move from Lunéville to the Reims area by train, was
ordered on arrival to join the Ninth Army. Its leading regiment arrived
at 4 a.m. on the 14th and was sent off in trucks to find the right of XLI
Corps.

On this day (the 12th) the Ninth Army, now involved at Dinant, had
ordered its one reserve, the 53rd Division, to move up in support of the
102nd Division: its leading infantry were already coming up behind the
148th Fortress Infantry Regiment. It had already been partly split up,
and its artillery lent to the 148th, while the 208th Infantry Regiment was
now marching up from Sissonne. Its commander, General Etcheberrigaray, was reassuming command. He expected to find the 14th Division
on his right about Villers-le-Tilleul and also the 3rd Spahis.

At 5 in the afternoon, General Lacaille spoke to La Ferté once more
to say that the alarm at Second Army had been a flurry and that there
was no urgency for reinforcements, but G.Q.G. saw no need to change
their orders.

[2]

At the same time that reserves were being ordered up to the threatened
parts of the Ninth and Second Armies, further divisions were on their
way to the First Army. On the 11th, the 32nd Division in reserve near
Cambrai was sent up to the Charleroi area. On the 12th, the 43rd was
ordered to move, during three days, to north of Maubeuge. At midday
on the 13th, the 2nd Armoured at Moivre was ordered to go by road and
rail to First Army at Charleroi, which the 1st Armoured should already
be reaching. The 36th Division near Bar-sur-Aube was ordered to move
to between Aubenton and Signy-l'Abbaye, in the Ninth Army area.
Long before its advance guards approached the Aisne, these two places
had been taken by the enemy. The 36th was redirected to the Aisne
between Attigny and Le Chesne.

[3]

During the night of 13th/14th, General Georges summoned the Major-
Général from Montry. Doumenc reached La Ferté about 3 a.m. to find
the Commander-in-Chief and most of his operations staff seated round
the telephone. 'The atmosphere was that of a family in which someone
has just died. Georges rose and went to meet Doumenc. He was ghastly
pale. "There's been a break-through at Sedan! the line has given way."
He dropped into an armchair and stifled a sob.' Doumenc did his best

to rally his chief. ' "Come, General," he said, "we've all seen incidents of this kind before. Come and look at the map and see what we can do." '
He sketched a countermove, to bring the 1st Armoured Division from Charleroi to attack from north to south, to detrain the 2nd Armoured now near Vervins to attack from west to east, and use the 3rd, already in the Second Army area, to engage at Sedan and drive the enemy back over the Meuse. Georges approved the proposals, and the orders were drafted. Included in the orders was one transferring Huntziger's Second Army from A.G. One to G.Q.G.N.E. as from midnight 13th/14th. Doumenc returned to Montry, and in furtherance of the plan, dispatched six training battalions to occupy a line between Liart and Montcornet, and ordered from the general reserve a number of artillery and armoured units to concentrate in the neighbourhood of Laon under the command of Colonel de Gaulle.[1]

7 DISMEMBERMENT OF THE NINTH ARMY, *13–15 May*

The rout of XI Corps

ON the morning of the 14th, the situation of XI Corps began to worsen. The 129th Regiment was pushed off the river by an attack at about 4 a.m., which left the flank of its neighbour, the 8th Infantry Regiment, exposed. The Meuse was lost as far as Profondeville. At the same time, Werner's group, holding Senenne and Point 190, drove what remained of the 39th out of Surinvaux Wood. They had also taken Haut-le-Wastia before midnight. A counter-attack by a battalion of the 14th Dragoons and some armoured cars recovered the village in the early morning, but owing to events elsewhere, II Corps later withdrew the garrison. During the day the much depleted 66th lost Hontoir and were gradually forced back to the line of the Flayon and the woods at Weillen.

That the attack ought to follow the Dinant–Philippeville road was obvious, and the key to it the village of Onhaye, five kilometres from the river. Rommel's engineers had repaired the broken span of the bridge at Dinant and by the morning of the 14th some thirty tanks were over the river to support the German infantry. To oppose them were still only the much-tried battalions of the 18th Division, though four more, just arrived from a night march of thirty kilometres, could be pushed into the battle on a line from Marteau southward to the Philippeville road. On their right, the mounted brigade of the 1st Cavalry, whose horses had just been killed by bombers, held Onhaye. The Germans pushed straight ahead from Dinant up the Philippeville road and thus came in behind an isolated party of the 18th Division, still fighting in Anseremme.

From somewhere south of the road, a battalion of the 5th Dragoons was in touch with the 22nd Division. In spite of starting a day late, the 22nd had taken up its line from Hastière to Vireux on the 13th. Owing to the fact that the attack was to be carried out by normal and therefore slow-moving Germany infantry divisions, the 12th and 32nd of Strauss's II Korps, it had not been disturbed. Only the reconnaissance unit of a German division had appeared on the 13th; while the main body closed up, it had done little, but towards evening some armoured cars appeared on the Chooz peninsula. Soon after 5 on the morning of the 14th, the French division was surprised by a sudden infantry attack across the river, men crossing in rubber boats, on rafts, on sheaves of straw, even swimming. The attackers pressed on and reached the line of battalion headquarters, in some cases before it was aware of an attack. The regiment on the left, the 19th, was outflanked, broken and thrust aside. Agimont, held by the 116th, was lost, the Chooz peninsula abandoned.

Givet was evacuated at nightfall. On the right, the 62nd Infantry Regiment, isolated and without orders, withdrew at midnight, having warned the 61st Division on its right of its departure.

[2]

In addition to the attacks at Houx and Dinant, General Corap, on the evening of the 13th, had other matters for anxiety in the news of the inroad at Monthermé, though the gravity of the attack was not yet known. There followed the report of the break between Sedan and the Bar, which threatened the whole of XLI Corps. Corap could do no more than order the 53rd Division to move up behind Mézières.

Thus, on the morning of the 14th, he had, uncommitted, only the 4th North African Division, the XI Corps reserve. This fine active division, commanded by General Sancelme, had begun marching up from the Trelon–St Michel area on the afternoon of the 12th (J/3), with the expectation of reaching the area near Philippeville on the 16th (J/7). The prospect of a leisurely approach had been shattered by the news of the passage of the Meuse. At 11 in the morning of the 13th, when a little beyond Chimay, the division received a peremptory order from Ninth Army to be on the line of the Mariembourg–Philippeville–Charleroi road next morning, in support of XI Corps. At 8 in the evening came an even more urgent message—this from XI Corps—requiring the arrival of the division's advance guards on a line north–south through Florennes, a further eight kilometres east, at dawn. Corap had asked Army Group One for lorries, but had been refused. Nevertheless, marching all through the night, the 25th Algerian Tirailleurs were east of Philippeville about 4 in the morning of the 14th. They were allowed to rest for a few hours.

Throughout the day the remains of the 1st Cavalry Division, aided by the reconnaissance group of the 4th North African, had hung on desperately west of Dinant against Rommel's infantry and tanks, and in spite of repeated dive-bombing. The German progress was not fast, but it was not halted. During the afternoon they took Anthée, six kilometres beyond Onhaye. Then the leading battalion of the 25th Algerians arrived, attacked and recaptured the village, only to lose it again. But Falaen, to the north of Anthée, still held and the Germans were stopped between Morville and Rozée on the main road.

Early in the morning of the 14th, General Billotte at Folembray, after much hesitation, decided to transfer the 1st Armoured Division, which was now concentrated at Lambusart north-east of Charleroi, to the Ninth Army. General Corap had already left his headquarters at Vervins to confer with General Martin of XI Corps at his new command-post at St Aubin, a short way from Florennes, from which he had been bombed out. The news of the transfer of the 1st Armoured was therefore not known to the Army Commander until late in the morning, and the movement orders reached General Bruneau of the 1st Armoured

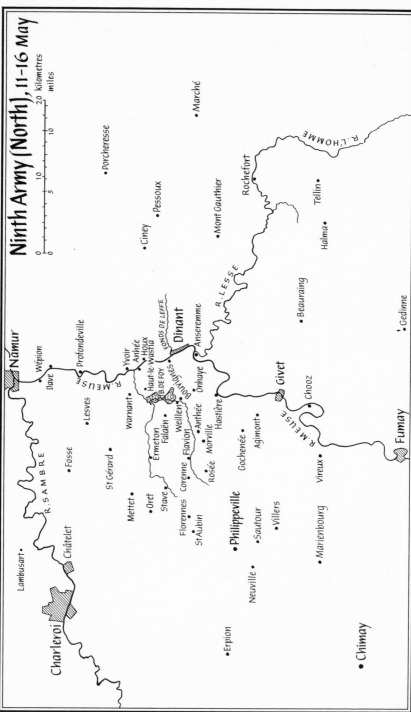

Ninth Army (North), 11-16 May

Charleroi
Lambusart •
Châtelet

R. SAMBRE

Fosse •
St Gérard •

Metret •
Oret •
Stave •
Florennes
St Aubin •

Neuville •

Erpion •

Chimay •

Philippeville

Sautour •
Villers •

Marienbourg •

Gochenée •
Agimont •

Vireux •

Fumay

Namur
Wépion •
Dave •
Profondeville •
Lesves •
Warnant •
Ermeton
Falaën
Corenne
Rosée •
Morville •
Anthée •
Hastière •

R. MEUSE

Yvoir •
Anhée
Haut-le-Wastia •
B. DE FOY
BOUVIGNES
Weillen •
Flavion
Onhaye •

FONDS DE LEFFE
Dinant
Anseremme •

Givet

Chooz •

R. MEUSE

Ciney •
Pessoux •

Porcheresse •

Marché •

Mont Gauthier •

Rochefort

Halma •
Tellin •

R. LESSE

Beauraing •

Gedinne •

R. L'HOMME

0   5   10
0   10   20 kilometres
                miles

© CASSELL & CO LTD 1968

only after midday. These were to leave his second echelon at Lambusart while the two armoured brigades were to move south in the direction of Mettet, followed by his artillery, six batteries of 105s, the 5th Battalion of Chasseurs-à-Pied and the refuelling companies. General Bruneau came ahead to take General Martin's detailed instructions, but on his arrival at St Aubin the XI Corps commander said he had received no orders as to the employment of the division.[1] The telephone centre at Florennes had been wrecked; there was no telephone at St Aubin. It took Bruneau some time to reach II Corps headquarters at Mettet and speak to the Army Commander. Corap told him to 'attack this evening with all you can put in' to take the pressure off XI Corps. Returning to St Aubin, Bruneau found that Martin was still ignorant of the situation of his two divisions. The best the two generals could do was to choose on the map a position where the armour could wait for morning.

In the meantime, the two B.1 battalions, the 28th and 37th, had set out from Lambusart, which is about twenty kilometres from Mettet as the crow flies. For hours they had to force their way through mobs of panic-stricken Belgian civilians, for dealing with whom the Belgian government had made no provision. The leading tanks reached Mettet about an hour before dark and were sent on to take up a position a little north of Flavion, about eight kilometres east of Florennes and four from Anthée, which the 25th Algerians had recaptured just before dusk. Bruneau placed the 28th facing east, a little north of Flavion, with the 37th on its left towards Ermeton-sur-Biert. Both were partly concealed by woods. They had fuel for no more than a couple of hours, and since the radio batteries only charged when the engines were running, radio silence was imposed. There was nothing to be done but wait for the arrival of the Hotchkiss battalions, the infantry, the artillery and, above all, the fuel *chenillettes*.*

About 6 in the evening (14th), it was reported at XI Corps Head-quarters that German armour 'seemed' to be over the river at Chooz and might be moving in the direction of Philippeville. Possibly what looked like the rout of the 22nd Division, coupled with the fighting at Anthée and Morville, may have influenced General Martin to summon an hour later his three divisional commanders to St Aubin and to order the withdrawal to a line five kilometres east of Philippeville, with the 18th Division on the north (including the remains of the 1st Cavalry), the 4th North African in the centre, and the 22nd to the south. Counter-attacks would be made by the 1st Armoured to cover the retreat of the corps. His own headquarters would open after midnight at Froidchapelle,

---

* The *chenillette* was a small tracked carrier employed for many services. Two *chenillettes* could replenish three B.1 *bis*. One could refuel three H.39. Each carried about 600 litres (132 gallons). The B.1 needed 450 litres. The *chenillette* had a crew of two side by side. The history of the 71st Infantry Regiment (Bretons converted to Alpine) records the individual attack of a sergeant driving a *chenillette* and firing a light machine-gun.

fifteen kilometres west of Philippeville. A staff officer was sent off to inform General Bruneau of the new dispositions and his new role.[2]

This took place between 8 and 9 p.m. On being informed, Army Headquarters was confounded. Here was a corps commander who, on his own initiative, had ordered the retreat of his divisions. At the same time, or thereabouts, reports arrived at Vervins that the Germans had broken in at Monthermé and Nouzonville—it was not true that Nouzonville had gone though it would go next morning. And last and most critical, the 148th Fortress Infantry Regiment at Mézières had been taken in the flank owing to the failure of the Second Army.

General Corap grabbed the telephone and asked to speak urgently to General Billotte. . . . I cannot report the conversation of the two commanders; General Corap was in his private office. The exchanges must have been stormy since their voices were unusually loud. The result was that General Billotte ordered a general retreat of the Army to the line Marcinelle [south of Charleroi]—Cerfontaine–Rocroi–Signy–L'Abbaye and what remained of our position near Omont. . . . How could a stand be made on a position represented by no more than a road, with no natural obstacles, no organization, no garrisons posted to occupy the strong-points ?[3]

Thus Colonel Véron, sub-chief of staff of the Ninth Army. The line, as he said, was no more than a string of names on an easily recognizable road. It had no tactical virtues, no natural defences, and there were no strong-points. Further, it was a good dozen kilometres behind the line selected by General Martin. General Billotte had also forgotten that, as a fortress formation, the 102nd Division had no transport and that much of its armament was fixed in position.

[3]

The débâcle of the Ninth Army

May the 15th or J/6 witnessed the end of coherent fighting by XI and II Corps, although their death-agony was prolonged for a few more days. General Bruneau spent an anxious night. He received no further orders. He had his two B battalions and no news of the rest. He saw passing eastward one company of the 23rd Algerians, which had marched some sixty kilometres in the last twenty-four hours and had no idea where they were going or why. About 10 p.m., the commander of one of his Hotchkiss battalions, the 26th, appeared. His tanks had been stopped at Fosse some twenty kilometres to the north by crowds of retreating troops and, in the night, in a country without road signs and from which most of the inhabitants had fled, most of his machines had gone astray; he had only a few with him. Bruneau sent a staff officer off to report his situation to XI Corps. The officer returned towards morning. He had found the headquarters at St Aubin deserted: no one could tell him when it had closed or where it had gone. At 3 a.m. the rest of the 26th Battalion turned up, having left five machines broken down on the way. It had picked up four Renaults from the Ninth Army Tank Group, which had lost their way. Soon after dawn, the general saw units of the 4th North African, which had received the orders to retreat, on their way westward.

About 5 a.m., the Armoured Division's fuel tankers were reported at Stave, only a few kilometres away, and at much the same time, the 5th Chasseurs-à-Pied and the artillery appeared. There was no news of the other Hotchkiss battalion, the 25th. The tanks began refuelling, company by company. At 8 a.m. an officer from XI Corps appeared with an order of the previous evening directing Bruneau to assemble his division west of Philippeville at dawn (i.e. four hours earlier), and attack eastward. Bruneau told the bearer of the order that he would move as soon as he had completed refuelling, but that this would require the whole morning. In preparation for his new task, he dispatched five of his six batteries to take up a position near Erpion, ten kilometres west of Philippeville. The battery he retained he placed near Stave, protected by the chasseurs west of Corenne. The refuelling went on. Suddenly, about 9 a.m., the single battery opened fire on targets it could see coming from Anthée down the Philippeville road.

After the crossings on the 13th, the commander of XV Panzer Korps, Hoth, believed that there was little except rearguards in front of him, but the fighting on the 14th alarmed him, and he directed the consolidation of the line Grange–Hontoir–Rostenne–Bouvignes. Rommel ignored his instructions, and when Hoth recognized the success he reinforced the attack. On the morning of the 15th, he ordered the 7th and 5th Panzer Divisions to advance westward, cross the Eau d'Heure, a stream about ten kilometres beyond Philippeville, and form bridge-heads at Cerfontaine and Silenrieux.

Rommel had brought most of his division over the Meuse during the night. In front of him were what remained of the much mauled 77th and 66th, the fragments of the 1st Cavalry, and Sancelme's 4th North African, some of which was fighting at Morville. He certainly did not know that behind the infantry were lying the sixty heavy tanks of Bruneau's 1st Armoured, partially immobilized across the valley from Morville. Covered by a team of Stukas, the 25th Panzer Regiment, with Rommel in his command car, moved off at 9 a.m. on the line of the Dinant–Philippeville road. This cortège was the target that General Bruneau's one battery had challenged.

Of the 1st Armoured, only the 37th Battalion had finished its refuelling. The 28th was still immobile, but it was obscured in the woods. It is doubtful if either this battalion or the 7th Panzer recognized each other for what it was. In any case, Rommel's objective was more than twenty kilometres further west. After a violent exchange of artillery and machine-gun fire, in which a number of French tanks were damaged, the German armour passed on towards Philippeville.

General Martin's orders of the previous evening reached the units of the 4th North African too late for fulfilment by dawn. The 25th Algerian, who had broken off their fight round Morville, got into position east of Philippeville, with headquarters in the town, about 7 a.m. The commander of the 13th Zouaves gave orders to move to the right of the 25th and hurried off to his new command-post at Sautoir to await his battalions. They never arrived. The Zouaves were caught by Rommel's Stukas before they had crossed the Dinant road. Smashed and harried from the skies, they scattered into the woods. The 23rd Algerians further north suffered very much the same fate, and they too were dispersed.

Having broken the North African infantry, Rommel's detachment turned northward, made a half-circle and descended on Philippeville, where they surprised and captured the headquarters of the 25th Algerians. A little later they roped in that of the 23rd.

On the evening of the 14th, General Sancelme had had his headquarters a few kilometres north of Florennes. His new command-post was to be at Neuville, some twelve kilometres to the south. It took him four hours to reach the place. Early in the afternoon, the village was suddenly attacked by Rommel's tank-escort company. This was driven off by anti-tank fire. Rommel himself, sending most of his force to Cerfontaine, rejoined his headquarters.

Rommel's advance had been lucky. But for the immobilization of General Bruneau's heavy tanks, he might have been involved in a serious battle instead of reaching Cerfontaine. He owed his immunity to Colonel Werner's 31st Panzer regiment. (The other regiment of the 5th Panzer division had not yet crossed the Meuse.) An hour after Rommel had passed the 1st Armoured, Werner's group came up. He at once decided to attack. Observing that the armour facing him was heavy, he drew back his light tanks and sent in his own heavies, thirty-five Mk III and thirty-two Mk IV, supported by his artillery. He was puzzled by the fact that the French tanks did not move, but failed to guess the reason. Bruneau's B's of the 28th Battalion had still not been refuelled. Further, some of its tanks had been damaged by fire during the brush with Rommel. Werner attempted to outflank the battalion, and in doing so he collided with the 26th Battalion of Hotchkiss, thin-skinned and under-armed. Informed of what was afoot, Bruneau ordered a company of the 37th which had completed its refuelling to help the 26th. Then, about 5.30, in accordance with instructions from XI Corps, he radioed the three battalions to retire to Oret and then to Beaumont. For the 28th, it was too late. It had now only two runners: these got away, and were able to pick up a few machines from the second echelon, but as a battalion the 28th was no more. The 26th had not picked up Bruneau's radio and was unaware of the situation until it noticed that the enemy now occupied the place of the 28th. When they moved, the companies found the enemy in their path. They tried to fight their way through, but only six tanks arrived at Mettet. The company of B's from the 37th was not seen again. The remainder of the 37th had moved off towards Ermeton-sur-Biert. A short way from the village they were ambushed by the anti-tank regiment of the 5th Panzer and finished off. Werner had been bold and lucky. Near the end of the fight his ammunition reserve was reduced to three shells per gun. He had these distributed and used. It was just enough. And his action had allowed Rommel to succeed.

There still existed scattered fragments of XI Corps: General Duffet vainly sought elements of his 18th Division, but failed to collect any coherent body. Parties of the 22nd were still being reassembled in the Anor gap and round Trelon. The units of the 4th North African were not so badly disrupted as the other two divisions. Soon after midnight General Sancelme and his headquarters staff reached Froidchapelle, said to be corps headquarters, to find it deserted. At Trelon, he heard that the corps commander, General Martin, was now at Wignehies. Reporting to him, he was told to establish his division (his division!) in the Fôret de St Michel and the Anor gap, with his headquarters at Mondrepuis, between Hirson and Fourmies, during the morning of the 16th.

Of the 1st Armoured there were still the 25th Hotchkiss battalion, still five batteries of 105s, still a few hundred men of the 5th Chasseurs in the neighbourhood of Solre-le-Château. The Hotchkiss battalion was found to have lost two of its companies. At 5 p.m. on the 16th General Bruneau received an order from the new Army Commander, General Giraud, to take his division (his division!) and clean up the enemy in the neighbourhood of Avesnes. The surviving seventeen tanks were sent to Avesnes with the artillery, and the chasseurs ordered to take up a position in front of Solre-le-Château.*

Twenty-four hours later the 1st Armoured ceased to exist.†

---

* Of the 6 Hotchkiss that escaped, 3, under the battalion commander, reached Maubeuge and fought in its defence until the 21st. Two others joined up with other stray tanks and were last heard of fighting round Hazebrouck. The few B tanks that had not been involved ran out of fuel and were abandoned.

† See p. 362.

8 THE SPLITTING OF THE CENTRE, *13–16 May*

The gap is not closed (14 May)

T HE 3rd Armoured Division had been formed under General Brocard as recently as 20 March. It was only partly trained, and suffered from all the evils of improvisation. Of the Hotchkiss battalions, the 42nd and 45th, one company had been detached from the former to the Norwegian Expeditionary Force and had not been replaced. Of the B.1 battalions, the 41st and 49th, six machines had been sent to the 1st Armoured and not replaced. Five more machines were in workshops and none had been run in. The track plates of the 45th Battalion were worn and could not be renewed until a supply came from the United States. Owing to the shortage of 37-mm. guns 1938 model, the Hotchkiss were armed with the old 1916 gun, of which the muzzle velocity was little over half that of the modern weapon.* As with the other divisions, the radio was ineffective. In 1st-line machines the division was twenty-three tanks below establishment. It also was without heavy trucks, heavy break-down equipment, tank transporters, tracked fuel tanks (it had only commercial ones), which led to enormous delays in refuelling. Also the nearest petrol depot was at Sillery near Reims, 150 kilometres from where the division was to be employed.

The 319th Artillery Regiment was still forming. The two groups had guns of different models which required distinct ammunition. Though the guns were tracked, the ammunition was on light lorries, which could not leave the roads; hence the usefulness of the guns was limited. The 47-mm. anti-tank battery never arrived. The infantry battalion, 16th Chasseurs-à-Pied, had received only half its carriers and the engines were not run in. It had no scout cars or motor-cycles for its reconnaissance group. There was no engineer company. The crew of the air squadron had reached Pau from Morocco, but it had no planes, and never arrived. Apart from the tanks, there was a deficiency of some 270 vehicles. Perhaps the most disconcerting feature was that the heavy tanks were the latest B.1 *bis* model, of which the armour had been increased to 60-mm., adding some eight tons to the weight, with a consequent increase in the size of the engine and a more rapid expenditure

---

* The Hotchkiss 35 was armed with a 25-mm. gun. But both Hotchkiss 39 and Renault were armed with a 37-mm. gun, in the case of the former with a 1939 model. Owing to the shortage of this gun, recourse was had to the 1916–18 model of which the muzzle velocity was only 402 m/s (1,306 feet), practically useless against armour. For the Renault, a quantity of the 1918 F.T. tanks were cannibalized. Their carcases were in a depot at Gien and were announced as a huge capture in the German communiqués, adding of course to the bitterness of defeat. (Cf. p. 345.)

of petrol. The eight-hour radius of the earlier model was reduced to five and a half at the best. A similar change had been made in the Hotchkiss.

But worst of all was the lack of training, of knowledge and of experience. The men—in two battalions they were from the Garde Républicaine Mobile—were staunch, but this was not enough.[1]

Ahead of his division, General Brocard reported to Second Army Headquarters at Senuc during the morning of the 13th. He gleaned little information, most of it vague but unfavourable. 'The Army commander seemed anxious, his staff was reticent.' The division began to assemble in its concentration area north of the Aisne, between Le Chesne and Tourteron, between 5 and 6 in the early morning of the 14th. Brocard had seen on the evening of the 13th and during the night that indescribable chaos reigned over the roads, which boded no easy movement for his division on the 14th. At 2.30 a.m., summoned again to Army Headquarters (at this moment preparing to move to a new headquarters* in Fort Landrecourt at Verdun),[2] he was told his division would be attached to XXI Corps, commanded by General Flavigny, who was believed to have a profound knowledge of armoured warfare. 'His tenacity and clear-sightedness,' we are told, 'had succeeded in forcing the creation of a Light Armoured division [*division légère mécanisée*] on a reluctant General Staff.' Indeed, he had built up and commanded the 1st Light Armoured Division. 'His coolness, his authority, his sense of command, were deeply valued by General Huntziger, who placed in him his complete confidence.' His relations with General Brocard started off on the wrong foot. Flavigny seems to have gathered that the 3rd Armoured was already just west of the Ardennes canal, that it could be brought across at once and could counter-attack in conjunction with the 3rd Motorized from the line Tannay–Stonne with, as the final objective, a line from Pont-Maugis to the northern edge of the Bois de la Marfée, the centre of the former stop-line. What he did not grasp was that the brigades had been moving all through the night, incidentally considerably hampered by stragglers and refugees, and needed to refuel. Brocard had already explained to Huntziger that his division was short of a large number of necessities vital to a combatant formation, that refuelling was a long and tedious process and that it would be impossible for him to be ready to attack at 11 o'clock: he could, however, arrive at the jumping-off line during daylight.

The approach march proved to be appallingly difficult. The roads had been shelled and bombed, driven into deep pits with explosive and were thronged with soldiers flocking back in disorder. The traffic police had enormous trouble in forcing a way for the columns, while the lack of

---

* The move to Verdun had been planned early in the year on the ground that this was far closer to the centre of the Second Army sector than Senuc. But to move in the middle of the battle was taken by lower formations to be a retreat, from which gloomy inferences were drawn.

pioneers drove the tank crews to leave their machines to fill up holes they could neither cross nor circumvent.

During the afternoon, while the division was assembling, the corps commander appeared complaining that the attack was taking too long to get under weigh and demanding an explanation. Brocard replied that, for technical reasons, the attack was delayed, but that the day was long, there was still plenty of daylight and anyhow the infantry had not yet arrived. On this Flavigny, with the notorious violence of baffled general officers, insisted that 'something must be done'.[3] He ordered the two divisional commanders to place groups of infantry and tanks on all the approaches, and effectively cancelled the counter-attack by distributing the armour in 'penny-packets' over a wide front, including an area west of the canal.

[2]

On the river (14 May)

The extension of the break on both sides of Sedan on the 13th called for immediate action to plug the gap in the line where, on that morning, the centre of the 55th Division had stood. Second Army had few reserves immediately available. The 71st Division had swung back its left, and on the morning of the 14th was on the line of Ennemane stream as far as Angecourt. East of the Meuse it was still on its original line behind the Chiers, which had not been attacked, and in touch with the 3rd North African. But on the other side of the gap, west of the Bar, the only Second Army troops were one battalion of the 331 Infantry Regiment in Hannogne and two groups of 75s from the 55th Division artillery. After the engagement and dissipation of X Corps reserves in Lafontaine's forlorn effort in the morning, the only body immediately available was Chanoine's group (the 5th Cavalry Division and 1st Cavalry Brigade), which after three days' fighting had been withdrawn into Army Reserve and was very tired. But the danger on the left was pressing. General Huntziger ordered Chanoine to cross the Ardennes Canal and defend it and the Bar River from La Cassine to St Aignan, with the further task of supporting what remained of the 55th Division further north.

By 7 a.m. the 5th Cavalry was in position as far as St Aignan, but had not made touch with either the Hannogne garrison or the artillery. The 1st Cavalry Brigade was placed in reserve along the edge of La Cassine wood.

On the left of the Second Army, the line of XLI Corps of the Ninth Army on the Meuse was still intact, though the enemy had crossed further north and was getting a grip on the Monthermé peinsula. But the German crossing in the Donchery–Sedan area had put the right of the 102nd Division in great peril because its defences had been constructed against only assaults from the east, and the crossing between Sedan and Donchery laid open its flank and rear. The only reserves of the Ninth Army as yet uninvolved were the regiments of the 53rd

Division and the 3rd Spahi Brigade.* There was also in the neighbourhood a 33rd Battalion of F.T. light tanks. And there were rumours that
de Lattre's 14th Division and the 2nd Armoured were on their way.

On 12 May, the 148th Fortress Regiment of XLI Corps was expecting
to be relieved by the 53rd Division, and part of the divisional artillery
was already on its way. The division was spread over a wide area. On
the night 13th/14th it was being reassembled by its commander,
General Etcheberrigaray. The heads of the columns of the 239th and
329th Infantry Regiment were on the Vence. The 208th, coming from
Sissonne, was still some way behind. At dawn on the 14th, the 239th
had joined the 148th at Flize, while the 329th was occupying the ridge
west of Sapogne and Villers-le-Tilleul. The 208th was between Poix-
Terron, Singly and La Bascule. It was 'a record in the art of dispersion',
says a commentator.[4] Between them and the Chanoine group, the 3rd
Spahi had been brought in to form a weak hyphen between the Second
and Ninth Armies. It had with it a company of the light tanks.

[3]

XIX Panzer Korps on 14 May

The infantry of Guderian's 1st Panzer Division had cleaned up the
south bank of the Meuse between Sedan and the Bar on the evening of
the 13th. On the morning of the 14th, there was again mist in the river
valley, which cleared very slowly. The armour had come over in the
night and was now joining the infantry between Bulson and Chéméry.
The 2nd Panzer was bridging at Donchery, but had not yet completed
it. About 8.30 its armour began coming over the Gaulier bridge. An
hour later its leading troops were at Pont-à-Bar and Villers. At neither
place had the bridge been destroyed and by 10 a.m. the Germans were
facing Hannogne. They also crossed at St Aignan and drove off a
squadron from the 5th Cavalry. They then captured the two groups of
75s of the 55th Division. The Hannogne defenders managed to hold out
all day, but the Dom-le-Mesnil position was submitted first to air bombardment about 9 a.m., followed by an assault of tanks from the south-
east. Its casemates, facing north, were taken in reverse and destroyed.
Fighting hard, the 3rd Battalion of the 148th fell back on the 1st Battalion at Flize and Les Ayvelles. The German tanks now turned back,
possibly to refuel, but returned later in the morning and resumed their
assault. Dom-le-Mesnil went down at 2 p.m., the Orangerie at 3; by
6 p.m. the Germans were past Flize and at dusk below the great Ayvelles
fort. Two of the battalions of the 148th had now gone, together with the

---

* On receiving the complaint of the premature retreat of the 3rd Spahis from
the Mouzaive ford of the Semoy on 11 May, General Corap at once ordered the
brigade to recross the Meuse. It did so, but too late to recover the Semoy ford.
It then occupied the bridgehead at Lumes. It was engaged here on the 12th with
advance troops of the 2nd Panzer, when it lost a squadron and half (four) of its
25-mm. anti-tank guns. It then withdrew to Poix-Terron.

239th Infantry Regiment from the 53rd Division and part of the 53rd's artillery.

The 1st Panzer, having in the morning broken the counter-attack of General Lafontaine's last reserve at Chémery, crossed the canal to Malmy and drove on past Vendresse in two columns north and south of the village towards Singly and Omont. In front of this force, the much weakened Spahis and Chanoine group could do no more than retreat fighting through the Bois de la Cassine. At dusk the cavalry were back on a line Chagny–Louvergny–Le Chesne, while the Spahis, with their mission to cover the Ninth Army flank, moved north-westward to La Horgne. With them were companies of the 33rd Battalion of F.T. tanks.

It was during this evening that the untimely order of General Martin of XI Corps to his divisions to withdraw induced General Billotte to instruct Ninth Army to bring XLI Corps back to the line Rocroi–Signy–L'Abbaye and south-eastward towards Omont.

[4]

It is of the nature of senior officials, both civil and military, to find scape-goats before they themselves can be designated. After giving orders to General Corap on the night of the 14th, General Billotte sat down and wrote a letter to General Georges, making Corap the sacrificial victim.

The Ninth Army is in a critical state; its whole front is giving way. It is absolutely necessary to put some spirit back into this dissolving army. General Giraud, whose energy we all recognize, seems to me just the man to take up this heavy task and administer the indispensable psychological shock. Because of the Ninth Army's withdrawal, I see that I am forced to order the First Army to pivot on its left (Wavre) and draw its right back to Charleroi. In addition to the 1st Light Armoured, I am about to bring two other divisions from the Seventh Army back behind my right.

This letter[5] was delivered to La Ferté between 4 and 5 in the morning of the 15th. General Georges consulted Gamelin, who arrived about 5.30, and gave it as his opinion that Huntziger, who had shown neither energy nor capacity and had failed to use the 3rd Armoured to counter-attack on the previous evening, should also be removed from his command. Gamelin deprecated this.[6] In consequence only Corap was told that he would be relieved. His command would be handed over to Giraud and he would take over the Seventh Army, which in the event was broken up before he could reach it. Gamelin also suggested that all the armour, both light and heavy, should be concentrated on the right of the First Army and ordered to attack southward against the flank of the Germans, who had crossed the Meuse at Dinant. How these for-mations were to be assembled, where and how soon they could be employed, would in Gamelin's philosophy be a mere matter of staff-work.

[5]

To the anticlimax of Flavigny's abortive improvisations on the 14th, Huntziger had no remedy but to resign his army to a defensive policy while trying to mask it as an active defensive. Georges, with a keener and wider appreciation of the situation, at 6.15 a.m. ordered that the attack should be renewed at once, and at 7 o'clock orders were sent to Flavigny to attack with the 3rd Armoured due north, with the Meuse at Wadelincourt as the objective. The armour would be supported by the 3rd Motorized. On the right of XXI Corps, he was to be aided by the 1st Colonial Division of General Roucaud, brought up from the Argonne, with, attached, the 2nd Cavalry Division. Zero was to be at 3 p.m.

The Germans were quite alive to the vulnerability of their situation until the position could be consolidated. Into the space evacuated by the 1st Panzer after its wheel to the right and over the Bar on the 14th, had come the 10th Panzer and the Gross-Deutschland Regiment. Early on the morning of the 15th, Guderian had arranged with General von Wietersheim that XIV Motorized Korps should take over the line as at present held. During the morning units of the German 29th Motorized Division came up to strengthen the 10th Panzer. Further, well aware of the importance of Stonne at the peak of the hills, the Germans at 7 a.m. threw the reconnaissance group and the battalion of the 67th Infantry Regiment (both of the 3rd Motorized) out of the village. An immediate counter-attack by the Hotchkiss of the 45th and one company of the 49th (B.1), backed by another battalion of the 67th, was followed by confused fighting. Stonne was recaptured at 11 a.m., but remained the centre of contention until at night-fall it was once again lost.

Nevertheless, Flavigny renewed his orders for the two battalions of B tanks to move forward at 3 p.m. accompanied by two infantry battalions, to each of which a company of Hotchkiss should be attached. Half an hour before the attack was due to start, the officer commanding the heavy tank brigade reported that the 41st Battalion attached to the Chanoine group across the canal had not appeared. On this, Flavigny, in alarm at what would happen to the Roucaud group due to start on his right, ordered the attack to be carried out with whatever B tanks could be got ready by half-past five in the afternoon.

At this hour only two companies of Colonel Préclaire's 49th Battalion were available, the third being heavily involved in the fight for Stonne. At the last moment, Flavigny realized that the attacking force was now reduced to one heavy and one light battalion of tanks and one infantry battalion, and cancelled the attack. This was at 5.15. The counter-order somewhat naturally did not reach the attackers. They set out, a company of Bs on each side of the Sedan road, accompanied by a few Hotchkiss. There had been no time to reconnoitre the ground or to arrange liaison with the artillery and infantry. They knew nothing of the French anti-tank ditch which ran across the front. When they discovered it, they tried to get into single file at the only crossing-point and thus offered a splendid target to the German anti-tank guns.

The attack, which was not followed by the infantry, was a fiasco. The Bs did not reach even the first objective. In the end, of the eleven machines which set out, five were either knocked out or immobilized. On the morrow morning, of a first-line establishment of thirty, the 49th battalion had eight runners.[7]

On Flavigny's report, General Brocard was immediately relieved of his command: his place was taken by General Buisson, the infantry commander of the 3rd Motorized.

[6]

It is possible, if not probable, that some serious riposte to the German attack might have been made if the commanders south of the Meuse had been other than Huntziger and Flavigny. The former, in shedding Brocard, wrote: 'I know the material difficulties with which the commander of the 3rd Armoured had to contend: they undoubtedly put paid to the desired mass action of the division. All the same, in the particularly critical situation of 14 and 15 May, the general officer commanding the division, in spite of the orders given him, sheltered behind *pretexts* in order not to act.'[8] As Brocard's chief of staff told the Commissioners on Events, all these fine phrases about '*missions de sacrifice*' and '*sans esprit de recul*' were so much moonshine. 'In the serious situation before our eyes, no officer doubted that duty would require sacrifice, but at the same time we all knew that with or without the duty of sacrifice, a tank without petrol can neither move nor fight.' General Ruby, then sub-chief of staff of the Second Army, admits[9] that while he thinks that Brocard might have harried his subordinates more, Flavigny, for whom he none the less expresses a warm admiration, was wrong in countermanding the attack on the afternoon of the 14th, while by subsequently dispersing the 3rd Armoured over twenty kilometres with units detached to several commands, he failed to take the one chance of counter-attacking which Guderian offered. 'The evening of the 14th probably registers the last opportunity for a great local success of which the repercussions at this tragic hour would have been felt far beyond the boundaries of the [Second] Army.'

[7]

Up to the evening of the 14th, neither the 52nd Demi-Brigade of Indo-Chinese machine gunners nor the 61st Division (apart from the battalions of the 248th Infantry Regiment lent to 102nd Division) had been seriously troubled. During the desperate battle at Monthermé on the 13th–15th,* the 52nd further south had suffered severe bombing,

---

* Cf. supra pp. 125-6.

Nouzonville had been attacked with incendiaries, which started a large fire, but in Mézières there had been no infantry attacks.

In the first part of the night of the 14th/15th, the 61st Division along the river from Fumay to Virieux was warned by the 22nd Division on its left that its centre had been driven in by the Germans and that it was abandoning its position on the Meuse.

About 4 a.m. on the 15th, in the usual morning river mist, German infantry tried to cross the Meuse in rubber boats and in spite of casualties secured a foothold. The elimination of part of the French machine-gun barrage allowed further infiltration, and thus the French strong-points were one by one taken from the rear. None the less, the line was still intact when General Billotte's order for the Ninth Army to retire was received. It was not yet known to the units on the right and left that the 42nd Demi-Brigade had succumbed and that armour from Kursten's 8th Panzer Division was already moving out from Monthermé. At this time it needed six or more hours for a message from corps headquarters at Rumigny to be delivered in the front line. The order to withdraw left Rumigny about 3 a.m., reached the headquarters of the 52nd at 7, and the companies in the line about 11. At this hour German armoured cars were already beyond Renwez and approaching the Hirson–Mézières road.

A similar order was dispatched to the headquarters of the 148th Fortress Infantry Regiment, establishing the first position in the withdrawal. This arrived soon after noon on the 15th. It affected only the three remaining companies of the 148th in Mohan, Villers-Semeuse and Les Ayvelles fort, the other six having been involved in the ruin of the Second Army on the previous day. Since here again the units were of the fortress type, the main armoury was heavy and static, and there was no transport. Somehow this was commandeered and the weapons put on board. The retirement began in the afternoon, but suddenly the German armour began to arrive. Wagons and light trucks were hastily abandoned, and the infantry scattered. Some of the infantrymen got as far as Thin-le-Moutier, divisional headquarters, and were captured next morning. Others staggered on, only to be picked up on the afternoon of the 16th. The colonel of the regiment accidentally walked into a German post on the following morning and was taken. Thus ended the 148th Fortress Infantry Regiment.

The 52nd Demi-Brigade received its orders earlier, while its front line was beating off the German assault. The second battalion got through to Mézières and marched westward all night, losing groups and individuals all the way. At 4 a.m., it had reached Lepren on the north–south road, assigned by General Billotte to the army, and found it unoccupied on both its flanks, while five kilometres to the west Marlemont, near which regimental headquarters should be, was on fire. The commander decided to make for the Aisne at Rethel. A few miles beyond Signy-L'Abbaye, the column ran into a number of German armoured cars and well-armed infantry. The French had few weapons. The fight was brief. The history of the 11/52nd was over.

Owing to the runner with the orders being killed, the 1/52nd was some hours behind the other on the same road. Having survived all through the 16th, it split up on the morning of the 17th into groups which were one by one intercepted. So ended the first battalion.

The headquarters of the demi-brigade were caught a few miles north of the Aisne at midday on the 16th. Small parties from the 42nd demi-brigade marched carefully and indomitably through the night only to be surrounded and taken by armoured cars somewhere north of Reims. As for General Portzert, at dusk on the 15th he was surprised in his headquarters. He escaped on foot and was taken next day.

The end of the 61st Division is similar to that of the 102nd, if anything more painful. At the back of its position on the Meuse lie large forests crossed by few roads. Ordered to withdraw south-westward and to occupy a line from Rocroi to Tremblois, a distance of twenty kilometres, it began to arrive, without difficulty, before midday on the 15th and to take up the position. But, first in dribs and drabs, and soon after in larger crowds, began the flow of fugitives from the north, from the 22nd and 18th divisions and from the 1st Cavalry, while from the east came the remnants of the 42nd Demi-Brigade and the two battalions of the 248th. This flow of debris did not halt, it drifted on westward, taking with it individuals from the 61st. An attempt by the divisional staff to set up collecting-points had no success: the flood moved on. And behind it, from Revin and Monthermé, came the advance guards of the 6th and 8th Panzer Divisions. In mid-afternoon, Ninth Army ordered a further withdrawal of some thirty kilometres to the line Aubenton–Rumigny, unaware that enemy armour was already in the rear of the infantry and on the point of entering Rumigny beneath the windows of the corps commander. Seeing that they had in front of them no more than a baffled and bewildered herd of soldiers, for the most part unarmed, the commanders of the 6th and 8th Panzers were driving forward without pause. South of them, Guderian's 2nd and 1st Panzer were doing much the same. Already the lines prescribed by General Billotte as positions to be held to the death, '*sans esprit de recul*', had been overrun. Almost contemptuously, commanders of the German armoured cars ordered the surrendered soldiery to pile their arms and stand aside, while their captors crushed the weapons before passing on, leaving them to escape or not as they could.

General Vauthier of the 61st, having with difficulty extracted himself from a bottleneck of transport, made for Army Headquarters at Vervins, where he reported to his new army commander, Giraud, as the sole survivor of his division, a statement which was not in fact true since already some hundreds had congregated at Sains and more would do so, but alas! without weapons.

[8]

On the 14th, General Touchon, who commanded XXIII Corps, at the moment in reserve in the Dijon area, was summoned to La Ferté and given the task of knitting up the rent at the junction of Ninth and Second Armies, and of building up the line indicated by General Billotte to Corap. To do this he was given command of such troops as were believed to be still fighting in this gap (no one was at all sure what there were), also the 14th Division, which had left Luneville on the 13th and was now just reaching Reims, and the 2nd Armoured Division, believed to be now on its way towards First Army. The only flesh and blood in these assumptions were six training battalions, without artillery.

Touchon set up his headquarters in the middle of the 15th, at Château-Porcien north of the Aisne, and set out to find the commander of XLI Corps at Rumigny. He failed to do this and on his way back was disturbed to find himself machine-gunned at a point some twenty kilometres west of the line he was expected to hold. At Château-Porcien he found General de Lattre of the 14th Division, who informed him that the best he could manage was a single infantry battalion. This, the 2/152nd, had come into the line at Bouvellemont on the night of the 14th.

During this afternoon, the Chanoine group was still hanging on to the road from Le Chesne to Poix-Terron, but weakening. On its left the 3rd Spahis, with a company or two of the obsolete tanks, were being slowly exterminated at La Horgne, but giving nothing away. Beyond La Horgne the 329th and 208th Infantry Regiments of the 53rd were between Poix-Terron and Hocmont. Beyond them to the west there was nothing at all except the fragments from XLI Corps. Into this huge uncharted area, the German Panzer divisions were now pushing. In front of them there was no organized body of any kind. To the south the 36th Division began to arrive on the Aisne east of Attigny.

9 THE DISARMING OF THE 2ND ARMOURED DIVISION, *13–21 May*

Movement of reserves, 13–15 May

WHILE the news from Second and Ninth Armies, such as it was, became hourly more ominous, the indications were insufficient to allow an interpretation of the German plans. The outflanking of the Maginot Line and the destruction of Army Group Two? A thrust at Paris? The rolling up of the right flank of Army Group One and its encirclement?

The difficulties of movement were enormous. The shortage of road transport forced an aggravated use of the railway, highly vulnerable to air attack and repeatedly cut. On the 10th and 11th there had been seventy more or less severe bombing onslaughts, particularly on the four lines into Belgium: St Quentin–Aulnoye–Jeumont; Soissons–Laon–Hirson; Reims–Rethel–Mézières; Vitry-le-François–Commercy–Audun-le-Romain. The plate-layers worked miracles, but even tireless devotion could not keep abreast of the damage. The demands on rolling-stock were huge. The move of a normal infantry division with 5,000 horses required forty-one trains. The tracked vehicles of the 1st Armoured Division needed twenty-eight. This was complicated by the problem of ammunition supply, twenty trains a day, and made more difficult by the loss of ammunition dumps, and thus accounts to some degree for the slowness in reinforcing and re-forming broken divisions.

On the afternoon of the 13th, the chief of 4th Bureau at Montry told General Vallet, of the Ninth Army staff, that four divisions were on their way to Corap; and added: 'It's twenty-four hours too late.' Of these, the nearest, the 1st North African near Soissons, got into action eighty kilometres north, on the 16th. The 14th Division from Lunéville got one battalion into line late on the 14th and another on the 15th, but nothing further. The 36th took up a position on the Aisne east of Rethel. Similarly, the 87th from Army Group Two did not arrive until the 20th and the 44th reached Fismes on the 18th.

[2]

Considering that his defences must be secured before he could launch a counter-attack, General Huntziger made no attempt to succour the remains of X Corps in front of the Second Army's second position. General Grandsard was withdrawn on the evening of the 14th and sent to extend the left of the army with command of the Chanoine cavalry group, and, when it arrived, the 36th Division (it was not complete until the 19th). His headquarters were at Machault. On the afternoon of the 15th, X Corps was transferred to General Touchon's command, which, first designated an army detachment, was now renamed the Sixth Army.

On this morning, the thin curtain provided by the Chanoine group, the battalion of the 152nd Infantry Regiment, the Spahis, and the 53rd Division, was in shreds, and the breach between Ninth and Second Armies wide open. In front of Guderian's two armoured divisions lay some thirty kilometres of hilly country, a chequerboard of woods and clearings. Beyond lay the wide valleys of Oise and Aisne and the northern part of the Châlons camp with the Sissonne ranges. The Germans pressed on. Chanoine's cavalry, now reduced to a third, slowly fell back. The 8th Chasseurs defended Chagny all day. Further north, Colonel Marc's Spahis, aided by the F.T. tanks, fought until dusk against repeated attacks of the 1st Panzer. Then about 6, with the village greatly destroyed by fire, with both the regimental commanders dead, the remnant, including the wounded Colonel Marc, were taken prisoner; only a few troopers escaped.

At Bouvellemont, the battalion of the 152nd, helped by the training battalions, without artillery, fought on late into the night before retreating. In blazing Bouvellemont the following morning, Guderian, hastening on after his advance guard, found French machine-guns still firing.

Further north again, the last of the 53rd Division, the 208th Infantry Regiment, a few remains of the 329th and the 1st battalion of the 152nd, were gradually driven back by the 2nd Panzer. Poix-Terron was abandoned, Raillecourt went at 4 in the afternoon, Launois and Neuvisy, the last crest, and the whole Vence valley was in German hands. What remained of the Touchon command fell back south-westward to the Aisne.

Further north, General Kempff's 6th Panzer Division from Nouzon-ville reached Montcornet at nightfall.

[3]

The 2nd Armoured Division, commanded by General Bruché, had been formed, like the 1st, in January with the same establishment. It had even been allotted six out-of-date observation planes, but the divisional commander never saw them. It had most of the rest of its equipment, and General Bruché claimed that it was a superb instrument of war, conscious and sure of its strength. Its tank commander, Colonel Perré, who later commanded the division, said that its young reserve officers were both keen and competent. From 11 May, the division in camp at Haut-Moivre, east of Châlons, had been on six hours' notice. It received no warning. At 12.30 on 13 May, it was abruptly warned to move at once, its wheeled vehicles by road, its tracked engines, artillery, and infantry by rail, at 4 p.m., from a number of sidings between Revigny and Ste Menehould, two hours' march from the camp. When it arrived at the railway it found that the transporters for the heavy tanks had not yet returned from carrying the 1st Armoured to Charleroi. In consequence, the leading group of 2nd Armoured did not leave the loading sites until the morning of 14 May, more than twelve hours late. Meanwhile the wheeled echelon, some 1,200 vehicles, was well away on the road to Charleroi, and General Bruché with his immediate staff had set off by road to report to First Army at Valenciennes.

On the 14th, headquarters at La Ferté attempted to carry out the Georges–Doumenc decision of the early hours. Believing that the 2nd Armoured had already reached Charleroi, G.Q.G.N.E. gave orders to First Army, repeated to Ninth, to send the combat echelon back to Signy-l'Abbaye (on the north–south line to which General Billotte had directed Ninth Army to fall back) and to turn the road transport to the same destination. The orders to the road transport were easily transmitted and duly obeyed. The trains had in fact not got very far, and Movement Control succeeded in stopping them, but since there were no means of unloading at Signy-l'Abbaye, the trains were ordered to halt in the neighbourhood of Hirson and move to Signy by road. The result was confusion. The non-combatant wheeled column, which had nearly reached Vervins, had turned about and was now bowling along as fast as it could into the arms of Guderian's XIX Panzer Korps on its way to Montcornet. As Novion-Porcien was approached, the officer in charge of the column observed growing confusion on the road, and learned from the stream of fugitives that the *boches* were coming. He therefore once more turned his column and sent it off to seek shelter south of the Aisne.

At the same time, the elements on the railway were detraining at various points, the two Hotchkiss battalions at Etreux on the Sambre–Oise Canal some ten kilometres north of Guise, the 15th (B) Battalion at Le Nouvion, eight kilometres east of Etreux, and the 8th Battalion (B) at Hirson, twenty-five kilometres south-east of Le Nouvion. General Bruché says that one half-company had just alighted from their wagons, which carried a couple of petrol containers, when the Germans appeared, whereupon the engine-driver set off at full speed and did not stop until he reached Niort several hundred miles away. On top of this some elements which, owing to lack of transporters, had not entrained at Ste Menehould, received no warning of these changes in the orders and had set off by road for Charleroi. General Bruché reached First Army Headquarters at 5 a.m. on the 14th, where during the next hours he received a succession of orders and counter-orders before he was directed to Ninth Army headquarters. He reached Vervins at nightfall, to be told to set up his own headquarters at Rocquigny twelve kilometres from Signy-L'Abbaye. At this hour he was not aware of anything other than his original orders, which he presumed had been followed. He wrote a report, which he sent off to Ninth Army, and to the Inspector-General of Armoured Fighting Vehicles, Keller, who also commanded the reserve armour of the whole French Army.

This second title General Keller seems to have adopted between January and May, entirely on his own authority. He was now turning up at any army headquarters which controlled armour and assuming command, treating these elements as his own private army. His ideas, like those of General Flavigny, seem to have been limited to the single sentence that 'something must be done and done quickly'. So, late on the following morning of the 15th, he came to Rocquigny and, rejecting Bruché's request to be allowed to collect his scattered forces, told him to take up a defensive position facing Signy-L'Abbaye with what he had. By now the 2nd Armoured was partly with Touchon's embryo Sixth Army and partly with the Ninth. General Bruché set off with the intention of rounding up his battalions. His peripeteia in search of them are too labyrinthine to be narrated here.[1] He got into touch with several headquarters, received innumerable inexecutable orders, pursued his soldiery from place to place, until after dark on 18 May he drove into Cambrai. Cambrai at that hour was being surrounded by Rommel's 7th Panzer Division. Bruché and his staff spent some part of the night hidden in a stable. Finally, towards dawn, by mingling with a huge column of fleeing villagers, they succeeded in making their escape to Arras and eventually on 21 May reached Armoured Headquarters near Compiègne.

Meanwhile the 2nd Armoured had been completely dislocated, its fuel tanks were south of the Aisne, its artillery had nothing to support, its *chasseurs* were fighting as an isolated infantry unit, and its armour was scattered. Part of the heavy battalions were snatched by Keller and placed in pairs along the west side of the Oise to guard the bridges. Here they were picked off group by group by the advanced guards of XIV and XIX Panzer Korps. It was not for another week that the division was reconstituted, to fight on steadily up to the armistice.

One minor success however fell to Bruché's tanks. Late on the night of the 15th Commandant Bourgin was discovered near Vervins by the newly arrived Ninth Army commander. Under the impression that he had the whole 2nd Armoured under his hand, General Giraud ordered Bourgin to attack the advancing Panzers at Montcornet at dawn. Bourgin had just two companies of heavy tanks, twenty machines, and a single company of the 17th Chasseurs. None the less, though 'somewhat uneasy at the illusions which the Army commander was cherishing as to the possibilities of this mission', he led his tanks from Marle to Montcornet on the morning of the 16th and skirmished round the village against the German screen, which retreated when attacked, for an hour and a half, anxiously asking himself how long his fuel would last. He then retreated to Berlaincourt near Marle where, from a village petrol pump, he was able to refuel, though it needed five to six hours. After this, he took his detachment over the Oise. It is probable that the small group that attacked Guderian's headquarters at Holnon Wood near St Quentin on the 19th were Commandant Bourgin's party, which later rejoined the other surviving fragments of the division on the St Quentin canal.[2]

10 THE END OF THE NINTH ARMY, *15–19 May*

General Giraud reaches Ninth Army

NINTH Army diary laconically describes the situation of the army on the morning of 15 May as: 'No information—communications cut—liaison unworkable—back areas blocked with convoys and wrecked columns—petrol trains in flames—wholesale chaos.'

General Giraud took over from Corap during the afternoon. 'There is no doubt,' wrote Voltaire, 'that sheep can be destroyed by spells and incantations, provided that these are accompanied by doses of arsenic.' Giraud, a fine fighting leader, had energy and courage but no arsenic. If such had been the remedies needed by the Ninth Army, he had enough and to spare, but unsupported by more material adjuncts they were of no avail. Probably the worst feature of the situation was the lack of information, or its unreliability, coupled with the slowness of its arrival. From the beginning, he was misinformed as to the position and strength of the enemy and misled as to the situation of his own troops. General Martin of XI Corps, having seen General Sancelme of the 4th North African *alone*, reported to Ninth Army that this division, now in fragments, had returned from Belgium with all its infantry and half its artillery. More fantastic was Giraud's belief that he had at his disposal the 2nd Armoured Division.

[2]

The retreat of II and XI Corps

On 14 May, while XI Corps was being driven off the Meuse, II Corps was attempting the impossible in holding from the river to the left of the 18th Division. In the attempt, made more difficult by the steep and narrow wooded valleys, General Bouffet divided his already much thinned command into two: on the left, under General Boucher of 5th Motorized, the corps reconnaissance group, the 8th Infantry Regiment and a couple of artillery groups, covering the Meuse from Wépion to Profondeville; on the right, swung back to face south-east, the survivors of the 129th Infantry Regiment, the reconnaissance group of the 5th Motorized, and the remains of the 4th Cavalry, under General Barbe. What remained of the 39th Infantry Regiment, except for the battalion near Avesnes in Army reserve, was with the 18th Division.

Early on the morning of the 15th, General Bouffet ordered the northern group to abandon almost the whole of its line on the Meuse and, pivoting on Wépion past St Heribert fort,* still held by its Belgian

---

* The fort did not surrender until the 21st; that at Dave, east of the Meuse, hung on until the 24th.

garrison, to take up a position Bois-de-Villers–Lesves–St Gérard. The Belgian 8th Division was already moving out of its defences between the forts on the Namur *enceinte*, and Altmayer's V Corps across the Sambre followed during the day.

This afternoon, after surveying at Vervins the catastrophic case of the Ninth Army, Giraud decided to withdraw what remained of II Corps into Army Reserve near Avesnes, behind the Maubeuge defence line. (The Sambre was the responsibility of First Army, the southern boundary running from Dave on the Meuse to Solre-le-Château inclusive.) To this end he ordered II Corps to get back to the line Fosse–Mettet and stay there until noon on the 16th. This was carried out on the following morning, with the Marioge detachment holding from Fosse to the Sambre. Later in the evening, dissatisfied with the prospect, Giraud sent a further order to II Corps to move back at once to the Avesnes area, some sixty kilometres. This order did not reach II Corps until midday. General Bouffet hastened to the head-quarters of 5th Motorized in a suburb of Charleroi and gave Boucher verbal instructions to march all his troops to the Avesnes area that night by way of Thuin and Solre-le-Château. On his return to his head-quarters at Bultia, he was surprised by German bombers. He and nearly all the staff were killed.* General Boucher became responsible for II Corps. He had already sent off his infantry commander, General Dunoyer, to Avesnes. He now summoned Colonel Marioge and told him to take over command of what he could salve of the 5th Division and with this and his own Moroccans to proceed that night to Solre-le-Château.

Except for a brush on the Acoz, the disengagement of II Corps was untroubled by the enemy ground troops. The Moroccans concentrated on the edge of Charleroi and set out soon after dark. Colonel Marioge reached Thuin during a violent air attack. The town was in flames. He was informed by Traffic Control that the direct road to Solre-le-Château was believed to be cut, and advised to cross the Sambre at la Bussière, where the bridge would go up at dawn. He could then march to Avesnes by way of Boussois in the Maubeuge fortifications. Following these directions, he reached Boussois during the morning, and his exhausted command came in slowly during the day. The infantry of the 5th Division followed during the afternoon. By now it was down to four captains and 970 other ranks of what a week earlier had amounted to 6,000. They had no anti-tank guns, no mortars, a few machine-guns but very few belts, and they could muster two light machine-guns per company. They were escorted by a collection of tanks of every type from at least four formations.

This was the morning of 17 May. Marioge could get no news of

---

* During the morning, General Barbe, of the 4th Cavalry, was killed, and command devolved on General Marteau.

Maubeuge-Arras, 17-22 May

0	10	20	30	40	kilometres
0	5	10	15	20	25 miles

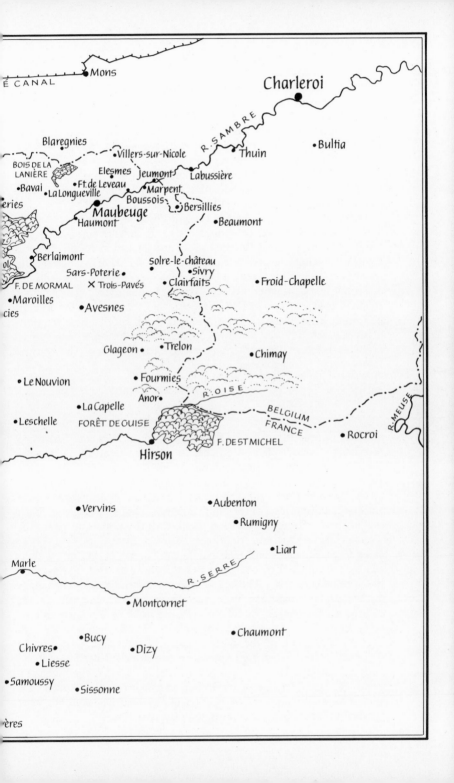

General Boucher or the future of the 5th Division. He reported to General Béjard of the 101st Fortress Division and commander of the Maubeuge defences, and was given charge of the Sambre between Maubeuge and Jeumont on the Belgian frontier. Here he and the survivors of the Moroccans and II Corps fought on until the 21st. By this day every unit to the north of Boussois had already been withdrawn. Having exhausted their means of defence, the gallant Marioge detachment surrendered.

General Dunoyer, infantry commander of the 5th Division, had failed to reach Avesnes. Eventually he joined General Didelet of the 9th Motorized, whose staff had been captured.

There still existed one unit of the 5th Division, the battalion of the 39th Infantry Regiment in Army Reserve. It did not survive long. It was caught by General Rommel in or near Avesnes. As for General Boucher, having reached Berlaimont a little south of Maubeuge, he found himself on the edge of a battle going on across his path, and cut off from his destination, Ninth Army Headquarters. He therefore reported to First Army at Douai. He was told that some of his division had reached Beauvais! He set out to find them. By this time the Germans had already reached St Pol, and some five German Panzer divisions blocked his path. So, beating back northward, he reached Dunkirk and boarded a boat intended for Dover. It is compatible with all we know of the Ninth Army that, instead of Dover, he was landed at Cherbourg.

[3]

On 12 May, the 1st North African Division of General Tarrit had been lying round Villers-Cotterets in G.Q.G. reserve. They were warned that they would move by rail during the next three days to the First Army. By the time the infantry was *en route*, its destination and future had been transformed. It began detraining at Valenciennes on the 14th, at the disposition of the Ninth Army. On the 15th General Tarrit was ordered to bring his division south, with the utmost speed, to the Trelon–Anor sector near Fourmies. A lorry convoy, big enough to carry three battalions and their equipment, would be put at the division's disposal: the divisional artillery was to move by road. The distance was seventy kilometres. The first detachment consisted of two battalions of the 28th Tunisians and one of the 5th Moroccans. The convoy was delayed again and again by columns of fugitives. The Tunisians arrived at Trelon at 6 in the morning of the 16th and found touch with the 84th Fortress Regiment to the north. On their right had come in the divisional reconnaissance group, which had attached itself to a small body of survivors from the 4th North African. Behind, there was one group of 75s. The line of unfinished casemates in the Trelon area should have been manned by infantry of the 53rd Division, but what remained of that body was now south of the Aisne.

On the next day, the German 12th Division of Strauss's II Korps attacked the Tunisians about noon and were beaten off. After an air bombardment, they attacked again at 4.30, and yet again at 5.30, without success, but the Tunisians had heavy casualties. After dark appeared another battalion of 5th Moroccans and one of the 27th Algerians, who went into support at Glageon. The actions of these five battalions were co-ordinated by the infantry commander, General Trabila.

Further away on the right, in the St Michel forest, the infantry commander of the shattered 22nd Division, General Béziers de la Fosse, was trying to patch up some kind of resistance with groups and stragglers from the east, particularly in the Passe d'Anor and behind, in the unfinished line of pill-boxes, men from the 62nd and 116th of his own division, from the 125th of the 18th Division, a bunch of Algerians from the 4th North African and now some of the 5th Moroccans.

[4]

Rommel's raid

On the morning of the 16th, General von Kluge of the Fourth Army ordered Rommel to take advantage of his success of the previous day and attack what was believed to be a northern extension of the Maginot Line between the Sambre and the Forêt de St Michel.

These defences bore little resemblance to the Maginot works. They consisted of two linked parts, the defensive sector of the Escaut and the fortified sector of Maubeuge. The former ran from Maulde on the Belgian frontier up-river to Condé, occupied by the 54th Fortress Infantry Regiment. Here it left the river and ran southward to Bry and Jenlain, where three heavily fortified works had been built. The Maubeuge sector began at this point. It was, in fact, like much else, a phlizz. It passed north of Bavai as far as the Salmagne work east of Bersillies, where it turned south to the Sambre at Boussois. South of the Sambre lay Marpent with four casemates,* whence the line ran on southwards to Clairfayts on the Belgian frontier. Most of this system consisted of a double line of constructions, one to four kilometres apart. Further south were similar casemates in the gaps between the woods at Trelon and Anor. It was these which had been left unfinished when the 4th North African set out on the 12th. The line from Clairfayts to the Sambre was garrisoned by the 84th Fortress Infantry Regiment of the 101st Fortress Division. All this defensive system was further strengthened by a switch-line from near Bavai across the north-east corner of

---

* Most of these strong-points can be identified from the 1/50,000 official map. Boussois-L'Epinette lay half-way between Boussois and Elesmes. Bersillies is left of the road to Villers-sur-Nicole, Crèvecoeur is west of the road. The Salmagne work was due east of Bersillies. That of Heron-Fontaine is 500 metres west-south-west of Fort des Sarts. At Marpent, south of the Sambre, the Rocq work, of three structures, is in the Bois de Faveux to the west of Ostergnies. Tous-Vents farm is due south.

the Forêt de Mormal as far as Berlaimont, which was to have been continued to Trelon.

That such a length of defences could not be held by the six battalions of the 101st Division had been recognized. Should this area be drawn by some mischance into the zone of active fighting, as was not seriously expected, then one or more field divisions would be brought up.

Although most of the first line was completed or nearly so on 10 May, it was far otherwise for the stop-line. Much of the concrete work was only just finished and the necessary additions, steel loop-holes, etc., had not been delivered. A third intermediate line, which had been conceived about Christmas, had nothing completed. As elsewhere, work had been delayed by the weather.

Rommel, with one armoured battalion, moved off on the afternoon of the 16th against Clairfayts. Sivry, just inside the Belgian frontier, was found deserted. Clairfayts, held by one company of the 84th Fortress, was subjected to a furious bombardment. All communications with the rear were soon broken, most of the casemates and pill-boxes smashed, the gun-emplacements torn open. By 8 o'clock it was all over, and the way to Avesnes lay open to the audacious Rommel. Engineers cleared the road of anti-tank obstacles, and preceded by motor-cyclists firing tracer ammunition and covered by artillery fire, Rommel and his tanks swept forward, apparently scarcely opposed, through the edge of Solre-le-Château, where they captured the five batteries of the 1st Armoured, which had never fired a shot. They passed on to Sars-le-Poéterie and Trois Pavés, bolting General Bruneau and some of his staff from Semousies. (He made for Wassigny, near which he was captured.) Advancing southwards towards Avesnes, Rommel met some slight opposition. He therefore took his own group round the town and stormed in from the west. According to the Panzer leader 'at least . . . a battalion of heavy tanks' were caught, but it is almost certain that these were the seventeen survivors of the 25th Hotchkiss Battalion. It was now about 4 in the morning of the 17th. Rommel decided to take his chance. He led his tanks forward to Landrecies, eighteen kilometres on, to occupy the Sambre crossing. The roads were crammed with civilian refugees, pioneer units, transport columns. Soon after 6 he was looking down from the Bois de l'Évêque on Le Cateau, having advanced seventy or eighty kilometres in the course of about eighteen hours.

All the same his mind was not easy. The fuel tanks of the Panzer battalion were nearly empty; it was short of ammunition and extremely vulnerable. The rest of the division had not followed up as ordered, and between them and their general stood numbers of unguarded French soldiers who had surrendered. Other French units, unaware of the situation, passed up and down behind him during the morning. He hurried back through Landrecies to Avesnes.[1]

[5]

General Martin, who on the 16th had moved his headquarters to Wignehies a little west of Fourmies, heard that the Oise had been crossed by German armour in strength. The origin of the message was unknown, and the general did not verify the fact. He was also told by General Tarrit that the first North African line in front of Fourmies had been entered. On this he ordered the division to draw back its right to cover Le Nouvion forest, and he told Tarrit to meet him at Pont-de-Sains on the Trelon–Avesnes road.

Tarrit issued the orders to his five battalions and set out for the rendezvous. As had happened before, General Martin had not waited but had flitted off in pursuit of his other divisional commanders: he came within sight of Avesnes, which at this hour was being visited by Rommel and the 7th Panzer. Avesnes appeared deserted, but as he approached he saw a line of French lorries burning fiercely, and a patrol of German armoured cars. He sped off to Wassigny in search of General Giraud, and so failed to meet Tarrit.*

By this time, the fighting at Trelon had blazed up again. At 6, the German 12th Division attacked once more. They did not break in, but the two Tunisian battalions, much weakened by casualties, became separated. Soon after midday, the Moroccans began to withdraw. They suffered an attack during the night at Rocquigny, but managed to make good their retreat to Catillon: they arrived here on the morning of the 18th. The Tunisians hung on all through the 17th. At nightfall, General Trabila brought them back to Le Nouvion forest, which they reached about 4 a.m.

The four remaining battalions of the 1st North African (one Tunisian, one Moroccan and two Algerian) had been delayed at Valenciennes, where the news of Rommel's descent on Avesnes on the morning of the 17th caused considerable alarm. Hence the four battalions were not sent off to Trelon, but placed in reserve—three battalions west of the huge Forêt de Mormal at Jolimetz, Louvignies, and Beaudignies, while one Algerian was sent to join a detachment of General Musse's approaching 4th Division at Pont-sur-Sambre. General Tarrit set up his headquarters at Le Quesnoy.

What remained of the 4th North African held on in the Forêt de St Michel up to 6 in the evening of the 17th. It was then overrun and General Sancelme captured.

[6]

At Ninth Army Headquarters, 15–17 May

On the evening of the 15th, a few hours after his arrival at Vervins, General Giraud was told that enemy armour was reported to have

---

* After having done much damage, General Martin was removed by Gamelin as soon as he could be pinned down. (Minart, *P. C. Vincennes*, II, 172.)

reached Signy-L'Abbaye, Liart, Brunehamel (the destination of the 36th Division) and Montcornet, the last a mere twenty kilometres from Vervins. To an anxious staff, he denounced their alarm as pessimistic and forbade the circulation of unverified reports. At the same time, he gave orders to prepare the defence of Vervins, a somewhat difficult undertaking since at least half of the headquarter staff of the army were non-combatant, and many were not armed, or else only with revolvers of the period of Napoleon III. And the telephonists were girls. These last were hurried away.

Whether the Ninth Army could survive depended on whether a defensible line could be found, and if troops could be produced to man it. During the night, as has been seen, Giraud had ordered Commandant Bourgin of the 2nd Armoured to clean out the wasps' nest at Montcornet, under the impression that the whole of this division was in the neighbourhood. A strayed battery of the same division now appeared. It was set to shoot up a village in which the enemy was reported. Another party of General Bruché's scattered division began detraining at Vervins and was sent off to La Capelle. Finally Giraud ordered the great part of the headquarter staff to St Quentin. The evacuation was carried out in order and without panic. The Germans entered Hirson and Vervins early in the afternoon. Meanwhile the General had set out to select a new advance headquarters. La Capelle proved useless and he shifted back to Bohain, recently abandoned by First Army and blessed with buried telephone cables. He was heartened by the information that the 9th Motorized of General Didelet was on its way from Antwerp and he planned a combination of this with the 1st Armoured, of whose disaster on the previous day no news had reached him.

But Giraud found Bohain too far from the troops. He believed that the place of an army commander ought to be no further from the battle than the line of battalion headquarters. He went forward again to Leschelle, half-way between La Capelle and Guise. Information was still scanty and unreliable. (In front the Tunisians and the broken pieces of the 22nd Division were fighting a desperate battle in the Trelon-Anor woods.) Giraud decided to withdraw them, and 'manœuvre from the rear' (never use the word retreat), counter-attacking from Etreux on the Sambre–Oise canal with the approaching 9th Motorized, the 2nd Armoured and, another hope, the 23rd Division, reported to be coming from Lorraine. (It was, but not to the Ninth Army.) Colonel Véron, assistant chief of staff, remained at the telephone centre at Bohain.[2] 'There was a visit from an English general—I forget his name—who had come in answer to a request from General Giraud for British air support. He came to say he could do nothing. I urged that we must not be deserted in this way and that intervention by the British Air Force alone could save us. He replied stiffly: "No. It's impossible, impossible." "Because you have not the means?" I asked. All he would say was that he could not tell me. At the time, I felt very bitter about that answer. I hated our English friends for abandoning us. It was much later that I understood the imperative reasons. . . .'

The British general was succeeded by a liaison officer from La Ferté with orders to the Ninth Army to mount a counter-attack on the Aubenton–Liart area. Both places had been in enemy hands for more than a day. At the same time, XI Corps commander announced to Giraud at Leschelle that his line could no longer be held. At 4 a.m. on the 17th, Giraud ordered what remained at his disposal to the Sambre–Oise canal.

[7]

The end of the Ninth Army

Soon after midnight on 14/15 May, Army Group One ordered Seventh Army to dispatch the 9th Motorized Division to the Maubeuge area, followed by the 4th Division, and the 1st Light Armoured, to north of the Sambre. General Didelet's division, of which only the reconnaissance group had been engaged in an abortive advance towards Breda, set out at once from Antwerp by road via Cambrai, to join the Ninth Army about the Guise–Hirson area. Everywhere, and perhaps worst of all in western Belgium, the roads were covered with military and refugee traffic. Also the division had to cross the lines of communication of the Belgian Army, the B.E.F., and the French First Army. The column took twenty-four hours to get its last instalment on the road, and the head of the division did not reach Cambrai until mid-morning of the 16th. Following an urgent call from the Vervins headquarters, General Didelet sent on a detachment of his reconnaissance group, a group of 75s and his 47-mm. anti-tank battery, to the upper Oise between Guise and Hirson, and himself set out to find General Giraud. The 9th Division infantry, now reaching Valenciennes, were deflected to the route through Le Quesnoy–Englefontaine–Landrecies–Le Nouvion. Moving all night, the leading battalions, two of the 13th and two of the 95th Infantry Regiment, were south of Landrecies, when Rommel, having created havoc in Avesnes, brought his tank battalion up the road with the object of securing the river-crossing at Landrecies. This was about 4.30 a.m. on the 17th.

The Ninth Army commander had remained at Leschelle during most of the night, but, as has been seen, the situation on his front had become much more precarious. About 4 in the morning, he sent off his order to the troops fighting in the woods, the North Africans and any others that could be reached, to fall back on the Oise–Sambre canal. He himself moved his advance headquarters to Wassigny five kilometres behind the canal and ten north-east of Bohain. From Wassigny, he sent a scribbled note to Bohain, which ran: 'Véron, send me some chaps who won't bolt, I mean, will get killed where they stand. In every case, the orders are to resist where we are and whatever happens to hang on to the end.' Bohain and Wassigny, so far as was possible, were put in a state of defence.

General Didelet reached Wassigny about 8. He was told to go to Etreux on the canal and deploy his division along it from Hanappes to Landrecies. From Landrecies as far as Berlaimont the water-line would be defended by XI Corps and, if he could be found, by General Martin. At this hour nobody yet knew that Rommel had burst through at Avesnes and, after passing through Landrecies, was on a hill east of Le Cateau with some armour, having cut clean through the middle of the 9th Division convoy. Warned in time, the next three battalions, one from each regiment, hurriedly debussed and took up positions north of the Landrecies–Le Cateau road, facing the Bois de l'Évêque. The last two battalions, both of the 131st Infantry Regiment, had been marching on foot from Valenciennes. At Le Quesnoy they were stopped and attached to the 1st Light Armoured.

During the day, the four leading battalions of the 9th, south of Landrecies, were brought back, and by evening of the 17th a number of men from Le Nouvion sector had been collected, some badly mauled Tunisians and Moroccans of the 1st North African and some of the dismounted dragoons of the 1st Cavalry. During the evening these last attempted to recover the Landrecies bridge without success. No attempt seems to have been made on the German tanks in the Bois de l'Évêque.

This numb situation was still unchanged when the Germans got their petrol and ammunition up and reinforcements.

Army Group One informed Ninth Army that General Picard's 1st Light Armoured, which had been moved from Antwerp by rail, was detraining at Solesmes, and ordered Ninth Army to move its head-quarters to Le Catelet. Giraud still preserved his optimism. He prepared plans as if the debris of his army were fully constituted formations, and went off to meet General Picard.

Le Catelet was not much. It was obviously indefensible. Colonel Véron began to organize the garrison. There were a few *gardes mobiles*, a few armoured cars and the headquarter staff. General Augereau, an Air Force general, whose group had been destroyed, joined as a volunteer. In the middle of the afternoon, German armour was seen coming down from the north (it was probably from the 8th Panzer Division). The town was shelled. The French armoured cars fought back. The signal station caught fire and flared up. The German infantry assaulted and stormed the headquarter office. The Chief of Staff, General Thierry-d'Argenlieu, was killed. So was General Augereau. The ammunition gave out. Some dozen other officers perished; the rest were captured. Ninth Army headquarters ceased to exist.

As General Giraud approached Le Catelet from the north, he saw the disaster and turned away. He realized his situation: an army commander and his personal staff, without an army, without headquarters, without a telephone or even a room, and that he was useless. He told his staff to fend for themselves. He himself got into a ditch and began to burn his papers. Here he was picked up by a section of tractors from the 2nd Armoured. But he was not to escape. On the following morning, the 19th, the party was snapped up by another Panzer detachment.

[8]

About midday on the 18th, the 1st Light Armoured had been ordered by Giraud to attack south-eastward across the Bois de l'Évêque, eject Rommel's tanks and line the Sambre-Oise canal from Landrecies to Etreux, the attack to start from north and west of the wood. Owing to delays, the western group under General Beauchesne did not set out until about 6.30 in the evening, and at once ran into trouble at Jolimetz from Germans who had pushed through the forest. The other group under Colonel de Causans never appeared; it had been held on to by General Tarrit's North African battalions in the east of the forest, where it was eventually destroyed.

The events round the Bois de l'Évêque are so entangled that their sequence is not to be determined: no two accounts agree. When he returned with another tank battalion to help the leading one, Rommel found a strenuous battle in progress between his tanks and French machines, perhaps Beauchesne's Somua. Knowing that reinforcements and supplies were coming up, he left the battalion engaged and took the one under his hand round through Ors, where he had some trouble with the dismounted dragoons before clearing the way south of Le Cateau to Cambrai. He reached the outskirts of the town in the afternoon. 'The enemy in Cambrai, unable in the dust to see that most of our vehicles were soft-skinned, apparently thought that a large-scale attack was approaching from the north of the town and offered no resistance.'[3] Which is very probable, since except for the old and sick who did not care to move, and General Bruché and his companions in the stable, the town was empty. Meanwhile the reinforced Panzer battalion held off the French and occupied Le Cateau before continuing southward to Le Catelet.

There still remained, south of the Cambrai road, a number of disorganized French groups. Of the 9th Division infantry, parties of the 13th and 95th Infantry Regiment were fighting all through the 19th at Ors, at Catillon, at Oisy. Some got back to Wassigny. A group of tanks from the 8th Panzer Division crossed the river near Tupigny. General Didelet, wounded, was captured early on the 19th. At a few places, parties of infantry and artillery held out during the 20th. But by that time, the battle had passed on and a new one was being prepared far to the north-west. The Ninth Army was no more.

11 THE LOSS OF MAUBEUGE AND THE OISE, *15–19 May*

The loss of Maubeuge, 15–20 May

GENERAL Billotte had begun to order the movements of the reserve divisions of Army Group One on the 12th, before he had any material knowledge of the course the enemy was pursuing. The 32nd Division (General Lucas) was directed from the neighbourhood of Cambrai to behind the Charleroi in support of III Corps. The 1st North African was destined for Binche, also north of the Sambre, but, as has been seen, was halted abruptly at Valenciennes on the 14th and immediately absorbed in the forlorn hope of bolstering up the smitten Ninth Army. The 43rd, the Strasbourg division of General Vernillat, round Épernay on the Marne, was told on the 12th to move by automobile and by rail to First Army north of Maubeuge. On the afternoon of the 14th, while still *en route*, General Vernillat was ordered to occupy the Sambre from Marchienne, a suburb of Charleroi, to Marpent on the edge of the Maubeuge defences, just south of the river. His division would be in touch on its left with V Corps. It was in position on the 16th. By that day the whole picture had changed.

The Belgians had retreated in reasonably good order into the Antwerp–Louvain line on the 12th. On their right the B.E.F. came in in front of Louvain, with three of their divisions in the front line, and in touch with the French III Corps. On the night of the 14th the French Cavalry Corps had withdrawn, leaving the infantry to face the attack of von Bock's Army Group B. This evening, General Billotte, now aware that the Ninth and Second Armies were in trouble, telephoned at 8 o'clock to General Blanchard at Valenciennes, warning him of a possible retreat. It was a precautionary measure: the fullness of the disaster was not yet clear, though much more was revealed a few hours later.*

On the following day, the 15th, von Reichenau's Sixth Army renewed their attack on the French IV Corps at Ernage and Gembloux, but failed to make any serious progress. In fact, for the German High Command (O.K.H.), what happened north of the Sambre was of relatively minor importance, provided the French First Army remained in position. Between Antwerp and Namur there were approximately fifteen under-armed Belgian divisions, eight British† and nine French,

---

* Cf. above, p. 142.

† The B.E.F. had the 1st, 2nd and 3rd Divisions in the line with the 4th and 48th in support, the 42nd, 44th and 50th in reserve. The 5th Division, which had been sent to Le Havre to embark for Norway, was now marching up towards Brussels. The 51st Highland Division was with the French in the Faulquemont sector of the Maginot line.

with three light armoured divisions, in fact the pick of the best troops, and practically the whole of the mobile forces. The German Chief of Staff, General Halder, wrote in his diary that opposite this Allied group they had fifteen divisions in line and six in reserve, and if necessary could reinforce with another army. The real battle was being fought south of Namur. As if in token of this, on the 16th, Hoeppner's XVI Panzer Korps was withdrawn from von Bock and sent southward to von Rundstedt's Army Group.

As yet, the completeness of the disaster between Mézières and Sedan was not fully comprehended at either Vincennes, La Ferté or Folembray, nor the vainness of substituting a Giraud for a Corap. On the morning of the 16th, General Georges ordered Army Group One to swing partly back on to the line Antwerp–Charleroi–the Sambre–the east face of the Maubeuge defences. At the same time, in order to delay the German armour in the region of the Vence, he ordered, for the morning of the 17th, a concentric attack of French armour towards Marle and Signy-L'Abbaye by the 1st and 2nd Armoured of the Ninth Army, reinforced by the heavy squadrons of the 1st Light Armoured, and by General Touchon from the south, with the de Gaulle armoured group. Of this collection, it has already been seen that the 1st and 2nd Armoured had been destroyed or scattered, and that the 1st Light Armoured was being distributed among various units round Maubeuge.

[2]

On the 15th, General Billotte, painfully conscious of the absence of any coherent body of troops between himself and the enemy, left his well-prepared Army Group One Headquarters at Folembray and betook himself to Caudry on the main road between Le Cateau and Cambrai. This was scarcely less insecure than Folembray. On the 16th, he moved to Douai.

On this day, General Lord Gort, somewhat disturbed by the little he knew of the situation, sent an officer to find out Billotte's intentions. Billotte had already prepared an order for the retreat of the whole of the Army Group, extending over the next three nights. These orders were given to both the British and the Belgians* early on the 16th. The movements were to:

Night 16/17   Charleroi–Brussels–Willebroek Canal
Night 17/18   Maubeuge–Mons–Dendre–river–Escaut to Antwerp
Night 18/19   French frontier defences to Maulde–Escaut–Ghent
                    bridge-head–Scheldt canal to Terneuzen.

---

* Gort's liaison officer saw the orders between 5 and 6; the Belgians got theirs by their liaison officer at 10. There seems to be no foundation for Gamelin's statement that the retreat was delayed one day owing to the king's reluctance to abandon Brussels.

At the same time, the Seventh Army, which General Corap had not yet reached, was dissolved. XVI Corps (General Fagalde) remained on the Scheldt, while I Corps, the 25th Motorized, and the 4th and 21st Divisions, became available to reinforce Army Group One.

The Escaut line was not a good position, but the best in the circumstances. First Army could use the two fresh divisions to cover the retreat, the 32nd now on the Charleroi canal at Nivelles, and the 43rd with three regiments covering twenty-eight kilometres of the Sambre from Charleroi to Marpent, and preparing the bridges for demolition. On the left of the 43rd, facing east, the 5th North African division, withdrawn from Namur, arrived on the night of the 16th/17th between the 43rd and the 12th Divisions. On the 16th, patrols of the 43rd met fragments of the dislocated II Corps and later skirmished with advancing armoured cars of the 5th Panzer Division. The bridges at Thuin and la Bussière were blown on the morning of the 17th, and V Corps began to fall back westward to the shelter of the Maubeuge defences.

[3]

The 4th Demi-Brigade of Chasseurs-à-Pied, the unit furthest east of the 43rd division, reached the Maubeuge defence-line late in the afternoon of the 18th. It had been a trudge of close on forty kilometres along bad and crowded roads. The chasseurs took up positions between Bersillies, Marieux and Heron-Fontaine, casemates and pill-boxes garrisoned by the 84th Fortress. The 3rd Moroccans were ordered to Feignies between Maubeuge and the Bois de Lanière, close to General Vernillat's command-post at Fort de Leveau. The southern boundary of the division was at the crossroads immediately north of Maubeuge, the junction of N.2 and N.49 roads. The division thus had no responsibility for the garrisoning of the town itself, which was the duty of the 101st Fortress Division and of the now anxiously awaited 4th Division. The third regiment of the 43rd, the 158th (Strasbourg) Infantry Regiment, came in by the riverside. As it reached the outskirts of the town, it came face to face with the enemy on the *north* side of the river. German armoured cars had thrust forward, and the 5th Panzer Division now had a spearhead inside Maubeuge itself. The 158th had expected to find some of the 4th Division on their right, but they now had to defend this flank. They took up positions partly at Boussois and Assevent overlooking the Sambre, partly further west near Les Sarts, and partly at Elesmes and in the northern suburbs. General Vernillat secured from V Corps the support of tanks from the 2nd Light Armoured.

Owing, no doubt, to the confusion of the retreat and the multitudes of fugitive Belgians, although the bridge in the centre of Maubeuge had blown, that at the western edge had been left intact. German armour had seized the chance and were now pushing reinforcements through, fanning out to both right and left. In Assevent the 158th were attacked from behind. It was here that the survivors of Colonel Marioge's detachment stood. With these he defended Boussois and Assevent and prevented the German armour emerging from Maubeuge.

The withdrawal of V Corps from Charleroi on the night of the 17th/ 18th had been slow and exhausting. 'Bottlenecks everywhere,' wrote the commander of the 14th Zouaves, 'over dozens of kilometres an uninterrupted procession of vehicles of every kind, military and civil. The infantry had to try to walk in single file along the sides of the roads, while the middle was monopolized by trucks struggling to pass the horse convoys.' The 5th North African took up a line on the left of the 43rd, round Givry down to Villers.

The Germans had once more forestalled the French further south. General Altmayer had borrowed the 8th Cuirassiers armoured cars from the 2nd Light Armoured. At daybreak on the 18th the regiment was at La Longueville with orders to patrol the Sambre from Jeumont to Berlaimont. The 4th Division had been delayed on its way from Belgium. Its units began to reach Denain and Valenciennes only late on the 17th. They were ordered to move to and hold the Sambre. The two leading battalions, one from each 72nd and 124th, set out for Pont-sur-Sambre and Haumont, but the Germans were already over the river as far as Les Mottes and Vieux-Mesnil, and, it was said, already west of the Forêt de Mormal.

On receipt of the information that the Sambre had been crossed and Maubeuge threatened, Billotte ordered the First Army (it was obviously beyond the capacity of the broken Ninth) to drive the enemy out of the forest. Blanchard entrusted the operation to the 5th North African, at this hour lying north of the 43rd Division and facing east.

The Forêt de Mormal is a solid block of woodland some fifteen kilometres from north to south and at its broadest about eight. The trees are fairly dense but are crossed by numerous rides. Across the waist runs the railway connecting Berlaimont with Le Quesnoy, while south of the track is a clearing in which stands the village of Locquignol. The Sambre flows past the east side, on the west runs the road, dead straight, from Bavai through Jolimetz and Englefontaine to Le Cateau, at the entrance to which, on this morning, Rommel had just brought a battalion of his Panzer regiment. Le Quesnoy, a charming brick-bastioned Vauban citadel, lies west of the woodland, and from here the country is open: compared with the east, it is little wooded. Normally the forest is deserted except for foresters, but on these cloudless May days of 1940 . . .

The enemy had already scoured the southern half with his light armoured columns, and the crack of shots echoed through the wood, while the northern end was undergoing a violent bombardment. Along the roads, under the trees, in the plantations and the clearings, scores of refugees had collapsed, haggard, exhausted, lamentable. There was a chaos of vehicles of every kind. There were old men sprawled on barrows, there were chicken and rabbit hutches, prams, old disused crocks drawn by oxen, lorries towing haywains, loaded with mattresses, sheaves of straw, stoves, anything and everything, the ill-assorted paraphernalia of terror and flight. The ground was littered with greasy paper, with disembowelled meat-cans, with filthy rags. The brilliant sunshine lent a holiday air to the scene, a fête in the Bois de Vincennes, both pathetic and nauseating. In the distance rose great columns of smoke and flame.[1]

General Mesny of the 5th North African withdrew the 24th Tunisians from the Bois de la Lanière, put the two remaining battalions of the 6th Moroccans to La Longueville, and was lent two battalions of the 3rd Moroccans from the 43rd Division. To these were added a battalion of Renault 35 and some of the 29th Dragoons' tanks from the 2nd Light Armoured, brought from Hargnies, north-east of the forest. The first objective was the Berlaimont–Le Quesnoy railway.

Harassing aircraft delayed the infantry on their way to the starting-line, and it was already the edge of dark when they began to move. They reached the first objective and waited for daylight. On the left, the 3rd Moroccans detached one battalion to join up with the garrisons of the casemates at Pont-sur-Sambre. The Germans between Berlaimont and Locquignol were reinforced, and succeeded in surrounding the French right. General Mesny decided to break out through Englefontaine under cover of night. By now the number of tanks was reduced by casualties and lack of fuel. What fuel could be got from the broken-down machines was shared out. On the evening of the 20th, the Mesny column set out, with the Tunisians leading, followed by the 6th Moroccan, with the 3rd bringing up the rear. Englefontaine was rushed, but a confusion of names led the advance guard down the wrong road. Nevertheless, after a sharp skirmish in which the French gunners beat off some German tanks, the great part of the column passed through the Escaut line on the evening of the 21st. Unfortunately part of the 3rd Moroccans had been unable to pass Englefontaine before dawn, and only a few got away.

The 43rd Division, reduced on the 18th to seven battalions, remained in position facing east and south through the next night. Two of the *chasseur* battalions, the 1st and the 29th, were brought down to Fort Leveau, which twice changed hands. During the afternoon of the 19th, General Vernillat recognized that it was high time to retreat. He ordered the 1st and 29th Chasseurs and the last battalion of the 3rd Moroccans to march westward, and the 158th, with the 10th Chasseurs, to hold the Bois de la Lanière. He himself joined the commander of the fortress troops, General Béjard, at St Waast, a little beyond Bavai. But early on the 20th Bavai was bombed and then stormed: all communications with his retreating battalions were cut. The Moroccans tried to work round Bavai, failed and ran into the enemy. One company was lost, the rest escaped to Estreux. Of the Chasseurs-à-Pied, the 29th Battalion, after in its turn storming Bavai, was captured, except for one company which got away to Eth with the 1st Chasseurs. The 158th and the 10th Chasseurs, with the last of the divisional artillery and some of the 87th Fortress, on the 21st made a determined effort to withdraw. The 10th Chasseur battalion, forming the rearguard, was cut off at Blaregnies and fought a long battle against a German infantry regiment. Their ammunition exhausted, the *chasseurs* burned their colours and were shot down attacking the enemy with the bayonet. The remains of the 158th were finished off on the 23rd as they approached Condé. Though a few from all three units are found later fighting on the canal line, 23 May saw the end of the Strasbourg division.

The third division of V Corps, the 12th (General Janssen), successfully withdrew, with little loss. On the night of 19th/20th it retired from its advance position to the north of the 5th North African, out of touch with V Corps Headquarters and without information. Moving southwestward, some of its leading infantry fell into an ambush near Bavai. When he discovered the situation, General Janssen changed the route, sent his columns northward and, unscathed, rejoined First Army through Valenciennes. The division was then transferred to III Corps.

When General Mesny took command of the operation against the Forêt de Mormal, the 14th Zouaves were occupying the divisional line below Givry to Villers-sur-Nicole and Battignies, supported by two groups of artillery and the 10th Anti-Tank Battery. During the 19th, pressure increased on the 14th Zouaves, as it had on its neighbours of the 43rd Division. On this day, the Zouaves were transferred to the 12th Division, which next morning ordered them to retire at the tail of their own 150th Infantry Regiment. As they approached Bavai, the Zouaves saw that the 150th were in trouble. They therefore swung away and, passing by Bry and Jenlain, where the great outworks appeared to be deserted, they marched through Valenciennes to Escaudain.

North of the Cambrai–Catillon road, the gradual withdrawal of the First Army was not seriously impeded. III and IV Corps were behind the Scheldt up to Valenciennes on the 20th. But General Altmayer had serious trouble in bringing back V Corps, or rather what remained of his divisions, the mauled battalions, the stricken companies, the exhausted sections of the 5th North African, and the 43rd. With them were the detachments of the 1st Light Armoured and the small groups of the last Ninth Army formations which had kept ahead of the now unresisted advance of Reinhardt's XLI Panzer Korps. Among these were fragments of II Corps, two reconnaissance groups, two battalions of the 131st Infantry Regiment of the 9th Division, which reached Bouchain, a group from the 1st North African, a battery, an engineer company, a few armoured cars, all moving north-westward. Here a line was building up along the Escaut to Bouchain, then north of the Sensée as far as the Canal du Nord at Arleux, on to the Scarpe at Biache, lined by a British infantry brigade, to Arras, garrisoned by a small scratch force of which the core was the 1st Battalion, the Welsh Guards.

AFTER their exchange of patriotic sentiments on the morning of 10 May, communications between the President of the Council and the generalissimo ceased. The President must henceforward rely on the Minister of Defence for news of the battle. Reynaud's personal military assistant, Colonel de Villelume, was critical of the wisdom of the advance into Belgium and had said so. On the evening of the 10th Reynaud said: 'I'm uneasy. Now we shall see what Gamelin's worth.' On the 11th, this uneasiness increased. He telephoned to Daladier and spoke of his disquiet. 'What do you expect?' came the reply: 'Gamelin's in charge. He is following his plan.' On Whit Sunday there was still no news. On the Monday, all Reynaud heard was that the French cavalry advance guards had been brought to a halt. About midday, on Tuesday the 14th, at the moment when Guderian was ordering his two leading armoured divisions to wheel westward and cross the Bar, news of serious trouble at Sedan broke, but not in detail. Between 5 and 6 p.m. Reynaud telegraphed to London asking for ten squadrons of fighters to be sent to France. It was not until the early hours of the 15th that the German passage of the Meuse in strength was confirmed, and the threat to the Allied armies north of the Sambre perceived. About 7.30 in the morning, Reynaud telephoned Churchill. 'He spoke in English,' wrote the British Prime Minister, 'and evidently under stress.' Reynaud blurted out dramatically that they had been defeated. Churchill remonstrated with what he took to be the exaggerated alarm of his interlocutor, but said he would come over to Paris on the next day and 'have a talk'.

In order not to offend Daladier's susceptibility, Reynaud refrained from telephoning to Gamelin. He asked Daladier for the reactions of the Commander-in-Chief. Daladier replied: 'General Gamelin has no reaction.' To Paul Baudouin, his under-secretary, Reynaud said: 'If only Marshal Pétain were here. He could influence Gamelin. His wisdom and serenity would be of enormous help.' Later in the day, Colonel de Villelume was told by Gamelin's *chef de cabinet*, Colonel Petitbon, that he, Petitbon, had had enough of Villelume's inquisitiveness, and that if it went on he would supply no information whatever. Reynaud was furious. 'It is time I put a stop to this farce. I ought to be Minister of Defence. Daladier shall go to the Foreign Office or get out.' In the evening a messenger was sent off to Madrid to fetch Pétain.

That evening about 9, William Bullitt, the United States ambassador, was talking with Daladier in his room in the rue St Dominique, when the telephone rang and Gamelin spoke with the Minister of Defence.

O N 16 May, the day on which General Billotte ordered his armies to begin their retreat to the Escaut, Brigadier A. B. Beauman, who commanded the Northern District of the British Lines of Communication at Le Havre, drove up to Amiens to consult the Commandant of No. 11 Military Area. General Lamson assured him that there was no cause for anxiety. Nevertheless, Brigadier Beauman preferred to trust his own eyes. The refugee traffic, including heavy military transport from the Dutch and Belgian Armies, on the Rouen road was impressive. At his headquarters, he began to organize the assortment of infantry at his disposal into the semblance of a fighting force. On the following day, the units of the British 12th Division, three infantry brigades with derisory artillery, were ordered by Lord Gort to occupy and defend a large area, the triangle Doullens–Albert–Amiens.

[2]

On the night of the 16th/17th, the situation of the French armies, though dangerous, did not yet appear catastrophic. Neither the Belgians, the British nor the French First Army was heavily pressed. Their retreat was being carried out with only local trouble. The 9th, 4th, and 25th of the late Seventh Army divisions were on their way from Antwerp and the 1st Light Armoured was joining the Cavalry Corps. Reserves were arriving on the Aisne, though not rapidly enough to remove General Touchon's anxiety. He was patching up with what he could get. General de Lattre's 14th Division had now concentrated south of the Aisne but had a bridgehead at Rethel. Divisions from Army Group Two were *en route*, the 10th and 87th (the last North African), but they had only insignificant detachments in position. In the meantime, the gaps in the defences between Rethel and the Oise were being plugged with bits and pieces, groups of training battalions without mortars or anti-tank guns, sent up by the optimist General Doumenc, escaped batteries, and sections led by indomitable subalterns and sergeants, specialist units such as gas companies, broken-down tanks from the 2nd and 3rd Armoured Divisions.

The railways were working magnificently in spite of severe bombing. The German Air Force was obviously aiming to prevent the reinforcement of Army Group One by blocking the Metz–Reims–Soissons and the Langres–Troyes–Mareuil-sur-Ourcq tracks. Of fifty-seven attacks on the 15th, 16th and 17th, thirty-eight had been effective enough to bring about long detours and force the withdrawal of detraining points. The attacks between the 17th and 20th were intended to keep open the breach between the now dissolving Ninth Army and whatever might be collecting south of the Aisne. The bombing of Tergnier, Chaulnes, Corbie, Longueau, Amiens, Abancourt, Canaples, Longpré, Eu completed the disjunction between Paris and the main bases on the line of the Seine and the northern railheads. On the 19th began the attacks on the *rocade* lines, on trains, sidings, platforms, junctions between Somme and lower Seine, at Montdidier, Beauvais, Amiens, Paris. Rails were cut and convoys delayed, it might be for twenty-four hours.

The French high command was baffled by their failure to penetrate the enemy's designs, indeed by their inability to understand the German theory of war, and this embarrassment created semi-paralysis, while the aggressiveness of German patrols led each local commander to the presumption that his sector was the next target.

On the evening of the 16th it was believed at La Ferté that there still remained a link between the right of the Ninth Army and the left of the Sixth, though very fragile, and that it would be possible to weld the two ends by introducing a new army. On the morning of the 17th, the commander of VIII Corps in Lorraine, General Frère, a very gallant officer with a fine 1914–18 record, and one of the few modernizers in the French Army, was summoned from Bitche to La Ferté and given the task of constituting a new Seventh Army to come in between Touchon's Sixth at Tergnier on the Oise and the Ninth, supposedly holding St Quentin. To form it G.Q.G.N.E. must draw on almost the last reserve not already committed. Five divisions were warned on this day. Four were in the east, the 23rd, promised to General Giraud, and already on rail in the neighbourhood of Troyes, the 19th from Mulhouse, the newly formed 7th North African from the Valdahon training centre near Besançon, the 4th Colonial in the Lunéville area. The fifth division was the 21st, which had been left in the north between Ghent and Terneuzen. One other division was set in motion, the 3rd Light, of two Alpine regiments waiting at Brest for shipment to Norway. At the same time, the staff of I Corps (General Sciard) was called from the Antwerp area, that of XXIV Corps (General Fougère) from Lorraine, and General Grandsard of X Corps from Second Army area.

Frère reached La Ferté at 5 in the afternoon and was given his orders in the presence of Gamelin. These were that the new Seventh Army should hold the line Coucy-le-Château–Péronne to bar the Oise valley and at the same time attempt to join the right of the Ninth Army somewhere about Ribemont. The British were said to have some infantry at Ruyaulcourt on the Canal du Nord. There, indeed, was one isolated and under-armed infantry brigade, the 70th, which was driven off and destroyed by the 8th Panzer division on the 19th.

Frère established a temporary headquarters with a skeleton staff at Roye and ordered his two divisions, with the 3rd Light on the left, to occupy the Somme from Ham to the Crozat Canal and the canal to the Oise. The 23rd Division was to try to form a link with the 87th Division at the junction of the Oise and the Ailette.

[3]

Early on the morning of 16 May, Guderian's two leading divisions, having taken Bouvellemont and Novion-Porcien, were sweeping forward unopposed to Montcornet, where they found the leading units of Kempff's 6th Panzer Division. Patrols were sent forward and reached Marle and Dercy on the Serre, without difficulty, on the morning of the 17th. It is possible that the XIX and XLI Panzer Korps could have crossed the Oise that morning, a mere thirty miles from Montcornet, but for the intervention of German O.K.H., which, looking at its unguarded left flank stretching for nearly sixty kilometres from the Bar, feared to allow a further extension westward until this was secured. They did not know that, south of the Aisne from Attigny onwards, except for the slowly approaching battalions of the 14th Division, no French force was capable of attacking. The 36th, which had been expected day after day, only began to reach the Aisne on the 17th. On the 18th, it claimed to have made a few small bridgeheads across the river on the right of the 14th Division, and that was all.

On this day, infantry detraining south of the Aisne were being hurried forward to reach the river, battalions of the 10th Division (General Aymé) between Château-Porcien and Neufchâtel, General Boissau's newly created 44th Division just assembling near Fismes, General Lestien's 28th Alpine near Soissons, with orders to occupy the Ailette canal, and, west of Compiègne, the 87th African (General Henri Martin) astride the Oise. Between the Aisne and the nearest Germans, Guderian's 1st Panzer Division, streaming westward towards the Oise, lay some twenty miles of open country, unoccupied but for one embryo force, the so-called 4th Armoured Division, otherwise the Groupement de Gaulle.

On 16 May, G.Q.G.N.E., 'imperfectly informed', as Colonel Lyet delicately expresses it, had conceived a strong armoured attack from four directions against the audacious German tanks, by the 1st and 2nd Armoured Divisions from the north, by the 3rd from Second Army and by the 4th coming from the direction of Paris. During the day it gradually became known that the first two were 'not available', that the 3rd was wholly occupied round Stonne, and only the embryonic de Gaulle group could be got into position. General Georges therefore proposed to cancel the attack, but General Touchon, much alive to the weakness of the Sixth Army, urged that his occupation of the Aisne needed covering for at least another two or three days. Hence Colonel de Gaulle was invited to attack the southern flank of the German armour between Montcornet and the Oise.

To the armoured group which was still assembling, G.Q.G.N.E. added a small reinforcement, which went into action on this day. General Petiet's 3rd Cavalry Division, which had been fighting on the Luxembourg frontier since the 10th, had been dispatched westward on 15 May.

While its horsed brigade moved directly to the Beauvais neighbourhood, its mechanized brigade (the 3rd Armoured Cars and the 2nd Dismounted Dragoons)[1] reached Pont Faverger, east of Reims, at midnight. Before dawn on the 16th, the armoured cars and the motor-cyclists went north to investigate the Serre between Montcornet and Liart. Finding the stream strongly held, the group fell back towards Dizy-le-Gros, where it was surprised by a body of German armour from 1st Panzer coming from its rear. At the end of a short sharp engagement in which the motor-cyclists suffered, two armoured cars extricated the rest of the regiment, which got away to Sissonne. The Dismounted Dragoons, which had not been engaged, had marched directly to the same rendezvous. The whole brigade was now attached to Colonel de Gaulle's group.

On 15 May, the Groupement de Gaulle was no more than a headquarters travelling from Paris to Bruyères, a few kilometres south of Laon. During the 16th there arrived at Bruyères the 6th Armoured Brigade, consisting of the 46th Battalion, only two companies of B tanks and one of D.2, twenty and fifteen machines respectively. The 8th Brigade, which followed, comprised the 24th Battalion and one company of the 2nd, in all some fifty Renaults. On the 17th appeared the 322nd Artillery regiment of 105-mm. and the 4th Chasseurs. The group was in truth a ramshackle outfit. Instead of 166 tanks, there were only ninety-three. The drivers of the 46th Battalion had been trained on light tanks and had never seen the complicated B. The battalion had done no formation training and the gunners had only once fired a 75-mm. gun. The Chasseurs had not been issued with their armoured carriers; they moved by lorry. There was no signalling equipment and, of course, no radio. In battle all messages had to be carried by dispatch-rider. 'The divisional artillery,' wrote the particular imp who invariably attaches himself to august figures, 'matched the rest. At Vernon between 3 and 5 in the morning of the 17th, some of us officers of the 322nd recruited chauffeurs, untrained motor-cyclists, gunners who had never laid a gun, while others, with faked requisitions, bullied and roared at the sleepy storemen, while they grabbed weapons.' The Hotchkiss anti-aircraft guns were found to have been issued with ammunition for the St Étienne models.[2]

So on 17 May, in pursuance of his mission (and his destiny), Colonel de Gaulle sent his two combat brigades towards Montcornet: the 6th Brigade on the left along the road from Laon; on the right, the 8th Brigade, the Renaults, through Boncourt and Ville-aux-Bois. Each column was followed by a detachment of the 2nd Dismounted Dragoons and some lorryloads of Chasseurs. The left column crossed the causeway over the marshes between Liesse and Chivres and at the far end met a group of German tanks. In this encounter an ammunition wagon was hit and blew up, which seems to have caused spectacular damage, but whether the wagon was German or French nobody seems to know.[3]

There followed trouble in the marshes and six of the twenty Bs slid off the road. The French appear to have reached the Serre, but not to have penetrated into Montcornet, which lies north of the stream and was defended by anti-tank guns. They modestly claim that one German tank was destroyed and a few prisoners taken. Otherwise nothing of significance happened. The battle went unnoticed by Guderian; he merely says: 'An enemy tank company which tried to enter the town from the south-west was taken prisoner. It belonged to General de Gaulle's division.'[4] At nine in the evening the French columns were recalled. On the way back they were chivvied by German aircraft and retired into the Forêt de Samoussy between Sissonne and Bruyères, where they spent a disturbed night. Five of the six tanks that got off the road were recovered. In the meantime XIX Panzer Korps continued its untroubled advance north of the Serre and on the next day reached the Oise. The delay in the German advance was in no way due to the action of the de Gaulle division, but to a pause imposed by General Kleist.[5]

De Gaulle was now reinforced by another motorized dragoon regiment, the 7th, made up as to half by men from the older classes, dug out from remount depots with unusable 25-mm. guns and machine-guns unsupplied with ammunition. There also arrived a group of the 3rd Cuirassiers with forty Somua and, of the 10th Cuirassiers, two squadrons of armoured cars and two of motor-cyclists. Unhappily many of these drafts, though full of pluck and energy, were amateur, while the tank commanders, just out of St Cyr, manned their machines for the first time: they had had three hours on the road but had never worked as a body. Nevertheless the reinforcement was welcome; on the morning of the 18th, the division had only twenty B and forty R.35 runners.

On the night of the 17th, the 3rd Cavalry's armoured cars had fallen back on the great cathedral-crowned *motte* of Laon, which overlooks the land to the north and east, and stayed there until the 20th. The town had not been completely deserted by civilians. On the 19th, de Gaulle was ordered by Touchon to cross the Serre and attack Guderian's communications. By this time the Germans had mined the approaches to the bridges and stiffened the river-line with plenty of anti-tank guns. The French tanks moved forward in three parallel columns. The Stukas appeared. Before nine in the morning the attack was halted, while on the right the covering infantry were roughly handled by reconnaissance groups of the 10th Panzer and the 29th Motorized Division closing up on the XIX Korps, and also by the dive-bombers. The French guns, in a wide arc south-west of the town, also suffered. De Gaulle asked permission to retire, but though Georges assented, Touchon asked for another twenty-four hours until the 28th Division was established on the Ailette. The infantry therefore held on until the next day, when the *chasseurs* had great difficulty in getting away and had to be brought off by the *cuirassiers*.

Laon was abandoned. As he was leaving, an artillery officer who had been observing from the ramparts was accosted by an elderly lady who appeared in a doorway, and said: 'Would you be kind enough to slip this letter in the post-box?' Somewhat staggered at the request, he obeyed.

During the slow withdrawal both artillery and armour were attacked again and again by light armour and dive-bombers. The absence of any system of communications added to the confusion. The order to retreat on the 20th did not reach all its destinations. Hence the fighting withdrawal of the remains of the 3rd Cavalry Division armoured cars and the dragoons, and the hurried retreat of the unprotected 322nd Artillery on the left.

By evening, the de Gaulle division was over the Aisne and concentrating round Fismes. Its losses had been moderately severe. It had accomplished nothing. There had been no miracle. No Frenchman had ridden the whirlwind. Colonel de Gaulle had appeared, reappeared and most disconcertingly disappeared at intervals, thus giving a false air of unity to what in fact was little more coherent than a succession of uncoordinated armed scuffles with flank-guards.

These indecisive skirmishes were inflated by Parisian editors laudably anxious to put heart into the civilians: stories which at least did not end in disaster could do something to stiffen opinion. In Colonel de Gaulle, the champion of the armoured fighting vehicle, they now had a figure they could build up as a commander who knew how to fight, thereby reflecting on the commanders of other divisions.[6]

THE British had not been seriously troubled in their retreat to the
Scheldt. But with the break in the south, of which Lord Gort was
imperfectly informed, he looked somewhat anxiously over his shoulder
to Arras, where his rear headquarters had remained. On the 17th he
became aware that a 'large gap of at least twenty miles existed south of
the Forêt de Mormal', and this was emphasized by a request from La
Ferté that the British should occupy more than twenty kilometres of
the Canal du Nord, north of Péronne. The British Commander-in-
Chief at once complied as far as he was able by sending a weak infantry
brigade to the Ruyaulcourt area, but he realized that the whole system
of communications was threatened. As has been seen, on this day he
had had the British 12th Division sent up from the Rouen area to
various points north of the Somme. He had sent the 1st Welsh Guards
to strengthen the details in Arras, and another weak infantry brigade
to occupy the Scarpe River east of the city, while the *bouches inutiles* in
Arras were sent off to Boulogne.*

The acuteness of the situation was further sharpened by the beginning
of the withdrawal of the Advanced Air Striking Force, three bomber
wings, from east of Reims to about the upper Seine, with headquarters
at Troyes. The Force had had heavy casualties and its strength was now
reduced from ten to six squadrons. On the following day, the Air
Component, some of whose airfields were almost in the firing-line, and
all of which were threatened, was withdrawn to England. On the 18th
also, Gort brought his own advanced headquarters back from Renaix
to Wahagnies between Seclin and Douai. General Blanchard had
established his own First Army Headquarters at Douai, while General
Billotte, who had retreated to Douai from Caudry, moved to
Béthune.

During the night of the 18th/19th, Billotte[1] came over to see the
British Commander, to explain the situation so far as he knew it. He
spoke of his measures to remedy what he now knew to be a disaster.
According to Gort, 'clearly he had little hope that they would be
effective.... I was unable to verify that the French had enough reserves
at their disposal south of the gap to enable them to stage counter-attacks
sufficiently strong to warrant the expectation that the gap would be
closed.'[2]

Lord Gort saw three alternatives for the Allies. Either, simultaneous

---

* 150th Brigade, cf. p. 184, fn.

attacks from north and south to close the gap. Or, a retreat to the line of the Somme, i.e. up the British and French lines of communication. This would impose almost insoluble problems and would undoubtedly face the Belgians with an intolerable dilemma, apart from there being no time to debate such a proposal. For the Belgians it would mean a choice between abandoning their country or fighting alone. It could easily lead to their surrender. Thirdly, a retreat towards the Channel ports, the formation of a bridgehead and possibly the withdrawal of the B.E.F. from France at a most inopportune moment. In the middle of the 19th, he told his Chief of Staff, General Pownall, to telephone to the Director of Military Operations at the War Office and discuss the situation.

[2]

The removal of Gamelin. Weygand

Reynaud had never believed in Gamelin's capacity. On 9 May he would have removed him but for the German attack. He had asked for a report on what had happened, and on the 18th received a fifteen-page document of explanation. On this day Pétain arrived from Madrid. With the marshal's help and pressure on President Lebrun, Reynaud succeeded in expelling Daladier from the War Office and the Ministry of Defence, compensating him formally with the Foreign Ministry. This would allow him to replace Gamelin with Weygand, on the latter's arrival in Paris, though it is possible he only intended to make the general his personal aide. He further strengthened his own situation by translating Georges Mandel, once feared as Clemenceau's *homme de main*, from the Colonial Ministry to the Interior. At the same time he removed Alexis Léger, summoning to his place Charles-Roux, a very experienced diplomat, who for years, because of the enmity of Joseph Caillaux, had been kept on the shelf at the Vatican. He offered Léger the Washington Embassy, but the Secretary-General declined.

That Weygand was a believing and practising Catholic, somewhat austere and peremptory, was well known—an embittered reactionary, according to Left politicians—but it had never been said that he had let his political views influence his military policies. Later it was recalled that he had never commanded so much as a brigade in battle, but from August 1914 had always remained in the shadow of Foch. This, of course, would not have been remembered had he won. At the moment when Reynaud cabled, he had been away from Beirut in consultation with Wavell in Egypt. He came straight to France, landing at Étampes in the mid-morning of Sunday the 19th.

This was the day on which General Didelet, his broken 9th Division fighting desperately on the Sambre, was wounded and captured; on which Ninth Army Headquarters at Le Catelet was overwhelmed, and on which Guderian's armour crossed the Oise and took St Quentin.

'Was all hope then lost?' wrote a cynical general, and answered: 'No, not yet . . . for on this very day, May the 19th, in Notre Dame, M. Paul Reynaud, head of the government, and M. Édouard Daladier, Minister of War, sang hymns and called on God to grant them the salvation of France. . . . The Lord, alas! did not answer their prayer. Perhaps they had not made the act of contrition.'[3]

The ministers had not been accompanied by General Gamelin. About 5 a.m. General Doumenc had telephoned from Montry to say that he had just returned from La Ferté, and that he believed it was time Gamelin intervened in person. The Commander-in-Chief agreed. At 6.30 he was fetched by the Aide-Major-Général of the Operations Bureau, Koeltz. On their way, Koeltz told him that orders had been issued just before midnight for a number of 'partial' counter-attacks but these would exhaust the reserves available[4] and an operation on a larger scale was needed. In obedience to a call from Gamelin, Vuillemin was waiting for him when he arrived at Georges's headquarters, and after rapidly sketching the situation Gamelin sent him off to warn his various zone commanders. He himself settled down to draft what were to be his last operation orders, his final *instruction personnelle et secrète*.[5] It began with the words: 'Without wishing to intervene in the conduct of the battle . . .' and went on to prescribe a full-scale attack from north and south which was simple on the map, but impracticable on the ground. The last line ran: 'The whole is a question of hours.' It was timed 9.45 a.m.

On Vuillemin's return Gamelin had the instruction read over to him, to Georges, and some of their staff. He himself says he added that if these measures were not successful, it would be difficult to make a long defence of French territory. Vuillemin rejoined: 'Then the government should be warned.' 'Time enough,' replied Gamelin, 'when things go badly. If we raise the possibility now, we shall be accused of pessimism and of losing the battle before it has begun.'[6]

A little later he was told that General Dill, now assistant Chief of the General Staff to Ironside, was in Paris, and he invited him to come to La Ferté to discuss matters with Georges. At the same time he was told of Weygand's expected arrival. Then they all went in to lunch where, in an atmosphere of gloom, the Commander-in-Chief, 'who by now knew he was condemned, thought it necessary to put on an act, talk about this and that, even to joke. It all seemed horribly false.' Gamelin ate heartily, drank his coffee and went off, still imperturbable, with the guard turning out and the appropriate bugle-calls.[7]

Before his departure, he exchanged a few words with Dill, who gave him a message from Ironside to the effect that whatever his orders might be, they would be strictly followed by the British. Alas, Gamelin's orders were in fact no more than suggestions which had been in every staff officer's mind for at least four days. And as for the British, Billotte, who had now moved from Douai to Béthune, telephoned to Georges

that the British were thinking of retreating on Calais and Dunkirk.*
On this Gamelin told Georges of Ironside's message. Then he hastened
back to Vincennes, which he reached about 3.30. Weygand was waiting,
and told him that Reynaud had summoned him to study and advise on
the situation: might he have a talk to Georges? Agreeing, Gamelin
suggested that Weygand should counsel Georges (who had served under
Weygand on Foch's staff) to pull his headquarters into better shape,
ignoring the fact that he himself had been the author of the confusion.
As he left, Weygand said: 'You know Paul Reynaud doesn't like you?'
Gamelin responded: 'I do.'

A little later he telephoned to La Ferté for news. There was none of
importance. One of his liaison officers, Commander Minart, had just
come back from La Ferté with the 'feeling that the personal and secret
instruction remained a dead letter'. At Vincennes business had practically ceased. 'Every man, thinking about his own troubles, was
hurriedly packing his bags. The filing-cabinets were nearly empty. . . .
At the first warning Vincennes would be abandoned like a fire-station
on a day of alarms.' Having reported, Minart suddenly broke the bounds
of his duty. He told Gamelin that G.Q.G.N.E. was at sixes and sevens
and suggested that he should replace General Georges with Huntziger.
'General Gamelin listened in silence. He unclasped his hands and threw
them up with a gesture which signified: "What's the use?" There was
nothing to do but salute and leave.'[8]

A little before 9 in the evening, an officer from Reynaud's secretariat
appeared and delivered the text of two decrees, the first suppressing the
post of Commander-in-Chief of the Ground Forces, i.e. of Gamelin,
the second nominating Weygand Chief of Staff of National Defence
and Commander-in-Chief of all theatres of war, earth, air and water.
With them was a courteous note conveying the thanks of the government
for Gamelin's services during a long and brilliant career.[9]

Weygand returned from La Ferté about 6.30, and saw Reynaud and
Pétain. At the end of their conversation, he said: 'Very well. I accept
the responsibility you are putting on me. You will not be surprised if I
do not promise victory, or even give you hope of a victory.' As he left he
said to Baudouin, who asked him his first impression of the situation:
'Bad. Very serious, but one must never despair.' When Baudouin
asked him what he was going to do this evening, he said: 'I'm dead
tired; I only had three hours' sleep in Tunis. I'm going to begin by
going to sleep, and tomorrow morning, I'll go to Vincennes and take
over.'[10]

On the following morning, Weygand, who during the evening had
spent some hours with Georges, took over from the dismissed general.
It perhaps throws light on the characters of the two men that, in their

---

* This seems to have come from the French monitoring service which had
probably picked up the conversation between General Pownall and the D.M.O.
at the War Office.

respective memoirs, Weygand scarcely mentions the meeting, while Gamelin asks at length for the reader's sympathy. 'We shut ourselves in my room. For me the moment was dramatic. Not a word from the heart. Has he one ? Joffre and Foch had. The general seemed sure of himself; his figure was younger than ever, even if age had sharpened his features a little. It was I who in August 1939 had entrusted him with the Levant command. He did not seem even to remember it. A man who is down does not count, especially when he can be an embarrassment.'

They discussed the situation, and various appointments, for some minutes. At one moment Weygand broke out: 'All these politics. It ought to be changed. We must get rid of all these politicians. Not one is better than the next.' Did Weygand in fact say this, or did Gamelin slip in this drop of poison ?

The contrast between the two men comes out sharply in the fact that Gamelin takes five pages to recount the conversation, while Weygand, although honouring the dignity of Gamelin in his fall, merely says that Gamelin did not mention his report to Reynaud of 18 May, a 'document which would have made matters clearer to me'. It is, however, very probable that at this date nothing could have been done to save the French Army.[11]

The two men parted, not to meet again until their encounter in December 1943 as prisoners of the Germans in the Itter Fortress. In the interval the Riom trial had been held, after which, even in prison, cordiality was impossible.

As General Georges was later to tell the Committee on Events, most of what Gamelin advised had been in hand for the past two days. He went on:

Between 3 September and 10 May, the Commander-in-Chief sent me not less than 140 communications of a general nature, notes, reflections, personal and secret instructions. . . . May 10 comes, the battle opens. No more orders from the Commander-in-Chief, except this one of 19 May, the day of his departure.

On the 19th, the situation was particularly grave. And the Commander-in-Chief proposed to take no responsibility for the conduct of the only battle being fought, on which depended the issue of the campaign and the fate of the country. He gave no orders; he limited himself to suggestion: he did not command. An odd way, at the hour of supreme danger of understanding the duty of the generalissimo. In a crisis of this kind, Foch, whose appetite for responsibility was always keen, would not, I think, have hesitated to fling himself into the fight, determined to bring to bear the full weight of his resolution and his authority.[12]

15 THE BRITISH AT ARRAS,
20–21 May

ON the afternoon of the 19th, as a result of Pownall's conversation with the D.M.O., which had set forth Gort's three various alternatives, with a leaning towards the withdrawal into a bridgehead, General Ironside, who felt decidedly opposed to the Gort proposal, obtained the permission of the Cabinet to go to France and talk to Gort. He reached Wahagnies at about 8 the next morning, and presented the Commander-in-Chief with an instruction from the Cabinet to move towards Amiens and 'to take station on the left of the French Army', a curiously obscure order. As soon as the two men had thoroughly examined the manœuvre involved, Ironside agreed as to its material impossibility. Seven of the ten divisions of Gort's command were engaged by the enemy. If they disengaged, as the cabinet instruction implied, a large gap would appear, into which the Germans would rush and finish off the Belgians. Lord Gort said, however, that he had a smaller scheme in hand with the 50th Division, to which he would join the 5th for an attack southward from Arras on the following morning, the 21st, when he received orders from the French. Ironside asked him under whose orders he was at the moment. Gort replied that he was under those of Billotte, but that he had received none for some time. Ironside then hurried off to see Billotte, whom he finally ran down at First Army Headquarters in Lens with Blanchard, 'all in a state of complete depression. No plan, no thought of plan. Ready to be slaughtered. Defeated at the head without casualties.' Eventually he forced Billotte to agree to plan and carry out an attack with two divisions on the left of the British. These two divisions would be from General Altmayer's V Corps.[1]

Once more the element of time played the devil with a paper scheme. None of the executants had been seriously consulted. The two British divisions had at the moment only two brigades apiece, and the tank brigade which was added had only two battalions.* On the morning of the 20th, General Franklyn of the 5th Division was summoned to Wahagnies, where he was told by the Commander-in-Chief that he was to 'operate round Arras'. He was to relieve the French light armoured formations holding the Scarpe between Arras and Arleux and to make Arras secure by driving back whatever German troops he might meet west and south of the city. 'To the best of my memory,' says Franklyn,

---

* The 3rd Brigade of the 5th Division was in Norway. The 150th Brigade of the 50th Division relieved the part of the Arras garrison which was on the Scarpe, east of the town. The 3rd Brigade of the 50th Division (the 25th) was in one of the scratch forces that Gort was improvising for his unprotected line of communication.

'he used the term "mopping up".' He was given no further orders, nor, apparently, was he told of the approach of the German armoured divisions. Having ordered the relief of the French east of Arras, Franklyn picked up General Martel, commander of the 50th Division and a leading British tank expert, and went on to Vimy to talk to General Prioux, 'pleasant, cheerful and obviously efficient'.[2]

Prioux had already been urging an attack by his three divisions, if he could recover them (half the 1st Light Armoured, as has been seen, having with difficulty returned from Belgium, had been seized on by the 1st North African at Berlaimont and with them destroyed)*. Georges had told him to discuss and arrange action with Billotte, but Billotte obviously hesitated, and Prioux thought that the dispositions of the First Army were not adequate for the situation. 'They delay the threats, but do not try to escape. We might possibly fight today [i.e. the 18th], but not tomorrow.'[3] On the 19th he received orders from Billotte which contradicted those given by Blanchard: in any case he had not yet recovered control of his divisions. On the 20th he was told to hold the line of the Scarpe, which meant that 'with death in my heart' he must countermand his orders. At this point, General Franklyn arrived.

With Prioux, Franklyn found General René Altmayer, commander of V Corps. Altmayer, 'a haggard and very worried looking' individual, showed the English general a map and told him that he, Altmayer, was proposing to attack southwards the next day, the 21st, and 'asked me if I would join in. . . . An attack on the scale proposed seemed quite outside the instructions from Gort, and when I explained this Altmayer seemed relieved. It was clear he had little faith in the project.'

The situation was all the worse in that V Corps had been in the thick of the fighting for the last week. It had only escaped behind the water-line at the last moment, a day behind III and IV Corps. Its 12th Division had been transferred to III Corps. The 43rd had been nearly annihilated. The 5th North Africans had been strengthened by the unexpected arrival of some 1,500 men from leave, but parts of it were still coming in. Altmayer had been promised the 25th Motorized from the former Seventh Army. Its infantry were said to be *en route* by train from Antwerp. But, owing to the closure of the Belgian frontier on the orders of the *préfet* of the Nord department in an effort to control the floods of Belgian civilians pressing into France, the railways had ceased to function and the trains with the 25th Division were motionless over the border. On the 20th the leading regiment, the 121st Infantry Regiment, was stuck on the railway between Torhout and Bruges with its rations dwindling. The 25th divisional commander, General Molinié, coming in advance by road with his divisional anti-tank battery and his reconnaissance group, had reached Douai on the afternoon of the 18th.

---

* Cf. p. 163. This was Colonel de Causans' combat group which was destroyed near Solesmes.

Ordered to attack and occupy Cambrai, and hold the Canal du Nord from Marcoing to Estrun, he found his objective already in the hands of Rommel's 7th Panzer, which had come up on the night of the 18th/19th. On the 20th the reconnaissance group had fallen back to the Sensée River.

The German XV Panzer Korps, the 5th Panzer on the right, the 7th Panzer, a little ahead, on the left, with the 'V' S.S. division, was moving up on both sides of the Cambrai road, towards Arras.

In view of Gort's urging, the revived energy of Billotte, and the pressure of Prioux, Blanchard on the night of the 20th sent Commandant Vautrin, one of the liaison officers with the British, to Altmayer with insistent orders to attack on the 21st, simultaneously with Franklyn. Altmayer responded that it was impossible before the 22nd, since the 25th Motorized was not in position . . .

In spite [reported Vautrin] of the fact that I had told him of General Gort's insistence that the attacks should begin next day, since in front of Douai and Arras there was only the rear of the German armoured divisions, and that the main body of normal divisions had not yet entered the area. . . . General Altmayer, who seemed tired out and thoroughly disheartened, wept silently . . . he told me that one should see things as they are, that the troops had buggered off, that he was ready to accept all the consequences of his refusal and go and get himself killed at the head of a battalion, but he would no longer continue to sacrifice the army corps of which he had already lost nearly half.[4]

Franklyn had drawn his plans, employing only British troops, with no expectation of a large operation. He could not use his tanks east of Arras because of the Scarpe. He could not send them through Arras as the streets might be blocked with débris. Therefore they must swing south of the city from the west and hope to join up with the 13th Brigade, which had relieved Prioux's 3rd Light Armoured on the Scarpe west of Biache, and would attack across the river. The 2nd Light Armoured held the line from Biache to Arleux with its dragoons and armoured cars. General Prioux was to cover the right flank of the British with what he still had of his 3rd Light Armoured. Much further west towards St Pol a few troops of British armoured cars of the 12th Lancers were doing what they could to stop the 8th Panzer Division. Franklyn's composite force (known as Frankforce) was commanded by General Martel, who accompanied the attack in an open car. It consisted of two territorial battalions of Durham Light Infantry, sixty-eight infantry tanks, of which sixteen were the heavy Mk II, but with six regiments of artillery. Though asked for, no air cover could be provided. The Air Component was on its way to England.

The attack opened in the early afternoon and swung round south of Arras. 'During the previous hours,' says Franklyn, 'accounts of the enemy's strength had become more depressing, but I still did not have any real conception of the hornet's nest into which I was about to be thrust'; and he had no knowledge that he was meeting the redoubtable Rommel. In spite of this, the attack was initially successful. The German armour was no match for the British, nor were the German anti-tank guns powerful enough to stop the I tanks. But when the British had nearly circumvented Arras, they ran into the German field artillery firing over open sights. 'No tank at that time was proof against such heavy metal and so inevitably the attack ground to a halt.'

The infantry were brought back into the villages they had captured, taking with them 400 prisoners; 'a small reward' says the general, 'for so much effort'.[5] But Rommel had lost nine medium tanks and some light and had been checked. On the British right, the 3rd Light Armoured had captured a battery at Agnez and driven back the Death's Head infantry, but heavy resistance at Berneville caused them to halt and later to retire. During the evening, there were heavy German bombing attacks on Arras and the villages, without opposition.

On the same day, further west, the 6th and 8th Panzer were also momentarily halted, but only momentarily. On the 22nd, they wheeled north, Rommel on their inner flank, with the intention of capturing the ridge on which stand the villages of Vimy and Souchez and which, sloping on the west, on the east falls away steeply and dominates the Douai plain. Here on this day stood the better part of the French First Army.

At dawn Franklyn relieved the 151st Brigade and the 3rd Light Armoured on the Dainville–Mareuil line with his 17th Brigade. He had no orders and was unable to resume the attack. No orders reached him from G.H.Q. Since, after the first conversation with Gort on the 20th, he received no other directive, and the only order for the attack was that written by himself, submitted to G.H.Q. and accepted, 'a case of the tail wagging the dog', it is impossible to make any serious conjecture as to what was in the mind of the British Commander-in-Chief before the Ypres conference on the evening of the 21st. In fact, it looks as if Gort reluctantly allowed himself to be pushed by Ironside and Mr Churchill into an operation in which he did not believe.

16 THE WIDENING OF THE GAP, *17–23 May*

The loss of the Somme

ON the evening of the 17th, General Frère, after collecting a single staff officer from the pool at Compiègne, went to Amiens, and finding the city unsuitable, moved to Roye, where he met the advance parties of his two divisions, the 23rd from the east and the 3rd Light, two Alpine regiments which had been waiting at Brest for transport to Norway. Except that he was told that the bridges on the Somme and the Crozat (otherwise St Quentin) canal were guarded by detachments of regional regiments, and that the Germans had arrived west of Bapaume, he was to all intents in the wilderness. He dispatched the advance parties to the Crozat Canal and moved his own headquarters, first to Breteuil and finally to Auneuil, a little south of Beauvais.

The 3rd Light and the 23rd, both of which were brought up by motor transport, took up their position on the Crozat Canal, from its junction with the Oise, on the 18th. There were no enemy in sight, but from St Quentin a vast mob of civilians and soldiers was hurrying south, including large numbers of young Belgians. Also there appeared fragments of General Bruché's dislocated 2nd Armoured Division. During the next two days these were collected and sent to Champlieu on the edge of the Compiègne Forest to refit.

The enemy, however, ignored the Crozat Canal. On the 17th and 18th, the Oise had been crossed from Moy to Landrecies. During darkness the German infantry slipped across the bridges concealed by the crowds of distraught refugees, took from the rear the tanks of the 2nd Armoured which General Keller had scattered up and down the right bank, and cleared the way. The slight delay imposed on Guderian by Kleist had not been serious. On the 18th, the 1st and 2nd Panzer Divisions were over the Oise. St Quentin had been passed and Péronne reached. They threw out bridgeheads across the upper Somme* at Éterpigny and Pont-les-Brie above Péronne, but an attempt at Ham was repulsed by the reconnaissance group of the 23rd Division. Péronne was occupied on the morning of the 19th and some tanks sent over the river. On the following day, when Gamelin was handing over to Weygand, the 1st Panzer moved on Albert where it captured the British battalion from Cléry. From Albert it passed on to Amiens, in flames

---

* The river was scarcely defended. The 28th Regional Regiment from Amiens and the 24th from Beauvais guarded the bridges in small groups of 20/30 men with a gun, either anti-tank or old model 75, and perhaps with an obsolete tank. The 1st Panzer appeared at Péronne on 18 May, and, having occupied the town, met on the far side a British labour battalion. The Germans did not press the attack and during the night the British were withdrawn to Albert.

from incendiary bombs, drove out two battalions of the Royal Sussex regiment, one of which suffered heavily from an air attack, and the French 28th Regional regiment, and occupied the Dury plateau to the south of the city. At the same time, the 2nd Panzer, practically un-opposed, rolled on to Abbeville, from which it swept out the British 35th Brigade and sent patrols thirty kilometres south to Eu on the Bresle. It also occupied the crossing at St Valéry-sur-Somme. There was little to oppose the two Panzer divisions. The reconnaissance group of General Sciard's I Corps, coming from Belgium, reached Moreuil on the Avre on the night of the 19th, and during the 20th fought a number of minor skirmishes with detachments of the 1st Panzer on both sides of the Somme between Corbie and Cléry. Groups of the 4th Colonial and 7th North African Divisions began to arrive, and similar passages of arms took place hereabouts, without much consequence, but the French were the weaker. Again the worst was the uncertainty at the head, the inability to act with speed and decision.

Late on the 18th, G.Q.G.N.E. had issued an order,[1] addressed to Seventh Army, Sixth Army and de Gaulle's detachment, which directed the establishment of a barrage on the Crozat Canal and on the Somme from Ham to Amiens. The Seventh Army was to avoid a disposition in line but to hold the bridges 'mined and ready to be blown' with anti-tank blocks and with the main bodies of the divisions echelonned in depth and prepared to counter-attack. The 2nd Region, which as has been seen had no serious means of action, was to prolong the barrage to the sea, and use the 21st Division from Belgium when it arrived. (The reconnaissance group of this division, or at least its motorized element, reached Abbeville on the 19th and went on to Blangy.)* The last paragraph of the order drew attention to the forward hazardous situation of the German armoured korps and the overstretched columns of motorized infantry; it ordered de Gaulle to attack north of Laon, and Billotte to throw in from the north all he could of the cavalry corps. But the order was scarcely peremptory; it was a message of slender hope rather than a command; it was no spur to action. In fact, as one commentator has observed, every line implicitly recognizes that the role of the Seventh Army will be defensive, and on the 19th, Frère was ordered to hold the Somme Line as far as Abbeville. The order 'mortgaged the future and accepted the enemy's initiative'. This is reflected in the build-up of the Seventh Army.[2]

On the same day that Frère reached Auneuil, G.Q.G.N.E. warned the railways they would have to move eight formations from Army Group Two to the Aisne–Somme region. A day later, one army corps with its constituent troops and two divisions were added. The railways rose nobly to the demand. Altogether, between 18 May and 4 June, they moved thirty-two infantry divisions in defiance of vicious bombing.

---

* The fate of the main body of the 21st is narrated below, p. 191.

But, to defend the detraining points and the junctions on the main lines, anti-aircraft guns had to be removed from less vital stations, and in any event the guns were not powerful enough to deter the enemy bombers and were far too few. The enemy bombing was bad, but more alarming was the fact that the German armour was in the forefront of the battle. The French staffs feared that the thrusting enemy might even raid railheads as the reinforcing divisions arrived. Therefore they withdrew the detraining points of the divisions urgently required on the Somme for the counter-offensive across the river, and the infantry detrained at absurd distances from what should be their jumping-off line.

The first two divisions from the east, the 19th from Dannemarie near Belfort and the 7th North African from Valdahon (Doubs), moved on the 17th. On the 19th, two battalions of the first, meant to come in on the left of the 3rd Light at Ham, detrained in the neighbourhood of Compiègne, sixty kilometres from their destination. The battalions that followed during the next three days were landed at various points of a wide arc even more remote, the extreme being L'Isle-Adam, eighty-six kilometres. The arrival of the 7th North African was even later. Although the first two battalions alighted on the 19th at St Just-en-Chaussée, forty kilometres from Amiens, the division was not at full strength until the 24th. The movement of three colonial divisions from the east, the 4th, 5th and 7th, was no more expeditious. After the first four battalions, six arrived on the 20th, twelve on the 21st, seventeen on the 22nd and the last six on the 23rd and 24th, the majority of them at a considerable distance from where they were needed.

On the morning of the 21st, Guderian's 10th Panzer Division relieved the 1st and 2nd Panzer in their bridge-heads at Amiens, Picquigny, Abbeville and St Valéry-sur-Somme, and the 1st and 2nd began to move northward, leaving light but effective defences.

Once again the inability to read the enemy's plans led to indecision and delay. Except for the seven armoured divisions, the country between the Scarpe and the Somme was empty, though there were innumerable assemblies of civilians and stragglers. (It was in the middle of one of these that a troop of the British 12th Lancers caught sight of a battery of German medium field guns on the move and blew it to pieces before it could extricate itself.) During the 17th to 24th, small bodies of French and British soldiers made good their escape. But rumour played the devil with the high command. Hence the opportunity, recognized as the only one, of cutting in behind the Panzer Korps was not seized. On the 22nd, von Wietersheim's Motorized Korps began to relieve the 10th Panzer, which then followed the 2nd Panzer northwards. The 2nd Motorized Division now held the Somme below Amiens, the 13th up to Péronne, and on the 23rd the 29th Motorized temporarily occupied the Amiens bridgehead while normal infantry divisions were coming up.

[2]

The end of the 21st Division and the loss of Boulogne

On 18 May, the 21st Division of General Lanquetot was ordered to move from the Ghent area to the new Seventh Army at Beauvais. It began to entrain at Thielt on the 20th. Its reconnaissance group started at once by road and was therefore able to cross the Somme between Abbeville and St Valéry, and escaped the embraces of the 2nd Panzer Division on the 20th. The main body of the 21st was less lucky. General Lanquetot, also travelling by road, found the Germans already in occupation of Abbeville. He turned back to Boulogne, from where he got in touch with Army Group One and was told to defend the approaches to the town on the line Samer–Neufchâtel. Owing to there being only enough rolling stock for less than two thirds of the division, the whole of the 137th Infantry Regiment and one battalion of the 48th did not entrain. They were eventually sent to Dunkirk and attached to the 68th Division. Also, one battalion of the 65th was stopped at Merville and fought near Strazeele on the 27th, while Lanquetot was able to halt some batteries and have them put to holding the bridges on the Aa between Watten and Arques. But other batteries, 75s and anti-tank guns, were detrained south of Boulogne at Nesle-Neufchâtel and were destroyed here by the 2nd Panzer on the 22nd. Another group was caught by the same division still on the train, and wiped out. Two battalions of the 48th detrained at Berguette, near Aire-sur-Lys, some sixty kilometres east of Boulogne, about midnight on 22nd/23rd, set out for Boulogne, fought a couple of small engagements with German infantry and armoured cars, but were at last rounded up during the morning. Of the last two battalions, both of the 65th, one was knocked out by the 1st Panzer on the 22nd, on the road from Desvres to Boulogne, the other beat off a Panzer attack at Desvres and tried to reach Boulogne by a circuitous road but was cut off and dealt with on the 24th, also by the 1st Panzer, which was making for Calais. On the 22nd, General Lanquetot got into touch with Admiral Abrial, who as 'Amiral Nord'* was responsible for coastal defence and who declared that the holding of Boulogne was of vital importance, but could offer no help. Boulogne citadel was held by some regional infantry, by five naval batteries of various calibres and by two British Guards battalions which had come over the Channel from Dover that morning, and beat off two attacks during the afternoon and evening. There was also some support from British light bombers.[3]

During the night, the German armour encircled the town and cut the road northward, down which a relief force from Calais was expected, and on the 23rd the units of the 2nd Panzer began to close in. The Fort de la Crèche was taken in the morning, after being deluged with smoke-

* 'Nord' is the sector north-east of a line from the mouth of the Coussnon at Mont St Michel to the Start Point.

shell. British and French destroyers kept up a constant bombardment. It was all in vain. About five in the afternoon the British were driven off Mont St Lambert east of the town, and during the night the majority of the British Guards and Marines were taken off by destroyers, with great difficulty and heavy loss. The town was now in flames. Some evacuation still continued. There were regrettable incidents between French and English, due to misguided orders. Lanquetot and his territorials, Marines and sailors fought on, but, still able to reach Dunkirk by telephone, he was given to understand that Amiral Nord could spare him no more destroyers. By this time, two destroyers and one torpedo-boat had been sunk and others damaged. By seven in the evening, the enemy's grip was tightening. The Calais Gate was still holding out, as was a party of Welsh Guards. On the morning of the 25th the Germans sent in an ultimatum that they would destroy the town if the Calais Gate, this last citadel, were not surrendered. General Lanquetot warned Dunkirk, then gave in. A few, very few officers and men succeeded in making their escape.

The British brigade commander, when ordered to re-embark his force on the evening of the 23rd, was unable to inform General Lanquetot in the upper town of what was about to happen, owing, it is said, to the occupation of the ground between the upper and lower towns by the Germans. This is thought by French historians to be debatable.

[3]

The loss of Arras and its consequences

While General Franklyn was redisposing his handful of troops in an attempt to prevent the overwhelming of the Arras garrison, Molinié's 25th Division had at last got away from Belgium. General Altmayer now ordered the attack across the Sensée River. The attacking force was to consist of five battalions, three from the 121st Infantry Regiment, and one each from the other two regiments, supported by the whole corps artillery, three reconnaissance groups and one battalion of Renault tanks. The intention was to reach Cambrai, about fifteen kilometres south of the Sensée, and there to organize a solid defensive centre from which further attacks could set out. After this, the two other regiments and everything available from the 5th North African would move forward to the Cambrai–Marquion road. But on the night of the 22nd/23rd, the other two regiments, the 38th and 92nd, had not arrived: they were marching from Douai, their road lighted by the blaze of the petrol dump at Courchelettes.

The attack started at 6 in the morning, led by the armoured cars and tanks. The infantry started at 9. They reached the line Blécourt–Abancourt–Cuvillers. There was little resistance on the ground but there were fierce attacks from the air. About 9.30, a radio message from the commander of the German 32nd Division[4] asking for help was picked up, and soon afterwards the attacking force was assaulted by groups of twenty-five to thirty bombers, followed by fighters with machine-guns. The reconnaissance groups were pinned to the ground. '*Notre offensive est complètement ratée, tuée dans l'oeuf.*'[5] Moving slowly, in small groups, the infantry reached the armoured cars about 4 in the afternoon, but got no further. The reconnaissance groups and the tank battalion were withdrawn. The latter had lost eight of thirteen machines. The reconnaissance groups suffered in the same way. The 121st Infantry Regiment lost 500. Though it held a large bridgehead, it had not reached Cambrai. Early in the morning of the 23rd, having learned that the British could now not help, General Altmayer ordered the 25th Division infantry to be brought back behind the canal.

The French were chagrined by the British reluctance to carry on the battle. But there were urgent reasons. The situation of General Franklyn's command (Frankforce) had changed. Hoth's XV Panzer Korps and the S.S. Division had swung round Arras and moved northward, attempting to turn the defenders' line. Following suit, Prioux's light armoured units moved northward, as the 5th and 7th Panzer moved towards Béthune. The 2nd Light Armoured, relieved on the left of the British on the night of the 22nd/23rd by the 5th North African, retired to the Haute-Deule and La Bassée Canals above Pont-à-Vendin. The 1st Light Armoured, to which the corps commander had attached the last twenty-one machines of the 3rd Light Armoured (1st and 2nd Cuirassiers), fought the pressing German armour round Mont-St Eloi, Souchez and eventually on the 23rd beat them off at Noeux-les-Mines before retiring behind the canals.

These movements left the Arras garrison in the point of an acute angle between the 17th Brigade facing west and the 150th and 13th facing south, the 150th along the Scarpe from Arras, the 13th* on the Scarpe as far as Biache, where it was in touch with the 14th Zouaves. The 14th Zouaves, with all three battalions in line, was on the water from Biache to Arleux and a little forward of the British. In the evening on the 23rd, the German 12th Division, which had come up during the day on the left of the 32nd, crossed the Scarpe and drove the 13th Brigade back on Gavrelle, which lies under the Vimy Ridge. Late that night General Franklyn, who had seen his brigades becoming more and more imperilled and had received no orders from G.H.Q., telephoned to Wahagnies and was ordered to bring his infantry out. There were now only two roads left, one of which, that through Douai, had been cut by the enemy, while the other, through Lens, was also reported to be cut. However, travelling radiator to tail-board, the whole of the force got clear during the night, and by morning were behind the Haute-Deule Canal. At the same time the Welsh Guards in Arras were withdrawn, but they had to fight their way out.

---

* The 13th Brigade had only two battalions, the third having been lent to the 151st Brigade which had had severe losses in the attack on the 21st.

The retreat of the British in turn bared the right of the 5th North African, causing the 14th Zouaves to fall back to the Sensée Canal from Moulinet to Corbehem. Altmayer's V Corps was therefore now in a pronounced salient, of which the bottom was the canal from Aubigny to the IV Corps at Bouchain. This was the night of 24/25 May.

Hatching a forlorn hope

ALMOST as soon as he had taken over on 20 May, Weygand, at La Ferté with Georges, met General Dill, who had brought with him from London the Cabinet's instructions, which, as has been seen, after talking with Gort, Ironside had much modified. Weygand, however, now spoke on the telephone to Billotte and ordered him to attack southwords towards Cambrai, regardless of loss. He also instructed General Besson, who on the 19th had taken over command of Touchon's Sixth Army and Frère's embryo Seventh as Army Group Three, to push the Seventh Army northward to meet Billotte's advance to Cambrai, using whatever troops were in contact with the enemy without waiting for the rest to arrive. He then decided that he must meet the commanders in the north, including King Leopold, and would fly up next day.*

For reasons that have not been explained, a great number of Weygand's messages never arrived. Also, the plane ordered for him at Le Bourget was not ready. When at last he set out, he was brought down at Norrent Fontès, an airfield which had been abandoned two days earlier. At last, after considerable trouble, he was picked up and driven to Ypres, where he met King Leopold and General van Overstraeten. To the king and his A.D.C., he insisted that the Belgian Army was too strung out and that the British were too far east. He recognized that the Belgians were too poorly armed and equipped to take the offensive. He therefore asked them to occupy more of the British line, so as to allow the latter to withdraw two divisions, which could then be employed with French divisions in a counter-offensive southwards. To enable them to do this he suggested that the Belgian Army should abandon its present position and retire to the much shorter line of the Yser. Van Overstraeten objected that the Belgian Army was much shaken by its repeated withdrawals: he feared that another, which must be carried out by night, would complete the disintegration. As in 1914, the withdrawal to the last fragment of Belgian soil would be bad for morale. There was also the annexed problem of supply, especially the removal of ammunition to new dumps. And there was the frightful imbroglio of the Belgian civilian refugees, which had been complicated by the closing of the French frontier on the previous day and the stoppage on the railways. On top of all this, there was only enough flour for a

---

* The last moves of the withdrawal of Army Group One on the night of 18th/19th had brought the Belgian Army back to the Ghent Canal from Terneuzen on the Scheldt estuary to a little north of Ghent, which it covered on the east as far as Wettern, returning to the Escaut River at Ecke. It then held the river to Audenarde, where it linked up with the British 44th Division.

fortnight, since all the Belgian reserves had been sent to France. The Belgians therefore proposed that they should retire towards the coast, from which they could be supplied.

Weygand countered that this was simply inviting disaster and was impossible. At this point Billotte arrived with General Fagalde,* part of whose XVI Corps was still on the Scheldt estuary. Although, on his return to Paris, Weygand was to say that Billotte was full of confidence, he was in fact a harassed and depressed man, who acknowledged that the German armour was invincible and that Blanchard's army was worn out. '*Nous crevons derrière les obstacles,*' he had said to Ironside, and he had not recovered. However, he accepted the essential plan of a counter-offensive by a joint Franco-British force, but no agreement with the Belgians had been reached before his departure.

Lord Gort had not been present—Weygand's message had gone astray. The British commander was at last found and brought to Ypres about 8 in the evening. He had already considered a form of Weygand's proposal and discussed it with Ironside, but had concluded that, however desirable it might be in principle, the southward attack was not practicable except, as he said, in the form of sorties. Now he was driven into acquiescence, since the only alternative was to fall back on the Channel ports; Abbeville had gone, and Boulogne and Calais were already in jeopardy. So he agreed that if the Belgians would take over the British left division (the 44th) and the French his two right divisions (the 2nd and 48th), the attack southward might be possible, and that the Franco-British combination would act on the 26th. The Belgians now agreed to cover the British left flank by with-drawing to the Lys, beginning on the night 22nd/23rd, and extending their front to Menin, while the French put two divisions in the line from Maulde to Bourghelles (thus freeing two British divisions), and the British swung back their left to Halluin.

It was a compromise, a poor one and no solution, for, whereas the Yser Line from Ypres northward would shorten and strengthen the defence, the line on the Lys would be a vulnerable re-entrant. If the hinge on the Lys at Halluin-Menin broke, the Belgian Army would be driven northward and a gap opened which the British would be unable to fill. 'You must do it, sir,' said Fagalde to Gort. And as he took his leave of the king, Gort was heard to say: 'It's a bad job.' Billotte was deeply despondent.[1]

More adversity followed. On his way back to Béthune, Billotte was involved in a car accident and two days later died without having recovered consciousness.

At Calais Weygand found that the aerodrome was so badly damaged as to be unusable. He drove to Dunkirk, where Admiral Abrial put him

---

* General Fagalde had been a liaison officer with the B.E.F. in 1914, and in 1918, military attaché in London.

on a small torpedo boat which eventually landed him at Cherbourg. He did not reach Paris until 10 in the morning of the 22nd, and it may be that he was only now fully informed of the loss of the Somme. It is probable that he received no more than a garbled account of the final arrangements, by telephone from General Champon, the French liaison officer at Belgian headquarters, who had been present at Ypres. This would explain the account of his intentions which he gave Churchill and Dill, who with Reynaud came to Paris this morning, outlining a Belgian withdrawal to the Yser, with an Anglo-French attack towards Cambrai and Bapaume at the earliest possible moment. He added that Besson's Army Group Three, which 'is advancing upon Amiens and forming a line along the Somme, should strike northward and join hands with the British divisions who are attacking southward.'

The consequence of this was a Churchillian epistle to Lord Gort, inflating Weygand's directions to read 'at the earliest possible moment certainly tomorrow [i.e. the 23rd, although the agreement was for the 26th] with about eight divisions'.[2]

The failure of Gort to meet Weygand at Ypres on the 21st undoubtedly had serious repercussions, made worse by Billotte's accident. Both men were alive to the need for action. But what action?

While Weygand was landing at Cherbourg on the 22nd, Lord Gort, who had moved his command-post to Premesques between Lille and Armentières on the previous evening, was visited, at 7.30 a.m., by Blanchard and General Fournel de la Laurencie, whose III Corps was to take over the British line from Maulde to Bourghelles. (Blanchard had moved his First Army Headquarters from Lens to Estaires on the Lys.) At Premesques, the plans for the attack on the 26th were discussed. After General Pownall, who did most of the talking, and Blanchard had agreed to the combination of the British III Corps (General Sir Ronald Adam) with Altmayer's V Corps, Gort 'with some deliberation opened the folding map which he carried in his pocket, spread it out on the desk, and tapping Cambrai with his pencil said slowly and emphatically, looking straight at Blanchard: "*Il faut tuer les Boches et il faut les tuer ici....*" Through the haze of theory in which he had lived, the chief's simple summing-up made, I think, a deep impression on General Blanchard. . . . I could not help overhearing later in the day General Blanchard's words to Colonel Alombert: "*Tiens, il a bien raison, Lord Gort*".'[3]

[2]

Weygand's exposition to Dill was not consonant with the facts. As yet the Seventh Army scarcely existed west of Ham. None of the divisions for this attack were on this day concentrated or in position. Between Péronne and St Valéry, the Germans were not in great strength, but there were practically no French. Why the former did not move forward out of their small bridgeheads (they had been drawn back since the 20th) was not understood until the 22nd, when the French radio picked up repeated German wireless directives: '*Nicht Abbeville, Calais. Nicht Abbeville, Calais.*'[4] Its meaning was confirmed by the fighting round Boulogne.

During these days, wrote General Grandsard, who was to attack Amiens, X Corps received a quantity of oddments, some from the rear, others withdrawn from the north amid a flood of refugees who blocked the roads. . . . 'On 20 May, one battalion from the 20th Division, which was at Breteuil, fifty-four kilometres from its destination, with no anti-tank weapons, elements from the reconnaissance group of the 9th Division, the 54th Machine-Gun Battalion, and one battery from XXV Corps (to go into action near Crèvecœur), a dozen 25-mm. anti-tank guns without teams, which were to be split up between two divisions, an armoured detachment consisting of two Hotchkiss, one Somua, one armoured car. Finally the 17th Reconnaissance Group was put under X Corps orders, but no one ever succeeded in running it down. By 22 May, when the aim of our operations was on the point of being changed, the corps had never been able either to build up a front or secure its flanks. The 7th Colonial was stretched from Poix to Esserteaux, occupying of course only the main crossroads on the line, with, at Granvilliers, twenty-nine kilometres north of Beauvais, a single company, this was to resist an outflanking movement which had been reported that morning. The rest of the division was still on the march.'[5]

Thus, at the moment when General Weygand was instigating Blanchard and Gort to move southward in force and join hands with the advancing Seventh Army, there were in fact no hands for them to take. Weygand's orders for the 23rd only reached Seventh Army Headquarters on the afternoon of the 22nd and were then detailed to X and I Corps, the former to clear Amiens, the latter to capture the Somme bridges east of Amiens and push its reconnaissance groups out to the line Corbie–Albert–Curlu.

On this day, the 22nd, General Frère lost his left formation, X Corps, which became, first, the nucleus of Group A, and then, with the arrival from Alsace of the headquarter staff of General Ihler's IX Corps, the right of the newly created Tenth Army. Of this army, the command was given to another of the apparently inexhaustible pool of retired cavalry generals, Robert Altmayer, elder brother of the despairing commander of V Corps. 'I cannot say,' wrote Brigadier Beauman, 'that I ever had much confidence in his leadership', a comment which the history of the Tenth Army indeed justifies. General Grandsard's command had consisted nominally of the 7th Colonial and 21st Divisions, and a dozen 75s from different regiments. That, on this day, the 21st Division was being extinguished round Boulogne, he was not to know until the morrow, when the 5th Colonial was allotted as a substitute, its main body still on its way from the east. To capture Amiens, Grandsard had only the 7th Colonial Division to which was added a squadron of Somua from the newly formed 7th Cuirassier Group under Colonel de Langle de Cary.* The capture of Amiens and its bridges was to be the preface to the crossing of the Somme by de Gaulle's 4th Armoured on both sides of the city and the clearing of the triangle Amiens–Doullens–Albert.

On the right of the 7th Colonial, I Corps was ordered to take Corbie and Bray. I Corps had four battalions of the 4th Colonial and three of the 7th North African. On its right it had the 19th Division in the angle of the Somme at Péronne. None of the attacking units appears to have been less than fifteen kilometres from the river.

X Corps put in two battalions of the 57th Senegalese. One of them received its orders at 5.30 a.m. and was then twenty-three kilometres from its jumping-off line. It was able to attack in the afternoon, supported by some of the Somua. It did not reach Dury, which is four kilometres from the southern edge of the city; and of the eighteen tanks, twelve were destroyed or crippled. The reconnaissance group which attacked Picquigny failed to drive the Germans off the south side of the river. Of I Corps on the right, no element reached the river, but the 4th Colonial pushed down to the great marshalling yard at Longueau. For the main part, however, the German outposts were not even forced off the Roman road along the ridge of the Santerre. On the right, two regiments of the 19th Division, which had detrained between sixty and seventy-five kilometres from the Somme, only reached Rosières and Chaulnes. On their right, the Germans, already over the river at Pont-les-Brie and Saint-Christ, now snatched Epénancourt.

Thus the fighting on the 23rd was everywhere unsatisfactory. Army and corps commanders became urgent in their orders for the 24th. Every directive was completed by moral appeals. Every cliché found a place: 'le sort de la guerre', 'aucune considération (longueur des étapes, manque de sommeil, etc.) ne doit compter que celle de la réussite de l'opération'. In front of Amiens, the 7th Colonial was again stopped short of Dury. The 7th North African cleared most of the ridge and reached the Somme in the Morcourt–Méricourt bend. Away on the right, the 19th Division got a small footing on the St Quentin road.

---

* It came from the Arpajon A.F.V. centre and had two squadrons of Somua and two of Renault, and one battalion of Dismounted Dragoons, but no artillery.

18 CONFUSED DISCUSSION,
23–26 May

The German 'halt'

DURING 23 May, General von Rundstedt, considering the situation of his armies, decided to close up his armour before continuing the attack northward, and from that evening von Kluge's Fourth Army, that is the von Kleist and Hoth Groups with II and VIII Korps, were ordered not to cross the general line north-west of Arras, Lens–Béthune–Aire–St Omer–Gravelines, the Canal Line. And although there were minor infringements, pressure on this sector was less, until the injunction was lifted by the German Fourth Army order of 9 p.m. on the 26th, with effect from early on the 27th. Much has been made of this order and its relevance to the evacuation from Dunkirk.[1] Guderian fumed, and claimed that, but for this unreasonable interference, he would have secured the capture of the whole B.E.F. and First French Army. On the other hand, Rommel welcomed the halt, since it allowed him to carry out the maintenance and repair of his armour.* Considering the fact that the armour of XV, XLI and XIX Korps had in fact done very little fighting of a serious nature, in spite of their spectacular advance, the extent of their casualties is surprising: 50 per cent for the Kleist group. It is clear that a good part of these are mechanical breakdowns.

[2]

On the evening of 24 May, the outline of the allied northern armies bore the shape of a gigantic shoulder with a fist at the bottom of the arm, the edge of the shoulder being the coast-line and the fist the tangle of water-lines from Maulde round to Corbehem.

Following their acceptance of the Weygand plan, the Belgian Army began its preliminary withdrawal, that to the Lys, on the night 22nd/23rd, and accomplished it without serious trouble, though the British 44th division at Audenarde had difficulties, owing to a German attack on the 22nd, a part of what, to O.K.H., was 'Reichenau's private fight with heavy losses and no serious advantage'.[2] The withdrawal was completed on the night of 23rd/24th.

The main Belgian Army was now on the Lys *dérivation* canal; the

---

* Although armoured divisions were engaged, the greater part of the fighting was done by the infantry. Guderian's armour saw little if any serious fighting except on 14–15 May. Apart from the fighting at Arras, Rommel's armour was chiefly employed in the pursuit of infantry broken and scattered by air attacks. All the river crossings were, of course, carried out by infantry. The German principle was that attacks on fortified points by armoured units should be avoided if possible, though the decision as to whether armour should lead the infantry, accompany or follow it depended on the enemy's dispositions.

area from its junction with the Leopold Canal to Breskens was patrolled by cavalry and cyclist detachments. To the Lys at Deynze, the Canal de Dérivation was defended by seven divisions. From Deynze to Menin, the river-line was occupied by four divisions with three in support. Royal headquarters was at St André, west of Bruges. The Belgian Army thus faced south-east, whereas the British II Corps covering Halluin faced north-east. It was not an easy position to defend. The re-entrant was undoubtedly weak. About here the river is perhaps twenty yards wide and winds considerably. Courtrai stands on the east bank and dominates the west side. The line was, of course, longer and weaker than that of the Yser, and, short of a miracle, if the Germans attacked at the southern end, the Belgian right would be separated from the British left.

From Halluin to Bourghelles the British had four divisions, the 4th, 3rd, 1st, and 42nd, the II Corps of General Brooke. At Bourghelles was the left of the French First Army, General de la Laurencie's III Corps, with the 12th and 32nd Divisions, as far as Rumegies, then, under the command of General Béjard, the former commander of the Maubeuge fortifications, a group made up of three battalions of the 2nd North African and whatever elements had escaped from the Maubeuge defences, the 54th, 84th and 87th Fortress Regiments, backed by an artillery group from III Corps troops. On their right, along the Escaut past Condé to Escaupont, was the 1st Division of General de Camas. From Escaupont, through Anzin to Prouvy, stood General Aymes's IV Corps, with the 15th Division on the left, the 4th on the right. Then came, round the peak of the salient, General Altmayer's V Corps with Molinié's 25th Division, which had been engaged on the previous day in the attempt to reach Cambrai. The 25th Division joined with the 5th North African at Aubigny-au-Bac. Of General Mesny's division, only two regiments still existed, the 24th Tunisians on the left; the 14th Zouaves lined the Sensée Canal to the point where it joined the Scarpe at Corbehem just below Douai. From this point northward, and then westward to the coast at Gravelines, detachments and improvised formations, French and British, faced the temporarily halted Panzer groups.

The Deule Canal, which meets the La Bassée Canal at Bauvin, was manned by part of the British 139th Brigade, by Colonel Tardu's 106th Infantry Regiment, lent by General de la Laurencie from the 12th Division, and by part of the 3rd Light Armoured. Between Bauvin and La Bassée was the remains of the Moroccan division, supported by General Vernillat's 43rd Division, now no more than a couple of companies of *chasseurs* with a few machine-guns, mortars and three anti-tank guns, and the two battalions of the 131st Infantry Regiment, which by being at the tail of 9th Division column had missed the disaster of the rest of the division on the 17th and 18th. The British 2nd Division, just relieved by the French III Corps, was arriving on the canal from La Bassée to Merville. In front was the Tarrit group, the last fragment of the 1st North African which had escaped from the fight at Maubeuge. It was now one assorted regiment, with four regional battalions and five companies of light tanks attached.

Beyond Hinges, four kilometres north of Béthune, the British were bringing in the advanced groups of the three relieved divisions, the 2nd, 48th and 44th, to occupy the area held by improvised forces, Merville, Hazebrouck, Houdeghem, Cassel, Wormhoudt, Bergues, not in fact the Canal Line proper. The canal (Aire–St Omer–Watten–Gravelines) was occupied only from Watten northwards: St Omer had been lost on the morning of the 23rd. Up to the 24th the only body of troops hereabouts was a battalion of 310 Infantry Regiment in Vauban's citadel at Gravelines, supported by four 155-mm. naval guns, and a battalion of the 6th Green Howards from the 23rd Division. On the 24th the line of the Aa River was reinforced by the battalions of the 21st Division, which had not been involved in the disaster at Boulogne, that is, the whole of the 137th Infantry Regiment, one battalion of the 65th and another of the 48th. There were also some British heavy gunners, who fought as infantry at St Pierre-Brouck.

Almost at once the enemy effected a crossing of the Aa at St Nicolas and pushed out a bridgehead. Further north, at Gravelines itself, a determined German attack was repulsed with the help of four British tanks.

Above Watten, held by the 1/48th battalion, the Germans were across at St Omer, Blaringhem and Aire, where they were with difficulty being contained by British cavalry units.

Looked at on the map, the weakest parts of the Allied position were the right of the Belgian line between Courtrai and Menin and the three corps of the French Army in the Condé–Bouchain–Douai salient. Until the latter was enlarged by the attack now being planned for the 26th, these formations would become more and more endangered.

[3]

After the withdrawal of the Seventh Army from the region of Breda and the islands, General Fagalde's XVI Corps,* the 60th and 68th divisions, had been left guarding the southern bank of the estuary from Terneuzen to Zeebrugge. At Ypres on 21 May, Fagalde had heard Weygand outline his plan for the double attacks against the Panzer lines of communication. XVI Corps was to be under Belgian orders. On 23 May, Fagalde was directed to move his headquarters and one of his divisions immediately, to the line of the River Aa from Gravelines to St Omer, to protect the rear of the Belgian Army, leaving the other division in the neighbourhood of Bruges. On this day, the 2nd Panzer Division was already finishing off the scattered elements of the 21st

---

* The 68th had lost the better part of the 224th Infantry Regiment and a group of 75s at Walcheren on 17 May. Of the 60th, pretty well the whole of the 271st had been wiped out on the same day, at South Beveland.

Division outside Boulogne, the 10th Panzer was investing Calais, and the 1st was advancing towards the Canal Line. On learning that the Germans were already on the Aa at St Omer, Fagalde decided to dispatch the 68th Division only as far as the Yser. But on the following morning, a telegram from Weygand appointed him Commander of all the ground forces in the area Boulogne–Calais–Dunkirk, under the authority of Admiral Abrial, including his own XVI Corps and the 21st Division, of whose annihilation as a formation G.Q.G. was still ignorant. A further message instructed him to leave the 60th Division in Belgium. The 68th reached the Yser on the evening of 23rd and the next day came on to the Mardyck Canal line half-way between Dunkirk and the Aa.

On his arrival at Dunkirk, Fagalde found that, beside the XVI Corps, he could dispose of the 272nd Demi-Brigade, consisting of three battalions of reserve troops from the garrison of the Flanders Fortified Sector, with two training battalions, three labour regiments (mostly old soldiers of 1914–18), two batteries of anti-tank guns, and the remains of the 21st Division, i.e. the five infantry battalions, six batteries of 75s and five of 155s. Except for the 21st Division units, all were indifferently armed. In the labour regiments there were not more than twenty-five rifles to a battalion.[3]

[4]

The history of the period between the evening of the 23rd/24th, when Frankforce and the Arras garrison began their withdrawal, up to the night of the 25th/26th is one of the utmost confusion of crossed lines, misinformation and absence of information, of contradiction, of leaping to conclusions without verification, followed by suspicion, distrust and accusation. In part this is due to the failure of Weygand either to appoint General Blanchard to replace the dying Billotte *par interim* or to nominate a more senior general, if such were available. Blanchard had not been present at the Ypres conference and only knew of the arrangements at second hand, probably from the liaison officer attached to King Leopold, General Champon, and he had no authority to direct either the Belgian Army or the B.E.F. Further, he could not speak to either Weygand or Georges, since the direct telephone (and telegraph) had been cut with the loss of Abbeville. All messages must now pass via Belgian headquarters and London.

During the night 23rd/24th, Weygand telegraphed to Blanchard: 'Seventh Army on the evening 23rd has reached the Somme, Amiens, Ham. On 24th, offensive action supported by *forces mécaniques* in the direction Albert–Bapaume.'[4] This was obviously a spur to the northern commanders to act. It was probably in reply to this that Blanchard telegraphed to Weygand a message to the effect that the British (i.e. Frankforce) had 'carried out, on its own initiative, a retreat of forty kilometres towards the ports, etc.'

On the morning of the 24th, at the usual conference in Reynaud's office, Weygand turned up obviously disturbed. As he came in he said to Baudouin: 'The situation is very serious. The English are turning back to the ports instead of attacking to the south.' And he reported to Reynaud that he had received a telegram with this information from Champon. The British move was, he said, contrary to the formal orders he had given. He added that after a telephone conversation he had had with Ironside in London on the previous evening he was not surprised. 'I could have smacked his face. It is impossible to command with an army which remains dependent on London for operations. Lord Gort has certainly not taken on himself to modify the disposal of his army.'[5]

Weygand and Reynaud then drafted a telegram to Churchill with the unverified statement that on his own initiative Gort had withdrawn his army twenty-five miles towards the ports, and so forth. At 4.30 in the afternoon, Weygand sent off a telegram to Blanchard anticipating the worst. 'If the retreat to the Haute Deule Canal makes the commanded manœuvre impossible, try to constitute as extensive a bridgehead as possible covering Dunkirk.'[6] In the evening he repeated all this and much more to Baudouin, including the suggestion that Paris could not be defended if the northern armies were forced to surrender and the French were left with no more than fifty divisions. Baudouin saw Reynaud later, and another telegram was sent off to London.

[5]

Between 5 and 6 on the afternoon of the 23rd, General de la Laurencie, whose III Corps had just taken over the line of the British 2nd and 48th Divisions from Bourghelles to Maulde, had become highly uneasy about the situation in which not only his four divisions but the whole of the First Army stood. He went over from his headquarters at Phalempin to those of First Army a mile or so away at Attiches to try to find out the Army Commander's intentions. He was considerably disturbed by the lack of direction. At Attiches he found General Prioux, with Blanchard and their chiefs of staff. 'I did not,' he says, 'discover any clear or firm resolve which the circumstances demanded, and I went back to my command-post having lost all confidence.'[7] Later in the evening he went back once more to Attiches. 'Profoundly shaken, I *begged* General Blanchard to study a withdrawal first to the Scarpe, then to the Lys, so that we could escape from the grip that was closing on us.' Blanchard replied that it was impossible to reach any agreement with the English and that it was difficult to regulate a movement as complicated as this one of withdrawing the strength of three army corps through so narrow a throat.

La Laurencie was so disturbed that he sat up through the night working out plans which he sent off to Army Headquarters between 3 and 4 in the morning. At the foot, he added that unity of command was vital: either Blanchard took over command of Army Group One or Gort did. 'We must disengage; today we can still do it, tomorrow it will undoubtedly be too late.' In the anguished notes he dictated to his P.A. at 6 on this morning of the 24th, he said: 'Unless we want to be driven to capitulation in the open field, the retreat of III Corps is unavoidable. The troops are in great form, but they are beginning to be short of ammunition and Army confesses that it cannot supply it, since all the dumps and wagons in the area have been emptied.'[8]

Blanchard was probably not the man Weygand would in any circumstances have appointed as commander of Army Group One had a more dominant figure been available and the choice been free. He had certain disabilities. He had been a professor at the École Supérieure de Guerre and he was a professor rather than a man of action. He was shy, and if he had made no errors, he had shown no positive qualities. It probably embarrassed him to take over two foreign armies before he was formally appointed. General Brooke of the British II Corps saw him on the morning of 24th at G.H.Q. at Premesques. 'He was standing studying the map and I gathered the impression that he might as well have been staring at a blank wall. . . . He gave me the impression of a man whose brain has ceased to function. . . . The blows that had fallen on us in quick succession had left him "punch drunk" and unable to register events. I . . . felt that if he were to take over the tiller, it would not be long before we were on the rocks.' Blanchard certainly appears to have been suffering from the 'mounting tide of despair', which, Marc Bloch wrote, 'seemed to lead to a kind of sleepy lethargy'. It was this that induced a subordinate general officer, almost certainly La Laurencie, to say in Bloch's hearing: 'Do as you please, General, but at least do something!'[9]

At 10 in the morning of the 24th, the persistent gadfly, La Laurencie, turned up again at Attiches, where he found Blanchard in conference with Colonel Humbert, the Chief of Army Group One staff, and Commandant Fauvelle, head of the Operations Bureau of Army Group One. There was an hour's argument, during which Blanchard with much bitterness said: 'The English Army thinks of nothing but using us to help them sail away the quicker.' La Laurencie protested vigorously at Blanchard's attitude, ending with: 'In any case, if General Gort refuses to take part in your scheme, you have only to put the First Army under his command and thus secure unity.' La Laurencie says that Commandant Fauvelle shared and approved his views. Finally Blanchard went off with Fauvelle to Premesques to talk to Lord Gort.

On the previous day, the 23rd, Gort had received a copy of a forceful telegram from Churchill to Reynaud, calling for vigorous pressure on all army commanders to act. Gort says[10] that he was not sure that the situation could be weighed up except on the spot and asked that General Dill should fly over at once. Most of the information about the French was inaccurate, and on this day the whole of the B.E.F. were closely engaged with the enemy, and until reliefs could be arranged and carried out, no British troops could be made available for the Weygand plan. It is, however, clear from the dispatch that the British Commander-in-Chief had not given up the joint attack with the French and had on the morning of the 24th already detailed General Sir Ronald Adam, the III Corps commander, to work out plans with the French First Army.[11]

When Blanchard reached Premesques with Fauvelle, he found that Gort had already left to meet Dill, but he had a conversation with Pownall during which he appears to have said that he could see only two alternatives, either the retreat to the Lys and the establishment of a great bridgehead covering Dunkirk and Ostend, or a renewal of the offensive southwards. In view of Franklyn's withdrawal, he thought the latter very difficult. Nevertheless he agreed to make the necessary plans. He mentioned that he was sending Fauvelle to Paris to report to Weygand and perhaps Reynaud.[12]

Generals Adam and Altmayer discussed the attack with Blanchard at Attiches during the afternoon. It was now to be made by five divisions, three French, the 25th Motorized, the 5th North African with Dame's 2nd North African in support, and the 5th and 50th British, now reorganizing south of Lille, against the line Plouvain–Marquion–Cambrai. The open flank towards Douai would be protected by the Cavalry Corps and such British cavalry as could be made available, and the R.A.F. would provide bomber and fighter air cover. The formations would concentrate during the next day, the 25th. On the evening of the 26th there would be a preliminary occupation of bridgeheads over the Sensée, which would be followed on the morning of the 27th with the advance towards Bapaume.

Already Blanchard's telegram implying that the British had abandoned the attack had had injurious consequences. On the morning of the 24th, the Seventh Army had renewed their attacks towards the Somme, with some minor success,[13] but on the evening of the 24th General Besson telephoned from Army Group Three to General Frère: 'Army Group One has had to withdraw northwards and the enemy is being reinforced opposite us. For the time being the offensive cannot be envisaged. Somme must be occupied and organized in depth.'[14] The Seventh Army attacks for the 25th were therefore cancelled.[15]

[6]

On 25 May, Weygand was a little more confident: at midnight Blanchard had telegraphed that after all the attack would take place next day. At the usual conference in Reynaud's office, Major-General Spears was introduced as the British liaison officer representing Churchill on the Allied Supreme Council. He was a man of considerable energy, who had been attached to and later head of the British mission to the French Army during 1914–18. In this office he had made both friends and enemies. With Weygand, he was on cool terms. Almost immediately after his admission, Commandant Fauvelle, who had left Attiches before the Adam–Altmayer conversation had begun, was brought in. He soon made it very plain that in his opinion the battle in France was as good as over. The French troops were exhausted, so were the staff, which led the British to distrust them. The First Army units had no more bread, although there was enough meat and wine. (The British had been on half-rations for some days.) All the heavy artillery had been lost.[16] All the horse-drawn artillery was immobilized by the slaughter of the teams by aircraft. Gun ammunition was down to one unit of fire. The British were preoccupied with thoughts about re-embarkation, and the Belgians were not to be relied on. 'He was,' says Spears, 'the very embodiment of catastrophe.'

'I believe,' Fauvelle said, 'in a very early capitulation.' ('*Il ne s'agit pas de ça,*' snapped both Reynaud and Weygand.)

At one moment during the meeting, Weygand, perhaps pardonably, lost his self-control. He burst out at Reynaud that France had thrown herself into the war without commanding the materials to carry it on, had gone to war in 1939 with an army of 1920. 'In such circumstances it was criminal to have declared war on 3 September. It is inconceivable that the men responsible for the French Army did not warn the government that the condition of the army at that date did not justify the struggle.'

Asked how many of Blanchard's divisions were fit to attack, Fauvelle allowed possibly three; only the 12th, 15th and 25th were well in hand. He added what everyone knew to be true, that all movement was hampered by refugees. He went on to air his views that there were only three alternatives: either to evacuate by sea all that could be saved and take Army Group Two to North Africa, or to fight a desperate battle in Lower Normandy and Brittany, or to request an armistice. In private after the meeting, Reynaud asked Fauvelle whether these were his own or Blanchard's views. Fauvelle admitted they were his own, and that evacuation to England and Algeria without loss of time was imperative if the fight was to continue. Reynaud then asked if it was possible to leave French troops in England. Fauvelle agreed it would be difficult, especially for the reservists separated from their families in the hands of the invader.

Before he started back to Army Group One, Fauvelle saw General Georges and asked that a senior officer should at once come north to report on the situation. He also stressed that Blanchard, until he was officially nominated to the command of Army Group One, lacked authority. This was at once agreed and a telegram sent off appointing Blanchard and directing Prioux to succeed him in command of the First Army. At the same time General Koeltz, of Doumenc's staff, was ordered to go north and advise on the establishment of a strong defensive bridgehead covering Dunkirk and Ostend.[17]

[7]

Reichenau's Sixth Army followed up the Belgian retreat quickly. Early in the afternoon of the 24th, the Germans opened a heavy bombardment, with aeroplane observation, on the Belgian IV Corps line from either side of Courtrai. They made their first crossing of the Lys below Courtrai, and at 5 p.m. another above the town. Belgian reserves thrown in were unable to restore the situation. Later the attack was extended northward as far as Deynze. At nightfall the Belgian line was swinging back. Although the 1st Belgian Division still held Menin and the river as far as Wulverghem, the Germans were well-established and had reached the line Iseghem–Hulste. There were other inroads further north.

On the right of the Belgians, the British II Corps covering Halluin had not been attacked. Its commander, the pessimistic General Brooke, had been none too easy about his left. Now his anxiety was justified. He was told of the German penetration of the Belgian lines at 2 a.m. the next morning, the 25th. 'I came to the conclusion that this was the beginning of a German offensive intended to push right through to our left rear and join up with the armoured divisions. . . . I am convinced that the Belgian Army is closing down.'[18] Brooke hurried from his headquarters in Armentières to G.H.Q. at Premesques to ask for reserves. G.H.Q., he found, was still absorbed with the prospects of the southern attack. With difficulty he obtained an infantry brigade, the 143rd, and the dispatch of the 12th Lancers (armoured cars) to Menin, but this was no more than very temporary and weak support against a major threat. At the moment, there was no intention of renouncing the southward attack. The British troops to be employed in it, the 5th and 50th Divisions, were on their way southward.

Gort had already warned London of the fragility of the situation. Early on the 25th, General Dill arrived from the War Office, and after talking with Lord Gort, reported to London that the situation was serious; he detailed the position of the Allies and the Germans, and stated emphatically that the southward attack 'cannot be an important affair'. At this point General Blanchard arrived at G.H.Q. At 2 a.m. he had received Weygand's telegram of the previous afternoon, giving him discretion to choose between the southern attack and the Dunkirk bridgehead.

In the meantime, however, Weygand had received Blanchard's telegram sent off on the evening of the 24th, with provisions for the attacks on the 25th, 26th and 27th,[19] and his hopes revived. General Besson was called to the telephone and ordered to resume his attack to the north to assure the Somme bridges. The British 1st Armoured Division* of General Evans, only just landed, was to be attached to the

* The British 1st Armoured Division had been split up. 1st Brigade had been with General Gort's force in the north. General R. Evans's command consisted of the 2nd Armoured Brigade, three cavalry regiments with light (5-ton) tanks, and the 3rd Armoured Brigade with two tank regiments. The third battalion

French Seventh Army, and the War Office in London, unaware of the matter of the Dill–Gort conversations, telegraphed to the British mission at La Ferté that it should be employed 'offensively and go all out'.[20] Finally Weygand sent a message to Blanchard that he was glad to see the decision to go on with the attack. These actions were taken before the arrival of Commandant Fauvelle in Paris.[21]

Meanwhile the news from the Belgian front grew slowly worse. It is significant of Gort's perplexity that he kept both Brooke and Franklyn at G.H.Q. without definite orders, thus allowing the British 5th Division to go on moving southward towards its battle-positions for that night. It was not until about 4 p.m. that he at last told Franklyn that he and his division were transferred to II Corps and General Brooke.*[22]

By evening the gap on the Belgian right at Zonnebeke near Wervicq was of the nature of ten kilometres, and the arrival of the 12th Lancers could do little to mend matters. The 5th Division could not come into the line on the open left of the 143rd Brigade until the afternoon of the 26th, only slightly ahead of the enemy. On the same day, General Langlois, who had succeeded Prioux in command of the Cavalry Corps, sent the 2nd Light Armoured to support the British near Ypres.

During the day, apart from the attacks on the Belgians, the German II, VIII and XXVII Korps had been active along the First Army front: violent bombardment of the Maulde forts, bombing of St Amand, attacks south of Odomez. Nevertheless, although he was aware of the Belgian trouble on the British left, Blanchard did not at once cancel the attack. After leaving British G.H.Q., he went to Belgian Head-quarters near Bruges. It was not until his return to Attiches that he knew of the end of British interest in the attack. Thereon he issued orders to Army Group One which did not go out until nearly midnight on 25th/26th.[23] These directed Army Group One to regroup behind the Aa Canal, the Lys and the Canal de Dérivation, and form a bridge-head covering Dunkirk. The First Army was to begin its withdrawal on the next day, the 26th, by bringing its reserves north of the Scarpe. The front line on the Sensée and Escaut would remain in position until the night 26th/27th. The Belgians were told to try to reduce the German 'pocket' near Courtrai.

[8]

On the 25th, following the meeting with Fauvelle and Spears, there was a meeting of the French War Committee.[24] Weygand said that he and Georges had examined the possibilities of shortening the line, but a

---

and the support group had been detached and sent to Calais. The Evans group landed at Cherbourg between 16–24 May. The 2nd Armoured Brigade had been hurried forward to the Somme.

* Dill returned to London. That evening, after a meeting at Admiralty House, Ironside resigned, to become Commander-in-Chief Home Forces, and Dill succeeded him as Chief of the Imperial General Staff from 27 May.

retreat south of the Seine would mean either the abandonment of the troops in the Maginot Line or the abandonment of Paris. The line suggested was the lower Seine–the Oise–the Nonette–the Marne–the Argonne–Verdun–Metz–the Maginot Line, but with their inferiority in numbers it would be difficult to occupy in good order. Lebrun asked what would happen should the armies be destroyed. True, there were agreements expressly forbidding a separate peace, but if Germany offered terms they ought to be examined, and the British should be consulted. Weygand said that the British should be consulted now. Pétain interjected that since the French had provided eighty to the British ten divisions, France had a strong claim to initiate talks. Campinchi disapproved of Pétain's view, but said that the military experts, Weygand, Darlan, Vuillemin, should at the right moment say: 'We can't go on.' He added that another government than Reynaud's might be less embarrassed at signing a peace treaty without British prior consent.*

Weygand agreed that it would be useful to inquire what sacrifices the British were ready to make to keep Italy out of the war, and thus free the divisions in the Alps. Finally Reynaud told the meeting that he was going to London on the following day and would put the question of the destruction of the French Army to Churchill. Weygand added that it was important to preserve the means of keeping order in case of defeat. In the meantime the committee had agreed that if the government was driven from Paris, it should retire to Bordeaux.

In London Reynaud was listened to by the Prime Minister, Halifax, Chamberlain, Attlee and Eden. He 'dwelt not obscurely on the possibility of a French withdrawal from the war'. But as Churchill remarked, one cannot easily make a bargain at the last gasp. So Reynaud returned to Paris empty-handed. There was another conversation with Daladier and Charles-Roux, 'confused and shattering'.

---

* This remark was to cause a lot of controversy after the war. The friends of Campinchi (who was assassinated on the Riviera after the armistice) claimed that he had never said this and that he could not possibly have said it. It was in fact a perfectly sensible comment. It in no way implies approval, and, in the upshot, it is what happened.

Into the Dunkirk bridgehead: First phase, 26 May

ON the afternoon of the 25th, the three relieved divisions of the B.E.F., the 2nd, 44th and 48th (the last without the 143rd Brigade left with II Corps) were moving to occupy the water-line from Bergues (behind the troops of the Flanders Fortified Sector) as far as La Bassée. Beyond La Bassée, one British brigade was holding the crossings at Carvin, and two battalions of the 25th Brigade (50th Division) were in reserve, waiting to move up into position for the attack. Blanchard was informed of Gort's order to transfer the 5th and 50th Divisions to the north only when he returned from Bruges. A copy of the orders of 11.50 p.m. was sent to British G.H.Q., but Gort had not seen it before he came to Blanchard at 10 on the following morning, the 26th. Then, in agreement with Blanchard, an order was worked out for the withdrawal on the next three nights. To reach the Lys, the British had less distance to cover than the French. Hence the British rearguard would remain during the night 26th/27th on its present line from Bourghelles, while the French rearguards came back to the Scarpe. On the night of the 27th/28th the French rearguards would come back to the Deule—that is from its junction with the La Bassée canal—and the British rear-guards would do likewise, the point of junction being in Lille. Both main bodies were to be on the Lys by the morning of the 28th. Last of all, on the night of the 28th/29th, all rearguards would fall back behind the Lys.

On these orders, two comments. First, ostensibly they envisage only a withdrawal to the Lys and, implicitly, the establishment of the great bridgehead. There is no indication of a further withdrawal or evacuation. On his return to his headquarters, Gort found a message from the Secretary of State warning him of the improbability of the French attack from the south being successful, and adding that in consequence the British might be forced to withdraw and re-embark.

Secondly, although the British forces were split between east and west, their situation was less perilous than that of the First French Army, particularly IV and V Corps in the pocket south of the Scarpe, the divisions which were to retire on the night of the 26th/27th. The need for speedy deflation of the salient which they occupied stood out in hideous urgency now that the British divisions were not to come in on the west of the Canal du Nord. The German pressure on the flanks would narrow the passage up which the divisions must pass. Their peril was increased by the fact that no supplies had reached them since the 20th. Their ammunition, especially for the 105s and 155s, was deficient, and although the French army cooks had worked wonders with what they could find in the towns and villages, food was insufficient. Moreover the removal of most of the motor transport of Army Group One to south of the Somme a week back meant that the divisions must rely on their wholly inadequate unit transport to carry out their withdrawal.[1] No less important was the almost total destruction of the central telephone exchange at Lille, which served the whole region.

A further telegram from London during the day told Lord Gort that Churchill had informed Reynaud of the possible evacuation and that Reynaud would inform Weygand, who would no doubt issue orders to Blanchard. Weygand may have seen Admiral Darlan during the evening, but no decision seems to have been taken. Blanchard was not given even a hint. Nevertheless, on the next morning, the 27th, Darlan sent off Captain Auphan to London, and Auphan was sent to Dover to see Admiral Ramsay who, since the 19th, had been preparing a flotilla to deal with this crisis.* Nevertheless, not only was Blanchard left in the dark; so too was 'Amiral Nord', Abrial, responsible for the defence of Dunkirk.

This morning, however, while Gort was discussing the withdrawal with Blanchard, Strauss's II Korps attacked between Pont-Mauduit and Oignies, the sector of the Deule Canal occupied by the British 139th Brigade, the Moroccan Division and the 11th Dismounted Dragoons. The Germans reached the Bois d'Épinoy and the suburbs of Carvin, from which they were eventually expelled with the aid of the British 151st Brigade. Later in the day, this brigade went back to the 50th Division, while the 139th rejoined the 46th Division east of Cassel.

[2]

The withdrawal to Dunkirk and the Belgian surrender

The country round Dunkirk is quite flat, very marshy, very rich agriculturally where it has been drained. The drains are everywhere and communication is governed by a criss-cross of dykes and bridges. This had a considerable effect on the movement of armour, especially in those areas subject to flooding. On the other hand, observation-points are hard to find.

General Fagalde's means were quite inadequate for the defence of the region for which he had been given responsibility: Dunkirk–Gravelines–Watten–Cassel–Steenworde. Only part of his 68th Division had arrived on the 24th, and the enemy was already attacking the five battalions of his composite division on the line of the Aa, and these might at any moment fly into fragments. But (as has been seen) on the previous day Rundstedt had forbidden the Kleist and Hoth groups to use their armour.[2] The fighting, however, had been hard, and the battalion of the 137th (from the dislocated 21st Division) at Gravelines suffered heavy casualties. At Watten, on the 25th, the infantry of Reinhardt's XLI

---

* The operation was named 'Dynamo'.

Korps won a small bridgehead from the two training battalions, but that was all. At the same time the 68th Division occupied the line Mardyck–Spycker–Bergues, and five tanks turned up and attached themselves. On this day Boulogne fell.

The 26th was relatively quiet. But the command in the bridgehead was now being troubled by the arrival of stragglers from the First Army, who added nothing to the strength of the defence but required food and shelter. Since all rations now came by sea and many boats were sunk by German aircraft before docking, the difficulties became irremediable. Moreover, the headquarters of Amiral Nord in Dunkirk citadel were restricted. Fagalde had only three small rooms at his disposal and most of his staff had to stay at Malo, five kilometres to the east.

Calais fell on this day, although the fact was not known for another twenty-four hours. The break-in on the right of the Belgian Army past Wervicq became more alarming. On the other hand, the lifting of the injunction on the employment of armour by the Kleist group had produced nothing spectacular. It was found that, even in high summer weather, Flanders mud persisted, and tanks were not irresistible. On the morning of the 27th the German radio announced to the defenders of Dunkirk that should they not capitulate, they would be destroyed. In earnest of this, gun-fire and divebombers began to transform the port and town into ruins. Waves of German aircraft succeeded each other, only temporarily stopped by the intervention of British fighters from England. 'Everything was burning, houses, docks, petrol reservoirs. Such was the smoke that, in spite of the sunny weather, there was scarcely more light than on a gloomy winter's day. The big naval dockyard was no better than a furnace. In the streets, the ground was strewn with bodies and it was impossible to remove them. It was like a scene from Dante! Moreover, the hellish bombardment was to persist during the 28th and 29th. At the end of three tragic days, Dunkirk had become just a graveyard and a memory.'[3]

On the 27th, Guderian's XIX Panzer Korps (now including the 10th Panzer) attacked the Aa position held by the 137th Regiment alone, supported by two artillery groups.* The tanks broke through between Bourbourg and Capelle-Brouck in the afternoon, and overwhelmed the battalion to the south, while the 8th Panzer pushed back a mixed body of infantry stretched over a long front. At nightfall, the defenders were back on the front Drincham–Wormhoudt, and cut off from the north at Looberghe.

[3]

First Army, 26/27 May

The main body of the First Army began its retreat towards dusk on the evening of the 26th. On the left, III Corps had little difficulty in carrying

---

* The other two battalions from the 21st Division had been sent further south with two of the artillery groups.

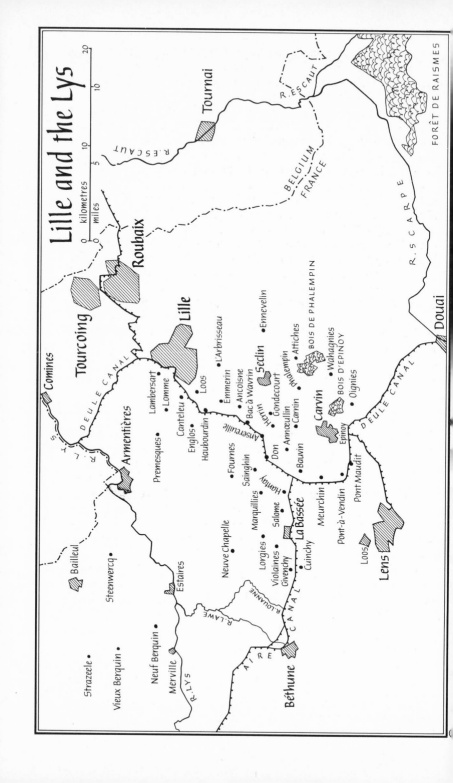

Lille and the Lys

out its withdrawal; its left division, the 12th, now only two infantry regiments and a little artillery, was firmly anchored to the British I Corps at Bourghelles, with the other divisions, the 32nd, the Béjard group (three battalions of the 2nd North African and the relics of the Maubeuge fortress infantry), and the 1st Division, swinging back to Cysoing–Pont-à-Marcq. Only the 1st Division rearguards had some fighting in the Forêt de Raismes and at St Amand.

In the morning General de la Laurencie had received an order to have the regimental colours burned. 'Why this act of despair?' he wrote. 'We are not yet on our knees, and the gate at Dunkirk is still open. My men trust their officers; they have ammunition; they *can* and *will* fight. They cannot do that without colours. I shall not carry out the order, and the regiments will march past with their colours on 30 May.'[4]

The other two corps were less fortunate. To retreat to the Lys and establish themselves, they must cross the Deule Canal westward between its junction with the La Bassée Canal and Lille. On the 26th, the Germans were already up to the La Bassée Canal. At best there were no more than four passages over the Deule south of Haubourdin (the south-western suburb of Lille), Don, Ansereuille, Bac de Wavrin, and near Ancoisne. On the afternoon of the 26th, the German II Korps (the 12th Division on the left, the 32nd on the right) faced the canals from La Bassée to Les Baraques near Bauvin and then south along the Deule. West of La Bassée lay Rommel's 7th Panzer Division, and at Béthune, Stever's 4th Panzer. During the afternoon of the 26th, Rommel's infantry got a very small bridgehead over the canal near Cuinchy.* The attack, by Strauss's II Korps on the 25th, on the canal salient Bauvin–Pont-à-Vendin–Pont-Maudit, held by the Moroccan Division, though eventually stopped, was not driven back. The Germans, part of the 12th and the 32nd Divisions, pushed northward, and though they were held by reinforcements sent up by the 2nd North African south of Carvin, the Moroccans north of the town were pushed back during the 26th to the line of the Don–Annoeulin–Camphin road. Bauvin was in German hands. On the west of the Deule, the La Bassée Canal as far as Robecq was occupied by French and British forces, largely fragmentary. The sixteen kilometres from the junction of the canal with the Deule, as far as La Bassée, was occupied by General Vernillat's patched-up 43rd Division: the 1st Battalion of Chasseurs, nine sections of riflemen and one machine-gun, in Salome and Hantay. Behind them, the two battalions of the 131st from Sainghin to Don, with the 29th Chasseurs (six sections of riflemen, one machine-gun and three anti-tank guns), and in reserve the last battalion of the 3rd Moroccans.

To the west, the British 5th Brigade, the left of the 2nd Division,

---

* Cuinchy, and across the canal Givenchy, were in the old British front line from 1914 to 1918.

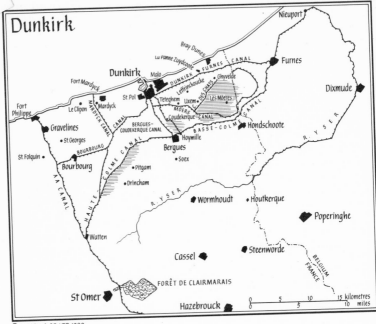

Dunkirk

Nieuport · Furnes · Dixmude · Poperinghe · Steenworde · Houtkerque · Wormhoudt · Cassel · Watten · St Omer · Hazebrouck · FORÊT DE CLAIRMARAIS · Bourbourg · St Folquin · Gravelines · St.Georges · Fort Philippe · Le Clipon · Mardyck · Fort Mardyck · Dunkirk · Malo · St.Pol · Teteghem · Uxem · Ghyvelde · Leffrinckoucke · Les Moëres · Hondschoote · Hoymille · Bergues · Soex · Pitgam · Drincham · Bray Dunes · La Panne Zuydcoote · DUNKIRK-FURNES CANAL · CANAL · DES CHATS · MOËRES CANAL · BERGUES-COUDEKERQUE CANAL · Coudekerque · BASSE-COLME CANAL · HAUTE COLME CANAL · MARDYCK CANAL · BOURBOURG · AA CANAL · R YSER · BELGIUM FRANCE

0   5   10   15 kilometres
0   5   10 miles

© CASSELL & CO LTD 1968

defended the canal between La Bassée and Béthune. The small bridgehead at Cuinchy was enlarged during the night by the infantry of the 7th Panzer and in the morning the German engineers were able to rig up a pontoon bridge over the canal, sheltered by the high steep banks from the fire of the defenders. Most of the Panzer regiment was passed over by early in the afternoon, and then Rommel was reinforced by the Panzer brigade of Hartlieb's 5th Division. The British were driven out of Givenchy and the 7th Panzer Armour sent forward to Violaines and Lorgies. The 5th Panzer came up on the right and drove the elements of the 43rd Division off the canal. By dusk, what survived of the British 5th Brigade (not more than a few hundred of the remnants of its three battalions) had been driven past Neuve Chapelle, and escaped during darkness to Estaires. The La Bassée–Lille road was open. While the tanks of the 5th Panzer swung eastward, Rommel's regiment went on through the night, and soon after midnight reached Lomme on the Lille–Armentières road, where until 8 on the previous evening General Brooke had had his headquarters. Before morning the tanks of the 5th Panzer were established at Englos between Lomme and Haubourdin. Thus, on the morning of 28 May, the path for the retreat of the main body of the First Army—three army corps, eight divisions and detachments of all arms, including light tanks— was commanded by the enemy on its left. General Vernillat made his way to Steenwerck and reported to General Prioux that his last companies had been destroyed and that the road from Lille was probably lost.

In spite of enemy attacks, General Aymes's IV Corps got away on the night of the 26th/27th. Such rearguards as they left were not greatly troubled. The two divisions, General Juin's 15th Motorized and General Musse's 4th, marched north-westward and halted in the early afternoon east of Seclin. General Aymes had little information as to the situation. All he knew was the order to move on the following night to the Lys between Estaires and Erquinghem. 'On leaving my command-post at Ennevelin at 2 a.m. on the 27th, I saw the sky reddened to the south-west towards Carvin and heard in the distance the dull uninterrupted sound of a violent cannonade, evidence that the withdrawal would not go without serious difficulties.'[5]

The situation of V Corps was far more troubled. The German attacks towards Carvin threatened the line of retreat of the 25th Motorized, the 5th North African, and Colonel Tardu's 106th Infantry Regiment detached from the 1st Motorized. On the morning of the 27th, the 2nd North African and the Moroccan Division held the western wall of the corridor from Oignies through the Bois d'Épinoy–Carnin–Annoeulin–Ponts-de-Don. The troops to the south of the Scarpe, covered by the reconnaissance groups, came away after nightfall on the 26th, and passing to the east of Douai, came up the Seclin road, under artillery fire from the west. From daylight, the columns were shadowed by German planes, and at intervals attacked by squadrons of bombers, especially at bridges.

At nightfall on the 27th, the Moroccans and the 2nd North African, believing the Don bridges to have been lost,[6] turned northwards parallel with the Deule, hoping to cross at Bac-à-Wavrin, which was one of the bridges by which IV Corps expected to cross. Hence, during the 28th, there was a monstrous confusion of infantry and artillery of five divisions moving both north and west, and as each pressed on to the road of the division on its right, the whole mass was moving parallel to the Seclin–Lille road.

On the night of the 27th/28th, the British divisions beyond III Corps, the 42nd and part of the 4th, came back to the Lys between Armentières and Comines, leaving only a rearguard on the Deule north of Lille.

Night came down, but the fighting, the shelling and the movement did not pause. It rained heavily, which added to the turmoil, but under it, elements of all arms managed to pass through. On the morning of the 28th, the British I Corps was back on the Lys with a rearguard on the Deule north of Lille. But the Germans were closing up on the city. During the night, the leading division of La Laurencie's III Corps, the 32nd, crossed the Lys, but part of his 1st Division was stopped by either the 7th or 5th Panzer Division, and driven back into Lille under the divisional infantry commander, General Jenoudet. On the other hand, the 8th Zouaves of the 12th Division ran into Rommel's tanks at Lomme and after some sharp fighting got away northward and reached Nieppe beyond Armentières during the afternoon. So did the other regiment, the 150th: under the cover of a violent storm it also wheeled northward and escaped behind the Lys.

[4]

Since the 24th, behind Fagalde's weak line from Gravelines up the Aa, there had been assembled a chain of British units. The line from Bergues to Cassel to Hazebrouck was held by the 48th Division, then as far as Merville by the 44th. On the left of the 44th was the 2nd Division, the destruction of whose 5th Brigade, along with Vernillat's 43rd Division, by the 7th and 5th Panzer has already been recorded. On the 27th, as has also been seen, the French left was driven back, and the Germans took the Forêt de Clairmarais and reached the foot of Cassel hill. They also penetrated north of Hazebrouck, occupied the Forêt de Nieppe and surrounded Merville, from which the British 6th Brigade was presently withdrawn.

On the 26th, after his meeting with Blanchard, Gort had appointed Sir Ronald Adam to organize the British share of the Dunkirk bridge-head in conjunction with Fagalde under the direction of Amiral Nord. A conference was called at Cassel for 7 a.m. on the 27th. It met as the Germans began attacking the town. It brought together, beside Abrial, Adam and Fagalde, Blanchard, Prioux and Weygand's representative sent off on the 26th, General Koeltz, the bearer of a long order to the commanders in Army Group One, which alas! offered nothing more material than a number of textbook principles.

It is clear that at the moment of Koeltz's departure, Weygand was contemplating nothing beyond a permanent occupation of the Dunkirk bridgehead and had given no thought to the question of evacuation. Owing to a series of minor obstacles, Koeltz did not reach Dunkirk through London and Dover until 5 on the morning of the 27th. He was at once conveyed by Abrial and Fagalde to Cassel. As had so often happened, even as they talked the situation was changing both rapidly and radically. Fagalde and Adam arranged that the French should hold the sector west of Dunkirk, and the British the east, simple enough on the map, but owing to the dispersion and intermixture of the troops physically impossible on the ground. But the Belgian collapse was imminent, and Calais was threatened. (It had fallen that morning, but this was not yet known.) Koeltz proposed that the town be relieved and incorporated in the bridgehead; a proposal warmly supported by Abrial, who considered Calais indispensable to the usefulness of Dunkirk.

At this point the German artillery began to shell the town in prepara-tion for an assault. The conference broke up.

Koeltz proposed to discuss the situation with Blanchard, but the latter replied that his headquarters was moving and he had not yet discovered where it was moving to. It was in fact going to Les Moëres between Bray Dunes and Hondschoote on the edge of the flooded area, by the road more than sixteen kilometres from Dunkirk. Koeltz therefore went off with Prioux to his command-post at Steenwerck. Prioux lamented the appalling difficulty in carrying out the retreat of the First Army, owing to the lack of roads, and foresaw that the rearguards would not get through. Koeltz then visited Belgian headquarters outside Bruges, where he received nothing except reproaches from General Michiels and van Overstraeten. Though nothing definite was said, Koeltz and General Champon were convinced the Belgians were on the point of surrender. However, they did not inform Paris; probably it was now impossible to telegraph.

Weygand's emissary now set off to find British G.H.Q., of which the location was unknown to all. At Dunkirk he found Abrial, who told him that the Belgians had just capitulated (they would not do so formally until the next day) and added that as things now were, evacuation could not be avoided.

Soon after this, Gort appeared. He had not yet heard of the Belgian surrender,[7] though he had had a warning earlier in the afternoon. To Koeltz he said: 'Since you come from General Weygand, what do you know about the plan for embarking 30,000 men a day?' Koeltz answered: 'I've never heard it mentioned.' Gort had been looking for Blanchard all the evening. Failing to discover him, he returned to his headquarters at Houtkerque, which, owing to the wave of retreating divisions, he did not reach until 4.30 a.m., considerably worried. 'I now found myself faced with an open gap of twenty miles between Ypres and the sea, through which many armoured forces might reach the beaches.'[8] The enemy, however, had all his armour opposite the southern side of the allied forces. On the northern wing von Bock's Army Group had one armoured and one motorized division.

The first Weygand knew of the surrender of the Belgians was at 6 in the evening, just as he was sitting down to a conference with Georges, Doumenc and Besson at Vincennes. He says that there had been nothing to allow him to foresee the Belgian action; there had been no warning, not a hint. Even on that very day Belgian headquarters had appealed for the help of a French division. The disappearance of the Belgian Army ended the prospect of the wide and deep bridgehead. The Lys would now be indefensible above Comines. The only thing to be done was to draw in the bridgehead and bring out as many troops as possible, but beyond telegraphing to Blanchard to dissociate the French and British from the Belgians, no orders went to Army Group One.

On the 27th, Gort had received from the War Office a telegram to the effect that his single task was to evacuate the maximum possible of his force. This he communicated to Blanchard, when he came to Houtkerque in mid-morning of the 28th. Blanchard, who had received no orders from either Montry or La Ferté, was horrified at the suggestion that he should not wait for orders, but act. Gort and Pownall rubbed it in that although the Germans would not be able during the next twenty-four hours to exploit the gap where the Belgians had stood, the whole of the line from Gravelines to the Lys, which was defended by bits and pieces of both nations and all arms, might go at any moment. The Allies must fall back to the line Ypres–Poperinghe–Cassel during the coming night. 'To wait till tomorrow was to give *two* days to the Germans to get behind us, an act of madness. We thought it unlikely that we could get even 30 per cent of our forces away.' In the middle of this, one of Prioux's staff arrived with the information that Prioux intended to remain between Béthune and Lille inside the quadrangle of the canals: his troops were too tired to move. On this Blanchard reiterated his refusal to withdraw, declaring that evacuation from the beach was impossible, and if the British fleet could do it, the French Marine would never be able to. 'I could not move him,' says Gort. At last he asked if Gort would withdraw the British without the French. Gort replied that he was going because he had been ordered by his government to re-embark, and to do that, he must retire at once. In another twenty-four hours they would be overwhelmed.[9]

The surrender of the Belgians, coupled with the decision of the British government to transport the B.E.F. back to England, led inevitably to the dissolution of Army Group One. General Blanchard recognized that he no longer had a command.[10] What would follow in the Dunkirk area must be under the authority of Admiral Abrial, while outside that there would remain only the First Army under General Prioux, determined to remain on the Lys and to recuperate such of the divisions in and south of Lille as could break through.

On this day, the 28th, Captain Auphan, who had returned from England after conferring with Admiral Ramsay, came with Darlan to tell Weygand exactly what was proposed about an evacuation. It was agreed that the French Marine would work in conjunction with Ramsay for the evacuation, though no one had much hope of success. Certainly it appeared impossible without the appropriate air protection and without the reoccupation of the coast-line as far as Cape Gris-Nez.

As yet Blanchard had received no instruction from Weygand. At 10 p.m. this night, he reported by telegram that part of the First Army was retreating towards Dunkirk and that numerous bodies were surrounded in Lille. It was not until the following day that Weygand replied that he should constitute a bridgehead between Dunkirk and Nieuport with whatever forces were available, in order to allow progressive evacuation by sea.[11]

[5]

The end in Lille, 28–31 May

On the morning of the 28th, the German divisions were pressing in on Lille and at the eastern entrances they had passed round the north and invested the citadel. They had cut the main road to Armentières, they were on the edge of Haubourdin and driving IV and V Corps into a narrowing circle. General Musse of the 4th Division, having heard from the *préfet*, Carlès, that the government had declared Lille an open town and that fighting must therefore cease, went off to find the regional military commander (a retired General Pagézy who had left the town a week earlier) and was snapped up by a German patrol. In return, some of the 25th Motorized picked up General Kuhne, commander of the 253rd Division. Command of the troops in Lille was now assumed by General Molinié. Fighting continued. General Mellier, with his Moroccans and the remains of the 25th Division, was fighting in Canteleu, and the 5th North African in Haubourdin: General Jenoudet, infantry commander of the 1st Division, with three battalions and one group of the divisional artillery in the suburb of Loos; and on the south, in Emmerin-Wattignies and L'Arbrisseau, General Juin with what was left of the 15th and 4th Divisions. On this afternoon, Molinié ordered an attempt to break out to the west by the seizure of the bridge from Haubourdin to Santes. A little armour was available, a couple of Somua, five Renault and two armoured cars. The attack was made at 8 in the evening by the 14th Zouaves and the 13th Algerians, but the exit from the bridge was now mined. The attempt to lift the mines led to heavy casualties. A tank driven on to the bridge blew up and blocked the crossing. All this led to German reinforcements, and at midnight the enterprise was abandoned. On the other hand, part of the 92nd reached Lomme and, unable to drive back the 7th Panzer armour, seized the park and château and held them for another forty-eight hours. During the next day, the 29th, ammunition began to give out, and eventually, with no means of defence, some of the Haubourdin battalions surrendered. Thereupon their captors drove them forward as a shield to their assault. On the night of the 29th, the Faubourg des Postes south of the town was lost, General Juin was captured and the rest of the 15th Division annihilated.

An attempt by the *préfet* to evacuate a large number of the townspeople had been successful until communications with the south were cut on the 20th, when some 800,000 came hobbling back. Many more had remained in the city and in quarters now being fought over. Children had been brought into the aid-posts of the 92nd holding Canteleu. Jenoudet's headquarters in Loos sheltered a group of nuns in charge of 300 orphans. The fighting went on, but as the supply of ammunition failed, the Germans were able to penetrate between the diminishing groups of defenders. With the fall of the Faubourg des Postes, the eastern end of Haubourdin was exposed. On the 31st, the redoubt here was still holding out, but Lambersart, Lomme, Loos had gone, and now Canteleu. Food and ammunition were finished. The artillery fired their last rounds over open sights and destroyed their guns. At 9 p.m. General Molinié surrendered with the honours of war.

On the following morning, two armed companies of the 2nd North African and one from the 5th, each a hundred strong with at their head divisional commanders, marched past the German General Wagner.

'In spite of the early hour, numbers of townspeople watched us pass. Women offered us cakes and tobacco, timidly, because of the *feld-grau* guards round us. In front of the station stood Generals Molinié, Dame and Mesny with the still-armed party. On the right, a German general, several officers, a battalion with a band, were drawn up to pay us honours. It is a rare compliment. In 1914–18 only the defenders of Fort Vaux received it. The Zouaves had the courage to parade at their best. It was a moving, pitiable spectacle, these haggard men, filthily dirty in their torn and ragged uniforms, marching in perfect step in column of fours, their officers at their head, under the eyes of the enemy.'[12]

From this confused and desperate combat, a number of groups, parties and individuals escaped. On the evening of the 28th, the 1st and 2nd groups of the 16th Artillery Regiment of the 25th Division, which had crossed the Deule at Bac-à-Wavrin, fell in at Fournes with the 1st Chasseurs-à-Pied in retreat from the La Bassée Canal. They encountered German tanks, probably of 5th Panzer, near Wavrin. The 2nd artillery group, which had part of the divisional 47-mm. anti-tank guns, got into position and opened fire. Though some were driven back, the majority beat off the enemy and found their way over the Lys. The reconnaissance group of the 25th Division reached Malo-les-Bains outside Dunkirk, but with others of the last defenders could not be taken on the over-loaded boats and were captured on 4 June. A squadron from the 1st Light Armoured, unable to get their tanks over the Lys, left them and swam the river.[13]

In the midst of this chaos of retreat, in which misinformation and rumour, as well as attacks by enemy aircraft, led to bewilderment, indecision and despair, at once heroic and absurd, in which the prospect of leaving France affected men with terrors more shattering than the expectation of death, wounds and captivity, the figure of General de la Laurencie of III Corps stands out as conspicuously as Kemmel Hill on the Flanders plain. A historian of the subsequent Pétain régime, relating a minor episode in 1941, refers to the general as a character from Courteline. In fact there is about him something of Don Quixote. On the 28th, when the 32nd, 12th and part of the 1st Divisions had crossed the Lys, he went to see the army commander, General Prioux, for his instructions. Prioux said that since First Army troops were still fighting in Lille, he, the army commander, could not desert them: he had buried his personal kit and papers and would remain with his staff where he was. La Laurencie asked permission to lead his own corps, of which four fifths were over the Lys, to Dunkirk. Prioux had no objection, but told him to add to his columns what he could find of the three light armoured divisions.* La Laurencie saw his generals, who were all in Steenwerck, that evening at 6, and pointed out to them that if their divisions stayed where they were they would be captured. But if they tried for Dunkirk, they might perhaps escape. He proposed that they should set out at midnight, since Poperinghe must be passed before daylight. The distance to the port was sixty kilometres. The generals, Janssen (12th) and Lucas (32nd), said their men were too exhausted to make the effort. (The 12th Motorized had lost all its transport; the 32nd never had any.) 'Very well, gentlemen,' replied La Laurencie; 'we will stay here, and I as your corps commander will remain with you, but I beg you to reflect on the consequences of your decision. Go and consult your regimental commanders. Meet me here at 7 o'clock, and if you persist in this answer, you will give me a signed report that your men are quite incapable of moving. And you will bear the full responsibility for our common surrender.' Janssen, a very good general, was shaken and answered: 'Let us try. Start at 11.' On this La Laurencie issued his orders, and at 11 the divisions began to move, covered by the remaining armoured cars of the 1st and 3rd Light Armoured.† Marching with no more than the normal halts, the columns covered the fifty to sixty kilometres and passed into the perimeter on the evening of the 29th.[14]

On the same afternoon, General Osborne, some of whose 44th Division was in position between Estaires–Merville and Hazebrouck, came to General Prioux at Steenwerck to learn his intentions. He was horrified to hear that Prioux proposed to remain where he was, but failed to shake him. Prioux, however, told him that La Laurencie's III Corps would move back next day. But on seeing La Laurencie, General Osborne was taken aback to find that III Corps was setting off in a couple of hours. Osborne, believing that his infantry could not manage to disengage and cover the whole distance to Dunkirk, withdrew them during the night to the Mont des Cats, a difficult withdrawal over unfamiliar ground. What remained of the division was brought in to Dunkirk the next day, the 29th, during which the other British rearguards also came within the perimeter.[15]

[6]

The defence and end at Dunkirk, 4 June

The second division of Fagalde's XVI Corps, the 60th, which had lost almost the whole of one regiment on 13 and 14 May in the islands, and on the morrow of the Ypres conference had been left attached to the Belgian Army, on the morning of 27 May, the day when the Belgians

---

* Weygand had ordered that priority in evacuation should be given to the armoured specialists. This unfortunately led to delays, with the consequence that some French ships left Dunkirk empty.

† The 2nd Light Armoured Division was further north on the Furnes–Loo Canal.

had reached the end of their power to resist, was holding a line along the Canal de Dérivation, with its left on the sea at Zeebrugge. Its artillery, three groups of 75s, had been lent to the Belgians. On this afternoon, foreseeing the Belgian capitulation, General Champon arranged for the infantry to be taken by Belgian lorries to the Yser. Owing to the now prevailing chaos, the transport was delayed, and the 60th did not start until the morning of the 28th, and then only slowly. The horse-drawn artillery was caught by German bombers on the Yser bridge at St Georges, near Nieuport, and almost wholly blotted out. Elsewhere the British 12th Lancers had already blown most of the remaining bridges, except that at Nieuport, where the explosives failed. Further, the Belgians had closed the flood-gates at Nieuport some days earlier before the water had risen far, and the mechanism of the gates was too damaged by bombs to allow them to be opened. Thus, on the morning of the 29th, the Germans found an easy prey in the 270th Infantry Regiment, much of which was surrounded. The 241st and other elements reached the Bray Dunes outside Dunkirk. A scratch battalion was formed and sent to join the 8th Zouaves of the 12th Division. The rest were ordered to points on the beaches, but no boats appeared. On 4 June, at 5 a.m., the last of the 60th surrendered.

On the 29th there came into the Dunkirk bridgehead the remains of III Corps of General de la Laurencie: two regiments of two battalions each and the equivalent of three batteries of the 12th Division; two to three battalions, but no artillery, of the 32nd Division; the artillery of the first Division nearly complete, its reconnaissance group, but no infantry unit; the 92nd Reconnaissance Group of the 2nd North African (now in Lille) and two improvised squadrons from the Cavalry Corps, one of Somua and one of Hotchkiss. Otherwise a large assemblage of soldiery. Fagalde had counted on the 60th Division to defend the eastern end of the perimeter, but it had never got clear of the clutches of IX Korps. The line of the Colme Canal was manned by General Janssen's four battalions (the 150th and 8th Zouaves).

On the morning of the 30th, Fagalde found the British concentrating on the port, while the flotsam of the French First Army were still coming. On all sides, the German divisions were closing in. But Guderian's XIX Panzer Korps was on its way out, to refit for other tasks, and as Guderian himself said, the ground round Dunkirk, with its maze of drains and its inundations, was unsuitable for tank operations. Parts of the XLI Motorized had also gone. On this day, the perimeter of the bridgehead was about forty kilometres, from Mardick to Nieuport: the depth from the Colme Canal to the sea, round which pressed one Panzer division and eight or nine infantry divisions, was perhaps eight kilometres.

The 68th was still a good fighting formation and had had its artillery augmented by a group from the 32nd. Eight or nine of the so-called battalions from the Flanders Fortified Sector were reduced to anything between a half and a tenth, but it still had four groups of guns. Of the 12th Division, there were two good battalions, though woefully short of weapons, but it was supported by five artillery groups. The three squadrons of tanks were held for emergencies. Between Bergues and Nieuport stood between thirty and forty British battalions. Except for a heavy attack by the 9th Panzer on the Haute–Colme Canal a little east of Bergues, held by the 137th Infantry Regiment, which lasted all the afternoon before being repulsed, the day passed with little other than bombing and shelling.

On the 31st a strong German attack was expected. Patrols with armoured cars tapped at the defences. The artillery fire increased, and the air bombardments. Fagalde says that he had hopes that the bridge-head was to be reinforced, since Lord Gort, in bidding him good-bye on this day, said that he was leaving three divisions under the command of General Alexander. The orders were obviously obscure. Lord Gort gave Alexander a free hand to act under Admiral Abrial, to assist in the defence of Dunkirk and to occupy himself with the arrangements for the evacuation of his command, bearing in mind that it was important for the French to share equally with the British.[16] He agreed with Alexander the night 2/3 June as the provisional date for evacuation. Gort left at 6 in the evening. Abrial told Alexander that he intended to hold the perimeter until all the troops were embarked. Alexander rejoined that the situation was deteriorating, that prolonged resistance was out of the question and that the front could not be maintained beyond the night of the 1st/2nd. Abrial and General Altmayer reacted hotly against this, which, they said, was not in conformity with Gort's orders. Alexander reported to the War Office in London and received orders that the British should be withdrawn as rapidly as possible on the basis of equal British-French numbers.

One of the main difficulties arose from the fact that, by agreement with the Admiralty, the main body of the French fleet was in the Mediterranean, and that there were very few French naval vessels available to Amiral Nord. In all, some forty were involved between 10 May and 4 June. Of the nineteen destroyers and the like, several had been sunk or badly damaged at Flushing and Boulogne, while a number of cargo vessels were sunk. It was not until mid-morning on the 30th that French evacuation began to be organized, when there were 63,000 awaiting shipment and the First Army troops just coming in.

The attack expected by both Alexander and Fagalde came on 1 June. Between Bray Dunes and Ghyvelde, it was made against the line of the 12th Division, through which the British 50th Division, with its 400 prisoners from Arras, had gone to the beaches: the 1st Guards Brigade retired from this line during the afternoon. What was lost was recovered after dark. At Bergues and Hoymille there was heavy fighting. The British to the east of the town had their line penetrated, but recovered it. The line eventually fell back to the Canal des Chats. Bergues itself was held by a mixed Anglo-French body, infantry from the British 139th Brigade, French engineers and companies from the two labour battalions. From the French point of view, the peak of misfortune was reached when all the British troops were withdrawn after dark—'By the morning of 2 June, they were all on the coast', wrote the British official historian—leaving the French to protect their own embarkation.

On the morning of 2 June, the bridgehead near Hoymille, east of Bergues, which on the previous day had been held by the British 139th Brigade, was apparently not handed over but evacuated. It was occupied by the Germans, who were counter-attacked by the French 21st Divisional Training Centre and an amalgamation of reconnaissance groups. The ground was waterlogged and the three companies of the training centre were reduced from 550 to sixty-five. The reconnaissance groups also lost heavily, and fell back on Coudekerque. Bergues, and its Vauban citadel, reduced to ashes by bombers and heavy guns, was lost at about 5 in the evening. By nightfall, the main line of the Flanders Fortified Sector was between Coudekerque and Teteghem. The enemy was now not more than six kilometres from the port, and the British had gone.

At the eastern end of the perimeter, the Germans failed completely against the 8th Zouaves and the 150th Infantry Regiment, and a counter-attack brought in sixty prisoners. Unhappily, the gallant General Janssen was killed that evening by a bomb.

At the west end of the line, the Gross–Deutschland Regiment, strengthened by tanks from Hubicki's 9th Panzer Division, attacked the 68th Division at Spycker. There was desperate fighting, with the French 75s firing over open sights. In the end, the Germans got into the village, but could get no further. Between Spycker and Bergues there was no change in the situation, though the Germans were now in the ruins of the latter. The most vulnerable point was in the centre, the position of the Flanders Fortified Sector, now three to four kilometres behind the Bergues–Furnes Canal. During the afternoon, Fagalde produced three battalions, one from the 68th, two reconstructions from the 32nd, the skeleton of the reconnaissance groups, all the armour he could find, and six artillery groups. Prematurely the battalion from the 68th Division attacked from Teteghem, supported by six Somua. It did not get very far, but held on to what it had won and waited for the next day.

Fagalde had expected that the evacuations would have been completed on the night of 1/2 June, but the shipping losses had been so heavy that embarkation was now restricted to night. The defenders must now endure another day. Fagalde mustered behind the Flanders Fortified Sector the last elements he could squeeze out of the 32nd Division under their infantry commander, General Alaurent, and stiffened them with the *Gardes Mobiles* from his corps headquarters. Fagalde was highly critical of the handling of the counter-attack on the previous night and this morning, and of the lack of co-ordination between the battalions and between infantry and tanks. 'In spite of these errors, the two counter-attack battalions, this forlorn hope, were going to surpass themselves.' True, they were held up short of the objective, but they had delayed the Germans for six hours at a juncture when every hour counted. Then they fell back on the remains of the 137th Infantry Regiment, which had been fighting for nine days, and of which the first battalion was now fifty strong.

On the flanks, other remnants of infantry somehow clung to a line running across the south-east of Dunkirk from Coudekerque to Leffrinckoucke.

To the west, the other battalions of the 68th prepared to stand on the line of the Bourbourg–Dunkirk Canal. All the morning they resisted in front of it, but were gradually driven back. The canal was now held by the elements of the two battalions, the divisional training centre and the reconnaissance group; their front was nine kilometres. The Germans attacked at the bridges. In only one place did they secure a shallow footing, but they could not enlarge it.

Opposite the 12th Division, Bray Dunes–Ghyvelde, the enemy failed completely, but on the right the reconnaissance group was driven off the end of the marsh and fell back to join the left of the Flanders Fortified Sector. At the end of the day, some units, such as the 1st Battalion of the 137th and the 21st Divisional Training Centre, no longer existed.

At 9 p.m. on the 3rd, as darkness fell, the French line was still in existence, but dangerously close to the town. In the centre, where were the Flanders Fortified Sector men, the enemy was no more than two kilometres from the quays. The French command feared the worst. As it chanced, it was a night of almost complete peace. On Fagalde's orders, the main body of the forward troops fell back behind a 'crust' in contact with the enemy. Behind the crust another was formed on the line Zuydcoote–Furnes Canal–Fort Mardyck. Then, at a later hour, both crusts, the outer first, were to come down to the quays and embark. The main bodies started at 8.30; the last crust left its position at 2 a.m. Between 3.30 and 4 the last ships moved out. At 4, British naval parties sank two boats in the channel. A few less than 53,000 had been taken off. With the last went the leading defenders of Dunkirk: General de la Laurencie, whose strength of mind had saved the better part of two divisions and the cavalry corps, General Fagalde and General Barthelemy, who had given all their strength to the protection of the operation, and Admiral Abrial, who had seen it through.

About a thousand men stood to attention four deep about half-way along the pier, the General and his staff about thirty feet away; and after having faced the troops whose faces were indiscernible in the dawn light, the flames behind them showing up their steel helmets, the officers clicked their heels, saluted and then turned about and came down to the boat with me and we left at 0320.[17]

[7]

The British, with justice, pride themselves on the courage, determination and discipline which allowed this prodigious feat to be accomplished. It was not, however, all as well-mannered, as coolly classical, as comradely as some writers would have us believe. There were many groups, especially at Malo, who considered they had been deserted. There were unpleasant incidents. 'Whoever remembers the horrifying mob at Malo and the approaches to the east jetty will agree that to produce order successfully, machine-guns were needed.'[18]

For the infantrymen of the 32nd Division left as a rearguard there was no room when they reached the quayside. A launch had been kept back for the twenty officers. They refused to leave their men and stayed. Led by General Alaurent, they tried to break out towards Gravelines. At Le Clipon they were surrounded and taken prisoner.

How many French soldiers were left is impossible to know. Fagalde makes no conjecture. The German figures do not discriminate between those taken here or hereabouts and in Lille, but von Bock's Army Group gives 30,000–40,000, most of them French.[19]

In the escape there were for the French, as for the British, many incidents of severity, if none as hugely calamitous as the later loss of the *Lancastria* at Ste Nazaire. There was the sinking of the French torpedo boat *Bourrasque* with 800 men, of whom 300 were drowned; the loss of T.-B. *Sirocco* with 750, chiefly from the 25th Division, among them the colour-party of the 92nd Infantry Regiment with the colours; there were the 400 who went down with the *Emile-Deschamps*, the 300 who went with the *Brighton Queen*, and the 300 lost of the 2,000 on the *Scotia*.

And as General Fagalde points out, while the British were returning to the comparative calm of their own land, the French escaped only to be within a few days once more in the battle.

[8]

Certain comments may be added to the above bald narrative.

German military specialists deplore Hitler's '*Halt befehl*', which stopped Guderian from sending his 1st Panzer Division against the French flank on the Aa, and rushing on Dunkirk. It may be that the port would have been captured and some 300,000 or so put in the bag. But it is not certain. After all, with little fighting, the armour of Guderian's XIX Panzer Korps had had 50 per cent casualties in a fortnight. The whole of the area round Dunkirk is a maze of drains and banks. It is possible that the final battle here might have done so much damage to the Panzer divisions as to postpone the assault that began on 5 June, with what consequences it is idle to speculate. The Germans preferred to make sure.

Weygand, as his memoirs show, was obviously partially stunned by the news of the unforeseen Belgian surrender. He certainly did not rise to the occasion. Perhaps with the little information available as to the situation of the French and British divisions, no commander except one on the ground could have acted. Koeltz obviously had nothing to suggest, and Blanchard, who had been at Belgian headquarters only two days earlier, was no better. Hence for forty-eight hours Army Group One was without direction. It is from this date that Weygand's pessimism of the 25 May conference became despair.

French writers on the Dunkirk evacuation incline to a certain bitterness towards the English over the whole affair. It is said that the British prepared for the evacuation long before the necessity appeared. The accusation of looking over their shoulder was made before even the 19th, when Billotte's anxieties were laid by him before Gort, and is not justified. On the other hand, the War Office began discussion with the Admiralty on the 20th, and Admiral Ramsay at Dover began his preparations between this date and the 23rd, but nothing was said until 7 p.m. on the 26th, when he received the message 'Operation Dynamo is to commence'. Gort had already taken the step of ordering the evacuation of the non-fighting troops and was warned of large-scale evacuation by Eden on the 26th. All this, of course, amounts to nothing. There could be no possibility of evacuation except through London, i.e. the British government, the War Office, the Admiralty and the Air Ministry.

On the other hand, Darlan did little; Weygand at first did nothing and then tried to impose conditions on the business of evacuation, with the result that three days were lost. From 29 May, when the direction that one Englishman should be embarked for one Frenchman was given, the removals were to all intents level-pegging, 139,732 English to 139,097 French.

It is, however, the final evacuation of the night 1/2 June, leaving the defence of Dunkirk to Fagalde's exhausted scraps, which is considered, if not a betrayal, at least an action difficult to justify. It appears that what happened is not what Lord Gort intended, but it must be stated that the orders are sufficiently ambiguous to allow different interpretations. They allow the French to consider the massive withdrawal of British troops and the abandonment of the defence of the bridgehead to Fagalde's depleted units, half of which were elderly reservists, almost a betrayal, and the British to consider the withdrawal a necessity imposed by higher authority.

Last of all, chance played its normal dissolute game. If on 24 May Reichenau had delayed his attack on the Belgians for another forty-eight hours, the whole of the reserve of the two Allied armies, five divisions, would have been committed to the forlorn adventure towards Bapaume and would have been impotent to disengage.[20]

20 FAILURE ON THE SOMME,
25 May–4 June

The Abbeville fiasco. Failure on the Somme

FROM the middle of May, the British 1st Armoured Division, of which one tank brigade had been sent to Calais and had there been lost, began to land at Cherbourg. Apart from the divisional headquarters of General Evans, with the anti-tank and anti-aircraft regiments, the first arrival was the Queen's Bays of the 2nd Brigade, which reached the Forêt de Lyon on the 22nd and was sent off on the 24th to reconnoitre the Somme west of Amiens, between Dreuil and Picquigny. To each squadron was attached a company from the 4th Border Regiment. The information was that French troops were on the river. None, however, were seen. The bridges were either broken, or guarded by German infantry. At Picquigny, they had patrols out as far as Fourdrinoy and Cavillon, five or six kilometres south of the river. At Ailly, two platoons of the Border Regiment got to the north side, but they were unsupported and had to be withdrawn. Minor attacks elsewhere had no success.

General Besson had cancelled the attacks ordered for the 25th, but on this day the infantry of the 19th Division, after six days of contradictory orders and counter-marching, had established themselves opposite Péronne: further upstream they recaptured St Christ Benoist across the river and Épenancourt and Pargny on the west side, with the aid of some tanks and *chasseurs* of the 2nd Armoured.[*] On the 26th an attempt by the 22nd Foreign Volunteers[†] to take Villers-Carbonnel failed. Small-scale fighting continued hereabouts for the next week.

The concentration of the Tenth Army now gathered pace. Between the 24th and 27th, the horsed brigade of the 3rd Cavalry Division was withdrawn from the Third Army and dispatched to the Tenth, rejoined *en route* by the dismounted dragoons and its armoured squadron, now equipped with new tanks. The division came in on the left of X Corps between Picquigny and Condé-Folie and spent five days clearing the south bank of the river. At the same time, the mechanized brigades of the 2nd and 5th Cavalry Divisions moved up opposite Abbeville, which was now garrisoned by the 57th Bavarian Division. Their horsed brigades did not arrive until the 29th. On the 26th, the 60th Infantry Regiment of the approaching 13th Division helped the 3rd Cavalry clear the enemy out of the area south of Picquigny, after which the

---

[*] It had been reconstructed and was now commanded by Colonel J. Perré, formerly commander of the armour.

[†] The '*régiments de marche de volontaires étrangers*', otherwise German exiles, were, says the historian of the 41st Infantry Regiment, 'very brave although untrained'. There were three: 21st, 22nd, and 23rd.

division occupied the south bank from Picquigny to the edge of Amiens (Pont de Metz).

Since the end of April, General Fortune's 51st Highland Division had been occupying a sector of the Maginot Line. On 20 May, it was warned that it would be relieved. The relief was completed on the night of the 22nd/23rd. It was moved by train to the Tenth Army, where it was to join General Evans's two armoured brigades. It arrived on the Bresle river on 28 May.

The ground south of the Somme opposite Abbeville offered no easy approach to an attacking force. It rises fairly abruptly from the river bed, or, perhaps better, canalized marsh, across drain-cuts and market gardens, to some 200 feet above the river. Just to the north-west of the Rouen road Mont Caubert stands with Caesar's Camp on the northern spur and commands the exits from Abbeville. This is the key-point. Beyond lie villages typical of Picardy, compact, largely concealed by orchards, difficult for infantry to overcome unless supported by strong artillery. The German bridgehead had been thrust out ten kilometres as far as Huppy with a fifteen-kilometre base on the river from Pont Rémy to Petit-Port. Another bridgehead was at St Valéry, sixteen kilometres down-river.

On the 26th, the 2nd and 5th Cavalry Divisions were ordered to join with the British armoured brigades in an attempt to wipe out the two bridgeheads. The British should have had a support group of two infantry battalions, but these had been sent to Calais and were now in enemy hands. The British 2nd Brigade, light tanks of five tons, went in with General Berniquet's 2nd Cavalry Division, the 3rd (Cruiser tanks) with the 5th (General Chanoine). The French and British accounts of what happened tally at scarcely one point so far as the attack on the eastern face of the position from east of the Rouen road, except that the attack was stopped by fierce and accurate anti-tank fire from well-dug-in positions, and that the small, lightly armoured cavalry tanks of the 10th Hussars and Queen's Bays suffered heavy casualties, sixty-five being knocked out and another fifty-five breaking down. North of the road, the 5th Cavalry and the 2nd and 5th Royal Tank Regiments took Saigneville between Abbeville and St Valéry, and reached Toeuffles and Moyenville, where they were stopped by minefields and gun-fire. St Valéry was not reached. The 5th Cavalry tried again on the 28th, with no more success.

[2]

On the evening of the 28th, de Gaulle's 4th Armoured, which had moved on the 20th from the Aisne to near Beauvais, came up to the area between Airaines and Merelessart, with orders to carry out the task which the British and French light divisions had been unable to fulfil, in chief to drive in the German bridgehead at Abbeville and seize the crossings. The general—he had been promoted temporary general

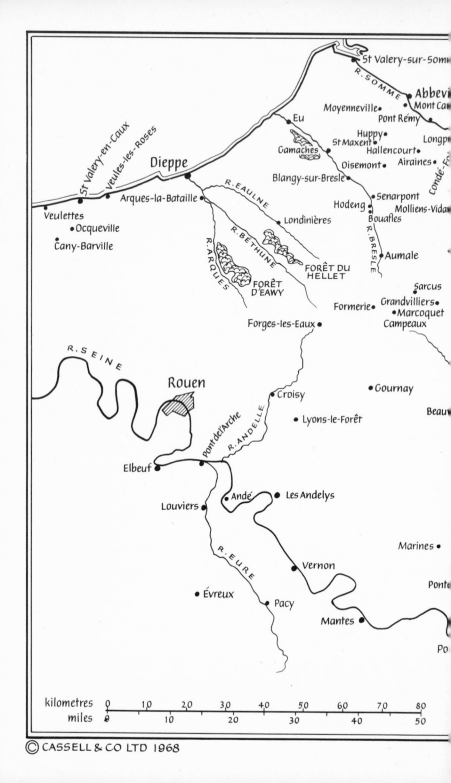

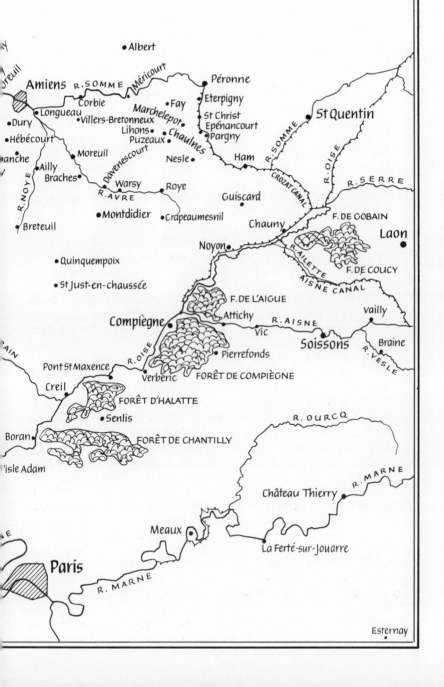

omme-Aisne-Seine- 18 May-8 June

Albert

Amiens   R. SOMME   Méricourt   Péronne

Corbie   Fay   Eterpigny

Longueau   Marchelepot   St Christ

Dury   Villers-Bretonneux   Epénancourt

Hébécourt   Lihons   Chaulnes   Pargny

anche   Puzeaux

Moreuil   Nesle   Ham   St Quentin

Ailly   Davenescourt   R. SOMME   R. OISE

Braches   Warsy   Roye   R. SERRE

R. NOYE   R. AVRE   Guiscard   CROZAT CANAL

Breteuil   Montdidier   Crapeaumesnil   Chauny   F. DE GOBAIN

Laon

Noyon   R. AILETTE   F. DE COUCY

Quinquempoix   AISNE CANAL

St Just-en-chaussée

F. DE L'AIGUE   Vailly

AIN   Compiègne   Attichy   R. AISNE

Vic   Soissons   Braine

Pont St Maxence   R. OISE   Pierrefonds   R. VESLE

Creil   Verbéric   FORÊT DE COMPIÈGNE

FORÊT D'HALATTE

Boran   Senlis   R. OURCQ

FORÊT DE CHANTILLY

'isle Adam   R. MARNE

Château Thierry

E   Meaux   La Ferté-sur-Jouarre

Paris   R. MARNE

Esternay

of brigade three days earlier—was to concert with the commanders of the 2nd and 5th Cavalry.[1]

His division was now much stronger than in the fighting round Laon. He had 140 tanks, three groups of artillery, thirty-seven anti-tank guns, two battalions of dismounted dragoons and one of *chasseurs*, the 4th, and an armoured car squadron of 10th Cuirassiers. At the last moment there was added the 22nd Colonial Infantry, the white two-battalion regiment of the 5th Colonial Division. The Tenth Army commander had left it to de Gaulle to agree with Generals Berniquet and Chanoine as to the methods of co-operation. He established his headquarters at Merelessart, between Oisemont and Airaines, and during the morning he reconnoitred the German positions. He decided to attack northward towards Mont Caubert, on the same axis as that followed on the previous day by the 2nd Cavalry Division and the British 2nd Armoured Brigade, starting roughly from the line already reached, St Maixent on the Rouen road–Limeux–Bailleul Wood. He put his heavy tanks on the right with the *chasseurs*, and the Renault half-brigade on the left with the colonial infantry. The attack was supported by three groups of the divisional artillery, one of 105s, two of 75s, two groups from the 2nd Cavalry Division, one of 105s, one of 75s, and one of 75s from the artillery general reserve, in all seventy-two guns. Zero was 5 p.m., when the armour was to move; the artillery bombardment was to last from Z/5 to Z/15. Orders reached the assault units only about 4 p.m. Also it rained. There were mechanical breakdowns. The roads were packed with refugees. The crews were tired from a night march. There were delays and the time of the bombardment had to be extended. Then the sky cleared and the German aircraft appeared. In the end the attack got under way between 5.30 and 6. There was no surprise and it was far too late to reach the objective before dark. Although advances were made and a number of prisoners taken, the attack was far from successful and a large proportion of the armour was put out of action. Only part of the first objective had been reached. The cavalry divisions had done better. The 2nd had taken Moyenneville, occupied and lost on the previous day, and Béhen. The 5th had reached the line Gouy–Cahon on the Somme.

The assault was renewed at 4 a.m. on the 29th with more success. The Rouen road was crossed, the wood at Bienfay reached by the 4th Chasseurs. For the rest, the Renault half-brigade, at the price of heavy casualties, took Huchenneville and Villiers-Mareuil, and reached the river at Mareuil and Caubert, but they were no nearer securing the ridge and Caesar's Camp. The 2nd Cavalry, trying to get forward from the Moyenneville–Miannay line, were thrown back by counter-attacks. The British 51st Division put the 2nd Seaforths in the line at Toeuffles. The 5th Cavalry made little progress. But the troops, who had been fighting since 13 May, were now extended. Nevertheless, the bridgehead had been reduced. De Gaulle prepared to renew the combat on the

30th. As on the previous day, a communiqué was issued *pour encourager les estaminets de province*, and in his memoirs the general claims 500 prisoners: 'it would be closer to the truth to say 250', says a less enthusiastic historian.

It was now thought that an attack from the west, where the ground was less exposed, offered better hopes. By now, however, the 4th Armoured was much reduced. On the left, a dozen armoured cars, some fifteen Somua and a battalion of dragoons were to move from Moyen-neville on Cambron. In the centre, a dozen 'B' tanks, all that remained of the 6th Half-Brigade with the *chasseurs*, would attack Mesnil-Trois-Foetus and Yonval, while on the right, the Renaults and the colonial infantry would try to reach Mont Caubert. Air support was promised, but proved both weak and uncertain. As before, zero was at 5 p.m. But on the previous evening, the Germans had received the formidable reinforcement of a group of 88-mm. anti-aircraft guns. The German artillery group commander sent two batteries south of the river during the night. Placed to cover Mont Caubert, the area north of Bienfay and the plateau north of Moyenneville, these powerful weapons were able to penetrate at 2,000 yards even the 60-mm. armour of the French 'B' tanks. The French attack ended almost as soon as it began, and the battered tanks were ordered to fall back. A German counter-attack about 8 in the evening, towards Moyenneville and Bienfay,[2] was stopped. At 4 in the morning the 22nd Colonial, with five tanks, made a further attempt at Villiers-Mareuil. The pair of 88s on Mont Caubert opened fire, and in a few minutes the attack was stopped dead.

On the left, some cavalry tanks and a company of the 1st Black Watch had reached the edge of Cambron, but they were isolated, and after the repulse of the 4th Armoured were withdrawn. On the following day, a Tenth Army inventory of the three French formations showed that between them there were only thirty-four runners; of these, only two were 'B' tanks. The 4th Armoured, except its artillery, was withdrawn to refit. A week later, on 5 June, General de Gaulle was appointed Under-Secretary of State at the War Office and left for Paris. The vacant command was occupied by General de la Font of the 3rd Light Armoured Division.

At the same time, the 5th Cavalry Division was relieved by the British 51st, and the 2nd Cavalry by the 31st Alpine, while further east the 5th Colonial Division began to take over the line held by the 3rd Cavalry Division from Le Catelet to Hangest.

It is not to be denied that de Gaulle had been given a difficult, even impossible, mission. On the other hand, at no time did the advocate of the *armée de métier* display that he had any real conception of the tactical handling of his chosen weapon. As a French officer has written of the attack on 28 May, 'Nothing could be more classical than his orders, nothing more conformist with French tank tactics, which were simply nothing more than the accompaniment of the infantry. De Gaulle even fell into the most obviously erroneous of French methods, that of underestimating the density of machine needed to break into a defensive position. . . . He was, of course, limited in his means, but in a large measure, he was master of the scale of his attack.'

The general, however, had no doubts about what ought to be said. In his memoirs,[3] he claims that 'we had not entirely liquidated the bridgehead at Abbeville, nevertheless reduced it by three quarters. Such as it was, at the moment, the enemy could not debouch in force, at least at first, to recover it. Our losses were heavy, all the same they were less than the enemy's. We brought back 500 prisoners to add to those from Montcornet.'

It may be so, but on 4 June, at the moment of the German attack on the Somme, the main body of the 4th Armoured was still near Beauvais. It had had too many casualties to be profitably re-employed. Of the original 135 Renaults (the establishment on 5 June) of the 2nd, 24th and 44th battalions only twenty-eight remained, and of the sixty-six 'B' tanks of the establishment of the 46th and 47th battalions, there survived but eight.

'These facts and figures allow one to doubt the argument of those faithful Gaullists in London who, by their articles, would have the reader believe that de Gaulle had practically won the war at Abbeville. . . . Eric Linklater, not without malice, since he had not to concoct an epic, did not hesitate to underline the fact that the French troops under Colonel de Gaulle's orders were unable to reach or hold the positions laid down for them. He was not thinking about the Rassemblement du Peuple Français.'[4]

In fact the most depressing aspect of this episode is the consequence of the attempts to bolster up a false reputation. Inflated by journalism, de Gaulle now took on himself to be the strategical adviser of Reynaud, which was far beyond his duties. Weygand may not have been better than average, but it was a disservice to the French Army for a political soldier, who had failed in the two restricted tasks assigned him, to presume to advise the President of the Council—even, as he later did, advise him to carry on the war. To the Cornelian hero such considerations have no significance: he marches on.

It is fair to say that de Gaulle in his memoirs makes more modest claims than do the *epigoni* on his tailboard. But what in fact did he do? Frankly nothing at all, except, at great cost in French lives, to take some 500 prisoners, a modest half battalion, little more than the bag taken by two British tank battalions and two infantry battalions at Arras on the afternoon of 20 May. He did not paralyse the German attack; the 'pulverized' 57th Bavarians were up and coming on 5 June. He did not hand over a defensible line.

What is a victory? I shall not try to teach de Gaulle; he has had too good a military up-bringing. To be victorious is to impose one's will on the enemy. What did the enemy want on 17–19 May? To resume his rush seaward without being delayed. What did he want at the end of May and the beginning of June? To hold the Abbeville bridgehead with a view to a further offensive southward. . . . In spite of the attacks of the 4th Armoured, he held it. In spite of the strong attack of the 2nd armoured on 4 June he kept it and took advantage of it.[5]

The 4th Armoured Division departed from the neighbourhood of Abbeville and was replaced by the reconstituted 2nd under the command of Colonel Perré. At the same time the Highland Division relieved the French cavalry. To this group was added the 31st Alpine. IX Corps ordered yet another attempt to reach Abbeville on the morning of 4 June. Information about the German positions was extremely sketchy and there were neither air photographs nor planes for reconnaissance. The 2nd Armoured and the 31st Division were sent against the key position, the Mont Caubert ridge and Caesar's Camp, with a British infantry brigade on either side. One, the 154th, was to occupy the Germans at St Valéry sufficiently to prevent the dispatch of reinforcements to Abbeville. The other, the 152nd, attacked Caubert village at the foot of the hill on the road into Abbeville. By this time the Bavarians were well dug in and had the advantage of knowing the ground. The attack had very little success and at nightfall the attackers were back on the starting-line. At dawn on this day, the Dunkirk operation had closed. Already the German Command had relieved the troops here, to employ them on the Somme, and they were arriving on the starting-line for *Fall Rot*, the second phase of the German strategic plan, which was to open on 5 June.

[3]

On 5 June the military situation of the French Army was hopeless. Though its leaders still shrank from admitting the fact, the losses had been mortal. The Belgian Army, if not powerful, had at least been strong enough to occupy a dozen German divisions. Except for one infantry division and two armoured brigades, the British force had disappeared. At best the British could send no more than two divisions to France. Of seventy-one field divisions, the French Army had lost twenty-two, including six out of seven motorized. Of five fortress divisions, two had gone. Eight (360 tanks) of the twenty armoured battalions, chiefly Renault, attached to the infantry, had disappeared. Of the four armoured divisions, two had been destroyed by French senior officers to no purpose, and the other two had been badly damaged. Although these four had been partly reconstructed, all were at less than half-strength. The three light armoured divisions of the Cavalry Corps had lost all their machines. The crews were already on their way back from England, but only a very small proportion could be re-equipped. Of the five cavalry divisions, the 1st and 4th had been destroyed, but had now been re-equipped as skeleton 'light armoured divisions', renumbered 4 and 7.

For the lost infantry divisions, there were no replacements, though an almost wholly weaponless XVI Corps was put together in Normandy under General Fagalde. Otherwise, there was one active division, made up of three demi-brigades of *chasseurs alpins* from the Norwegian Expeditionary Force, two North African divisions on their way from Algeria, two Polish divisions, partially trained and not fully armed in Army Group Two (a third was being mobilized in Brittany). There were three 'light' infantry divisions made up from those Second Army formations broken at Sedan, and seven similar divisions, numbered 235 to 241, consisting of two infantry regiments, one regiment of 75s and a reconnaissance group, drawn from draft-finding units, training battalions, instruction centres.* There were still most of the fortress regiments in the Maginot Line, and there were numerous unincorporated units, machine-gun battalions, anti-aircraft batteries, pioneer regiments, etc.

Between the mouth of the Somme and the junction of the Ailette Canal with the Aisne at Bourg-et-Comin, some 180 kilometres of river and canal were held by one British and thirteen French infantry divisions, with another seven in reserve. With them were three weak armoured and three even weaker cavalry divisions. Outnumbered two to one in infantry, and by far more in armour, they awaited the attacks of von Bock's Army Group B, thirty infantry divisions with six more in reserve, and six armoured divisions, six motorized (one of them S.S.) and one cavalry division. Between Bourg-et-Comin and the Meuse, a little over a hundred kilometres, there were nine French divisions in the front line, with perhaps a like number in reserve; this included the 3rd Motorized, much depleted and without transport. There was also the much-reduced 3rd Armoured. Facing them was von Rundstedt's Army Group A with twenty-five divisions up to the Meuse, plus Guderian's armoured group of four armoured and two motorized divisions. Six more divisions held the line between the Meuse and the Moselle. There were eight divisions in reserve. Von Leeb's Army Group C, which faced the Maginot Line and the Rhine, had twenty-four infantry divisions and four fortress.

And there still remained to the Germans the Eighteenth Army of six divisions and two groups, one in Flanders of eight divisions, and one east of the Meuse with five more.

The German strength was, of course, overwhelming. In the air it was even more so. The British had withdrawn the Air Component to England, except for one fighter and one reconnaissance squadron near Rouen: it had lost seventy-four planes in combat, but 122 damaged planes had to be left in France. A depleted Advance Air Striking Force of six squadrons had retreated to the region of Troyes: there were

---

* Some were not even as strong as this. The 240th Light seems to have consisted of six North African infantry battalions, with no divisional artillery and no divisional commander.

with them three fighter squadrons. During May and June the A.A.S.F. lost 229 machines.

Beyond the fact that General Vuillemin, either directly or through Weygand, repeatedly asked for large numbers of fighters, on the ground that the French Air Force was destroyed, it is impossible to know what, in fact, the air strength was. The losses in the first days after 10 May were crippling, and though replacements and new American machines filled up the gaps, the major problem was to provide pilots. New bombers, Glenn Martin and Douglas, were introduced, but the main work fell on the Lioré 45 and Breguet 693. Between 11 May and 22 June there were 1,469 bomber sorties, of which some seventy were abortive owing to weather. Nearly every one was against troop concentrations and lorry columns. On 29 and 30 May, at the time of the attacks by de Gaulle's 4th Armoured, bridges at Abbeville and elsewhere on the Somme were bombed, but no successes were claimed and can certainly have been no more successful than against the Maastricht or Sedan bridges. The total losses from these sorties amounted to 123 machines.

French air defence was ineffective. The fighter groupings, Nos. 21 and 23, the first west, the second east and north of Reims, were under separate command from the ground defences. At the beginning of June, the Germans made a full effort to smash the air defences, regardless of casualties. On 1 and 2 June, heavy attacks were concentrated on the Rhône valley and Marseille. On 3 June Paris was the target, carried out in the early afternoon. Their task was eased by the failure of the ground forces to warn the fighter groups, although such raids had been expected for the last ten days. At a number of airfields, the first knowledge of what was happening was the passage of the German bombers overhead. As elsewhere, the anti-aircraft batteries round Paris were unable to do anything serious. It is reported that the French lost twenty-one machines to the German nineteen, but on balance the French losses were more severe. The raid had been chiefly against the arms factories in the west of the city. The west wing of the Citroën works was badly damaged, and there were nearly 1,000 casualties, of which 250 were dead.

21 'FALL ROT'; TO THE OISE, *5–10 June*

'Fall Rot', first phase, 5–8 June

THE first part of the German final offensive was entrusted to von Bock's Army Group B on a front that extended from the mouth of the Somme to the junction of the Ailette Canal with the Aisne. It consisted of Kluge's Fourth Army, Reichenau's Sixth, and part of the Ninth, now commanded by Strauss, hitherto of II Korps. It amounted in all to ten army corps with three in reserve, and included six of the armoured divisions. This force was faced by Robert Altmayer's Tenth Army with IX and X Corps, Frère's Seventh with I and XXIV Corps, and on the right XVII Corps of Touchon's Sixth Army. In all there were roughly fifteen divisions in the front line and ten in reserve, of which three were the already much tried and weak cavalry divisions. Also in reserve were three reconstructed armoured divisions: the 1st, 2nd and 4th, not one of which was at full strength; all were west of the Oise. With the Tenth Army were the two British lightly armoured brigades.

In the first days of June, the Luftwaffe had carried out heavy air-raids on Paris, its airfields, its factories and its railway girdle, with a view to isolating the city, which they intended to mask and pass on both east and west.

The infantry in the front line facing the Somme were under no illusions as to the German intentions; the only question was the date. On the morning of 5 June, at various times after 2 a.m., while the river was still shrouded with mist, the German artillery opened, at first against the French artillery. Between 3.30 and 4, this turned to a general artillery preparation, followed by the infantry assault on the defended villages, 'too far apart', according to the Highland Division, 'to give each other effective support'.[1] On the left, the 154th Brigade was attacked in force from the St Valéry bridgehead. Saigneville was lost, and most of the villages in the angle between the sea and the river. On their right, the 153rd Brigade and the 31st Alpine Division were gradually driven out of the villages captured earlier. On the right, the 152nd Brigade of the Highland Division was also slowly driven back. By the evening of the 6th, all were on the line of the Bresle from Eu to Blangy.

Further to the right, the dismounted dragoons of the 2nd Cavalry Division, 600 men on a twelve-kilometre front as far as Longpré, were attacked out of the Abbeville bridgehead and fell back to the line of support-points held by the 5th Cavalry through Hallencourt. All these formations, though retreating, were resisting stubbornly.

It was beyond Longpré that the disaster began. Between Condé and Hangest two railway bridges cross the Somme. These had not been blown, and on the night of the 4th/5th were occupied by infantry units from Hoth's XV Panzer Korps. During the same night, the horsed brigade of Petiet's 3rd Cavalry was being relieved by the two Senegalese regiments of General Sechet's 5th Colonial Division. The relief was not complete at the hour of the attack and the 6th Dragoons were still in the line with the 44th Senegalese. Further, the Colonial Division's artillery was not yet in position. The rifle regiments of the Panzer Korps came straight on after crossing the railway bridges, while the engineers removed the rails to allow the tanks to follow. Rommel's account says that the tanks were delayed by the steepness of the banks beyond the Somme. It was not for long. The unhappy African troops were overrun in a few hours, and a gap, eight kilometres wide, developed between Hangest and Airaines, through which the German armour advanced rapidly towards Le Quesnoy. General Petiet recalled his mechanized brigade, but it was too late. Already the 7th Panzer armour was past Le Quesnoy and moving up the Laudon valley. The first group of the 72nd Artillery, twelve 75s, took on the tanks, but though they claimed to have knocked out a large number, the group was overrun and captured in the evening. Tenth Army put the Langle de Cary armour at Petiet's disposal and then withdrew it before it could be used. The Panzers came down both sides of Airaines and east of Le Quesnoy and reached a line a little short of Molliens-Vidame, where Rommel, fearing they might run into a Stuka bombardment, halted them. At nightfall, Aumont, headquarters of the 5th Colonial, was still holding out, as was a battalion of the 53rd Senegalese in Airaines. But General Sechet had lost touch all round.

East of the 5th Colonial, the 13th Division occupied a sector of great awkwardness, with its left on the line of the Somme from St Pierre to Breilly and Ailly, but the Germans held Dreuil and the line then ran south until it linked with the 16th Division of X Corps. The loss of Hangest towards midday compromised the defence of the river-line. The attack by Manstein's XXXVIII Korps reached the Bois de Cavillon, Fourdrinoy and Saissemont, which isolated the 60th Infantry Regiment of the 13th Division in a salient. For the time being they were able to maintain themselves, although the left of the division was extending further and further south as the 7th Panzer pushed on. Their right was to some extent covered by the 16th Division. Here, after an early artillery preparation, the attack began soon after 5, with tanks from the 3rd Panzer Division at Dury, Rumigny, Hébécourt, as far as Oresmaux. These attacks were repeated during the morning. The support-points were isolated and attacked from the rear. Oresmaux, deep in the position, was lost, but recovered late in the afternoon. At nightfall, though some of the forward position was lost, many of the 16th Division strongpoints were intact and the divisional headquarters was still where it had been at dawn, though the enemy had got within a couple of kilometres.

The situation was better beyond Amiens. The 4th Colonial had not been seriously attacked. At evening its left was still at Longueau and attacks towards Villers-Bretonneux had failed. At Cagney and Boves the division had thrown out flank guards as the German armour came through the 16th Division's strong-points, but there had been no crossing of the Avre or the Noye. On the front of General Sciard's I Corps, where the attack was initiated by von Wietersheim's XIV Panzer Korps,* the fighting was extremely bitter. The first attack from Aubigny against the 7th North African was broken, though Méricourt was smashed by gunfire before being stormed. At Proyart, a little to the south-east, the Tunisians, in spite of being surrounded, held out, and towards dusk the attackers withdrew.

On the other hand, the 19th Division to the right of the Tunisians was slowly destroyed. The division (two active Breton regiments and the 22nd Regiment of Foreign Volunteers) had been fighting hard since its entry into position on the 24th, particularly on the river south of Péronne. On the 30th, its right had been taken over by the 29th Division. It was in a salient of which the peak was the villages of Belloy, Estrées and Berny. On 1 June, a dawn attack with flame-throwers on Fay was repelled by the 41st Infantry Regiment, and the Germans lost rather more than half their assault force. As elsewhere, each village had been converted into a strong-point and the whole line was covered by the divisional and corps artillery, but there was little cover, and on 5 June, the dive-bombers dealt thoroughly with the batteries. The French fired a short counter-preparation before dawn, but the German guns opened at 3.30 and included incendiaries. The armour—it was Hoeppner's XVI Panzer Korps—came down half an hour later, passed between the defended villages and attacked the supports. They were followed by lorry-borne infantry. All telephone lines were soon down and each strong-point fought as a separate detachment. By 10 a.m. the situation was critical. In places the armour had reached the gun positions. At one point, a successful counter-attack was carried out by two tractors with light machine-guns. Belloy, held by the 117th, was lost at 11, Berny at 2, and Estrées at 5 p.m. Déniécourt, behind Berny, was fighting at nightfall, but the ammunition was exhausted and the garrison had had severe losses. On their left, the 41st Infantry Regiment and the 31st Algerians held on, and Chaulnes and Ablaincourt were still in existence at nightfall.

The 29th Division further up-stream had their position intact at the end of the day. Beyond Ham, the enemy did little. The Crozat Canal was to go of itself, when the flanks were broken.

While the flanks were still holding, across the Oise, the right of the Seventh Army and the left of the Sixth were attacked by Strauss's

* XIV Korps was now made up of 9th and 10th Panzer Divisions and the 29th Motorized, under von Wietersheim. It was attached to Reichenau's Sixth Army. For the reorganization of the Panzer divisions see Appendix B.

Ninth Army on the Ailette and Oise–Aisne Canal, held by the 87th African Division and the 7th. As to the west, the bombardment began between 3.30 and 4 a.m. Covered by thick mist, the Germans crossed the canal on rubber boats and rafts. Far from universally successful, they infiltrated deeply enough to be able to establish positions for exploitation, and during the day were able to push the infantry back from the canal. The line was not broken, but the Germans secured enough ground to be able to reinforce a more formidable attack on the following day, although a number of strong-points were still holding out.[2]

[2]

The situation on the morning of 6 June might have been considered satisfactory except for one sector, that of the shattered 5th Colonial Division, through the gap into which Hoth's XV Korps was now pushing hard. Except for the garrison of Airaines, which still held out (it went during the night), and that at Molliens-Vidame, which escaped, covered by de Langle de Cary's *cuirassiers*, the two Senegalese regiments were gone, dead or prisoners. In front of Rommel's 7th Panzer there was nothing but the Dismounted Dragoons of Petiet's 3rd Cavalry on the Poix road, with, on their left, the horsed brigade of the 2nd Cavalry; on their right at Briquemesnil they had touch with the 13th Division. The 13th Division was still in touch with the 16th Division, but the break on the left was causing an extension southward to Poix with a consequent thinning out of battalions. All posts on the Somme had gone on the previous evening.

To the west, to the other side of where the 5th Colonial had been, the Highland Division was on the Bresle with the 31st Alpine on its right. On the right of the 31st, there now came in the 40th Division, nine battalions of *chasseurs alpins* recently brought back from the Norwegian Expeditionary Force. All these three divisions were on the Bresle. The Bresle, a small marshy stream, wandering through bushes, reeds and trees, runs to the sea at Le Tréport, from the south-east, its headwaters being nearly due south. Therefore, by treating it as an anti-tank ditch, IX Corps command were widening the gap where the 5th Colonial had been, between the 40th Division, of which the right in the afternoon of the 6th was at Aumale, and the 13th clinging desperately to X Corps. Between Aumale and Poix were more than sixteen kilometres, sketchily occupied by the three cavalry divisions. During the day, these were slowly driven westward and southward towards the upper Bresle, Liomer–Guibermesnil–Tronchoy, by the 5th Panzer.

On this same day, the 6th, Rommel's division, with von Hartlieb's on his right and the 6th Division of Manstein's Korps on his left, crossed the Poix–Aumale road practically without a fight. Poix was captured in the evening by XXXVIII Korps. On the other hand, the XVI Panzer Korps ran into far stiffer opposition against Grandsard's divisions. Hoeppner's tanks had made very little impression on the villages south of Amiens. Although it lost heavily, on the 5th the 16th Division had held most of its posts. Grandsard ordered the 4th Colonial to take over from the 16th whatever it could find east of the road from Amiens to Estrées, and told the commander of the 24th Division, in reserve behind the 16th, to take over the area between the Noye and the right of the 13th Division. But from early morning the enemy had resumed his attacks. Dury was at last lost, Hébécourt surrounded, Oresmaux threatened. Orders were given to abandon these villages and others still holding in the Celles valley. Fighting continued during the afternoon and evening. By dusk the 16th Division was almost obliterated. What remained fell back through the line of posts of the 24th Division, from Conty through Le Bosquel to Ailly-sur-Noye. During the evening orders to retreat to a line from Ailly to Braches were sent to the 4th Colonial in touch with the 7th North African.

These two divisions had withstood the enemy, XL Korps of Reichenau's Sixth Army, during the whole day. But by 2 p.m. General Sciard, of whose I Corps the 7th North African was the left division, saw that the 19th Division on its right was being annihilated, and that the two divisions, still for the most part on their positions of the 5th, would in a short time be cut off. He spoke to the Seventh Army commander and in consequence orders were sent to the two divisions to withdraw at dawn the next day, the 4th Colonial whose left was already near Ailly to bring their right to Braches, and the 7th North African from Braches to Davenescourt. The infantry came back reluctantly: during the days before the attack they had brought up rations and ammunition to last for some time, and were furious at being forced to abandon them.

The right of the North Africans was in touch with the 47th Division, I Corps reserve, of which the line ran through Warsy and Crapeaumesnil, in touch with the 7th Colonial.

[3]

As has been seen, of the 19th Division, the 117th Infantry Regiment had been wiped out on the 5th, but on the 6th, the 41st at Fay had held out all day, in touch with the 31st Algerians of the 7th North African. On the right everything had gone as far as Marchelepot, which still sheltered the 22nd Foreign Volunteers. But the XVI Panzer Korps had reached Lihons, Chaulnes, Puzeaux and Nesle. Two battalions of the now reconstructed 1st Armoured (General Welvert), ordered to attack towards Chaulnes at 4 a.m., did not start until 8.30, in full daylight and without air cover. They had scarcely started before they were attacked by Stukas, and almost immediately lost thirty-eight machines. They reached Liancourt-Fosse about half-way to Chaulnes before turning back. They had succeeded in delaying the enemy, but nothing more.

The Foreign Volunteers holding Marchelepot were at last crushed at 3 in the afternoon, having fought to the death. By evening only seven of the 75s of the divisional artillery were still in existence. The air attacks on the villages were continuous. Roye, Nesle, Rethonvillers, Roiglise, were all in flames.

On the morning of the 7th, the posts of the 41st Infantry Regiment were ordered to withdraw. This was carried out between 2 and 2.30, but the isolated garrison at Fay did not pick up the order on its radio. At 10.45 a.m., the Germans sent in a white flag to invite surrender. The garrison was now without food or ammunition and half of them were wounded. They destroyed their weapons and the last fifty then surrendered.

The remainder of the division was now withdrawn behind the 47th. The Germans had reached Roye.

At the same time, the 29th Division, which had been badly mauled, was withdrawn, having covered the evacuation of the salient Ham–Tergnier–Chauny, occupied by the 3rd Light and the 23rd. These divisions also fell back, the 23rd to Guiscard, and then, on the next day, behind the 7th Colonial, which faced east on both sides of Noyon.

[4]

At midnight on the 6th/7th, the IX Corps line was approximately from Eu to Gamaches on the Bresle, occupied by the Highland Division, thence to Senarpont by the 31st. Next to the 31st, a little east of the Bresle, the 40th held from Senarpont to Guibermesnil and Caulières, past which the 7th Panzer armour had swept during daylight. East of these were detachments of the 5th and 2nd Cavalry Divisions, engaged by the 5th Panzer and 2nd Motorized Divisions. There was then an extensive emptiness. Possibly there were still men of the 13th Division at Frenoy-au-Val, some ten kilometres north-east of Poix, but it is unlikely; there were, however, still elements in Pissy and Guignemicourt, north of the Poix–Amiens road. From Guignemicourt across the Celles in X Corps area there were garrisons of the 29th Infantry Regiment in Vers, Bacouel, Buyon and Nampty on the Celles, facing Manstein's 46th and 27th Divisions.

On the morning of the 7th, the Germans resumed their advance on the Tenth Army front between Caulières and Conty with the 7th Panzer and the 6th Division from XXXVIII Korps. Rommel started from south of Poix, and, except for a small party of four infantrymen who took on the armoured cars, met no resistance. Rommel ordered the advance over open country, avoiding villages and scaring refugees and peasants in the fields. On the left the 6th and 46th Infantry Divisions also began to hurry: ignoring the fragments of the 13th Division on their left, they kept on the tail of Rommel's units and reached the line of the Thérain.

On the morning of the 5th, General Ihler had had his IX Corps headquarters at La Chapelle-sous-Poix. The break-in of Hoth's Panzers bolted him to Sarcus, fifteen kilometres to the south, on the

6th, and a further irruption of German armour drove him first to Campeaux south of Formerie and finally late on the same day to Londinières, about eight kilometres from Breteuil, near which were the new X Corps headquarters. He had begged Tenth Army to withdraw what remained of the 13th Division to a line further back—in vain. IX Corps was split into two. One of its formations, the 5th Colonial, was no more, the Langle de Cary armoured group had been almost annihilated in the Colonial Division's catastrophe, while the 2nd and 5th Cavalry Divisions were being pressed back on to the line of the Bresle. During the day the Germans were widening the gap every hour, against weakening resistance.

During the 6th, the 2nd Armoured Division of Colonel Perré had been put at the disposal of X Corps. It had marched on the nights of 1/2 and 2/3 June, and had fought through 4 June, when it lost thirty-eight tanks: it had been sent back to between Aumale and Londinières and was required once again on the night of the 5th/6th to march to Beaudeduit, ten kilometres east of Grandvillers. It had now eighty-six runners. Knowing that the division needed to service its armour, Grandsard gave it twenty-four hours. It was, however, taken from X Corps and given to I Corps on the evening of the 6th, in order to close the gap.

Attacks persisted on the 24th Division throughout the 7th. By nightfall much of its left had been driven back, but the right was still in Ailly-sur-Noye in touch with the 4th Colonial. The command-posts of the 50th and 89th regiments were surrounded. When the division went into the line, it had been short of two fifths of its anti-tank guns. By evening on the 7th the rest had gone. The whole left of X Corps, including the 13th Division and 2nd Armoured—neither formally under General Grandsard—was being gradually eaten away. The corps commander reported his situation to Tenth Army, but received neither orders nor help. Nevertheless, the 24th Division, in desperate straits, with all its anti-tank guns, both 25s and 47s, gone, half its 75s and a number of its 155s lost, and a severe shortage of ammunition, did not crumble. On the next day, the 8th, Grandsard attempted a reorganization which would allow the position to be maintained until evening. For this he called on the 2nd Armoured, but Colonel Perré, under orders from his group commander, could not move. By noon, therefore, the 24th Division was dissolving, the 13th falling back, and the enemy in Breteuil. X Corps advance headquarters fell into German hands. New headquarters were opened at Fay-St Quentin from which at 4 p.m. orders were sent to divisions. But by this time every divisional headquarters had moved, and the 4th Colonial was cut off by German armoured cars which had raced on beyond Breteuil to St Just-en-Chaussée.

Thus [wrote General Grandsard] at nightfall [on the 8th] the disaster was complete. On the left Beauvais was in flames, on the right Clermont was burning. The enemy were in St Just and Ducamp. There was no touch with subordinates or neighbours. Army headquarters was silent.

Two staff officers in liaison, sent off last night, returned at 11 this morning, but brought back nothing, no orders, no warning, no information. Another sent off during the day has not returned.[3]

With four tanks and two companies from a 16th Division regiment, X Corps Headquarters organized the defence of Fay-St Quentin, while through the night search was made for the vanished divisions. All three, the 24th, 13th and 16th, were found south of Fay-St Quentin round the Forêt de Hez between Beauvais and Clermont. At 6.30 in the morning, a liaison officer from Tenth Army arrived with an order of the previous day, directing retreat to the Oise and transferring X Corps to the Seventh Army. The withdrawal was to be covered by the newly created XXV Corps, consisting of the 2nd and 4th Armoured Divisions. The divisions of X Corps were to move at once and cross the Oise on the night of 10th/11th between Boran and L'Isle-Adam. The remains of the three divisions marched through the 9th and 10th and crossed the Oise as ordered. By this time they were shreds of what they had been. The 13th Division was reduced to eight small battalions, but there were still thirty-two out of thirty-six 75s, eight 105s, and three 155s. The 16th Division had six much diminished battalions, but it had lost nearly all its guns. The 24th had only eleven out of sixty pieces. One of its infantry regiments, the 78th, when it crossed the Oise on the night of the 9th, had ten officers, 220 other ranks, seventy-four draft horses, forty-three weapons, eight automobiles and four lorries.[4]

Grandsard's fourth division, the 4th Colonial, when, on the 8th, it fell back from the Ailly-sur-Noye–Braches position, had found that the enemy had outpaced them in following up the withdrawal of the 24th Division. And when the remains of the 2nd Colonial Regiment and the 24th Senegalese reached Paillart, they found it already occupied by the Germans. They therefore carried on their withdrawal, but their flank was threatened. At 3.30 p.m. the Germans were at St Just-en-Chaussée, and they reached Clermont about 4.30. The colonials retreated all through the night. They had had no rations since they had quitted the Somme. The roads were a chaos of transport and guns. At dawn on the 9th, they were in Brunvilliers and the Bois de Morlière. The Germans caught up with them and stormed the villages. They shot the Senegalese prisoners, including the wounded, and a number of their white officers with them. All that escaped of the division were 150 men of the 2nd Colonial Regiment, 350 from the 16th Senegalese, and fifty of the 24th. Of the divisional artillery, nine 75s and twelve 105s rejoined X Corps later, together with thirty guns of attached regiments. The Germans appear to have been from the Gross Deutschland regiment.

When the remnant of the 19th Division was withdrawn on the 7th they came through the line of the 47th Division. Marching all day, they came to Rubescourt and Domfront south of Montdidier in the evening, paused, and at 8 p.m. started again. They reached Quinquempoix at 1.30 next morning and lay there until the following night, when they once more set out to cover fifty kilometres to Pont-Ste Maxence. They crossed the Oise after midday on the 9th, in blazing heat. The division now consisted of the 41st Infantry Regiment, 1,000 men (the whole of its 1st Battalion and two companies of the 3rd had been lost); the 117th had between 200 and 300 men; the Foreign Volunteers did not exist. There were still a few 75s and 105s, but no 155s.

While the survivors of the 19th Division were marching south, the 47th Division between Warsy and Lagny was heavily engaged by enemy armour coming down from Roye to Crapeaumesnil. Hard fighting continued here all day, but though Crapeaumesnil was lost, the attack went no further. On the right, the retreating 23rd got back to Lagny and north and south of Noyon, the 7th Colonial, facing east, held on to villages between Sermaize and Porquericourt on the Oise until the evening of the 8th.

During this afternoon, in view of the situation of the Tenth Army to the west and the left wing of the Sixth Army on the Aisne,* General Besson ordered General Frère to bring his army across the Oise during the 9th and 10th. As soon as darkness had fallen, the 47th broke contact with the enemy. The regiments marched all night. The covering force expected on the Aronde was not there, but the 4th and 7th Colonial Regiments on the right engaged the pursuing enemy on the Matz. At dawn on the 9th, the tired soldiers had still twenty-five kilometres to the river crossing at Pont-Ste Maxence. They now knew that the enemy was past Compiègne and on the other side in Clermont, and that they must pass through a defile which might close in a few hours. The infantry were exhausted. The pace of the march dropped to two kilometres an hour. 'The driblets that came by at long intervals were rocking in their tracks; their packs had gone, but they still clung to their weapons. The response to the command to march was scarcely perceptible.' Not a grumble was heard. With bent heads and blind eyes they marched on. When they came to the great Paris–Cambrai road, the columns were broken up. 'Vehicles of every kind, huge horse-drawn guns, took the whole width of the *chaussée*, moving a hundred yards, then stopping for long minutes. The edges of the road were crowded with civilians moving south.'[5] The leading groups of the division began to reach the Oise bridge towards half past three. Some crossed, but a little later a bomb from an aeroplane detonated the demolition charges. The bridge went up. A ten-mile column of retreating transport was halted on the enemy side of the river. A footbridge was discovered a mile or so up-stream and the retreat continued—in single file. Heavy weapons were brought to the water's edge and pushed in. The lighter guns were carried over, but the 25-mm. anti-tank guns could not be saved. The teams smashed them. The division marched on another dozen kilometres to Senlis.

---

* See below, pp. 242–3, and 249.

The 7th Colonial, after a heavy fight on the 9th on the Matz, came down by lesser roads, as did the 23rd. They crossed at Croix-St Ouen, where the bridge was blown on the next day. The crossing at Verberie was held all day by a regional regiment and an active battalion of the 94th, borrowed from the 42nd Division.* On the next day the 33rd Senegalese fought stiffly to hold off an aggressive enemy.

At 8 a.m. on the 10th, the Seventh Army was on the Oise from Boran to Pont-Ste Maxence, and then from Verberie to the eastern horn of the Forêt de Compiègne. All its divisions were weak, some now operationally useless. The artillery was much depleted. The 1st Armoured had few tanks, but some damaged ones might be repaired. Behind were coming up, in front of Paris, the 57th Division and the 239th Light.

[5]

The right of the Seventh Army east of the Oise, the 87th, and the left of the Sixth, the 7th Division and the 28th Alpine, resisted the attacks of six divisions of Strauss's Ninth Army through the 5th, 6th and 7th. On the evening of the 7th, they were told to fall back across the Aisne, the line of which was now occupied by the 11th Division from Compiègne to Attichy, by the 8th between Vic and Ambleny, and by the 27th Alpine covering Soissons. All the infantry had suffered severely.

---

* The straits to which the French were reduced is exemplified by the fact that this battalion of the 94th was brought from Villers-Franqueux, north of Reims, a matter of ninety kilometres.

The end of IX Corps

DURING the 7th and 8th, while the Highland Division with some battalions attached from the British troops at Rouen and Le Havre bases defended the Bresle Line against a not too pressing enemy, the French division on their right were being forced back, as the German armour and infantry wheeled westward and outflanked them. On the right of the Highlanders, the two Alpine divisions fought on, while the 5th and 2nd Cavalry Divisions extended and protected the right flank, and then extended again, gradually moving further south and west.

During the same days, Petiet's 3rd Cavalry had slowly fallen back westward. At dawn on the 7th its armour was at Conteville a little north-west of Formerie; at Formerie the leading units of the 17th Light Division, hurriedly brought up by train from Dreux, were caught at the station by Hartlieb's 5th Panzer and scattered. Most of the division's single artillery regiment went at the same time. Only seven guns got away and joined the other infantry regiment, the 90th, at Forges-les-Eaux, from which they were withdrawn to become part of the group now being organized by General Duffour (yet another of these retired generals, 'elderly and very troublesome', says Brigadier Beauman). This retreat was covered by the 3rd Cavalry, which moved south on the evening of the 8th and crossed the Seine, partly at Pont-de-l'Arche, partly at Pont d'Andé. On the same night the horsed brigade crossed at Les Andelys.

On 29 May, Weygand concluded his note to Reynaud with the warning that the moment might come when, in spite of everything, France would find herself incapable of continuing to provide an efficient military protection of her territory. He added verbally that though he hoped to resist on the Somme–Aisne line, 'it is my duty to tell you that I am by no means certain. I must therefore prepare for misfortune, for the misfortune may be irreparable.'[1]

During 5 June he had driven to La Ferté and Ferrières. At these headquarters and at Montry the reports were encouraging. The infantry were holding and the 'hedgehogs', though surrounded and shelled, often with incendiaries, were continuing to fight. There remained the question: could the French reserves destroy enough of the German armour to keep the garrisons of the villages intact? Though the 19th Division was reported as holding in the Péronne salient against a mass of tanks, the break in of Hoth's XV Panzer Korps between Hangest and Airaines does not appear to have been known. Again on the following morning, the 6th, although the withdrawal of the Highland Division and the 31st was reported, the Commander-in-Chief appears to have heard nothing at all about the fighting east of the Oise except that the main positions were still resisting. He learned that General Touchon had already ordered part of the Sixth Army artillery to withdraw and was bringing the rest back to the Aisne during the night. It was not until the afternoon that the menace to the Tenth Army began to appear. In his memoirs he adds a footnote that the penetration into the Tenth Army defences was deeper than he knew; in other words, than had been reported. He could not know that IX Corps headquarters, having abandoned La Chapelle-sous-Poix for Sarcus and fled from Sarcus, was now *en route* for Campeaux, another twelve kilometres south. Nevertheless, about 6 in the evening, he accepted the fact that the defences of Army Group Three must be progressively drawn back to the line Bresle–Hornoy Ridge–Poix–Conty–Ailly-sur-Noye–Moreuil–the Avre–the Aisne, a line much of which had already been reached, while the stretch between the Bresle and Conty no longer existed.

Still disturbed by the absence of news from the Tenth Army, on the next afternoon, the 7th, as soon as he could get away from Paris, Weygand drove to Tenth Army headquarters at Lyons-la-Forêt in order to urge General Altmayer to greater efforts to arrest the German advance down the coast. While he was here, a minor raid by German aircraft succeeded in cutting all the telephone lines, leaving the army commander bereft of the means of communication except by inefficient radio or by messenger. Weygand now learned for the first time that Hoth's Panzer Korps had broken through between Hornoy and Aumale on the previous day, and that a German order found on a prisoner taken by the 40th Division revealed that the enemy were moving on Forges-les-Eaux. He had a conversation with General Evans, who was preparing, with a much diminished force of cruisers and light tanks, to attack the German left flank. In spite of the protests of the British general that he had already been deprived of his defensive weapons and that his force was only suited to a counter-attack, Weygand insisted that the British armour should hold the line of the Andelle. The significance of the fact that the enemy was not advancing down the coast but in the centre of the Tenth Army seems to have escaped him. On his return to Vincennes he telephoned orders to Montry to put all available reserves at the disposal of Army Group Three. But he still failed to discern the danger threatening IX Corps, the cornering of three infantry and two cavalry divisions.[2] Or did he? For that evening he sent Colonel Bourget, his personal assistant, to Reynaud to warn him of the possible loss of IX Corps, 'which might involve grave consequences'.

According to General Altmayer, the Commander-in-Chief repeated: 'Continue the battle of the Somme, continue holding at every point where you are. I need until 15 June to effect my plan.' There is, however, no indication as to what Weygand was envisaging for 15 June.*

---

* The date apparently refers to the arrival west of Paris of the reinforcements *en route* from the south: viz. the 236th Light Division to the Duffour Group,

Before leaving Lyons-la-Forêt, he authorized Altmayer to destroy the bridges on the 'lower Seine', which means *above* Rouen, since there are no bridges below the city. Since the whole of the Tenth Army was north of the river, the authorization appears to have no relevance to circumstances.

Perhaps he may have understood when, on the next day at Montry, he read in the morning summary of operations that General Altmayer and the Tenth Army staff had quitted Lyons-la-Forêt at 7 o'clock and sped to Marines, fourteen kilometres north-west of Pontoise at the eastern end of the Tenth Army area and wholly out of touch with IX Corps. General Altmayer's staff had not even seen fit to inform the commander of the British armoured division of their flit, although he was in the same town. Weygand removed IX Corps from Tenth Army and put it directly under General Besson. At the same time he ordered General Ihler to withdraw IX Corps from the Bresle. It was two days too late.

With the disappearance of Altmayer's headquarters, IX Corps was isolated. It was directed by Army Group Three to withdraw to Rouen. Ihler had spent the greater part of the war in the Maginot Line and had no experience of the speed at which the Germans moved. He proposed to take four days to reach Rouen.[3] He was apparently unaware that on this day, von Hartlieb's 5th Panzer Division was fighting some of Beauman's scratch battalions on the upper Andelle, perhaps thirty kilometres from Rouen, while Rommel, with a pursuit force, was racing towards the Seine with the intention of capturing the bridge at Elbeuf.

The end of IX Corps and General Ihler can be briefly narrated. Left without orders until midday on 8 June, the Highland and 31st Alpine Divisions remained on the Bresle between Eu and Senarpont, while the 5th Cavalry and the 40th Divisions faced the German 12th Division a little further east on the Liger. The 2nd Cavalry guarded the right flank, west of the Basse Forêt d'Eu. Beyond this point, or, better, to the south, was a gap in which the remains of the 17th Light Division was retreating towards Rouen, protected to a small degree by the 3rd Cavalry Division, of which the Dismounted Dragoons were still between Formerie and Aumale. The 3rd Cavalry had been ordered to regroup south-west of Forges-les-Eaux, and on the 8th was directed, first to cover the crossings of the Seine, and then, in the afternoon, itself to cross. On the same day (the 8th), General Evans's tanks also passed the river at Elbeuf. Thus the right of the IX Corps was now wholly without protection.

On the morning of the 8th, at his headquarters at Marcoquet, one kilometre south-east of Formerie, Rommel agreed with General Hoth's

the 237th Light to III Corps, the 84th North African and 8th Colonial to X Corps, and the 85th African to XXV Corps.

headquarters to drive onward towards Rouen as if to enter the city, but near Croisy to turn left and make a dash for the Elbeuf bridges. The 7th Panzer were held up for a short time by some of Brigadier Beauman's pioneers on the Andelle, and other bold French and British detachments also caused delays. Night fell. The Panzers lost their way and also lost touch with the advance troops. At 2 a.m. Rommel reached Elbeuf to find in the north part of the town a wild confusion of armoured cars and transport and the bridge not taken. No one quite knew what was happening and a French woman ran up to Rommel to ask if he was English. He sorted out the trouble, but before he could get his assault party forward, the bridge went up. The explosion was echoed up and down the river from the destruction of other bridges.[4]

Undefended, Rouen fell to von Hartlieb in the morning. The civil authorities along the Seine had not expected, not believed in time, that the Germans would come so fast. The normal trains were running into Rouen and the Germans came like tourists down N. 28. In Louviers, when the 3rd Cavalry Division came in on the afternoon of the 8th, people greeted them with bouquets of flowers as though they were conquerors. 'We looked with longing eyes at the windows of the cafés, at the pâtisseries crowded with customers as if the enemy was a hundred kilometres away. Alas! twenty-four hours later, the poor citizens of Louviers would understand and would fill their part in the unsuspected drama which was being played at their door.'[5]

On the morning of the 9th, Hoth ordered the 5th and 7th Panzer Divisions and the 2nd Motorized to leave the Seine and move north-westward to cut off IX Corps. The news of the capture of Rouen and the destruction of the Seine bridges reached the commander of the 51st Division, General Fortune, early. At once he changed the destina-tion of his division (and in consequence that of the French divisions) to Le Havre. He quickly dispatched by lorry a mixed force of British infantry, artillery and engineers, and two battalions of the 31st Alpine Division, to occupy a line covering the port between Lillebonne and Fécamp. This body, 'Arkforce', started from Arques-la-Bataille (*'Pends-toi, brave Crillon; nous avons combattu à Arques et tu n'y étais pas'*) and reached Le Havre undisturbed, except for its last vehicles.

On the 10th, Rommel, von Hartlieb and the 2nd Motorized moved westward against IX Corps, which was already engaged in front by the German 31st, 12th and 32nd Infantry Divisions. IX Corps had begun to leave the Bresle line on the 7th, with its right flank protected by the 2nd and 5th Cavalry leap-frogging each other. Since most of the roads the cavalry were using were in wooded country, Basse Forêt d'Eu, Forêt du Hellet, Forêt d'Eawy, now in full leaf, they were able to travel undetected. Roads and tracks were deserted and there were places full of civilians still going about their normal occupations. There were villages which had been forgotten or ignored by the civil administration. 'Hodeing and Bonafles . . . in spite of the lateness of the hour watched us from their doorsteps with the wistful anxiety which by now we knew only too well. . . . Many of those who had fled had been replaced by evacuees from the Boulogne or St Omer part of the world, who had installed themselves in farms deserted by the original occupiers. All these unfortunates, abandoned by their authorities, asked us if they should go, and we dared not tell them that we were continuing to withdraw before the invader.'[6]

With the entry of Hoth's XV Korps into Rouen, the end of IX Corps was assured. On the night of the 9th, everyone knew that the Rouen road was closed, yet Weygand persisted in sending orders which implied that the lower Seine could be held. On the 10th the 7th Panzer reached Cany and Veulettes and closed the coast road to Le Havre. British ships sent to take off the soldiers were shelled from the coast. On the night of the 10th, the Highland Division had now only part of one day's rations. The French divisions were in like straits.

Gradually the circle tightened round St Valéry-en-Caux and, a little further east, Veules-les-Roses. To the latter came a squadron of the 3rd Dismounted Dragoons, one from the 18th Cuirassiers, some guns, and the last companies of the 22nd Colonial Regiment.* The 5th Cavalry Divison held Manneville, the 31st was in Ocquevile and Crosville, the 40th out at Angiens. The enemy held the cliffs to the west of St Valéry and dominated the town. All attempts to capture or neutralize them failed. On the 11th, General Berniquet, commanding the 2nd Cavalry, was hit and died the following morning. The plan to evacuate on the night of the 11th/12th was frustrated by fog. On the morning of the 12th, in spite of British protests, General Ihler[7] ordered the surrender. It was his first decisive action.

---

* The last fragments of the divisions: the 22nd Colonial Infantry was 600 strong; the 3rd Dismounted Dragoons about 200; the 2nd Armoured Car Regiment had two armoured cars, two Hotchkiss tanks and three or four light machine-guns. All the anti-tank guns had disappeared.

23 REYNAUD RECONSTRUCTS. ITALY DECLARES WAR. PARIS EVACUATED, *6–10 June*

The sharp horns of the dilemma

REYNAUD'S political vulnerability, due to his isolation, had led to his filling his ministries with men from all parties of whom few owed him any political loyalty, with a consequent incoherence of government. His attempt to conceal this by giving the command of the army to a general of a high military reputation, backed by another with a great national reputation, demonstrated his own blindness on military matters. Within a week he discovered that his recruits were no wizards, not even Napoleons. Now he was helpless. As he told the Commission on Events, he could not appoint a new Commander-in-Chief every few days.

When they failed to work miracles, he put their failure down to their political opinions rather than to the material facts. It should in no way have surprised him that Weygand lost his temper, scratched and bit, was rashly insulting about the British, about the R.A.F., about Churchill, 'living', in Spears's phrase, 'in a kind of demented dream world'. Weygand's temper was certainly not improved by inappropriate suggestions from the British Prime Minister or from his personal representative in Paris. On 19 May the situation was already irremediable. Weygand's error was not to have recognized it sooner, and, when he had, his diffidence or reluctance to say so clearly. His note of the 25th on what might happen was conditional and allowed Reynaud to persist.

In Pétain, Reynaud had found no wise supporter, but an elderly, petulant and jealous egoist. At the age of eighty-four, the defender of Verdun was mentally alert only at intervals. Weygand certainly showed him the deference due to his age and rank, but certainly did not consult him. On the 28th, Pétain had told Reynaud that if the Somme–Aisne position were lost, he ought to negotiate with the enemy.

At the meeting of the War Committee on the 25th, it had been decided that if the line now being organized were broken, the government should retire to Bordeaux. At the meeting on the 29th, Reynaud wondered whether Bordeaux was really suitable; perhaps it would be better to organize an area on the sea from which it could be supplied, and he discussed the question with the committee in front of a map. He suggested the Cotentin and Brittany, or perhaps one of the two. Weygand replied that while this idea of a continuance of the war suited his own temperament, its feasibility must be examined. As Reynaud left the meeting, he told Baudouin how glad he was that Pétain had changed his mind and that both he and Weygand were ready to go on with the resistance. 'If the French Army is completely defeated, I would not be opposed to requesting a suspension of hostilities, but I am convinced that the enemy would try to impose dishonourable terms. Then we would have to prolong the battle in the Breton redoubt.'[1]

But on the next day (the 30th) Weygand demonstrated that to hold the Armorican peninsula they would have to rely wholly on imports of food and ammunition, and that the British fleet would have a far from easy time with the Luftwaffe. Also it would be difficult to withdraw divisions from the battle and bring them back to the west. For the moment no steps were taken, except that Reynaud told Colson to prepare telephone and radio communications.[2]

[2]

Italian movements now appeared more threatening. Like a rising gangster, Mussolini was saying: '*Le grisbi, je suis assez grand pour aller le chercher moi-même.*' Ciano told François-Poncet that it was useless to talk of concessions, and Churchill had stoutly refused to make any approach to the Italians. On 30 May, Daladier, now at the Quai d'Orsay, sent a letter to Reynaud requesting him to open direct negotiations with the Italian government and enclosed a note to be handed to Guariglia, the Italian ambassador in Paris, declaring France's readiness to make concessions. Daladier had not consulted François Charles-Roux, Léger's successor at the Foreign Office, who, when he saw the document, pointed out that it had not been shown to the British and that it contravened the alliance. Pétain commented that it was extraordinary that a Foreign Minister should draft a note without consulting the Secretary-General. Although Daladier was reminded that, only the day before, Ciano had told the British Ambassador in Rome that Mussolini was refusing to engage in any conversation, Daladier insisted on its dispatch. Two days later Pétain declared to Reynaud that he could no longer suffer the presence of either Sarraut or Daladier in the cabinet, that is to say, of two leading members of the Socialist-Radical party. Reynaud said he would drop them at the appropriate moment. He had partly reconstructed less than a fortnight ago, on 19 May, when he introduced Pétain and transferred Mandel to the Interior. Now, on 5 June, after the chairman of the Senate Foreign Affairs Committee had requested Daladier's removal, he carried out the second execution. This evening he forced the resignation of Sarraut, Daladier and three other ministers. He had invited Pétain to take over the Foreign Office. On his refusal he took it over himself. Baudouin refused the invitation to become Minister of Finance, and remained Under-Secretary to the President of the Council.

De Gaulle's appointment to the War Office this same day infuriated Pétain. But since Reynaud at once sent de Gaulle off to England to try to get hold of more British fighter squadrons, Pétain did not set eyes on on him for some days.[3]

[3]

The assault on the Somme–Ailette line by von Bock's Army Group B, at dawn on the day Reynaud reconstructed his cabinet, continued during the 6th and 7th.* Weygand had hopes that the defence would hold, and although there were breaks-in, he believed that the German advance was being not only delayed but stopped. It is very probable that the true situation of the Tenth Army was not reported. Hence it was a shock to Paul Baudouin to be rung up at 10.30 p.m. on the 7th by Weygand's chief personal assistant, Colonel Bourget, and told 'that an accident of a tactical nature' had happened, which circumlocution was after some time unfolded into the statement that two Panzer divisions had that afternoon entered Forges-les-Eaux. Baudouin told Bourget to report to Reynaud directly, and in the meantime warned the President of the Council of what he might expect. 'Is it possible that our hopes are fading? No. It is impossible!' 'It was not Paul Reynaud's usual voice,' says Baudouin, 'it was not his head; it was his heart.'[4] Forges-les-Eaux, that pleasant, sleepy old-fashioned watering-place on the road to Dieppe, a mere couple of hours' run from Paris; thousands of citizens knew it. Its appearance on the official communiqué brought the immediacy of the danger home to the Parisians; they watched with growing apprehension the flight along the outer boulevards of cars from Seine-Inférieure and Oise, and then from Seine-et-Oise.

On the next morning, Weygand, much disturbed by General Altmayer's unheralded removal of his headquarters to Marines at the eastern end of his command, instead of across the Seine, divided the Tenth Army line on the Seine into two, that of the Rouen region under the regional commander, Duffour, and from Elbeuf to Vernon eastward under General Fournel de la Laurencie, who had returned from England and had just reported. He also consulted General Doumenc about moving to the prepared headquarters at Briare. The war committee once more moaned over the negligence, muddle and laziness of the back areas and the wholesale lack of preparation for war.

About 6 in the evening of 8 June, Pétain summoned to his office[5] General Bernard Serrigny, who had been his personal assistant, and later chief of staff from early in 1915 to the end of 1917, the man he called 'my imagination'. He showed his visitor the situation map. Serrigny asked where were the reserves, and on being told there were none, asked how long the front could hold.

'Weygand says about three days on condition we don't go all out.'

'What do you expect to do in the circumstances?'

'Push the government to request an armistice. There is the meeting of the central committee tomorrow evening. I shall draft a proposal.'

'That's too late,' Serrigny returned. 'Action ought to be taken while France still has the façade of an army and Italy has not yet come in.

---

* Cf. Chapter 21.

Get hold of a neutral to intervene in the approach. Roosevelt seems the obvious choice. He can bring his power to bear on Hitler.'

Pétain agreed and said he would see Reynaud that evening, but it was not until the next day (the 9th) that he produced his proposals at the morning meeting of the war committee.

The morning of 9 June had already seen the opening of the second phase of '*Fall Rot*', the attack of von Rundstedt's Army Group A from Bourg-et-Comin to the Meuse. To Pétain, Reynaud returned that no honourable terms were to be expected from Hitler, and that it would be imprudent to separate from their allies. Pétain retorted that French interests should take precedence over British. 'The British have got us into this situation.' Weygand, when he appeared, said that the army was fighting its last defensive battle. If the battle was lost, it would be broken into fragments and rapidly destroyed. Once more no decision was reached. Again Reynaud evoked the possibility of the Breton redoubt, to which the expected British divisions would be sent, and Weygand replied that at the conclusion of the present battle the troops would be in no condition to be got to Brittany. The only outcome of the meeting was permission to Dautry to withdraw all the young men from the war factories in Paris, and send them southward. It was agreed that the dispensable ministries could be withdrawn from the capital.

When the war committee met on the morning of the 10th, Pétain had already left Paris for Nitray, a château near Montrichard on the Cher. On the other hand, the new Under-Secretary of State for War, Brigadier-General de Gaulle, appeared at it. The completeness of the disaster to the armies east of Paris was not yet visible, but north and west of Paris the situation was desperate. On the previous evening, enemy detachments had been reported at L'Isle-Adam, almost a suburb. Weygand said that the soldiers were exhausted. After five days of battle, even those of Frère's army were no longer what they had been. Not only was the German mastery of the air weakening both the strength and determination of the soldiers; it was destroying communications and hampering control and direction. The telephone lines to centres such as Evreux and Caen were broken, and he warned Reynaud that a complete rupture might occur at any moment. At the end of Weygand's declaration, Reynaud commented that it offered no positive conclusion. To this Baudouin interjected that if Marshal Pétain were present he would insist that the terms of an armistice should be discussed, first, with the British government and then with the German. 'The situation is getting worse every day,' he ended. 'If the situation is getting worse,' interjected de Gaulle, 'it is because we let it worsen.' 'What have you to propose?' returned Weygand sharply. 'It is not my business to propose anything,' de Gaulle answered smugly. Later, to Baudouin, Weygand said he distrusted the new Under-Secretary of State, who was 'more of a journalist than an officer', and whose self-satisfaction amounted to blindness.

[4]

Once more appeared the familiar frieze of soldiers waiting, fighting, retreating, marching; worn, hungry, sleepless, trudging further into France under the relentless sun, wondering if it will ever rain and stop these vigorous young troops, triumphant in their well-prepared success. Once more in the background to the frieze of stubborn defenders, there is the civilian population, men, women and children, from Brussels, from Lille and Roubaix, from Arras and Laon, and now from St Quentin, from Amiens and Abbeville, from Compiègne, Chantilly and Pontoise. In many places there were those who still believed that some miracle would stand in the way of the marauder. From Paris, the wealthy, often those who had some knowledge of the power of Germany, had gone early, but the great majority, whose livelihood depended on their presence in the city, had perforce remained. The communiqués had never been illuminating. There had been a moment when the name of Laon had appeared in them, but the enemy had not turned towards the capital, and the names of Amiens and Abbeville had caused no tremors. But now places in the Île-de-France and the Multien began to appear, and on both sides of the capital the adversary's columns were threatening an embrace.

In the preparation of 'Fall Rot', Hitler, like Weygand, worried over the believed turbulent and revolutionary population of Paris, in which wasps' nest he was reluctant to involve his armies. The Germans must by-pass the city on both sides. From other motives, both Reynaud and Weygand preferred that Paris should not be the scene of battle. Fight before Paris, yes; fight behind Paris, yes; but in Paris, no. Beliefs had changed since the days of Clemenceau. If Paris could not be held from the front, then, said Weygand, it must be declared an open city: the retreating divisions of the Seventh and Tenth Armies would pass round by the outer boulevards, and not through the centre, and there would be no destruction of bridges and similar installations. A new army was formed under the Military Governor of Paris, General Héring, to become a field formation, the link between the Seventh and Tenth Armies. It would retreat with them. Paris was to be left in the charge of the Prefect of Police, Roger Langeron, and General Dentz, Héring's chief of staff.

No orders, however, were given as to evacuation of the population or the ministries. Vuillemin had put the question to Weygand, but it was not until the 9th that Weygand told Reynaud he could see no solution. All he would advise was the removal of children below the age of sixteen. However, on the evening of the 8th, Reynaud ordered all ministries inessential to the battle to retire to the various towns and villages on the Loire which had been earmarked in the first days of the war. Only Reynaud himself, Laurent-Eynac of the Air, Campinchi of the Marine, and, of course, Mandel at the Interior would remain.

A number of special trains, forty-five for passengers, fourteen for archives, had begun moving since the 6th. 'If the train movements were made discreetly, it was far from so with the preparations for departure of the ministries or their employees and the hurly-burly round government offices contributed to the beginnings of panic.'[6] Baudouin notes in his diary that he was staggered to find that neither at the War Office nor at the Interior, nor at the Police Préfecture, had any plan been thought out or any preparations made. 'Everything had to remain ostensibly secret to prevent panic in Paris, since people would inevitably be disturbed at the sight of departure of the government without warning.'[7] The alarm of the Parisians was heightened by the reticence of the High Command as to the part to be played by the capital; was it to fight to the death like Warsaw and Rotterdam or to be spared? The uncertainty had been kept alive by the knowledge that gangs of civilian labourers were being sent out to fortify a line on the perimeter of the capital, while the orders regulating the withdrawal of the younger workers from the arms factories to mobilization centres caused immense confusion. From 11 June, the main-line railway stations were besieged, and on this and the next days the doors had to be closed against the frenzied crowds. There were additional special trains for lunatics, and for criminals. The railwaymen worked as they had been doing since 10 May, without haste, without rest. 'From midday [on 12 June] there was a real mass evacuation, the trains leaving one after the other without consulting any time-table; trains of all kinds, passenger, parcels, military, goods.' It is certain that very many trains marked '*messageries*', '*marchandises*' or '*militaires*' were used either wholly or in part by evacuees.[8] This was succeeded by the mobs of those who tried to escape by road, by car until their petrol was exhausted, by cart, by bicycle or on foot. It was not until the 13th that the flow of refugees was turned off by the announcement that Paris was to be considered an open town. This morning the last train from the Gare Montparnasse left for the south-west at 8.30, and after a circuitous route over three different systems eventually reached Tours.

Many thousands, of course, did not go. At the tail of the exodus came those characters one never sees, at least by day, the *clochards*, hairy, filthy and savage. At the sight of their wolfish faces, the shopkeepers in the rue Mouffetard hastily put up their shutters and retired indoors to wait for the enemy.

June the 14th saw the crowds swelling to their maximum between the Seine and the Loire, particularly in the triangle between Melun, Sens and Pithiviers. The worst swarming came at Montargis and Gien.

Undoubtedly part of the chaos lies at the door of the Ministry of the Interior. True, Mandel, least *capitulard* of ministers, had only been at the head of this all important office since 19 May, but he had set his face against the flinching of civilians or civil servants. He had ordered all local authorities to oppose movement of the civil population and dealt severely with *préfets*, police, *maires* and magistrates who ignored his orders. The *préfets* of Aisne and Oise, the *sous-préfets* of Vouziers, Montdidier and St Omer, had been harshly removed. So too had Amédée Bussière, director of the Sûreté, one presumes for failure to control the refugees. Hence, when the crisis came, the people remained without information, without guidance or orders. No doubt little could have been done, but the impediment to troop movement by crowds of errant *bouches inutiles* made the prosecution of war even more hazardous.

[5]

The government and the commands left their various offices during the afternoon and evening of the 10th, General Georges and his staff for Vaugereau and Briare, General Weygand for the same destination. Reynaud went to Chissay near Montrichard on the Cher. He had intended to go with de Gaulle, by way of Army Group Four, to see Huntziger at Ancy-le-Franc, in the hope that he would find a Commander-in-Chief less pessimistic than Weygand. At Orléans he received a message that Churchill was on his way to France. He therefore sent de Gaulle to interview Huntziger and himself drove to Briare, which he reached between 6 and 7. He had already heard of Mussolini's speech from the Palazzo Venezia in Rome, announcing the Italian invasion of France.

Mandel said good-bye to Langeron, the Préfet of Police, last thing at night: 'We have no intention of throwing in our hand,' he said. Langeron reminded him of a conversation some months earlier. Mandel had said that Weygand might well replace Gamelin, and added: 'but don't you think if things go wrong he would be ready to play the Hindenburg?' Langeron had answered: 'The place is already taken. Pétain will be our Hindenburg. If he succeeds, he will give up everything and . . . my job will soon be over.'

Mandel set out for Tours.

The Under-Secretary of State for War reached Arcis-sur-Aube and, according to Huntziger, invited him to take command of the shattered armies, concentrate the pieces, and organize a bridgehead in the Cotentin peninsula south of Cherbourg. Huntziger considered such a project derisory, on which de Gaulle transferred his scheme to the Breton peninsula, which Huntziger said was no less absurd. On this de Gaulle left him.

General Gamelin had left for the south a week earlier.

O N 10 May, General Prételat of Army Group Two disposed of three armies, ten army corps, twenty-six field divisions and two cavalry divisions. There were also available eleven battalions of tanks, nearly all Renaults, and one of D.2. In the static defences, there were thirty-seven fortress regiments apart from the technical teams of the Maginot *ouvrages*. In March some of the fortress regiments had been grouped into a fortress division, the 103rd, on the Rhine. On the right from Rhinau to Pontarlier, directly under G.Q.G.N.E. was the Eighth Army (part of Army Group Three), commanded by General Laure, from Pétain's staff, with two fortress corps, XLIV (the 54th Division and the 104th Fortress Division) and XLV (the 63rd and 57th Divisions), and also a number of fortress regiments. Behind these lay a number of corps and divisions at the disposal of G.Q.G.N.E.

With the opening of the battle, the transfer of divisions began almost immediately, first, the corps and divisions from G.Q.G. reserves, then Army Group Two's own reserves. At the same time, the composition of Army Group Two was several times changed. On 17 May, Huntziger's Second Army, which had been directly under G.Q.G., was attached to Army Group Two. On 20 May, the Eighth Army was also transferred to Prételat, as the result of the move of Army Group Three (Besson) Headquarters to the west. Then, on 28 May, the Fourth Army of General Requin was withdrawn from the Rohrbach–Saarguemines sector into G.Q.G. Reserve. Its front was divided between the Fifth Army and the Saar Group, otherwise XX Corps. Finally, on 6 June, Second Army was removed from Army Group Two and with the Fourth and Sixth Armies made into Army Group Four under General Huntziger, with headquarters at Arcis-sur-l'Aube. The command of the Second Army fell to General Freydenberg of the Colonial Corps. The Fourth Army now held the Aisne from Neufchâtel to Attigny with XXIII and VIII Corps; the Second from Attigny (exclusive) to Margut, where it joined with the Third Army of General Condé.

[2]

The Second Army front continued to be active during most of May without any serious loss of ground. Divisions came into position, resisted attacks and were relieved. From about 20 May fighting momentarily died down on the high ground between Meuse and Bar, but on the 18th the Germans had opened a bombardment with heavy guns against a small isolated *ouvrage*, La Ferté, on the right of the Second Army. The fortress was damaged and the wrecking of the turrets and the craters caused by the shells made the use of the fort's guns difficult, even impossible. During the night of the 18th/19th German patrols crept up to the walls and succeeded in pushing explosives into the embrasures, which destroyed part of the fortifications, destroyed the communication system and finally killed the garrison. Although this was followed by savage fighting in the Montmédy bridgehead, the enemy got no further. But the fact that a fort of the impregnable Maginot had been rendered indefensible became known and spread alarm in the area between Meuse and Moselle. In the great steel centre of Thionville there was panic. 'In twenty-four hours, the unhappy town emptied, like a pricked blister. . . . A few grocers and provision shops and two or three cafés stayed open. The rest were shut and locked. No more cinema, no more newspapers, I couldn't get into the public baths. . . . Since yesterday there have been no trains, and the railway staff, since it is hopeless, have left the station. The factories have closed down. Even the brothel is shut. . . . Thionville is not officially evacuated. So no one has any rights. Remain under the bombing and wait. If you are too alarmed, go and your blood be on your own head. There is no free travel, no receiving centre, no compensation. You have nothing.'[1]

The wall in which all Alsace had placed its trust had cracked.

> A leurs poignets ils ne liront plus jamais l'heure
> Reniant le monde moderne et les machines
> Eux qui croyaient avoir la muraille de Chine
> Entre la grande peste et leurs bateaux de fleurs.

[3]

While Huntziger's Second Army and the left of Condé's Third were fighting to hold the hills between Meuse and Bar and to prevent the outflanking of the Maginot, the reserves of Army Group Two were being drained away. By the 19th three army corps and their corps troops, with twelve divisions earmarked as G.Q.G. reserves, had moved west. Eighth Army had lost a corps and three active divisions. Prételat had lost two corps, eight infantry and two cavalry divisions and six out of eleven battalions of modern tanks. Moreover, with the extension of his responsibility to include the Second Army on the 17th, he found himself forced to support Huntziger's weakening defences. Since 10 May Army Group Two had been bled and, alas, to little profit. In view of the relative quietness of his sectors, he could not but submit to the exigencies of G.Q.G., but as the situation in the centre deteriorated, he became alarmed at the rapid depletion of his forces. At his first meeting with Weygand on 26 May at La Ferté, he pointed out that since 10 May, he had lost two thirds of the formations at his disposal and suggested that he should withdraw the troops in the intervals between the Maginot defences to form a mobile reserve. Weygand refused, on the ground that these troops had not the necessary equipment for movement and that they were therefore better in their defensive positions. Besides, public opinion would not accept with indifference any abandonment of the Maginot Line. Prételat protested that he was not thinking of abandonment, but merely of the earmarking, among the troops in the intervals, of those units which might be appropriately employed in the event of a withdrawal from the Maginot. Weygand replied that it was useless to think about withdrawal, since on the previous day he had agreed with Reynaud to put all they had on the line they were holding at the moment. 'We shall fight without a thought of withdrawal.' (This, of course, was before the Belgian capitulation and the relinquishment of the joint Cambrai–Bapaume attack.)

'But,' returned Prételat, 'if we are driven from this line ?'

'If we are driven from the Somme . . .'

'Which we don't hold,' interjected Prételat.

'If we are driven out of the positions we hold to the south of the Somme, at that moment we shall take whatever decisions are forced on us.'

Prételat considered the decision to stand where they were, '*sans esprit de recul*', highly dangerous. Weygand was not to be swayed, and Prételat returned to his headquarters at Metz infinitely depressed. 'By refusing to admit the possibility of a retreat and authorize preparatory steps, an attitude from which he was not to withdraw until 12 June, the Commander-in-Chief had already sealed the fate of the forces in the east of the country, which three weeks later would leave more than 400,000 prisoners in the hands of a bold enemy.'[2]

[4]

The enemy did not relax his determined attacks on the Second Army and Prételat, fully alive to the fact that a failure at this point would jeopardize the whole area to the east, continued to reinforce Huntziger with whatever he could spare. From 23 to 26 May the fighting between the Bar at Tannay past Stonne and Beaumont to beyond the Meuse to Margut persisted with no decisive result, but it was terribly costly. Everything was thrown in to stop the enemy, including cavalry and spahi brigades. On the 24th, the losses of the advanced troops were so heavy that the XXI Corps commander, Flavigny, proposed to withdraw his line, which implied the abandonment of the jumping-off line for the attack on Sedan. Huntziger considered that, in the general situation, an attack towards Sedan now would be pointless and would make heavier demands on his forces than would be profitable. With Prételat's consent, the front line and the high ground were evacuated. Two days later, the Germans made a powerful thrust against the 6th North African east of the Meuse: it was stopped, but again the losses were heavy, and the links with the Montmédy bridgehead much strained. Huntziger said that G.Q.G. had delayed giving the order to the armies in Belgium to withdraw, with consequences of which all were cognisant, and now they would delay giving it to the armies in the Maginot. On 2 June, he was called to G.Q.G. He gave Weygand his opinion, and was rebuffed, as was Prételat. A day or so later, he was told to take over command of a new Army Group (Four), consisting of his own Second Army, and Touchon's Sixth, with inserted between them Requin's Fourth. It stretched from Montmédy to Attichy on the Aisne. Its headquarters opened at Arcis-sur-Aube from the morning of 6 June.

From Prételat's point of view, the new creation gave neither relief nor aid. He had bolstered up Second Army with most of his best divisions (it now had three corps and ten infantry divisions, of which five were active and five A). It had not held the high ground, and in consequence of its withdrawal, the Montmédy sector of the Maginot defences had been partly abandoned and its fortress regiments converted into a mobile division under its sector commander, General Burtaire. Prételat was acutely conscious that if the new Army Group lost its present position, the huge area of Army Group Two would be compromised. He complained bitterly to Georges. Georges's reply was an instruction to Huntziger to 'ensure the liaison between Army Group Three and Army Group Two' by clinging to the Montagne de Reims on the left and on the right to the line Montmédy–Longuyon, the Meuse and the northern Argonne. The instruction was in fact not worth the paper it was written on. It was made worse by the fact that the best of the Army Group Two divisions, including the reserves Prételat had placed behind Second Army, were now lost. He was left with only three armies for 'the imperative task of defending the fortified position and the course of the Rhine'.*

On the front facing north from the Rhine to Longuyon, the most vulnerable part was that previously held by the Fourth Army, particularly the lightly fortified sector Faulquemont–Saaralbe–Wittring, the Sarre sector, now occupied by the 58th (B) Division, two regiments of colonial machine-gunners, the 41st and 51st, and the 1st Polish Division, only partly trained and inadequately armed. On the night of 5/6 June, the German 258th Division attacked in the Saaralbe–Holving re-entrant and captured Willerwald and posts in the neighbourhood, but the enemy did not press on, and on the next day the 51st retook the village. The raid, however, showed up the weakness.

---

* On 9 June, apart from the fortress regiments, Army Group Two comprised the 30th Alpine and 26th Divisions (A), the 51st, 52nd, 54th, 56th, 58th, 62nd, 63rd, 67th, 70th Divisions (B) and the 1st and 2nd Polish Divisions. The 20th Division was sent to the Sixth Army on 8 June, the 41st on the 7th.

25 ARMY GROUPS FOUR AND TWO, *9–12 June*

O N the morning of 8 June, the Germans were pressing heavily on the Seventh Army and the XVII Corps on the Oise and south of the Aisne. The defence, however, were spared attacks from German armour, since Hoeppner's XVI Panzer Korps (the 3rd and 4th Panzer Divisions) had been withdrawn from the left of Reichenau's Sixth Army and was being transferred to von Rundstedt's Army Group. But the situation of the French was serious enough. While the remains of I Corps were painfully coming down to the Oise bridges below Compiègne, XXIV Corps was preparing to defend the Aisne from Compiègne to Vic. The main strength on the river was the 11th Division of General Arlabosse, the 'Iron Division' of Nancy, which had seen little fighting since it had attacked on the Sarre in September. The 87th Division, after fighting on the 5th and 6th, had come back over the Aisne on the evening of the 7th and was now recovering itself near Pierrefonds on the edge of the forest. On the Oise the crossings were watched from Montmacq down to Verberie by various bodies, parts of the 7th Colonial, reconnaissance groups, the 141st Alpine Regiment from 3rd Light, and a few details of the retreating 47th. Further south, the lack of reserves had led to the hurried transfer of a battalion of the 94th Infantry Regiment from the 42nd Division, on the Aisne north of Reims, to hold the river crossing at Creil.

For the XXIV Corps the situation was worse on the right flank. As has been seen, the 7th Division was broken on the Ailette. It was only remains that crossed the Aisne. The 28th Alpine Division (General Lestien) crossed the river between Vailly and Bourg-et-Comin. The fresh 8th Division,* holding at Soissons and Ambleny, was overrun, and the 27th Alpine, south of Soissons, was hard put to it to maintain its position on the left of the 28th. There was thus a large empty space on the right of the 11th and 87th Divisions. Below Ambleny there was nothing to fill the gap. By the evening of the 8th the 27th was fighting ten kilometres south of Soissons, with the last of the 8th Division, its 12th Foreign Legion on its left. It was brought back to Ourcq during the night of the 8th/9th. On its right, the 28th, driven off the Brenelle plateau, came back to the Vesle in front of Fismes.

Thus on the morning of 9 June, the French armies between Reims and Le Havre showed deep penetrations by the enemy on either side of Paris. The salient between them was covered by one complete

---

* It was very much a '*division de marche*', being composed of a regiment made up of four training battalions, an ex-fortress reserve regiment, 12 *Étranger*, and 23 Foreign Volunteers.

division, the 11th, and a number of more or less broken ones, depleted of infantry and without most of their heavy weapons.

[2]

The attacks which completed the conquest of the French armies were directed to cutting off and possibly encircling the whole of Prételat's Army Group Two. The assault was made by the German Second (Weichs) and Twelfth (List) Armies of von Rundstedt's Army Group A, with, as the *schnell Verbände*, the pursuit force, Guderian's new Panzer group, Reinhardt's XLI Panzer Korps (the 6th and 8th Panzer Divisions and the 20th Motorized) on the right, Schmidt's XXXIX Panzer Korps (the 1st and 2nd Panzer Divisions and the 29th Motorized) on the left. The Second Army had two corps of two divisions each, the Twelfth three corps, also of two divisions each. In reserve there were six divisions.

This formidable German striking force of sixteen infantry divisions, four armoured and two motorized divisions, was faced across the Aisne by six French infantry divisions with, in support, the corps troops of four army corps, eight infantry divisions of different categories, one battalion of Renault tanks, and a mobile group consisting of the 3rd Armoured Division (now 30 B and 45 Hotchkiss tanks) and the former 4th Cavalry Division, made up with some Somua and Hotchkiss tanks, strengthened by a battalion of Renaults, into the simulacrum of a light armoured division, which was retitled the 7th Light Armoured. With this was also the severely battered 3rd Motorized, the last of the seven motorized divisions of 10 May, much reduced in numbers and without transport. From the east the position of the new Army Group was

Second Army:
  XVIII Corps (line Margut–Inor)
    Burtaire Division (formerly Montmédy fortified sector)
    6th North African
  XXI Corps (line Inor–Oches)
    1st Colonial
    6th Division
  Colonial Corps (line Oches–Attigny)
    35th Division
    36th Division
  Reserves: 3rd Motorized, 3rd Colonial, 6th Colonial, 3rd North
      African, 1st Cavalry brigade, 3rd Spahi brigade
Fourth Army:
  VIII Corps (line Attigny (Exc.)–Thugny–Trugny)
    14th Division
  XXIII Corps (line Biermes–Avaux)
    2nd Division
    10th Division
  Reserves: 3rd Armoured, 7th Light Armoured, 235th Light, 82nd
      African

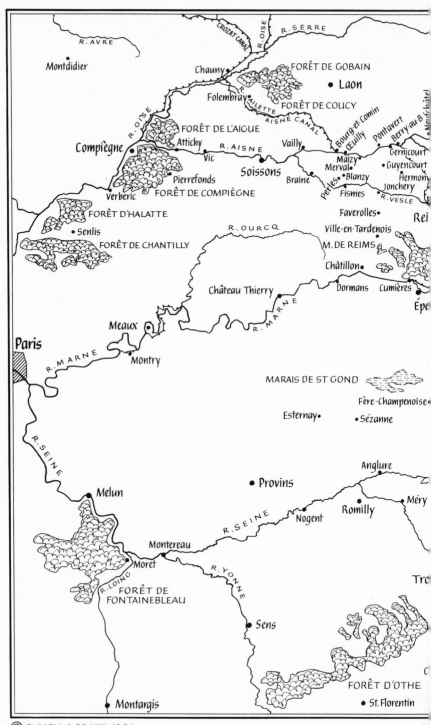

R. AVRE

Montdidier

CROZAT CANAL

R. OISE

R. SERRE

Chauny

FORÊT DE GOBAIN

Laon

Folembray

FORÊT DE COUCY

AILETTE

AISNE CANAL

FORÊT DE L'AIGUE

R. OISE

Attichy

R. AISNE

Vailly

Bourg-et-Comin
Œuilly

Pontavert

Berry-au-B

Neufchâtel

Compiègne

Vic

Soissons

Braine

Maizy

Gernicourt

Pierrefonds

FORÊT DE COMPIÈGNE

Perles

Merval

Blanzy

Guyencourt

Hermon

Verberic

Fismes

Jonchery

R. VESLE

FORÊT D'HALATTE

Faverolles

Rei

Senlis

R. OURCQ

Ville-en-Tardenois

FORÊT DE CHANTILLY

M. DE REIMS

Châtillon

Château Thierry

Dormans

Cumières

Meaux

R. MARNE

Épe

Paris

R. MARNE

Montry

MARAIS DE ST GOND

Fère-Champenoise

Esternay

Sézanne

R. SEINE

Anglure

Provins

Méry

Melun

Romilly

R. SEINE

Nogent

Montereau

Moret

R. YONNE

Tro

R. LOING

FORÊT DE
FONTAINEBLEAU

Sens

FORÊT D'OTHE

Montargis

St. Florentin

© CASSELL & CO LTD 1968

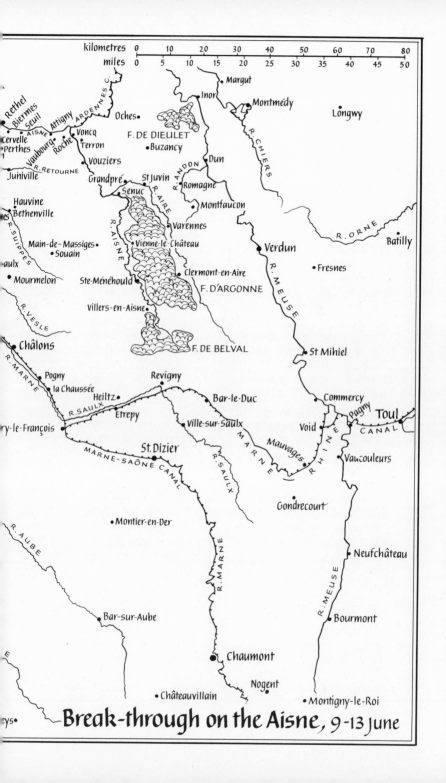

kilometres 0 10 20 30 40 50 60 70 80
miles 0 5 10 15 20 25 30 35 40 45 50

Margut
Inor
Montmédy
Longwy
Rethel
Biermes
Seuil
Attigny
Oches
ARDENNES C.
F. DE DIEULET
R. CHIERS
Cervelle
Perthes
Voncq
Roche
Terron
Buzancy
Dun
R. AISNE
Vouziers
R. RETOURNE
Grandpré
St Juvin
Romagne
R. ANDON
Juniville
Senuc
Montfaucon
R. AIRE
Hauvine
Bethenville
R. AISNE
Varennes
R. ORNE
Batilly
R. SUIPPE
Main-de-Massiges
Souain
Vienne-le-Château
Verdun
Fresnes
aulx
Mourmelon
Ste-Ménéhould
Clermont-en-Aire
R. MEUSE
F. D'ARGONNE
R. VESLE
Villers-en-Aisne
Châlons
F. DE BELVAL
St Mihiel
R. MARNE
Pogny
la Chaussée
Revigny
Commercy
Pogny
Toul
Heiltz
Bar-le-Duc
Void
CANAL
R. SAULX
Etrepy
Ville-sur-Saulx
Mauvages
R. RHINE
ry-le-François
MARNE
Vaucouleurs
MARNE–SAÔNE CANAL
St. Dizier
R. SAULX
Gondrecourt
R. AUBE
Montier-en-Der
R. MARNE
Neufchâteau
R. MEUSE
Bar-sur-Aube
Bourmont
Chaumont
Nogent
Châteauvillain
Montigny-le-Roi
eys

Break-through on the Aisne, 9-13 June

Sixth Army:
  VII Corps (line Brienne–Maizy)
    42nd Division
    45th Division
    44th Division
  XVII Corps
    28th Alpine Division
    27th Alpine Division
  Reserves: 53rd Light Division, 3rd and 10th Battalions of A.F.V.

Few of these divisions had been in position on the Aisne for any length of time: de Lattre's 14th had had its infantry in action on 15 and 16 May, but most of the others came later. The position of the Fourth and Sixth Armies was far from strong. The Aisne, doubled by a lateral canal from near Vailly to Rilly beyond Attigny, is a sluggish stream, neither particularly wide, nor deep, and in June 1940 shallower than normal.

Behind the Fourth Army lay the fields of many spectacular fights of 1914–18, places such as Moronvilliers, Mesnil-les-Hurlus, Butte-de-Tahure, Main-de-Massiges. It was easy country for armour, and except for the Aisne (and the lateral canal on the south side), which the French looked on as an anti-tank ditch, there were few obstacles except the small Retourne tributary which flows through marshes from Junivelle to Neufchâtel. The villages along the Retourne had been bombed and were now deserted. These, and the villages between the Retourne and the Aisne, Avançon, Tagnon and so on, were being hastily converted into strong-points. On the river itself, little defensive work had been done. From 15 May to 1 June, the river bank from Neufchâtel to Attigny had been occupied by the 10th and 14th Divisions, which were not strong enough to guard fifty kilometres of river and canal and prepare them for defence. When the 2nd Division took over the centre of the position, the twelve kilometres from Herpy to Biermes, on 1 June, the defence had not been organized. The closing-up of the German divisions to the canal, much of which was masked by bushes, demanded constant patrolling. Little digging was done. Some mines were laid, but they were insufficient. The artillery was none too strong; simply the divisional field regiments, thirty-four 75s and twenty-four 155s, augmented by sixteen medium guns.

[3]

'*Fall Rot*' was an exemplary operation. The initial break-through on the extreme west was the condition of the final destruction of the French armies in the extreme east, and largely contributed to by the losers. '*Ce qui nous a manqué, ce n'est pas le coeur; c'est la tête*', wrote Renan after 1870. The choice is offered; the victim selects the method. The disaster which overtook General Requin's Fourth Army was the direct consequence of the dissolution of Touchon's Sixth, which itself came from the attempt of VII Corps to bolster up the dislocated XVII.

On the evening of 7 June, General de la Porte du Theil of VII Corps had three divisions on the Aisne, from Neufchâtel to Bourg-et-Comin, the 42nd, 45th and 44th. Two regiments of the 45th (the 113th and 31st Infantry Regiment) had taken over the line from Berry-au-Bac to Pontavert a few days earlier. On 7 June, the desperate situation of the Seventh Army retreating from the Somme had caused the dispatch of one battalion of the 94th Infantry Regiment of the 42nd Division to defend the Oise bridge at Creil. On the evening of 8 June, the situation of the XVII Corps, with two divisions shattered, and two retreating obliquely from the Aisne to the Vesle, i.e. facing north-west, threatened even worse. The 44th Division had put its 26th Demi-Brigade of *chasseurs alpins* into a switch-line from Maizy on the Aisne to the right of the 28th. VII Corps had no reserves. Its commander therefore decided to withdraw the 45th from the front line and concentrate it north-west of Reims in support of XVII Corps. So, at 8 p.m. on 8 June, General Keller* of the 42nd was directed to relieve the battalions of the 113th and 31st Regiments during the night. All he had available were his own reserve, one battalion of the 80th Infantry Regiment and the last battalion of the 94th, both of which had to move some distance from east of the Laon–Reims road. The undertaking led to chaos. The battalion of the 94th was to take over from the further regiment of the 45th, the 113th; the battalion of the 80th was to relieve the 31st immediately on the left of its own front-line battalion.

The German attack began at 3.30 on the 9th. The bombardment opened in darkness before the 31st had been relieved. In consequence, two battalions of the 31st were intermingled with one of the 80th in the sector between Gernicourt and Berry-au-Bac; the left battalion was already fighting when the relief arrived. Those companies that were in the line remained with the companies of the 80th. Those that were not, including the headquarters, departed. The only reserve left to the 42nd Division was the divisional training centre, which General Keller flinched from employing, especially as the situation towards Pontavert was far more menacing. Here the 113th had withdrawn before the arrival of the relieving battalion of the 94th, rolled up its telephone lines and gone off in lorries. At dawn, the 94th contingent had got no further than the line Roucy–Bouffignereux, still three kilometres south of the river. The 42nd Divisional Artillery Group was still on its way. The only defenders were a single group, three batteries, of the artillery of the 45th Division, which stayed in position and, in spite of heavy casualties, covered the approach of the 94th.

Fighting here went on all day. Roucy was lost in the afternoon, but Guyencourt was held. On the left no touch was found with the 44th Division. The 44th had one company still clinging to the river at

* General Pierre Keller, to be distinguished from the Inspector-General of Armour.

Concevreux, but the rest of the division was gradually moving to face west rather than north. At nightfall it stood on the line Revillon–Merval–Blanzy–Perles. The divisional commander at Montigny-sur-Vesle, General Boissau, had no reserves except a few motor-cyclists. Liaison officers sent by General Keller could find no formed bodies of infantry, only small groups. Beyond the left of the 28th Alpine yawned a gap. Not less than thirty kilometres to the south-west, the right of the 27th Alpine was on the Ourcq, already deeply bitten into by the German Ninth Army. On the morning of 10 June, while the right of the 42nd Division was in close touch with the 10th at Aumenancourt, its left was at Pévy, more than ten kilometres south of Pontavert.

[4]

Although the attack on 9 June involved the whole of Huntziger's Army Group Four, the bombardment was selective: some units appear to have escaped. The Aisne valley was shrouded in mist and the German gunners had added a percentage of smoke shell. Combined with the half-light of dawn, this increased the difficulties of the defenders. German infantry on the Fourth Army front seem to have begun crossing with the barrage, bringing their rafts and rubber boats to the river bank, and although many were sunk, entries into the French lines were made before the mist cleared.

The 10th Division on the right of the 42nd resisted successfully for some hours, but about 6 in the morning infiltration began, especially near Asfeld. Worse, however, came at the right-hand end of the line through the junction with the 2nd Division.

As has been said, the 2nd Division had taken over its sector as recently as 1 June and had been unable to improve the position. The ground south, between the Aisne and the Retourne, is very bare, with few villages, isolated farmhouses and sparse woods; admirable targets for bombers. Across the Aisne and the canal, the divisional front included the large village of the Château-Porcien and the town of Rethel, through which flowed the river and of which a suburb extended over the canal. The 2nd had four battalions in front and five in support.

The bombardment lasted from 3.30 to 5 a.m., at which hour the artillery lengthened range and the front line was subjected to dive-bombing attacks, while the German infantry swarmed over the canal at Taizy and Nanteuil and, in spite of counter-attacks, reached the artillery positions near Avançon, where the gunners were firing over open sights at the advancing infantry. At the same time on the left, in the 10th Division area, the Germans broke in at Blanzy.

On the right of the 2nd Division, beyond Rethel, there was a similar German inroad in the line of the 14th Division. The village of Thugny-Trugny was lost but recaptured. Further east, beyond Attigny and east of the Aisne, the Germans made a deep penetration, capturing Voncq and Terron from the 36th Division, but the villages were recovered

by the two cavalry brigades and a detachment of light tanks. In the
evening a second attack west of the Aisne resulted in the loss of Ste
Vaubourg and Roche. Attigny was held.

During the afternoon, companies of Renaults of the 23rd Battalion
and armoured cars from the reconnaissance group counter-attacked
towards Taizy, but the infantry, 'which had never been trained to work
with tanks, did not follow them'.[1] The Germans had already brought
up their anti-tank guns. The counter-attacks faded away; the majority
of the French Renaults had been knocked out.

By evening the Germans were firmly though not deeply established
south of the Aisne on the Fourth Army front. During the day, the 2nd
and 14th Divisions had made a number of prisoners, among them
soldiers from Guderian's armoured group, who said that the Panzers
would attack next day.

Except for the attacks in the bend of the Aisne, the Colonial Corps
had suffered only bombardment. But further east there had been fighting
in the XXI Corps area, in the Forêt de Dieulet and at Oches. Oches
was lost, but retaken, together with some 500 prisoners.

At the conference held at Twelfth Army headquarters before the
attack, Guderian had asked that the infantry and engineers of his
armoured divisions might carry out the preliminary assault, in order
to establish bridgeheads over the Aisne from which his tanks might
break out. He feared that otherwise the supply columns of the infantry
would block the roads and delay the armour. List refused. When, on
the afternoon of the 9th, Guderian saw the divisions between Rethel
and Attigny had made so poor a showing, he was furious. Later in the
day he found that a shallow bridgehead between Blanzy and Acy on
either side of Château-Porcien would be just deep enough to concentrate
400 or so tanks of the XXXIX Panzer Korps.

The German infantry had not in fact penetrated as deeply as Guderian
believed, but the French had lost heavily. On the left of the 2nd
Division, the Germans were near enough to the French batteries to
prevent the guns being brought off, and these had to be put out of
action. Of the twenty-four 155s, thirteen were abandoned and five of the
nine batteries of 75s had been lost.

[5]

During the night, General Requin made what preparations he could
for the heavier assault foreseen for the morning. Two battalions from
the 235th Light Division were ordered up to the 2nd, while the 82nd
African Division (General Armingeat), on the wooded Montagne de
Reims, was sent to the south-west of the city, to cover the army's flank,
in view of the growing discomfiture of the Sixth Army. During the 9th
a strong counter-attack by the Buisson Armoured Group had been
planned for the following day, its axis depending on the position of the
enemy. In spite of the fact that no more than 150 machines could be

got together, the tank commanders were confident, particularly as the German forces had not proved as formidable on the 9th as had been expected. Nevertheless there was disquieting evidence of enemy infiltration during the night, towards the Retourne, and soon after daylight on the 10th tanks and lorried infantry (the 1st Panzer Division) were seen coming down from the Reims–Rethel road. Village after village was attacked from both air and ground. Soon they were in flames.* Alincourt went about 11.30 a.m., but parties from the garrison which fell back into the marsh behind the village were not finished off until evening. Neuflize, too, did not succumb until towards dark. Here a German Panzer officer patronizingly told the captured subaltern in command of the strong-point: 'Your anti-tank defence wasn't too bad.' Juniville, further east, held out all day and the garrison got away. At the same time, the 'hedgehogs' further north, La Cervelle, Tagnon, Perthes, gave the Germans a lot of trouble. Tagnon held out until the afternoon; the last message ran: 'Ammunition finished; still holding.' Colonel Terrier of the 33rd Infantry Regiment surrendered two hours later. Perthes, headquarters of the 127th, was still resisting.[2]

It had been intended that the Buisson Group, which lay south of the Retourne, should attack early in the morning. It expected to cross the stream by bridges east of Juniville. These were found destroyed. The 3rd Armoured therefore had to make a long detour east. Long before it was in position, its moves had been detected and its attack anticipated. 'Passage of orders, the detour and the taking up position, had required more than *five hours*, and from this single fact the operation from which so much had been expected, had already lost most of its chance of success.'[3]

The armour advanced in two columns. Each consisted of nine or ten B tanks and a battalion of Hotchkiss, the 42nd on the right, the 45th on the left. The northern group was accompanied by the 16th Chasseurs. There was no artillery support. (There was one bombing attack by nine Douglas from No. 2 Grouping in the area between Avançon and the river, and one of eight Lioré near Château-Porcien.) The Germans of the 1st Panzer Division, warned of the approaching attack, had prepared a line of anti-tank guns which opened as the French came over the ridge east of Perthes. In the northern group half the Hotchkiss were destroyed in a few minutes. The French never reached the first objective, the Reims–Rethel railway. But the heavy Bs made some progress. It was here that Guderian tried in vain to knock one out with a captured 47-mm. anti-tank gun. 'All the shells simply bounced off', and the German 37-mm. and 20-mm. were equally ineffective. At the same time, the 16th Chasseurs in their armoured carriers made a dash for

---

* The German Air Force appear to have used considerably more incendiary during '*Fall Rot*' than in '*Fall Gelb*'. Villages well behind the combat lines were constantly bursting into flame. All types of vehicle were attacked. It is as if they wished to flush out any armour.

Perthes and rescued the last parties of the garrison, the headquarters of the 127th Infantry Regiment, seven officers and thirty unwounded other ranks of the 300 of the morning of the 9th. The *chasseurs* remained in the village until dark, and then brought off the garrison, including the wounded, with three light machine-guns and two mortars. Attempts to reach the few detachments still fighting in Sault-les-Rethel and Biermes had to be abandoned.

On the same day, south of the Retourne, the 7th Light Armoured, together with the 10th Battalion of Renaults, attacked towards Juniville against the German tanks, without success, but temporarily blocked the way southward.

East of the 2nd Division, de Lattre's infantry had held the line of the Aisne throughout the 9th. Although Thugny-Trugny was surrounded early in the morning, the *chasseur* battalion holding the village beat the enemy off and the position was restored in a counter-attack by the reconnaissance group and a section of Renaults. Further east, fighting went on all day, and at nightfall the position was intact. Some 800 prisoners had been taken. Though east of Attigny, as has been seen, Voncq and Terron in the buckle of the river had been recaptured, the enemy broke in behind Attigny and had not been ousted at nightfall. On the 10th, in a renewed attack, the Germans enlarged their bridgehead significantly, almost reaching Vouziers. Although this occurred at the boundary of VIII and Colonial Corps, it spelled none of the dangers elsewhere. The line of the 14th Division remained unchanged.

In the XXIII and VII Corps areas, pressure was renewed on the 10th, before daylight. Again this came in thick mist. The right of the 42nd Division was still linked with the 10th Division, which even now had some of its 5th Infantry Regiment still on the river. But the main bodies were being gradually manœuvred back. General Keller had the two battalions of the 424 Pioneers in Bourgogne and Fort Brimont* of evil memory, covering the withdrawal of the 151st Infantry Regiment. To their left, part of the 31st of the 45th Division was in Hermonville. Then the line swung southward to Pévy and Prouilly. Later in the morning, the 44th withdrew from Fismes to a line from Jonchéry to Faverolles on the right of the 28th.

During the day, the battered and much weakened 42nd Division became more and more extended as claims were made on it by both its own VII and the XXIII Corps. General Keller visited the local area commander in Reims, who, insisting that he was under Fourth Army, refused all relationship with the 42nd Division. By evening, touch with the 10th Division was gone completely. The defenders of Bourgogne and Brimont had been submerged and Reims was being

---

* Where, in April 1917, an earlier VII Corps lost 15,000 men in attempting to capture it.

evacuated. In XXIII Corps, the 235th Light* had come up in support of the 10th to a line between Pont Faverger and Reims.

General Huntziger, keenly alive to the fact that the battle of the Aisne was lost, believed that the only salvation lay in a rapid retreat to the line of the Marne and thence to Ste Menehould and Clermont-en-Argonne. It was all the more urgent in view of the situation of Sixth Army. So, on the 11th, the Fourth Army and VII Corps began to retire southward. The situation of the Fourth Army was particularly difficult, and the engagement of its only reserve, the 82nd African, on the left south of Reims could do nothing for the centre.

[6]

11 June

The disengagement of the Second and Fourth Armies started early on the 11th towards the general line from Les Islettes through the Forêt de Belval (south of the Argonne) across to the Marne. The Second Army began to move at dawn. The 3rd Colonial was taken in lorries into reserve between Montfaucon and Ste Menehould across the Argonne. The 3rd North African was sent to the area between Ste Menehould and Vitry-le-François. East of the Meuse, there still remained the Burtaire group of fortress infantry between Margut and Stenay. West of the Meuse, the divisions withdrew without much difficulty to the line Buzancy–Vouziers–Mazagran (due south of Attigny).

The retreat of the Fourth Army was far more difficult. The 14th Division and the 3rd Motorized came back to a line from Machault to Bethenvillers, covered by the 7th Light Armoured, while the 2nd came out of the line to the Suippe river, covered to some extent by the 10th, and the 42nd, which had crossed the Vesle on the previous evening, came back to the northern slopes of the Montagne de Reims. But the vicissitudes of the VII Corps appeared to General Huntziger so menacing that at 6 a.m. he ordered the 7th Light Armoured to move with all dispatch to Damery, near Épernay on the Marne. Before General Marteau could collect his regiments, Guderian's as yet unemployed XLI Panzer Korps was over the Aisne and hastening southeastward to catch up with the XXXIX Panzer. It caught some of the 35th Infantry Regiment in Machault and finished them off. It drove the 51st Infantry Regiment of the 3rd Motorized southwards, and caused General Marteau to leave half his division behind in support of the VIII Corps infantry. On the same day, another battalion of the 14th Division, from the 152nd Infantry Regiment, was wiped out at Hauvine. By evening VIII Corps was back on Mourmelon and Souain.

By the morning of the 11th, VII Corps had for the most part gone.

---

* It consisted of the 9th and 108th Infantry Regiments (otherwise six training battalions) and the 323 Artillery regiment from the debris of the Ninth Army artillery, two groups of 75s and one battery of A.-T. guns. The division was nevertheless a good one. Its commander was General Trolley de Prévaux.

The 28th Alpine, out of touch with all commands except by radio, waited on the Vesle to be relieved by the two regiments of the 45th Division withdrawn on the night of the 8th/9th. These did not arrive; part had retired close to Reims, while the other part strayed across the rear of the 44th and eventually reached Dormans on the Marne. On the other hand, the 173rd Demi-Brigade of the 44th Division, the Corsicans, retreating, joined with the 28th.*

In the immense confusion on the night of the 10th/11th on both sides of Reims, neither General de La Porte du Theil nor General Germain of XXIII Corps could be sure who commanded what, and the position of any formed body at the boundary of the Sixth and Fourth Armies. Orders somehow filtered down to divisions and regiments to retreat from Vesle to the Montagne-de-Reims, where the 82nd African had taken up position. Much of the movement was completed during the morning of the 11th, during which everything moving was harassed by aircraft. The left of the 45th made an eccentric retreat to the south-west, finally crossing the Marne at Dormans. The 44th passed Ville-en-Tardenois and found the enemy already at Châtillon. These they drove off, and, passing the river, took up position between here and Épernay. In and round the forest of the Montagne-de-Reims were mingled groups from all sides: the 82nd facing north-west, elements of the 42nd east of Ludes, another fragment of the 45th, some of the 10th at Verzy, one regiment of the 235th Light in the angle of the Aisne–Marne canal (the other had been destroyed on the 10th), the remains of the 2nd at Sept-Saulx, the 14th near Mourmelon camp, and away towards Souain the 3rd Motorized. A vestigial 3rd Armoured south of Suippes watched the right flank of the army, while the 7th Light Armoured moved across to Épernay. What, except the enemy, lay beyond the 3rd Armoured was unknown.

As Huntziger had said, the orders to retreat were given too late. On the 11th, the Second Army was already in danger. The intention of General Freydenberg was to cling to both left and right. In fact, it was Army Group Two which must cling to the Second Army, by withdrawing from the left of the Maginot fortifications. In obedience to Weygand's instructions, Prételat had withdrawn nowhere, though he had taken other precautions. But, as someone has said, he was too well disciplined. Freydenberg's attempt to fill his dual role was doomed. He withdrew the 6th North African on the right bank of the Meuse, intending to dispatch it southward towards Verdun by rail, leaving only Burtaire's scratch division of fortress infantry and machine-gunners. By the night of the 10th, it was obvious that the Fourth Army was swinging its weakened right flank away and that the German armour would press

---

* The 27th Alpine had been driven off the Ourcq on the 9th. It was short of ammunition and the infantry had had no food since the 6th. On the following day the great part of one regiment was surrounded and captured near Château-Thierry. The rest of the division crossed the Marne near Chézy on the 11th.

into the gap, which would then endanger the left of the Second Army. Second Army headquarters had foreseen the appearance of such an emergency and had prepared to retire to Ville-sur-Saulx, a little south-west of Bar-le-Duc, where an appropriate system of communications had been installed. Scarcely, however, had the staff settled in than it was found that the 1st Panzer Division was rapidly approaching Vitry-le-François, a mere thirty kilometres to the west. Second Army Head-quarters shifted to a second prepared headquarters at Châteauvillain near Chaumont.

At the same time, the Second Army formations sent southward were unable to find touch with the right of Fourth Army, and matters were made worse by a number of unexpected factors, confusion of orders, failures of transport. Part of the 1st Colonial, withdrawn from XXI Corps and sent off on the night of the 13th/14th towards St Dizier, ran into a series of disasters. The move was complicated by a violent storm, the first for more than a week, lasting all night, followed by an air attack at dawn which destroyed a number of trucks. On passing Bar-le-Duc, it learned that German armour (it was Kirschner's 1st Panzer and the 29th Motorized) was already across the Rhine–Marne canal and almost in St Dizier. The 1st Colonial could get no further than the line of the Saulx.

[7]

Army Group Four, 12 June

On the morning of the 11th, a report reached General Requin that a long column of German armoured vehicles was stretched along the road from Corbeny to the Aisne at Berry-au-Bac waiting for the broken bridge to be completed. He asked for a bombing attack to be made on this splendid target. It was refused 'on account of the atmospheric conditions'.[4] This probably was part of Hoeppner's XVI Korps (3rd and 4th Panzer Divisions) brought from the Péronne–Ham area via Laon. 'The roads,' noted von Bock in his war diary, 'are hopelessly obstructed; one can scarcely understand how XVI Korps got through and how XIV will.' They crossed the Aisne, and some appear to have been engaged during the day west of Reims against the retreating 45th. By the 12th they were on the Marne at Dormans.

The 12th was the crucial day. Much of the Fourth Army was still north of the Marne. Between Dormans and Damery the 45th and 44th had blown the bridges. The 7th Light Armoured and the 82nd were spread in a tenuous semi-circle across the western side of the Montagne-de-Reims. The 10th and 42nd were still facing north at Rilly, but touch had been lost with the 14th. The Germans were reported to have taken Bouzy (they had not), and the 235th was to retire over the river. This they did during the day. Its remains were amalgamated with those of the 2nd under General Klopfenstein and withdrawn to hold the Marne between Condé and the Montagne. They fought here throughout the day. At one moment, in defence of the bridge at Cumières, the 6th Algerians drove the enemy back at the point of the bayonet. Further to the east the 4th Moroccans held on at Rilly with the rearguards of the 42nd and the 10th. The 235th and a few Renaults held the Aisne–Marne canal, but there was still no touch with the 14th believed to be at Sept-Saulx and Mourmelon. Here the 2nd Panzer Division broke in between Mourmelon and the Vesle, but the detachment of the 7th Light Armoured, that had remained with the 3rd Armoured, succeeded in holding the Panzers back for some time

After midday, however, the situation changed for the worse. XXIII Corps had lost all touch with the Sixth Army. Only three bridges remained intact on the Marne behind the 42nd and 10th; all the others had been blown as far as Pogny. The 82nd covered the retreat and stayed north of the river until the next morning. The rest of the corps occupied the southern bank, the 42nd and 10th to Condé: from Condé to St Gibrien below Châlons was defended by the mixed force of survivors from the 2nd Division, the 235th Light and training battalions grouped under the command of General Klopfenstein. The retreat of VIII Corps was carried out with great difficulty. Armoured detachments of the 2nd Panzer had advanced up the river between the two corps and outpaced the 14th Division still fighting behind Mourmelon. Everything available was thrown in: the 7th Light Armoured party, reconnaissance groups, the 3rd Motorized and the 3rd Armoured, covered the infantry of the 14th as they struggled back towards Vitryle-François. The 3rd Motorized and the 3rd Armoured made a long detour, only crossing the Marne at Vitry-le-François during the morning of the 13th. The 14th, covered by the light armoured group, kept closer to the river and were able to cross at Pogny and La Chaussée. The Marne as far as Vitry (but not Châlons, which lies on the east bank) was occupied by the 53rd Light Division, the two remaining regiments of the division that had fought Guderian's corps on the Vence in May.

While the Fourth Army was being split into several parts, the Second Army was now attempting to hold the impossible. During the 9th and 10th it had fought the German XXIII and XVII Korps. The order for its withdrawal came after 'a delay which unhappily compromised the manœuvre'.[5] The 3rd Colonial and 3rd North African were on their way towards the right of the Fourth Army. On the 11th, the Colonial Corps, the neighbour of VIII Corps, began to retire towards Vouziers, XXI Corps on to the Stenay–Buzancy road. The 6th North African was entraining to be transferred to the Chaumont area. The Burtaire division passed under the orders of the governor of Verdun, General Dubuisson. The XVIII Corps headquarters of General Doyen disappeared from the line. The general was sent southward to organize a barrage on the Aube. With the irruption of the XLI Panzer Korps at the junction of Fourth and Second Armies, the latter could not avoid swinging its left back on to the Argonne forests. On the night of the 11th/12th, the 3rd Colonial was in the Andon valley with its right on the Meuse between Dun and Montfaucon. The retreating 1st Colonial came back on its left about Romagne. The 1st Colonial's left was protected by the 6th Division about St Juvin: then came the 36th and 35th. On the night of the 10th/11th, the Second Army reserve, the 6th Colonial, had had some touch with de Lattre's 14th Division near Somme–Py, but that went under the impact of the German armour, the 8th Panzer Division, as it wheeled left. By nightfall on the 12th, the Second Army appears to have had no formed bodies west of a line Vienne-le-Château–Ste Menehould–Revigny. Although Requin believed that there was still touch between the two armies it is improbable.

26 ARMY GROUP TWO ISOLATED,
13–15 June

Behind the front

THE great military area between Aisne and Marne is not thickly populated and most of the villages east of Reims had emptied themselves during the week following the attack. But further south, and also on the Marne and Seine, especially in the rich farmlands of the Brie, there had been no large-scale clearance. From the 9th onwards the evidence of defeat became more and more convincing. The ambulances had been working at full pressure. Wounded had been brought in in large numbers. And now, on the 9th itself, the ambulances, the casualty clearing stations, were packing up, and the hospitals were evacuating all movable patients.

The roads were horribly congested; the streams of refugees had swollen to considerable proportions in the short space of an afternoon, and there were not only lines of people on foot, but in addition a large assortment of barking dogs of all sizes, goats, cattle, and poultry. Heavy military vehicles too, were on the move, and when I looked closer I saw petrol-lorries, radio cars and the ground staff of air-fields going south. It was an alarming sight. . . .[1]

South of Vitry, the stud farms began to march.

Two huge-four-wheeled wagons to which four stallions were harnessed, carried with the baggage the wives and children of the stable-men; a little cart heaped with the stud books, a manure cart and the old station wagonette which had not been out for a long time (it had been fashionable about 1880) sheltered the children, the babies and their mothers during this improvised exodus. To each vehicle was hitched a stallion. Then came the grooms, twenty-nine of them, also each with a stallion. There were a few women and children on bicycles and in the van the manager himself in his car to reconnoitre the road . . . a procession which had left, of a population of fifteen-hundred, no more than sixty individuals.[2]

The air raids had now grown heavier. The British Advance Air Striking Force, such as it was—the few fighters left were reserved as escorts for the bombers—had moved to Saumur. The French Air Force could not stop the Germans, who bombed railway junctions, cross-roads, bridges, all of which involved villages. Many small hamlets were on fire.

[2]

On the morning of the 13th, the Fourth Army was behind the Marne from Damery up-river to Vitry-le-François. Châlons-sur-Marne was in the hands of the 2nd Panzer Division, while the 1st Panzer was about to cross the Rhine–Marne canal at Etrepy, thus completing the fissure in Army Group Four: its headquarters had retired the previous day from Arcis-sur-Aube to Ancy-le-Franc. Reckoning up what the Fourth Army comprised, General Requin was well aware that the Marne could not be held. On the left, the 44th, now attached from the Sixth Army, covered the flank from Damery southward, and the 82nd, worn down to half its strength (the 4th Moroccan had lost the whole of its European cadre), was falling back to the Marais-de-St Gond. On its right, as far as Châlons, were the remains of four divisions, the 42nd (down to 1,600 infantrymen, but with most of its guns), the 10th (two infantry battalions and three artillery groups), the 2nd (300 infantry and 200 gunners with seven guns), and the 235th Light, one battalion (400 strong, and two batteries of 75s).* The 7th Light Armoured was at half strength. This was XXIII Corps. Defending the river from Châlons to Vitry, VIII Corps had the 53rd Light, not yet engaged. Still retreating, and not yet wholly over the Marne, were the remains of the 14th and 3rd and the 3rd Armoured. The last still had twenty-five light tanks, four or five B tanks, and 300 of the 16th Chasseurs.

Guderian's thrust with four armoured divisions and the motorized infantry had already severed communications with the east. The arrival of Hoeppner's XVI Panzer Korps on the Marne at Dormans completed the divorce of the Fourth Army from whatever still existed of the Sixth. 'I know I ought to be covering your left,' telephoned General Touchon to Requin. 'My VII Corps is broken. Between Montmirail and Sézanne, it's simply nothing but a tank circus.'

In quoting Touchon's despair, Requin comments on the impotence of Army Group and Army headquarters: 'the pace of war in 1940 did not allow preparation, writing or despatch of orders'. By the evening of the 13th, Hoeppner's leading elements were across the Seine at Romilly, and before midnight on a level with Troyes. This was not known even at divisional level.

During the 13th, the front of the Fourth Army remained relatively quiet, but the progress of the German armour on both flanks made the army's future more insecure. Two divisions, or parts of them, the 20th and the 41st from Army Group Two, appear to have come in on the Marne, as well as some Polish armoured cars, to the support of VII Corps. They seem to have been involved in the general mêlée into which the right of the Sixth Army had been forced by the thrust of XVI Panzer Korps. Pushed eastward, the 44th Division came in behind the retreating 82nd and hindered its withdrawal. During the afternoon, however, most of the formations succeeded in getting back to the area behind the Marais-de-St Gond and as far as Vitry, with the left of XXIII Corps covered by the Africans and the 7th Light Armoured. On the right, VIII Corps troops crossed the Marne, manœuvred by the 2nd

---

* Part of the 235th Division artillery was separated and engaged elsewhere.

Panzer, while the 1st Panzer drove on towards St Dizier. By evening there appeared to be more than twenty kilometres of open country between Vitry and the Saulx river, empty but for uncontrolled and unco-ordinated elements of French divisions. On the left, Vitry was burning fiercely, and though screened by anti-tank guns was obviously lost. In front of Schmidt's XXXIX Panzer Korps across the Rhine–Marne canal, the road to St Dizier was apparently free. Apparently only, for on that morning a column of French trucks had deposited, at the village of Heiltz-l'Evêque on the north bank of the canal some fifteen kilometres from Vitry, a battalion of the 12th Zouaves of the 3rd North African, commanded by a figure from the pages of Stendhal, the combative Commandant Loustaunau-Lacau. This group was joined by a wandering 75-mm. gun team just at the moment when six German armoured cars appeared. Having satisfactorily demolished three of these and driven off the others, the French commander annexed two more errant 75s and a pair of light tanks, probably from the 3rd Armoured detachment on its way to St Dizier. 'Are we fighting?' asked the tank officer, 'then I'll stay.' By this time more German A.F.V. were appearing, but, no more alert than the earlier group, were speedily dealt with. Presently three companies of the 15th Algerians from the same division were delivered by the wayward French transport service. At nightfall these unsupported fragments were still holding the canal though they had retired to the south side. Here they stood through the morning of the 14th against various infantry assaults. However, the presence of such a hornet naturally attracted enemies. A company of tanks from the 2nd Panzer appeared, but it was not until 5 in the afternoon that they finished off the audacious defenders and broke the last link between Second and Fourth Armies.

[3]

The main body of the over-stretched Second Army retreating through the Argonne was slowly pressed back and across the Meuse. Stenay fell on the 11th, Dun on the 13th. General Dubuisson, Governor of Verdun, commanding a mixed body, the Burtaire Division, local regional regiments, pioneers, retreated and covered the left of General Condé's Third Army. Two regiments from the 3rd Colonial, fighting on Côte 305 and the Mort Homme, were being slowly driven down the *Voie Sacrée*. On the morning of the 14th, the Second Army was nearly back to the river. The left of the 3rd Colonial was protected by the remains of the 6th Division. On the left of the 6th, the 35th faced northward from Clermont to Ste Menehould. Here the line turned sharply southward. Driven from the Main-de-Massiges, the 6th Colonial had reached Villers-en-Argonne and was holding the edge of the Forêt de Belval to Nettancourt, with on its left the 36th Division. The 3rd North African, which should have continued the line, had, as has been seen, been thrown piecemeal into the battle and was now being exterminated on the Rhine–Marne canal. The left flank of the army, such as it was, the remains of the Colonial Corps and the cavalry brigades, faced west, covering Bar-le-Duc along the Saulx. The left of the 1st Colonial was some ten kilometres east of St Dizier, driven back by the eagerly insistent 1st Panzer.

In an attempt to block the rush of the German armour, General Freydenberg had sent General Doyen, whose XVIII Corps had been absorbed in the Dubuisson Group, round to Chaumont to organize whatever troops he could find between Montier-en-Der and Bar-sur-Aube. There was not very much: the reconnaissance group and two battalions of the 56th Division,* such of the 14th Algerians as had not been involved in Loustaunau-Lacau's battle, a few oddments of corps troops, twenty tanks from the 3rd Armoured, which Huntziger had transferred from the Fourth Army, and six North African training battalions without artillery and without even a commander, designated by courtesy the 240th Light Division. Freydenberg ordered them to attack south-westward. There was no response; there scarcely could be. The attempt to stop Kirschner's tanks was derisory. Doyen's detachments were eliminated one by one, and the general escaped with a few armoured cars to Dijon.

General Pagézy, former military commander of Lille, now in charge of the 8th Military District (Burgundy), had been told to organize a defensive line from St Jean-de-Losne along the Burgundy canal up to Montbard, for which he was allocated various non-existent units. All he had in the flesh were three battalions of a regional regiment and five thousand young soldiers from the artillery reserve depot at Is-sur-Tille. The 6th (Lorraine) and 13th (Auvergne) Districts were already in retreat. On the 15th, 8th District abandoned a hopeless project, left Dijon and set out for the hills, protected to some extent by VIII Corps —that is, by this time, the remains of the 7th Light Armoured, the 14th Division and some batteries from the 235th Division.

On the 14th, General Freydenberg, finding Châteauvillain far south of the region into which his Second Army was being driven, spent the night at Bourbonne-les-Bains. He was still out of touch with both XXI and Colonial Corps and with Army Group Four. Next morning he set out for Third Army headquarters at Flavigny, south of Nancy. Here he was told that Colonial and XXI Corps had already been transferred by G.Q.G. to Third Army, and that Second Army was now to occupy the Saône, from Jussey to St Jean-de-Losne and thence to Dijon, with a motley assembly of infantry believed to be on its way southward from Metz, Haguenau and St Dié. His headquarters would be Besançon. The orders were neither practicable nor even plausible. No troops arrived. Besançon was occupied by Guderian on the 16th. Second

---

* The 56th division (B) had been withdrawn from the Longuyon sector to the region of Metz during the past three days.

Army Headquarters retired to Arbois and thereafter played a minimal part in the battle.

[4]

While XXIII Corps was putting up a not altogether unsuccessful resistance against German infantry, it was being passed on both flanks by Hoeppner's and Schmidt's armour. It was only about 9 p.m. on the evening of the 13th that General Requin at Troyes learned that Hoeppner's advance guards had crossed the Seine a couple of hours earlier, a bare few kilometres west of XXIII Corps headquarters at Méry. The bulk of the German divisions were up to thirty kilometres further north. Withdrawal was imperative, but '. . . three officers with orders left corps headquarters in succession. Not one reached the divisions, not one even succeeded in returning later to the command-post. During the day, the formations, exhausted by repeated movement, having for several days received no regular rations, completely out of touch, knowing the situation only from shreds of imperfect and contra-dictory information which they were able to pick up, finally disinte-grated.'[3] On the left, General Armingeat, trying vainly to co-ordinate the moves of his hard-fighting 82nd, was captured, early on the 14th. Left without orders, the regiments fought on until the middle of the afternoon, helped to some extent by a Polish Armoured Brigade which had lost its way, and which vanished at the end of the day. The 4th Moroccan and the reconnaissance group held on until nightfall and then, under cover of darkness, marched across country to Arcis-sur-Aube. The rest of XXIII Corps, the Klopfenstein group, the 42nd Division and the 53rd, also fell back to the Aube. The Infantry of the 3rd and 14th were brought back by lorry. The situation of the Fourth Army was now beyond repair. The single main road to the west from Troyes had been cut. Its only main road southward had been made useless by bombing and anyhow was blocked by refugees. Henceforth, the Fourth could only fall back to the Loire, while the Second Army, its left entirely in the air, was about to be driven over the Meuse and away towards the Moselle.

On the afternoon of the 14th, General Klopfenstein saw his corps commander, General Germain, for the last time. Both knew there was little hope of resisting what was coming. The corps commander instructed Klopfenstein to hold on within the angle of the Seine and Aube and after dark to fall back up the small Barbuisse stream. It was already too late. The Kleist Group (von Wietersheim's XIV Korps had now been reunited with Hoeppner's) crossed the Troyes–Sens road and by early morning of the 15th had its advance-guards through the Forêt d'Othe and moving on St Florentin, not far from Branches, where Requin spent the night. This was some fifty kilometres west of the place he had expected to occupy.

From now onwards, the divisions, without orders, moved in whatever direction they guessed to be that intended by higher authority. The most northern, the 82nd, moved in two columns. One, the remnants of the 4th Moroccans and 6th Algerians, fought to the death on the edge of Troyes, the other, composed of the last of the 1st Zouaves and a party of Colonial Pioneers with a couple of guns, was wiped out trying to cross the Seine. On the right of the North Africans the 42nd hung on near Arcis until late on the 15th, when General Keller, finding his division without neighbours, brought it back up the right bank of the Seine past Troyes, turning about at intervals to beat off the pursuit. It lost half its artillery but crossed the river below Bar and made for Chaource. Here it had a glimpse of the still wandering Polish brigade, but failed to make contact with it. But the enemy caught up. There was fighting all night. The division was dismembered, and the fragments were surrounded near Les Riceys. Most of the men who survived were captured. General Keller, who made his escape, was able to remain free, but he was captured after the armistice.

The VIII Corps formations were to some extent sheltered by XXIII and were able to move southward ahead of the enemy, though by no means all succeeded. General Klopfenstein, with the motorized part of his headquarters and some of the 2nd Division artillery, eventually reached Arbois, fifty kilometres south-east of Dijon, and reported to Second Army. General Trolley de Préveaux of the 235th fell into an ambush, escaped and dodged about inside the German lines for another three weeks before reaching the French zone. Some 400 of his division reached Beaune, but more than half his artillery crossed the Loire. The 8th Dragoons of the 7th Light Armoured still had a few armoured cars. They were caught in the narrow forest roads of the Morvan between Montsauche and Saulieu, where they lost their last cars, but succeeded in slipping away with a party of the 14th Dismounted Dragoons to Decize. The 14th Division also came through the Morvan. It was still a fighting body. The infantry seized every chance that was presented to equip itself from depots and supply-points. It is said that General de Lattre recruited 500 gunners from an artillery depot on his way. It is a fact that, with the 53rd Light, the 14th came over the Loire near Nevers still in reasonable strength.

[5]

'It is at this point,' wrote the historian of the 2nd Division, 'that we end the history of this fine formation. After the evening of the 15th, our units received no further orders from the General. The last effective liaison would be made by Captain Augais of the divisional artillery and Lieutenant Koehl with the batteries. They did not come back to us, but threw in their lot with that of their units, and with them were made prisoners.'

On the 15th the morning communiqué of the German wireless ran: 'Today the third phase of operations begins, the pursuit of the French armies up to their total annihilation.'

At 6 this morning, finding that the enemy was already south of his proposed command-post, and hearing that G.Q.G. had reached Briare on the Loire, General Requin drove there for instructions. At Briare, he was joined by General Besson with his two army commanders, Frère and Touchon, and by General Huntziger. Huntziger reported the complete dislocation of Army Group Four and the impossibility of reuniting his three armies. After a short conference, General Georges told them to bring their divisions south of the Loire, the one obstacle behind which it might be possible to rally and reorganize. All recognized the necessity of this daunting march, but they were full of misgiving. Requin was to open his new headquarters at Lapalisse, thus registering the fact of the break with the Second Army. Georges told Frère that he had shown the last Seventh Army report to Reynaud, saying: 'Read this, M. le Président, this is the situation reported by the most optimistic commander in the French Army.' 'But,' Georges went on, 'Reynaud is stubborn against us all. He wants to hold the Breton redoubt—and with what?—and to take our retreating armies to North Africa! How?'

It was not only the exhaustion of the soldiers that alarmed the army commanders, but the chaos of refugees. 'At the Bordes cross-roads opposite Sully, there was a wholesale stoppage. An army convoy was blocked on the north–south road, and on the Briare road civilians were halted to wait their turn to cross. You could see children dying in their mothers' arms and from a roadside house the groans of a woman in labour.'[4]

Over the Loire, 13–16 June

FOLLOWING the decision of General Georges to bring what still survived of the Fourth, Sixth, Seventh and Paris Armies behind the Loire, orders were given, so far as orders could be communicated to the scattered units, to extricate themselves as rapidly as they could. For the divisions of the Fourth and Sixth, the problem was to escape from the overtaking German armour, a race between French soldiers almost everywhere on foot and Germans in their tanks and trucks. Continually passed by the enemy, liaison officers, dispatch riders and runners were forced to long detours only to find the headquarters they sought already abandoned. At an early hour on the 15th, while it was still dark, the Chief of Staff of the 2nd Division at La Chapelle-Vallon, south of Arcis-sur-Aube, was wakened by the report of a gun. Investigating, he was staggered to see a shadowy line of enemy tanks emerge from the village and pass on its way unchallenged by two Renaults, whose exhausted crews were sunk in sleep.

Although broken, reduced in numbers and badly mixed, regiments and companies struggled on. The remains of the 9th Infantry Regiment of the 235th Light, largely wiped out between the 11th and 14th, crossed the Seine at Bar on the 15th, and retreating up-river came to Nuits-St Georges on the next night. Somehow during the next forty-eight hours, the regiment, now little over a hundred strong, turning westward, crossed the Loire and reached Gannat.

An officer from the staff of General Bourret's Fifth Army sent ahead to organize a line to be occupied at the end of the withdrawal from Bitche, watched a small group of *chasseurs alpins* from the 28th Division, led by a sergeant covered with dust, their uniforms in rags, marching on in order and in step, the men bent forward, pulling with both hands at the straps of their equipment. Some were wounded, the dressings stained with blood and dirt. Some slept as they marched, ghosts bowed under the weight of their packs and their rifles. They passed in silence, with an air of fierce determination. 'Three months before he had seen the Lestien division coming out of the line, the berets and the weapons dipping to the quick-step of the hunting-horns . . . between two hedges of Alsatian head-dresses under the slender apple-trees not yet in bud. No one dreamed of defeat and the division looked invincible. Today this handful of *chasseurs*, wasted by battle, at their last gasp, formed the one group in France to wear the guise of warriors.'[1]

The better part of the regiments of the Sixth and Fourth Armies crossed the river between Cosne and Digoin. General Requin set up his headquarters at Lapalisse and stayed there until the 17th. There was not much to command. Of six infantry divisions, the 2nd, 3rd, 10th, 14th, 42nd, 44th, of two light, the 53rd and 235th, and the 3rd Armoured and the 7th Light Armoured, scarcely one could be described as fit to go into battle. The 14th was still a fighting body, but General de Lattre had recruited part of an artillery depot and very sensibly plundered abandoned stores for equipment on his way south. The remains of the 3rd Armoured retreating towards Dijon were surrounded and captured, with their general, on the 18th. The 7th Light had lost all its armour. A few artillery regiments, and small parties of infantry joined with local forces and regional regiments in an attempt to hold the eastern slopes of the Massif Central.

[2]

Seventh and Paris Armies, 11–16 June

The Seventh Army, which had crossed the Oise and the Aisne, had not been pursued over the rivers by Kleist's armoured group: this, as has been seen, had been transferred east. The 11th Division, with its flank partly covered by the 87th, had held on during the 9th and 10th to its position in front of the Forêt de Compiègne. General Frère, however, saw that with the disaster of the Sixth Army the Oise position was compromised, and ordered the withdrawal of XXIV Corps through the 11th and 12th. With the declaration that Paris was to be treated as an open city, the left of the Seventh Army was covered until it had passed the southern edge. The retreat was not easy. There was hard fighting on the Nonette at Senlis for the 47th Division and the 7th Colonial. The retreat across Ourcq and Marne was covered on the right by two fresh units, the 57th from near Bâle and the 239th Light. During the 13th and 14th, Seventh Army crossed the Seine into the Forêt de Fontaine-bleau.

[3]

On his way to the Loire on the 10th, Reynaud received at Orléans a message that Churchill wished to meet him and Weygand on the following day. The Churchill party, which included Eden, Dill and Spears, reached Briare in the late afternoon of the 11th and went to Weygand's headquarters in the Château du Muguet, where were waiting Reynaud, Weygand, Pétain, de Gaulle* and Villelume. The conference lasted from 7.30 to 9 p.m. There was much unhelpful talk. Churchill enlarged on the British intention to fight on whatever happened and spoke of the British forces now reaching France, which were in reality but a drop in the torrent needed. He had nothing with which to sustain the reeling armies. His interest, naturally, was to prevent the French fleet falling into German hands. Weygand's account of the situation was

---

* De Gaulle had come back from seeing Huntziger. His report to Reynaud on the commander of the Fourth Army Group was a, '*Bien. Pas plus.*'

infinitely discouraging. While insisting that there had been no break-down, he said that he now expected the enemy to cross the Rhine and attack towards Belfort, while the Italians attacked in the Alps. The French Army might hold their positions but '. . . There is nothing to prevent the enemy from reaching Paris. We are fighting on our last line and it has been breached. . . . I am helpless, I cannot intervene, for I have no reserves. There *are* no reserves. *C'est la dislocation.*'² At Churchill's request, Georges, who had his headquarters near Briare station, was summoned, and confirmed all that Weygand had said—the number of divisions wholly lost, the divisions now seriously disabled by losses, some no more than a cipher. As for the air force, the French had at most 180 fighters and the pilots were worn out. Although the British squadrons were doing all they could, the aircraft daily crossing the Channel could give no support as effective as it would if based in France. Churchill said he would examine what could be done.

The conversation went on, a mixture of recrimination and regrets politely expressed. It was clear that the British would not dispatch their last fighter squadrons to be swallowed up in the holocaust, and that they had neither infantry nor armour in quantities sufficient to put up any resistance to the German divisions. There was much eloquence, but it lacked body. There were vague references to the Breton Redoubt but no facts.

The conference was renewed early on the following morning. On this occasion, Darlan and Vuillemin appeared and the British Air Force commander, Barratt.³ Once more the arguments ranged over a wide field with at the end no satisfying answer being given to the questions.

At their last meeting, Georges, who had come over to say good-bye to Churchill, told him quietly that the battle was almost at an end and armistice inevitable.⁴ To send British fighter squadrons would not remedy the disaster. Churchill also saw Darlan, to whom he said: 'I hope you will never hand over the fleet.' The admiral replied that there was no question of this; 'it would be contrary to their naval traditions and dishonourable'.

At 6 this evening, the 12th, the French cabinet met at Château Cangé which housed Lebrun. For the first time, the members showed signs of disillusion and discontent, especially after hearing Weygand and Pétain's note on the necessity of an armistice. Some, Ybarnégaray the Basque, who had been appointed in the belief that he was a die-hard, and the newspaper proprietor, Prouvost, opposed the continuation of the war either in the Breton Redoubt or in North Africa. Campinchi, Dautry, Georges Monnet, Marin, stood by Reynaud. On the proposal of Chautemps, it was agreed to await the return of Churchill.

Reynaud went to the château at Chissay near Chenonceaux with Baudouin, who told him he was being too uncompromising. He spent the night here and with his immediate staff. Before leaving to sleep elsewhere, de Gaulle lectured him for a long time on the feasibility of the Breton defences, which Darlan had already proclaimed untenable without serious anti-aircraft protection.

Churchill, attended by Beaverbrook and Halifax, arrived at Tours in the early afternoon of the 13th, where he was joined by the ambassador, Sir Ronald Campbell, and Spears. Once more he spoke with confident eloquence, but he raised no responsive flicker in Reynaud, who asked whether, should a French government ('which would not include me') be driven to capitulation, the British would agree to the abrogation of the pledge not to ask for a separate peace? Churchill said no more than that if France remained in the fight with her fleet and the French Empire, and if the Germans did not destroy England, National Socialism would be swept away. 'Given immediate help from America, perhaps even a declaration of war, victory was not so far off.' And to Reynaud's reply that this was in fact no help, Churchill said that the British would waste no time in reproach or recrimination, but that this did not amount to liberating them from the agreement. Let Reynaud approach Roosevelt. Only after his reply could they consider the situation. Without seeing the French cabinet, the British party flew back to London.

At the subsequent meeting of the cabinet at Cangé, Reynaud was severely criticized for his failure to bring Churchill with him and for his statement that the French government had decided to continue the struggle. There were protests from Reynaud's own nominee, Bouthillier, the Finance Minister, and from Chautemps. On the basis of a rumour he had picked up, Weygand announced that the Communist party, headed by the fugitive Thorez, had set up a provisional government in Paris, which led Mandel to telephone Langeron in the capital to get a denial. The meeting was further soured by Weygand telling Campinchi that if he, Weygand, had been a politician he would have remained in the capital and behaved like the Roman senators faced by the barbarians. 'I would have awaited the invader in my senatorial chair.' (At a later date Weygand admitted he had been stupid to have said this.) Pétain read out a denunciation of the proposition to carry on the war from Africa, and proclaimed that for his part, he would not 'abandon the soil of France but would accept the suffering which will be imposed on the country and its sons. . . . In my eyes, the armistice is a necessary condition for the survival of eternal France.'

As before, there was no decision except to wait for Roosevelt's reply to Reynaud's appeal. That night Reynaud broadcast an appeal to the United States asking the American people to give France a hope of common victory. And in the early hours of the 14th, he dispatched another appeal to Roosevelt, which he knew could avail him nothing. It was merely an attempt to postpone the choice between two repugnant alternatives in the hope that something would turn up. In spite of de Gaulle, who was now in Brittany, it had already been decided to abandon the Breton Redoubt and to transfer the government to Bordeaux. That morning Reynaud set off by car down the main road swarming with refugees and their vehicles. Passing through Angoulême at 2 in the afternoon, Reynaud was handed by the *préfet* of the Charente Roosevelt's sympathetic but unhelpful reply. He reached Bordeaux at 8 p.m.—the 300 kilometres had taken some ten hours—and put up at the army headquarters in the narrow rue Vital-Carlès, where, in the *préfet's* private residence, the President of the Republic was housed.

In the controversies over responsibility that raged in June 1940, and even now have scarcely calmed down, no solution to the dilemma appeared then or has appeared since. Accusations pass to and fro, insults are exchanged, personal vanities alleged, so on and so forth. It was not only the obstacle of the Anglo-French agreement of March which stiffened the *durs*; it was the knowledge of what would happen to French citizens at the mercy of the Gestapo and the S.S.: the latter had already shown its quality. On the other hand, what the politicians feared, the professional soldiers did not imagine. All they could see was the continuing squandering of battalions and companies, the deaths of men, the abandonment of wounded to the enemy, and all to no purpose, because defeat was not only inevitable but present. It was all very well for Reynaud to talk of the Breton Redoubt, but he seemed not to have the faintest inkling of the fact that even if it were possible to build it up with divisions—and that implied, for the most part, British divisions—it would be no better than an enlarged Dunkirk, difficult to supply from the sea and impossible to protect from the air. It was simply a fantasy of de Gaulle's, and in the eyes of Pétain and Weygand this political soldier, journalist and adventurer was exceeding the bounds of his office.

The case against North Africa was still stronger. Such a move was perhaps even more difficult to execute. Five minutes' reflection demonstrated that even if the numbers of Frenchmen suggested—half a million—could be transported, they could be armed only by Great Britain, itself since Dunkirk in a parlous state for weapons, or by the United States, as yet incapable of supply. And there were other objections, particularly political. It was alas! a dream. 'The Empire,' raged Weygand to Louis Marin, 'just a pack of blacks over whom you'll have no control from the moment you're beaten.' That this was prescient, the episodes of Indo-China and Algeria have since testified.

In Alsace-Lorraine

As has already been narrated, Prételat was fully aware that the defence of Lorraine depended on the protection afforded by the Second Army, and to strengthen that, he had moved Colonial Corps head-quarters to Senuc. His further intention, should the withdrawal which appeared to him inevitable be ordered, was to hold the perimeter of his command so long as it was possible with a defensive crust of which the strongest features would be the fortified sectors and the line of the Rhine, while the mobile divisions and the infantry between the *ouvrages* were gradually brought back. At a point south of Nancy, the front would be narrowed. Fifth Army headquarters would then be extracted and sent back to the vicinity of the Loire to organize a new position. The scheme was sensible enough on paper, but its success depended on the maintenance of the east and west sides of the corridor down which most of the northern troops would be brought. This in turn depended on speed. Little motor transport was available. The railways were vulner-able to bombing and there was a dearth of rolling-stock.

On 11 June, Weygand at last prepared the secret instruction to be issued if the front along the lower Seine, the Paris position and the Marne should be dislocated. If that occurred, the Commander-in-Chief alone would order withdrawals. For Army Group Two the general direction was Sarrebourg. The aim was to regroup the armies on the line Caen–Tours–the middle Loire–Clamécy–Dijon, or along the Perche hills, the Loire from Tours to Nevers, the Morvan and the hills and woods behind the Doubs.

Prételat had become increasingly alarmed at the situation ever since 9 June, and the subsequent troubles of Second Army made it worse. He spoke with Georges on the telephone, pointing out that his last free division, the 20th, had been taken from him. 'You have nothing to complain of,' retorted Georges, 'you have the fortress troops. You should just see the rags on our left.'

In view of the withdrawal of Huntziger's Army Group to the Marne and the threat to his left, Prételat made tentative changes in his dis-positions. He had abandoned the Montmédy bridgehead. The switch-line from near Longuyon to Mangiennes had been occupied by parts of the 51st Division since mid May, and he had also put the major part of the 58th Division below Spincourt. Now he took more field units from the defences. If the Third and Fifth Armies were to retreat, their rear must be covered, particularly in the open sector Faulquemont–Puttelange–Wittring. He concentrated parts of the 26th and 30th Divisions behind either end of this gap, and prepared the 56th Division near Metz to move up by truck. Further to the south, he brought what he could from the Jura to the Eighth Army, to ensure the defence of the Vosges cols and the Belfort gap, the loss of which would threaten the retreat of the Third and Fifth Armies.

He had sent a staff officer to General Georges at La Ferté on the 11th to obtain his comment on the orders he had drafted in case of emergency. On the next day this officer returned with Weygand's hitherto secret instruction, to be put into action at once. Prételat quickly sent out preliminary orders to his three army commanders while he amended his already drafted orders in the light of Weygand's decisions. In particular, he told General Condé to organize a task force to prevent the crossing of the Rhine–Marne canal in the area between Toul-Vaucouleurs–Mauvages. Condé hastily collected an infantry regiment, a group of 75s and an anti-tank company from the 56th Division assembled round Metz, together with other anti-tank units and a battalion of tanks.* This was scarcely organized before Huntziger telephoned to say that his Second Army was dangerously stretched near Vitry-le-François and could no longer assure the flank of Army Group Two. Georges had told him to get reinforcements from Prételat; he wanted a division. Prételat had only the unemployed regiments of the 56th, which he had already destined for the Eighth Army, but in view of Huntziger's urgency, he agreed to dispatch these, though warning Huntziger that they could not reach St Dizier in time.

Further in view of the insecurity of his left, he asked permission from G.Q.G.N.E. to see the Commander-in-Chief on the next day. His intention was to remind him of their conversation of 26 May and to obtain the precise orders that 'the situation required'. Before setting out, he ordered Fifth Army to send troops from the Haguenau sector to take up a position between Chaumont and Nuits-sur-Ravières. It was an operation requiring at least a week; at best he had two days. At 8 next morning, the 14th, Balck's Rifle Brigade (the conquerors of the Meuse on 13 May) took Langres, seventy kilometres south of Chaumont, with 3,000 prisoners, and, wheeling eastward, swept on to the Saône at Gray.

[2]

The flight from the towns

Hitherto, in spite of the stampede from Thionville which followed the annihilation of the La Ferté *ouvrage*, most of the civilians in Meurthe-et-Moselle, Moselle and Vosges, had placed unreserved faith in the protection of the Maginot Line. In particular, those who lived west of the Vosges in Épinal and Nancy, and who remembered 1914–18, had remained confident. Except for the early withdrawals in May from near the Rhine and the Maginot, the authorities had in no way varied the

---

* These were Estienne's 70-tonners of 1929. There were only six. They were sighted by German bombers on a railway siding and blown to pieces without ever having been in action.

precautions laid down before the outbreak of war. But on 10 June, Army Group Four (General Huntziger) ordered the evacuation of three zones west of the Meuse, and although these were to be carried out *seriatim*, the third group, the citizens of Verdun, bolted at once, taking all the available transport, with the consequence that the evacuees from Grandpré and Buzancy had to move on foot and in due course were overtaken by German armoured cars. The civil authorities had not foreseen where and how the blow would fall, and the German thrust west of the Meuse threw all their earlier plans into confusion. What route should a Verdunois take to get to La Rochelle, when Guderian's tanks were careering across the roads to the west ? Moreover, the withdrawal of the Second Army divisions east of the Meuse induced the civilians to do likewise and get ahead of the troops, thereby impeding those retreating from the north.

As early as the 13th, people in the northern towns such as Metz were surprised and thrown into confusion by the preparations for departure of the army depots and ancillary services. The steel-workers and their families, essential producers, were up and off as trains became available. The alarm spread. On the 14th the school-leaving examinations for the *baccalauréat* were in full swing at Nancy, when the rumour spread that the *préfecture* services were packing up. At once parents rushed to the examination hall to extract their children, hurry them to the station and join the crowd already besieging the building —in vain, since no train would start before midnight. Nor was it likely that many got past Besançon, since Besançon was reached by XXXIX Panzer Korps on the 16th. The panic flight of the Messins was in some measure due to the recollection that they had been German citizens up to 11 November 1918, and they did not welcome the embrace of the Nazi party.

Many refugees, of course, never reached a place of refuge, but for the determined it was not impossible. On the 14th a train carrying the guns and gunners of a heavy battery set out from Batilly near Briey. It reached Épinal that evening and went on to Jussey, where the railwaymen took up their wives and families before passing on southwards, displaying as it passed the nappies of the babies drying in the sunlight on the gun barrels. Except that the train was shot up in Besançon station by a roving tank from the 1st Panzer Division, which had just captured the city, the party appears to have crossed the battlefield in tranquillity and finally reached Lons-le-Saulnier.

Others were less fortunate. The youths of two classes that Reynaud had talked of calling up, sent southward, found the Germans in Dijon and drifted back to Alsace.

[3]

Facing the French defences between the Moselle and the Rhine waited Witzleben's First Army, with three army corps concentrated almost

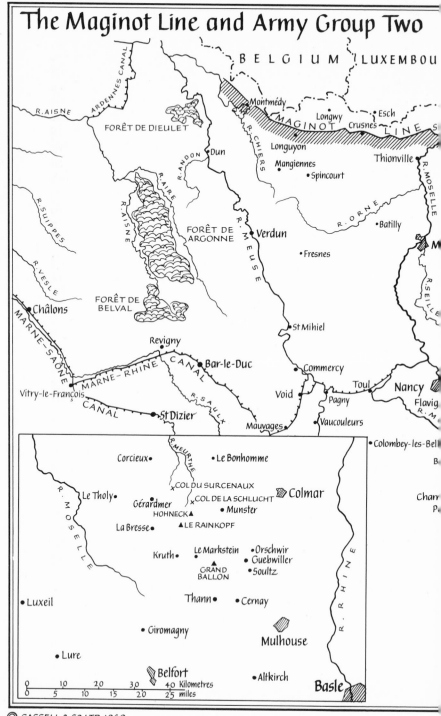

The Maginot Line and Army Group Two

BELGIUM ·LUXEMBOU

R. AISNE
ARDENNES CANAL
FORÊT DE DIEULET
R. RANDON
R. AIRE
R. AISNE
R. SUIPPES
R. VESLE
FORÊT DE ARGONNE
FORÊT DE BELVAL
R. CHIERS
MAGINOT LINE
Montmédy
Longwy · Esch
Crusnes
Longuyon
Thionville
Mangiennes
·Spincourt
R. ORNE
·Batilly
R. MOSELLE
M
Dun
R. MEUSE
·Verdun
·Fresnes
R. SEILLE
Châlons
MARNE-SAÔNE
MARNE-RHINE CANAL
Revigny
Bar-le-Duc
CANAL
R. SAULX
Vitry-le-François
St Dizier
Mauvages
·St Mihiel
·Commercy
Void
Pagny
Toul
Vaucouleurs
Nancy
Flavig
R. M

·Colombey-les-Bel

B

Corcieux·
·Le Bonhomme
R. MEURTHE
×COL DU SURCENAUX
Le Tholy·
×COL DE LA SCHLUCHT
Colmar
Gérardmer
HOHNECK▲
·Munster
La Bresse·
▲LE RAINKOPF
R. MOSELLE
Kruth·
Le Markstein
·Orschwir
·Guebwiller
▲ GRAND BALLON
·Soultz
R. RHINE
·Luxeil
Thann·
·Cernay
Charr
P
· Giromagny
Mulhouse
·Lure
Belfort
·Altkirch
Basle

| 0 | 10 | 20 | 30 | 40 Kilometres |
| 0 | 5 | 10 | 15 | 20 | 25 miles |

© CASSELL & CO LTD 1968

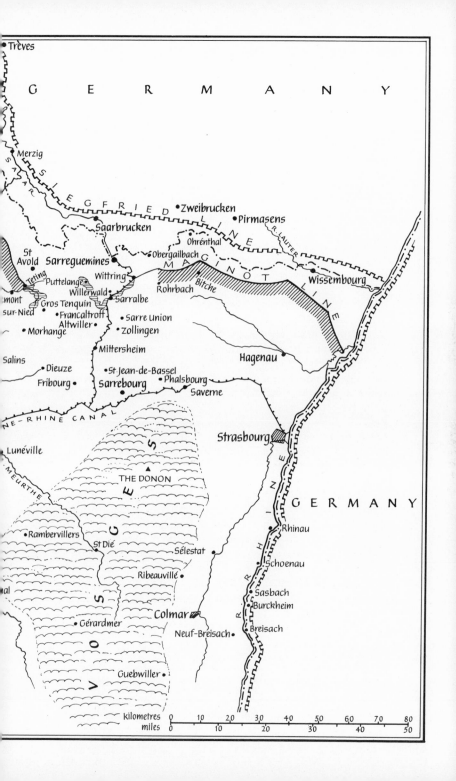

298 THE DISASTER

wholly between Saarguemines and St Avold, and a corps headquarters on either flank. The three centre Korps from west to east were XXX, XII and XXIV. The outer Korps were XXXVII opposite Haguenau and Bitsche, and XLV astride the Sarre, facing the Crusnes fortifications. These two had no corps troops. In all there were fifteen infantry divisions, but no armour.

Early in June there had been minor attacks in the Willerwald–Holving pocket against the colonial machine-gunners* and Willerwald had been lost. Now, following Weygand's tardy decision to manœuvre, the retreat from the Sarre and Faulquemont sectors† was ordered by General Girval to begin at 9 p.m. on the evening of the 14th. During the day, the Germans had attacked at several points. Posts had been lost and retaken. There was heavy fighting in the sector north of Bitsche held by the 30th Alpine Division, and advanced posts were overrun. In the Haguenau sector outlying blockhouses and casemates repulsed tentative attacks with the support of skeleton infantry battalions. West of the Sarre from Puttelange to Holving, after a heavy bombardment during the afternoon, the Germans attacked and were repelled. As darkness fell, the withdrawal began. No serious attack had been made further west on the *ouvrages* north of Faulquemont.[1]

On the morning of the 15th, the rearguards stood on the line Han-sur-Nied–Landroff–Gros-Tenquin–Francaltroff, with the colonial machine-gunners and the Poles at Altwiller and Zollingen astride the coal-mines canal, which joins the Sarre to the Rhine–Marne canal. Next day, the 'crust' was roughly from Morhange south-eastward through Bourgalstroff to Mittersheim and St Jean-de-Bassel. The retreat went on. The German evening report announced that their advance elements were a little north of Château-Salins and facing Dieuze, Fribourg, Sarrebourg and Phalsbourg.

To the south-west, the situation on this day had become so threatening that General Condé ordered Colonel Reviers de Mauny, the commander of the 51st Machine-Gunners, to hasten with a battalion southward to the Moselle, between Bayon and Portieux south of Nancy, to organize an anti-tank cordon with such troops as could be got together, a divisional training centre, a battery of mountain-guns, a battalion of obsolete F.T. tanks, parts of the 30th and 70th Divisions, and of the Haguenau fortress garrison, destined for Gray-sur-Saône. Colonel Reviers de Mauny reached Bout-du-Pont opposite Charmes on the 17th. It was too late.

On the 15th, the leading troops of the 1st Panzer Division had reached

---

* Cf. page 265.

† The Fortress regiments were roughly as follows: from Kerfent to Teting, 156 F., 146 F.; Leling–Biding–Cappel, 69 F., 82 F. with, intermingled and in support, 52nd Division units: Puttelange–St Jean-de-Rohrbach, 174 F. From Puttelange southward to the Sarre, 41 Col.M.-G., 51 Col.M.-G. with the 1st Polish Division in support from Holving to Oermingen, east of Saaralbe.

the Saône at Gray between Dijon and Vesoul. On the 16th, the whole XXXIX Korps had crossed the river. The 1st Panzer had swept into Besançon and then wheeled northward up the Doubs towards Mont-béliard, while the 29th Motorized dashed on to Pontarlier to reach the Swiss frontier the next day. At the same time, the XLI Panzer Korps was also on or across the upper Saône and preparing to wheel north-ward against the Moselle between Épinal and Charmes. On the 15th, too, the German Sixteenth Army had taken Verdun. The fragments of the French Colonial and XXI Corps (now transferred to the Third Army) were fighting desperately in the woods east of the Meuse, in front of Toul, round Colombey-les-Belles, and south of Neufchâteau—small unco-ordinated pockets of Frenchmen, Moroccans, Senegalese, exhausted, hungry and with their ammunition running low. South of Bourmont, to which the 1st Colonial Division was retreating, there was nothing. In front of the XLI Panzer Korps, as it turned north, there were no troops at all.

[4]

The crossing of the Rhine

The Rhine defences consisted of blockhouses close to the river bank ('almost *in* the river', says the historian of the 54th Division) with casemates at the crossings. The principal position lay on the Strasbourg–Neuf-Brisach–Mulhouse road (N. 86), with large ferro-concrete case-mates as well as minor shelters. The third line was on the Rhine–Rhône canal with blockhouses at the locks and intersections. Further defensive measures intended by Prételat were overtaken by events and remained unfulfilled. He had made it clear to General Laure that at all costs Eighth Army must prevent an incursion from the east, which would imperil the retreat of the troops from the Maginot.

On the 14th, the infantry holding the blockhouses on the Rhine had observed that the enemy across the river were cutting lanes through their own barbed wire, a certain announcement of immediate attack. Since, however, at dawn on the 15th there was no bombardment and no attack, the French assumed the operation had been postponed. It had, but only until 9 a.m., when after a sharp twenty-minute bombardment in which smoke-shell was used, the German Seventh Army sent storm-detachments in fast motor-boats over the Rhine at Neuf-Brisach, Burkheim, Sasbach and Schoenau. Although at Neuf-Brisach they were twice driven back, here and at other places they eventually secured a footing and gradually isolated and paralysed the strong-points east of the Rhine–Rhône canal. By evening on the 16th, all these villages had been surrounded, and at Sasbach a bridge had been thrown across. On the 17th, the leading troops entered Colmar. The French XIII Corps (General Misserey), the 104th and 54th Divisions, retreated into the deep narrow wooded valleys from Ribeauvillé to Guebwiller. Further north the 62nd Division was falling back into the hills towards the Donon.

On the western side of the Vosges, Witzleben's three corps were pushing southward towards the Rhine–Marne canal and had detachments both east and west of Nancy. Far to their rear however, pressure on the isolated Maginot forts was not enough to induce the garrisons to surrender.

By now the area of Army Group Two presented scenes of fantastic and irremediable disorder. Parts of regiments, let alone divisions, would be engaged in desperate fighting in the neighbourhood of Saarguemines or Boulay, while other parts of the same command might be counter-attacking south-west of Nancy and others again attaching themselves to troops defending the Loire. At the end of a long retreat on 17 June, the 35th Division found near Toul men returned from leave who should have reported on 10 May.

When, on the 16th, the 1st Panzer Division turned northward after occupying Besançon, it crossed the Doubs, and on the following day reached Montbéliard. The French XLV Corps on the Swiss frontier, with the greater part of the 2nd Polish Division and elements of the 67th, tried to move down the Doubs from Lisle to Besançon, but it could not arrest the advance of Kirschner's tanks.

The Eighth Army was now facing east, south and west. From the east, the Germans who had crossed the Rhine had reached the foot of the Vosges. From the south, the 1st Panzer Division was moving on Belfort, while parallel to its march the 2nd Panzer, having reached the Saône at Auxonne, had also wheeled and was now hastening northward towards Remiremont and Gérardmer. General Laure had his Eighth Army command-post at Malvaux at the foot of the Ballon d'Alsace on the road to Giromagny, some twenty kilometres north of threatened Belfort. On the 14th, he had sent a composite force, a Polish infantry regiment and the reconnaissance group of the 2nd Polish Division, with the motor-cyclist elements of the 67th and 63rd Divisions, to the area east of Belfort. To this he added a battalion of Renault tanks. The 63rd Division to the north of Belfort was turned about and sent to face the enemy advancing on Lure and Luxeil. The XLV Corps made no serious progress down the Doubs and was driven back towards La Chaux-de-Fonds on the frontier.

[5]

On 13 June, General Prételat did not cover the road to Briare as rapidly as he had hoped: he did not arrive until 1 p.m. and Weygand had already left. He did not get back to his headquarters at Villers-les-Nancy until 9 in the evening. Nancy itself was now threatened and Third Army headquarters had shifted to Flavigny, behind Prételat's. Prételat also found a message from G.Q.G. saying that German armour was at St Dizier and urging him to hasten the withdrawal. It was clear that he could no longer remain in the suburbs of Nancy, and at 7 a.m. on the 14th he set out with his staff to Dijon. Before doing so, he issued a number of orders, which in view of the kaleidoscopic situation of his armies might, but probably would not, be implemented. On the 16th he was cut off from his armies.

29 FROM SEINE TO LOIRE,
11–16 June

The retreat from the lower Seine, 9–16 June

WHILE General Besson's Army Group had been striving to stem the attack of von Bock's Fourth Army, Weygand had summoned every reserve he could lay hands on to strengthen the line of the Seine below Paris. Two fresh divisions had been brought from North Africa, and the only active division left to the Army of the Alps, the 2nd Colonial, had been drawn on to produce a Light Colonial, while an 8th Light Colonial was improvised from European, Moroccan and Senegalese units. From training centres, three new light divisions were organized and sent up to support the troops falling back on the Seine. To Weygand's mind, time at the moment was all important. 'I need until 15 June,' he had told Altmayer on the 8th. He was not to get it.

This was not the fault of the transport services, which were still working heroically. On 6 June, the 17th Light Division had detrained at Dreux and marched over the river. On the 7th, the 57th began to arrive at Provins, the 239th at Meaux, both for the Seventh Army, the 85th North African came to the military government of Paris, and the 8th Light Colonial began to arrive at Houdan. On the 8th, the 2nd Light Colonial joined the Seventh Army, and on the 9th the 84th North African came in between Vernon on the Seine and Boran on the Oise; a single regiment of the 83rd Division detrained at Montereau and G.Q.G. was taken from La Ferté to Briare.

Transport was immensely complicated by the arrival of the troops being repatriated after Dunkirk. They were landed at Brest, Cherbourg and other ports, to be brought to Évreux and other concentration-points. Between 29 May and 7 June, 89,000 arrived, and on 11 June there were still 30,000 to be disposed of. Their reorganization was hindered by the dispatch of gunners and engineers to their depots. This, since the infantry was being re-formed in Normandy, deprived all the reconstructed formations of most of their artillery. General Fagalde, for example, was trying to reconstruct his XVI Corps out of the ghosts of four infantry divisions of the First Army somewhere between Honfleur and Pont-l'Evêque, in all thirteen battalions, the strongest contingent being that from the 43rd, which produced five armed and three unarmed battalions. Similarly the cavalry corps was being patched up near Rambouillet on a skeletal basis. The *brigades de combat*, which on 10 May had consisted of eighty-seven Somua and eighty-seven Hotchkiss, now had ten of each type, while the *brigades de découverte* had four or five armoured cars and a single weak battalion of dismounted dragoons instead of three.[1] None of the light armoured divisions had either artillery or engineers, and there were no supply trucks.

[2]

On 9 June, after the capture of Rouen, von Bock had sent Hoth's XV Panzer Korps to hunt down Ihler's IX Corps at St Valéry-en-Caux. At the same time, the XVI and XIV Panzer Korps (the Kleist Group) had been withdrawn to be sent to von Rundstedt's Army Group A to complete the rupture of Huntziger's three armies. This had left Kluge's Fourth Army with only two Korps, v. Stulpnagel's II and von Manstein's XXXVIII, in all six or seven divisions, to deal with the retreating French. He was allotted the Eighteenth Army from reserve, which needed some days to come into the line between Kluge's Fourth and Reichenau's Sixth Army.*

On the night of the 8th/9th, on the heels of a mixed crowd of Dutch, Belgian and French refugees, Petiet's 3rd Cavalry crossed the Seine with some of the British tanks. Before the river defences could be organized, on the morning of the 9th advance parties of von Manstein's XXXVIII Korps were over, helped by thick mist, at Muids, a ferry on the Les Andelys peninsula, and on the 10th at Vernon. Petiet reported to General de la Laurencie, who had now arrived at Louviers via Dunkirk–Dover–Tidworth–Southampton–Cherbourg–Paris and Caen. III Corps had been given the responsibility for the defence of the river from Pont-de-l'Arche to Vernon. At the moment La Laurencie had no more than two reconnaissance groups, two groups of 75s and one anti-tank battery to defend a matter of sixty kilometres of winding river. The enemy had not yet crossed the river in force below Pont-de-l'Arche.

Tenth Army Headquarters had moved from Marines to Vaucresson near Versailles, and on the 10th was directed to Orbec just off the Le Mans road, sixty kilometres south of Rouen. General Altmayer's force consisted of the Duffour group, a thoroughly irregular command, a heterogeneous collection of extemporized bodies, the remains of the 17th Light (one infantry regiment and seven field guns), a battalion of a regional regiment, two of *douaniers*, an infantry and a cavalry depot, two groups of 75s, two of high-velocity heavy guns, and, commanded by a captain, four armoured cars, a detachment of motor-cyclists, four anti-tank guns of various calibres, and two groups of machine-gunners. On the 10th began the arrival of the 236th Light Division with one group of 75s. It held a wavering line from near Pont-Audemer through Montfort and across to Pont-de-l'Arche.

On the right of the Duffour group, III Corps was reinforced during the 9th by Brigadier Beauman's scratch C Brigade, part of which had been left north of the river when the Pont-de-l'Arche bridge went up,

---

* Von Manstein's Korps had attacked south-westward between the 5th and 9th, but the XIV Panzer Korps on his left attacked southward. Hence there was a gap which became wider with the withdrawal of XIV Korps. It was into this that the Eighteenth Army was directed.

and was with difficulty recovered. The other two brigades, which had crossed the Seine on ferries below Rouen, followed. There were also some of General Evans's tanks, and, in the evening, the first battalions of the 237th Light division. But there were sixty kilometres of river to Vernon to defend, extremely sinuous, the north bank often dominating the south. In addition to their crossing at Muids, the Germans had already built a pontoon bridge just above Les Andelys, which could not be approached. On the right they had enlarged their bridgehead at Vernon, which was only contained with great difficulty by the Cavalry Corps.

Beyond Vernon was the Army of Paris. On the left the river was held by the 84th North African (Zouaves and Tunisians) as far as Poissy, and then up the Oise. This enormous stretch was taken over on 10th/ 11th by General Grandsard with a transformed X Corps consisting of the 8th Light Colonial (Moroccans and Senegalese) on the left, and after concentration the 84th North African. In addition the corps was supported by the 2nd Light Armoured. The other Army of Paris corps, General Libaud's XXV, was on the 9th still holding the Oise from its junction with the Seine as far as Boran with the survivors of the four divisions of X Corps and another recently arrived division from North Africa, the 85th—Zouaves, Algerians and Senegalese—against a not very thrusting enemy infantry in front of Pontoise. These were temporarily protected by the Delestraint group, the 2nd and 4th Armoured, both much depleted. All these detachments were withdrawn from the Oise behind the Seine on the 11th, following the declaration that the capital would be treated as an open city.

To those on the river it was quite clear that the Seine could not be held. As General Grandsard says, the river, winding through sixty kilometres with seven bridges and a number of other crossing-places, had no natural features to help the defence.

During the 10th, with the help of some British armour, Petiet's cavalry held the attacks near Louviers, and the Light Armoured divisions contained the enemy between Pacy and Bonnières. But this delay could be no more than temporary.

[3]

In the hope that the French would still be able to defend their country, the British had landed the first contingent of a new Expeditionary Force at Cherbourg, the 52nd Lowland Division, and, further west, advance parties of the Canadian Division. One brigade, the 157th of the 52nd, was sent forward at once, on the 12th, to III Corps at Conches. During the day, the Duffour group had had its right driven back to Le Neubourg. In consequence, La Laurencie brought his left back to Le Neubourg–Évreux–Pacy, with the Scottish brigade in the centre of its right on the now flaming town of Évreux.

The commander of this new British Expeditionary Force was General

Brooke, formerly of II Corps. He landed at Cherbourg on the morning
of the 13th and after calling at British Headquarters at Le Mans was
taken on to see Weygand and Georges at Briare. (This was the day of
the last meeting of Churchill with Reynaud at Tours.) Brooke's journey
in face of the universal traffic blocks was slow. He did not reach French
G.Q.G. until the evening, too late to see Weygand. He had only the
vaguest picture of the situation and was aghast at the map which Georges
let him see the following morning, showing the penetration of the
German armoured corps deep in the French line. He was shaken, too,
by the statement that all reserves were now engaged. For the first time
he was told about the Breton Redoubt. From the map before him, he
could see that there was no prospect of a French recovery and that the
Breton Redoubt, which the British troops would have to defend, was
quite phantasmagoric, a dangerous illusion—an opinion already arrived
at by the two French generals. Weygand as good as admitted that
organized resistance was at an end. Nevertheless, Brooke had no
alternative to signing a document about the concentration of the British
troops now in France in the neighbourhood of Rennes. On his return
to Le Mans, he telephoned to the War Office and gave his view of the
seriousness of the situation. After some argument and the intervention
of Churchill, his advice was accepted. He was freed from subordination
to the French and instructed to prepare the withdrawal, embarkation
and return of all British troops to England.

On the previous day, Weygand's directive of the 12th for the withdrawal to the Perche hills and Loire had reached Tenth Army and been
communicated to the corps. The Duffour Group had already been
forced back that morning, carrying with it the left of III Corps to
the line of the Risle, while at the same time the cavalry were no longer
able to contain the enemy at Pacy. Tenth Army order instructed its
formations to fall back southward in liaison with the Army of Paris.
On the 15th, the task of the Tenth Army was complicated by the
withdrawal, first, of the Beauman Division to Carentan on its way to
Cherbourg, and then by the extraction of the 157th Brigade from III
Corps and its crossing the back areas of the Duffour group.*

[4]

While the Tenth Army was still holding the enemy attacks, the Army
of Paris, on the appearance of the German Eighteenth Army, had begun
to withdraw XXV Corps from its position on the Oise. The 241st Light

---

* The 155th and 156th brigades of the 52nd division had not left the Cherbourg area. They were re-embarked on the 16th. Brigadier Beauman was
instructed to move on the 15th. He had collected enough transport to move his
three brigades, and after a night at Carentan reached Cherbourg on the 17th.
With difficulty he got orders to embark. The 157th Brigade withdrew on the
evening of the 16th and got away from Cherbourg the next day, only an hour or
so before the arrival of the 7th Panzer Division.

and the 85th North African remained on the Seine while the last elements of the 13th, 16th and 24th Divisions came through Enghien and then marched round the capital by the outer boulevards, coming out by the Porte d'Orléans and retiring to the neighbourhood of Corbeil. The depleted divisions were to be transported to the Loire by train. But the trains were already fully employed. The divisions set out on foot, considerably hampered by the mobs of refugees. Some were lucky. Parts of the 13th Division were picked up by lorries and taken to Pithiviers, whence with some help from the 2nd Armoured they marched to the Loire. Others, the 16th Division for one, were overtaken north of Pithiviers and captured, except for such motorized elements as still existed. On the 16th the 2nd Armoured was surrounded north of the Forêt d'Orléans and had to fight its way out.

In the meantime the Army of Paris withdrew slowly. On the 13th, the Germans were at Meulan to the south of Versailles. On the 14th, XXV Corps was on the Chevreuse valley and in touch with X Corps, near Houdan. Thanks to the 2nd Light Armoured and the Cavalry Corps, X Corps still had a link with Tenth Army. On this afternoon, General Héring was ordered to withdraw to the Loire. Between the Chevreuse valley and the Loire lay the Beauce, on which there was no possible defensive line against armour. The army order was to entrain the main bodies of infantry and artillery and cover these with light troops to be brought back by road transport. This proved impossible. The trains could not be provided. The army fell back to the line Châteauneuf–Maintenon–Rambouillet, with the 2nd Light Armoured near Senonches, in touch with the Cavalry Corps.

On the 16th, Hoth's two Panzer divisions were brought over the Seine, and on the 17th Rommel was told to make a dash for Cherbourg, moving by Argentan before turning west. The 5th Panzer was ordered to go straight to Brest. They met with little opposition. On this day between the right of Fagalde's XVI Corps and Duffour's left there was an unoccupied gap of twenty-four kilometres. Into this, Tenth Army sent from reserve the mechanized brigade of Petiet's 3rd Cavalry. Under the impression that there were no enemy within fifty kilometres, it took up positions in the quadrilateral Rânes–La Ferté–Macé–Couptrain–Carrouges. It was attacked by the 5th Panzer making for Rennes and there followed a long confused fight, at the end of which the French groups, a mixture of armoured cars, motor-cyclists and dismounted dragoons, managed to escape. The northern party ran out of petrol and was captured at St Fraimbault. The southern took refuge in the grounds of a château between Fougères and Rennes, where they hid until after the armistice.

In the meantime, General Altmayer had withdrawn his headquarters via Orbec to Rennes. Here he was visited by his brother, the former commander of V Corps, who had been sent by Weygand to do something about the Breton Redoubt, of which the Tenth Army commander had heard rumours. He was also visited by General de Gaulle on the same business. Having given a number of orders, totally impracticable in the circumstances, the Under-Secretary for War hurried on to Brest, where he left for England, his business there to arrange for shipping to North Africa. How the Redoubt was to be organized and with what no one quite knew. There was some talk of a Polish division.

This day, the 17th, at 12.30, Marshal Pétain broadcast to the world that fighting must cease and that he had proposed a cessation of hostilities to the German government.

The broadcast was used by interested parties to announce that the war was over. No one was very sure. German tanks carrying white flags seemed to confirm it. Many surrendered without more ado. Many who tried to fight were impeded either by their comrades or civilians. General Bethouart, commander of the Chasseur Brigade of the Norwegian Expeditionary Force from Narvik, had landed at Brest with two battalions of *chasseurs alpins* and two of the Foreign Legion with instructions to report to the Tenth Army. On reaching Rennes and observing the hideous confusion, the general turned about, re-embarked his troops and sailed off to North Africa.

[5]

The retreat of the Seventh Army to the Loire

Shielded on its left by the great conurbation of Paris, after it had crossed the Oise the Seventh Army had not had to face Kleist's armour. Although it had had to fight, it had succeeded in reaching the Forêt de Fontainebleau without further heavy losses. But in the forest its troubles were considerably increased. On 13 June its forward divisions had been on the line of the Marne from La Ferté-sous-Jouarre (now abandoned by G.Q.G.N.E.) to Lagny. On the following day they had retired behind the Seine from Corbeil to Montereau, with the right on the Yonne protected by the 1st Armoured Division. On the morning of the 15th, the Seventh Army, like the Tenth Army and the Army of Paris, was ordered to fall back to the Loire.

The withdrawal was carried out in excruciating circumstances. All Paris, it seemed, was tramping southward. All roads were blocked by civilians, and the obstructions increased as driver after driver abandoned his car for lack of petrol. From now on the pitiful, pitiless crowds hampered and distorted every movement of the soldiers. Fontainebleau forest was filled with refugees. The war diary of every unit speaks of the hideous chaos to which it was subjected by the mobs struggling to escape. At Champagne-sur-Seine, on the edge of the forest, the colonel of the 9th Zouaves watched a flood of humanity pushing carts and cars into a mass of other vehicles, running over pedestrians, overturning cyclists, building up inextricable barriers hundreds of yards deep. When the Zouaves were seen to be preparing the bridge for demolition, the panic-stricken crowd stormed the barriers at the moment the charge was fired. Dead and dying were hurled into the air to fall back into the stream with the débris of the bridge.

Here too the railwaymen worked without pause. Trains for both military and civilians were dispatched from La Ferté-Alais, Malesherbes and La Chapelle-la-Reine, one behind the other as quickly as they were filled. Trains were overloaded and broke down. Engines had to be repaired. Impatient columns of infantry, knowing the pursuit at their heels, started to march, only to be overtaken by the motorized pursuers. As the Loire was approached, the traffic blocks became longer and denser.

The march to the Loire was a long purgatory, a slow marking-time in which the machine-gunning from the air and the deluges from summer storms alone punctuated the monotony of the endless hours of the longest days of the year. On they limped, the sad crowds. And now, with the crumbling of the front, they were hustled, or, worse, pushed aside by the imperious needs of the infantry, themselves driven and harried by the armour, the terrible armour of the enemy. Dazed civilians, frightened and thirsty—the Beauce peasants were dispensing water at five francs the glass—did not attempt to look for alternatives to the main roads to the south, N. 20, N. 51, N. 7, N. 5. The bridges were few and far between. From Châtillon to Orléans there are six in eighty kilometres, from Orléans to Tours seven in 114. At La Charité, fifty kilometres above Gien, the Germans bombed and stopped a train with a cargo of interesting War Office documents from which they later published a selection. Long before the enemy reached the river (16 June) great mobs were struggling for a footing on the bridges. As early as 11 June, the flood of refugees foretold catastrophe. The convoys evacuating the arms factories in and round Paris, organized by Dautry, were treated as privileged and passed over the Loire. Up and down the river Italian aviators bombed and machine-gunned towns with no anti-aircraft defences.

The easiest passage was at Orléans itself, since the city, parts of which were burning, had been evacuated. Some of the battalions of the 47th Division crossed here on their way to their positions at Jargeau. The 11th Division, on the other hand, although its horsed column crossed at Châteauneuf, had its entrained infantry delivered, some at Gien, some south of Orléans and some at Châtillon. The 87th, covering the entraining of XXIV Corps units, picked up trucks at the Croix-du-Grand-Maître in Fontainebleau forest at 4 in the morning of the 16th and set out for Sully. Thirty kilometres short of the Loire, the convoy was stopped, caught in a dense column of stationary vehicles, many of them abandoned. Eventually they succeeded in getting within ten kilometres of Sully bridge, by now partly damaged by bombs. The commander of the divisional infantry tried to clear the road by sending all the civilians and the military horse-convoys up-river to Gien and pushing the abandoned cars into the ditches. Most of the infantry crossed at Sully on foot. But before the road was clear the Germans were through the Forêt d'Orléans; the commander of the infantry and his headquarters were captured.

On the 17th, there suddenly appeared opposite the 107th Infantry Regiment (23rd Division) at Jargeau, where the bridge had been blown, some 400 gunners and infantry from the 13th Division, who either swam the river or were brought over by row-boat. Similarly on the 16th, a party of the 87th Division, believing Gien to be occupied by the enemy, swam the river at Nevoy.

On the 15th, Orléans city was a chaos. There were stragglers from the army, either alone or in groups, either armed or disarmed, either drunk or sober. 'Some were on bicycles. Officers in cars with their family and luggage . . . a complete fire-brigade passed, three vehicles with the firemen and their families. A woman, bag on shoulder, pushing a pram in which a baby slept, at her skirts a little girl of five or six, tells us that she has come from Paris on foot, that she lost her mother during a raid as they came through Étampes three days ago. She is hurrying on before dark in the hope of finding milk in a village, for in Orléans there is nothing left. Everything is on fire.'[2] Late-comers were pillaging the brothels in the faubourg de Bourgogne, the quarter where Charles Péguy was born and brought up.

Of all the towns on the middle and upper Loire, the worst to suffer was Gien. Lying as it does on, or rather just off, N. 7 (Paris–Nevers–Lyon) on the north bank of the Loire, it was to Gien that the great part of the hordes from Paris came. Not only the pell-mell undirected mobs, but official refugees, such as the 1,800 War Office clerks and 400 typists. On the 14th the town was put in a state of defence by the local regional regiment. Towards midnight, the order was given to evacuate the old, the children and the sick. At midday on the 15th, a dozen Italian bombers with fighter escort attacked the bridge. There were a hundred dead, followed by a panic in which frightened refugees flung themselves at the bridge, where the Italian airmen machine-gunned them. Trains no longer came from Orléans, Auxerre or Argent, but there were departures towards Nevers and Moulins, trains of all kinds, petrol, rations, coal, ammunition, with military and civilians clinging to their sides. The hospitals and *asiles* were cleared. By the evening, there were no bakers, no police, no doctors and no grave-diggers, while the prisoners escaped from Melun jail plundered the abandoned shops and houses.

The Italian bombing was renewed on the 16th. The hospice was set on fire, which compelled the nuns and the patients to attempt the road to Bourges, more than seventy kilometres to the south, moving on foot at the tail of a column of children from the Montreuil nursery school, which had been evacuated to this haven. A bombing during the afternoon fired the petrol dump. A second and a third again damaged the bridge, which the authorities could not decide to destroy until the following day. During the week, the better part of three divisions crossed, the 23rd, 57th and 3rd Light. The Germans were now in full cry. Three hundred men of the 102nd Infantry Regiment of the shattered 7th Division were caught at Dampierre a few kilometres down-river from Gien, where there was no bridge, and having exhausted their ammunition surrendered. Finally, the Gien bridge was blown at the moment when it was being crossed by civilians sent up from Sully.

As they came over the Loire, the infantry were distributed along the river in improvised positions. Most formations were not only depleted but mixed; stragglers and small groups attached themselves to any organized body; *chasseurs*, Tunisians, Moroccans, Senegalese, two Czech regiments, newly equipped. A few days later these last were withdrawn for transfer to England: they handed over their equipment to the 41st Infantry Regiment, which thereupon proclaimed itself motorized.

On the afternoon of the 16th, the German 33rd Division reached Orléans, where it found the main bridge intact and crossed, driving out the 241st Light Division. General von Bock, who visited the town on the 17th, reported a long line of French troop-trains laden with batteries and ammunition, supply trains and columns of prisoners and refugees, 'a complete picture of a break-down'. Late the same evening, the Germans reached the Loire at La Charité and Nevers. They crossed at Nevers and on the next day pushed out towards Bourges. Seeing that his army was threatened on both flanks, General Frère ordered the retreat to the Cher and after that to the Indre.

Reynaud's resignation

THE transfer of the government to Bordeaux opened the last political crisis of the Reynaud administration. All that remained was to decide between transferring the government to North Africa and continuing the fight, or asking the Germans for their terms for a cessation of hostilities. At the cabinet meeting which lasted from 4 to 7 p.m. on the 15th, Chautemps said that if it was the President of the Council's purpose to transfer the government to Africa, those ministers who accompanied it would need the sanction of public opinion, and for that the German terms for an armistice must be known. To obtain them, the question must be put. At the same time, the French pledge to the British must not be broken, hence a request should be made to the British government for their authorization of the inquiry to the Germans. Reynaud was against the proposal, but for the first time a vocal if minor opposition to him appeared. Pétain and half a dozen minor ministers supported the Chautemps proposal. Another half-dozen rejected it. No decision was reached. It was agreed to wait for Roosevelt's answer to Reynaud's latest telegram.

Roosevelt's reply reached him during the evening. It was sympathetic but negative. A long message was sent to Churchill asking the permission of the British government to inquire through the United States for the German and Italian terms for an armistice.

During the evening, Reynaud had told Weygand that the ministers were in favour of a capitulation of the land forces only, and that this must be asked for by the Commander-in-Chief. Weygand refused hotly and there was a fierce controversy between Weygand, Reynaud and the President of the Republic. At the cabinet meeting on the morning of the 16th, Pétain insisted that they were coming to no decision and that he would resign. He was asked to wait until the American reply was received. Roosevelt's sympathetic cable promised the dispatch of material aid, but pointed out that the declaration of war could only be made by Congress.

Late in the morning, Sir Ronald Campbell brought a message from Churchill. After reminding Reynaud of the injunction against separate negotiations, it offered, *provided and only provided* that the French fleet sailed to British harbours at once, that the British government would agree to the French government asking the German terms for an armistice. On hearing the message, Reynaud wryly remarked that it was silly: how could the French fleet quit the Mediterranean at the very hour when the French government was being invited by the British to go to North Africa.

A second message in the afternoon elaborated the morning telegram and included a paragraph on the duty of the French to extricate the Polish, Belgian and Czech troops in France. While these messages were being discussed by Reynaud with Campbell and Spears, a call from de Gaulle in London announced that Churchill was proposing the union of France and Great Britain. Reynaud produced this offer to the cabinet, which met almost at once after the receipt of the British proposal. It demanded too much mental and moral effort on the part of men on the path to surrender. They shrank from their ally's embraces. Very few ministers deigned to give it serious consideration. Chautemps renewed his earlier suggestion. Reynaud put it to the cabinet. It was voted by what was taken to be a majority, and Reynaud announced his resignation. He went to see Lebrun, who asked his advice. 'Call Marshal Pétain,' said Reynaud bitterly, 'he has the majority of the cabinet with him, and besides he has his own ready.'

Reynaud resigned at 9 p.m. President Lebrun asked the advice of the presidents of Senate and Chamber as to whom he should invite to take over the government. They replied, 'Reynaud.' Since this was impossible, the Marshal was invited. He at once accepted. He, indeed, had his list of ministers ready, or at least the names of the chief ones, many of them confidants of the last few days. The list, which he discussed with Weygand and Baudouin, showed the latter at the Quai d'Orsay and Laval as Minister of Justice. Soon after this Laval appeared, and insisted that he be appointed to the Foreign Office. Pétain weakly surrendered, on which both Weygand and Charles-Roux, the Secretary-General, told the Marshal that Laval's appointment would amount to a break in relations with Great Britain. Weygand said that it would throw France into the arms of Germany. Baudouin was therefore designated.

All this wasted time. It was not until after midnight that Lequerica, the Spanish ambassador, who had been warned of what was likely to happen and was waiting in the Spanish consulate, was invited to ask his government to intervene and to approach the Germans with the request, not for the terms of an armistice but for the cessation of hostilities and the terms of peace, coupled with a plea to stop their air force from bombing towns. At 12.30 on 17 June, yet another day of blazing heat, without consulting any of his ministers, Pétain broadcast to the French nation.

'*Ici Radio-Journal de France.* . . . M. Lebrun has called on the Maréchal Pétain to assume the reins of government.' There was a gasp of mingled surprise, horror and satisfaction, but before the assembled company could recover, the voice announced the Maréchal himself addressing the nation. We listened to the cold quivering tones of a tired old voice. 'Frenchmen, at the appeal of the President of the Republic, I have today assumed the direction of the government of France. Convinced of the affection of our admirable army . . . convinced of the confidence of the whole nation, I give myself to France to assuage her misfortune. . . . It is with a heavy heart that I say we must end the fight. Last night I applied to our adversary to ask if he is prepared to seek with me, soldier to soldier, after the battle, honourably, the means whereby hostilities may cease.'

Critical as the situation was no one expected this blow. They did not know whether to rise to their feet while the National Anthem was played. As the last note sounded, the moment had come for a gesture. But what should it be? . . . they all hesitated between relief and revulsion. Then one man, quicker than the rest, raised the cry of: 'Vive la France!' At first only a few voices took up the refrain. Then suddenly with a shout the whole room echoed the phrase; afterwards there was silence again while the news bulletin was read. . . .

The crowd started to eat, then to talk. What had the Maréchal said? Did it mean that a state of armistice already existed? Were the English also suing for peace? Were hostilities to cease against Italy too? These were the questions on everybody's lips. We had all heard the same speech, yet no one had rightly understood. It was a masterpiece of ambiguous phraseology. . . .[1]

The ambiguity of the phrase, 'the fight must stop', horrified and alarmed the Marshal's entourage. No reply had as yet been received from the German government, but the sentence was enough to cause such soldiers as wanted to stop fighting to lay down their arms. Amendments to the text were proposed and later versions of the broadcast attempted to undo the rash words. But the substitute, '*le moment est venu de tenter de cesser le combat*', was scarcely an improvement. Those five little words, said Léon Noel at the Pétain trial, 'cost us thousands of prisoners and even dead, for in the villages people stopped taking shelter from aircraft, believing the war to be over.'

[2]

Hitler received Pétain's request at a station on his way from Charleville to Munich, where he met Mussolini on the 18th. Mussolini had not had any French note. In his discussion with his partner, he proposed grandiose claims for Italy: annexation of France east of the Rhône, Corsica, Tunisia, French Somaliland, naval bases at Algiers, Oran and Casablanca, the surrender of the French fleet and air force. Hitler would have none of this. His object was to bring the war to a conclusion by offering Great Britain what he hoped would be acceptable conditions: for the same reason, the armistice terms with France would be severe, but not harsh enough to be less preferable than the end of hostilities. The working out of these required time. It was not until 6.25 a.m. on the 19th that the French government received the German reply. It was to the effect that the German government was ready to propose conditions, and, if the French would name their delegates, would make known the date and place for meeting, on condition that the French entered into parallel negotiations with the Italian government.

The French therefore nominated Léon Noel, until lately ambassador to Poland, General Huntziger, Admiral Leluc, Chief of the Naval Staff,

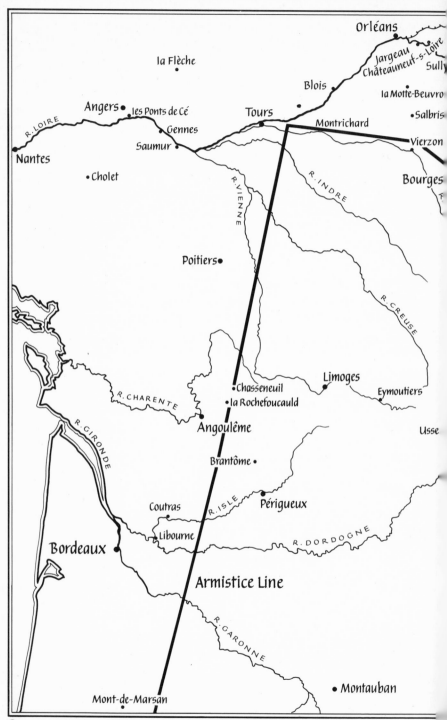

Orléans

la Flèche

Jargeau
Châteauneuf-s-Loire
Sully

Blois

R. LOIRE

la Motte-Beuvro

Angers • les Ponts de Cé

Tours •

Salbris

Gennes

Montrichard

Vierzon

Nantes

Saumur

Cholet

R. VIENNE

R. INDRE

Bourges

Poitiers •

R. CREUSE

Limoges

Chasseneuil

Eymoutiers

R. CHARENTE

la Rochefoucauld

Angoulême

Usse

Brantôme •

R. GIRONDE

Coutras

R. ISLE

Périgueux

Libourne

R. DORDOGNE

Bordeaux •

Armistice Line

R. GARONNE

Mont-de-Marsan

• Montauban

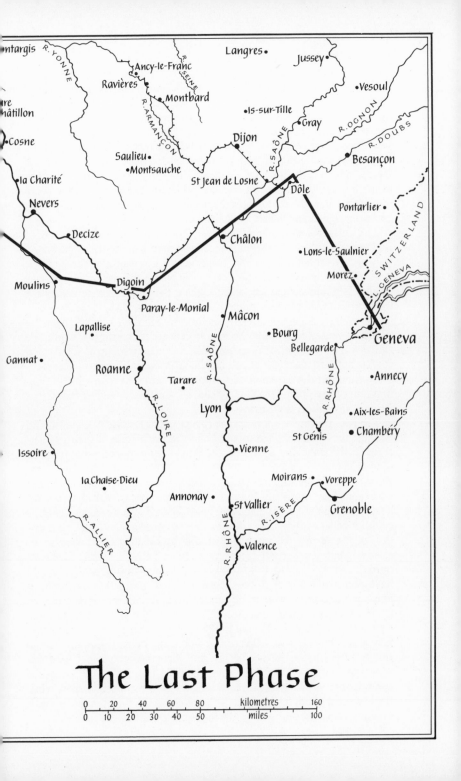

The Last Phase

0 20 40 60 80 kilometres 160
0 10 20 30 40 50 miles 100

General Bergeret, Chief of Air Staff, and General Parisot, former military attaché in Rome. At 2.30 p.m. on the 20th, the delegation set out for the north, up a corridor twelve kilometres wide in which the 'cease-fire' had been ordered. They crossed the Loire at Amboise, the bridge of Tours having been blown, in spite of the protests of the civil authorities. The city was, in fact, not yet occupied by the Germans. Under German escort they were driven to Paris, which they reached at 7.30 a.m. At 1.30 p.m. they were once more *en route* for Compiègne, and with heavy Teutonic irony were taken to the clearing at Rethondes, the scene of the surrender of 1918. Here they were introduced into the identical railway carriage in which the 1918 terms had been signed and where Hitler and his staff now sat.

The delegates were harangued by General Keitel, Chief of Staff of the Armed Forces. Having denounced the crimes of the Allies, he stated that his government's aim was to prevent a reopening of the conflict, to provide Germany with the guarantees which the pursuit of the war against England demanded, and to create the conditions necessary for the establishment of a new peace, the object of which was to be the repair of the wrongs done to the German Empire. He then handed them the terms, saying there would be no modification: argument would be futile. A permanent armistice commission would be set up at Wiesbaden to which objections might be submitted, but were unlikely to be accepted.

Considering the situation of France, the terms were less harsh than might have been thought. This, of course, was due to the fact that Great Britain was still in the fight.

The first trouble arose from the fact that the French delegates could not sign the document but must obtain the permission of their government. It was only after a stormy scene that they were permitted to recite the terms over the telephone to Bordeaux. This entailed further delay. Furthermore, they were told that the armistice with Germany could not come into force until the French had come to terms with the Italians. The fleet was not be handed over, but disarmed and interned—Hitler's advisers believed that a demand for its surrender would lead to a rejection of the terms. All prisoners of war in French hands were to be released, but the French prisoners were to be held by the Germans until the return of peace (750 Luftwaffe prisoners in France who should have been handed over to the British had not been). Political refugees living in the country were to be handed over. France was to be occupied by the German armies north and west of a line from Dôle through Besançon and Paray-le-Monial to Bourges, and thence to a point twenty kilometres west of Tours. From this point, the demarcation line would run twenty kilometres east of the line Tours–Angoulême–Libourne–Mont-de-Marsan–Orthez to the Spanish frontier. The wretched commission, as Noel says, was weighed down by the fact that, while they vainly argued, fighting was still going on, the invasion was spreading, and fugitives were being machine-gunned along the roads.

The dictation of the terms to Bordeaux was only completed late at night. Then the delegates were taken back to Paris. The French cabinet, Pétain, Weygand, Darlan, Baudouin, Bouthillier, Alibert, discussed the terms at once. The Secretary-General, Charles-Roux, wished to reject them and to move the seat of government to Algeria. On this Pétain threw his arms in the air and exclaimed: 'This silliness again!' Eventually four amendments were proposed. The first that the occupied zone should have its bounds much further north and that Paris should be excluded. The second that the French naval boats now in ports in France should be allowed to proceed to North African harbours for disarmament. Thirdly, that the delivery of political refugees to the Germans was dishonourable and humiliating and the demand should be expunged. Last, a proposal from Weygand, that instead of being handed over, aircraft should be warehoused under German supervision. Only the last of the four was accepted by the Germans.

On this morning, the 22nd, after three hours' sleep, the delegates were taken back to Rethondes. During the day various points were discussed with the Germans or with Bordeaux. At 6.30 p.m. Keitel brusquely told them that if the terms were not accepted during the next hour, he would treat the matter as closed. On hearing this, Weygand ordered the delegation to sign the convention. This done, they were to go to Rome. At 4 a.m. on the 23rd, the Noel Commission left Le Bourget, and via Munich and Padua landed at Rome that afternoon. Here the negotiations went more smoothly. Much of the schedule was identical with the German document. The Italians agreed that the demilitarized zone should extend to fifty kilometres beyond the points reached by their troops. Since, except at Menton, they had scarcely advanced beyond the frontier, the proposal was agreed to. The main Italian preoccupations were over their African possessions. The terms were signed on the evening of 24 June to commence at twenty-five minutes after midnight of the 24th/25th.

On 18 June, in reply to Pétain's broadcast, and in defiance of Germany, there was heard on the air a French voice: 'I, General de Gaulle, at this moment in London, invite French officers and soldiers at present on British territory, engineers, and skilled workers, to get into touch with me. Whatever happens, the flame of French resistance must not be quenched. Nor shall it be.'

The collapse, 17–25 June

THE consequences of Pétain's pompously pathetic broadcast were all that his immediate auditors foresaw; and the more astute Germans at once perceived the advantages. Up and down the front, German armoured cars and tanks appeared covered with white sheets, approached groups of French soldiers, often without officers, surrounded and disarmed them. The German High Command halted the centre armies (Sixth, Ninth, Second and Twelfth) on the armistice line, though they continued to pursue the retreating French divisions at their leisure. The German Fourth Army on the right was sent to clean up Brittany on the 18th/19th; while the Eighteenth, to which the XIV Panzer Korps had now returned, was ordered to advance down the coast as far as the Spanish frontier, where it would be joined by Rommel's division. Rommel was already on his way in pursuit of the vanishing British at Cherbourg. He was held up by various contingencies and his own caution, and reached the outskirts of the great naval port at midnight on 18th/19th, twenty-four hours after the last British troops (1st Armoured Division) had embarked and sailed. In the same period, the 5th Panzer advanced towards Rennes.

The Tenth Army was now split into two. Fagalde's XVI Corps, isolated at Fougères, was surrounded and captured. The Duffour Group, never seriously organized, had liquidated itself. Its commander found a fishing-boat at Le Croisic and reached the Île d'Yeu, from where he got back to the mainland to make his way to report to General Georges at Montauban. Before escaping, he had told those who could reach it, to join La Laurencie's III Corps. On the 19th the 5th Panzer Division captured Rennes, and General Altmayer with it, and went on towards Brest.

The left of III Corps was now completely bare. Of Petiet's Cavalry Division, only the headquarters still existed. At midnight on the 18th/19th, the corps was taken directly under Army Group Three, and given orders to defend the Loire, i.e. to abandon the Tenth Army. At this date, III Corps consisted of the Cavalry Corps, the 1st and 3rd Light Armoured, the 3rd Cavalry Division, now composed entirely of gunners, the 237th Light, very much depleted, and some reconnaissance groups. Withdrawing across the lower Loire, General de la Laurencie opened his headquarters at Chalonnes, a little west of Ponts-de-Cé.

By this time, 10 a.m. on the 19th, the presumption that the Marshal's broadcast would at once bring hostilities to an end had been distorted by the civilian population into the belief that it was already all over and that the army should now stop fighting which merely invited reprisals and endangered the lives and property of honest citizens. On the other hand, there were professional soldiers whose creed was that they should obey orders and fight as long as required by the Commander-in-Chief. As soon as he had occupied his headquarters, La Laurencie received one of the *adjoints* to the *maire* of Angers, who requested him to withdraw the soldiery preparing to defend the city. The general, whose old-fashioned sense of duty has already been observed, said to the emissary: 'Sir, be assured that I shall not expose your town to the terrors of bombardment uselessly. But you will be good enough to inform M. le Maire, that in circumstances of this nature, my decisions are derived from my conscience alone . . . and from God, who will judge us. Will you please go? I have nothing to add.'

However, half an hour later, General Langlois, commander of the Cavalry Corps at St Clément-de-la-Place, some fifteen kilometres to the north of Angers, received a telephone call. His interlocutor proved to be a German general (possibly von Manstein) at La Flèche, who asked if he, Langlois, proposed to defend Angers. General Langlois replied somewhat stiffly: 'Sir, I have been entrusted with a duty. I shall carry it out.'

'It will be sad for the population, sir. German aircraft will be bombing Angers at midday, and at the same time tanks will be reaching the town. . . .'

'Quite.'

After this, General Langlois was approached by every civilian of local importance, the *préfet*, the senator, the bishop, who all insisted that Angers was an open town. When Langlois reported to him, General de la Laurencie approved his determination, but at 11 a.m. the corps commander rang up Langlois and told him that a higher authority had now decided that Angers was not to be defended. He was therefore to leave the city, retire to the Loire at Ponts-de-Cé (which is practically the southern suburb) and organize its defence. At once General Langlois realized that he must discover the German officer who had telephoned to him. Fortunately the same voice replied from La Flèche. Langlois told him that he would not now defend Angers, but that he could not possibly withdraw his units before midday. 'I should not like the death of German soldiers from the fire of the defence to bring reprisals on the people of Angers. I need more time.' 'Of course,' the voice replied. 'My leading trucks shall not pass Seiches cross-roads until 2 p.m. Will that do?' On this, Langlois with some difficulty withdrew the two battalions of Senegalese on his front, who crossed the Loire with little time to spare. The Germans appeared at the first of the bridges at 2.45, and the French engineers blew the charges.

This happened on the 19th. As yet no order had emanated from G.Q.G. as to the defence or otherwise of large towns, although an order to this effect had been signed on the previous day. Without instructions, many officers had already made preparations for defence, in spite of the protests of *maires* and municipal councils. On the other hand, at Nantes, General Griveaud, Commander of the 11th Region, circulated an order to the effect that the government had decided that places of more than 20,000 inhabitants should be declared 'open towns', which should neither be defended nor prepared for defence by demolitions and obstructions. This directive ('most culpable', thought General de la Laurencie) resulted in Nantes being entered by the German 32nd Division without a blow being struck. La Laurencie tried to enforce the destruction of the bridges, but it was too late.* In any case, the defence of the Loire was hopelessly compromised. All the same, a number of crossings were contested. At Saumur the cadets of the cavalry school put up a gallant fight between Candés and Gennes. It was all without avail.

Orders of all kinds, for withdrawal, for 'open towns', etc., reached corps, divisional and regional commanders from various authorities, from Weygand, from the Minister of the Interior (Pomaret), from *préfets*, from *maires*, from *police-commissaires*, and in Tours from a sapper officer who had gone off his head and claimed to have secret orders from Pétain. These led to many misunderstandings between French and Germans and between soldiers and civilians. There were 'incidents' on all sides. Jean Moulin, *préfet* of Eure-et-Loire, had almost to quell a riot at Chartres, led by a collaborator. The *maire* of Cholet, having been told that a French cavalry patrol had established a post on a level-crossing outside the town, made a fuss and by various stratagems, including contacting the Germans, forced the officer commanding the patrol to withdraw. The officer then took up a position on a crossroad south of Mazières, the *maire* of which told him that though he was opposed to the armistice, he didn't want war in his borough. In another village, five French infantrymen were handed over to the enemy.

At Tours there were similar dissensions between the military and civil authorities as to the demolition of the Loire bridge, particularly as the water supply of the city came by pipes from the north side. The *préfet* claimed that the Minister of the Interior had declared Tours to be an open town and that there should be neither defence nor destructions. General Bougrain of the 2nd Light Armoured said his orders were to defend the city, and appealed to General Grandsard, who confirmed Bougrain's orders. To the dismay of the population, the bridge was blown on the 18th. The order declaring open every town of a population of 20,000 did not reach X Corps until 8 a.m. on the 20th.

The Loire was abandoned on the 19th by the Seventh Army, which fell back first to the Cher, then to the Indre. With it came back the

---

* The partly built battleship, *Jean Bart*, was with immense difficulty extracted from the naval dockyard at Ste Nazaire and taken to Casablanca.

Army of Paris, the Sixth, and whatever survived of the Fourth. When the Indre had been relinquished, the enemy gave up the pursuit. But in the Rhône valley, Hoeppner's XVI Panzer Korps (3rd and 4th Panzer Divisions, the 13th Motorized, the Adolf Hitler S.S. Division and the Gross Deutschland Regiment) continued to press on.

The terms of the armistice as regards those taken prisoner made it imperative that all who could should escape. From the 18th, therefore, every effort was made to disengage. Notice was circulated that there was no armistice, no suspension of hostilities and that the fight was still on. Everywhere the infantry was falling back.

[2]

The end of Army Group Two

On the morning of 17 June, G.Q.G. addressed a telegram to Army Group Two for transmission to the Third, Fifth and Eighth Armies, encouraging them to attack, whereas they had much ado to escape being overwhelmed. Prételat, near Lons-le-Saulnier, was told to try to rejoin the Eighth Army at Belfort. He asked the Commander of the Eastern Air Zone for a plane and was told that all the air-strips west of Belfort had been already destroyed and the only one still existing was too small for a modern plane to land on. He now made an attempt to go by road, by Morez and Pontarlier, but soon found that the Germans were already at the latter place and returned to Bourg-en-Bresse. From now the only means of communication with the encircled armies was by radio.

General Condé of the Third was given command of the three broken armies, but he could contrive no control. On the 14th he had moved his headquarters to near Épinal, and after Prételat's failure to return, on the 17th, he retreated to Gérardmer.

General Bourret's Fifth Army had been dispersed, and he set out for his new headquarters near Digoin. He just avoided capture at Bain-les-Bains. Doubling back, on the 15th he joined Condé at Épinal. Some of his divisions were still fighting round Haguenau, and parts of the 30th Alpine and the 70th had reached the upper Moselle. The line his army was to occupy would never be filled. Similarly, Colonel Regard, commanding the Fifth Army detachment, ordered to Belfort, reached the city alone. His troops never arrived. The Eighth Army was being driven in on all sides. General Daille's XLV Corps, having failed to recover Besançon, was penned up against the frontier. Seeing that it was impotent to make any impression on the German armour, the general ordered the division to cross into Switzerland, and on the 19th, with all their arms and equipment, 12,500 Poles and nearly 29,000 French marched over the frontier near St Hippolyte and were interned.

On the previous morning, General Laure had moved his headquarters from Malvaux to La Bresse south of Gérardmer. Belfort had been broken into by the 1st Panzer and the forts were being taken one by one.

The divisions of XIII Corps, the 54th, 104th and 105th, were being driven up the Vosges valleys. The 28th Fortress Regiment on the outskirts of Guebwiller and Orschwihr, and the 10th Chasseurs Pyrénéens, linking with the 10th Fortress holding Soultz and Cernay, temporarily stopped the way to the Grand Ballon. The 302nd held Munster below the Col de la Schlucht. On the Bonhomme, the 42nd Infantry Regiment, reduced to eighteen officers and 320 infantrymen, had only 700 rounds per light machine-gun and twelve per rifle. On the 18th, Munster was lost and the 42nd's training battalion retired up the ridge, destroying the bridges as they went, to the steep windings of the Schlucht. But on all sides the enemy was slipping round and through. On 20 June, the Schlucht, only fifteen kilometres from Gérardmer, fell, and the Col de Surcenaux, even closer, was lost. On the same day, the remains of the Altkirch Fortified Sector were surrounded on the Ballon d'Alsace. The German advance from the south continued inexorably. The 105th Division headquarters at Kruth behind the Markstein went. The 28th Fortress were still fighting hard round the Rainkopf and Hohneck. The Markstein fell at last, after all the ammunition had been spent.

The northern arc of the circle was closing equally fast. On the 18th the enemy was on both sides of Luneville; the 26th Division, the 52nd, the Sarre contingents, the 1st Polish, the 49th Alpine Battalion from the 30th Division, were all south of the Rhine–Marne canal and falling back up the Meurthe. The water lines provided no obstacle. It was all open fighting. The French had lost all their entrenching tools and were husbanding their ammunition. The roads were blocked by the transport of six divisions; the woods were full of discarded equipment. The Alsatians watched this disarray with angry malice. 'As we passed through Nessancourt, a farmer's wife who was preparing to stay here with her two young daughters, screamed at us for cowards.'[1]

To the west, Épinal and Charmes were taken by the 6th and 8th Panzer on the 18th. In the former, the staff of VI Corps was captured. On the same day, the 2nd Panzer, which had raced up from Auxonne through Plombières, reached Remiremont: the few detachments from the 30th and 70th Divisions could not stop them. The town was lost, and with it General François of the 70th. On the 20th, too, Le Tholy, ten kilometres west of Gérardmer, went. On the 21st, the 42nd Infantry Regiment was surrounded, and the 242nd. The 330th of the 54th Division was still fighting on the Col de Ste Marie-aux-Mines, but the enemy was already behind them. The command-post of the 54th Division in Corcieux, of XIII Corps in Gérardmer, of XLIV in La Bresse, were all isolated.

Since the 18th, all three army commanders had been warning Army Group and G.Q.G. of the fact that food was running out and a million and a quarter mouths had to be filled. 'Civilian and military reserves will be finished on the 22nd, in spite of rationing.' On the night of the 21st/22nd, G.Q.G. radioed that when all means of defence were exhausted, the three armies might surrender. General Bourret decided not to pass on the message. Other formations did not receive it. Among these were the commanders of XXI and the Colonial Corps, Flavigny and Carlès, who still fought on west of the Moselle at Sion–Vaudemont, '*la colline inspirée*', and General Lescanne, retreating up the wooded Donon.

Late on the 22nd, General Condé radioed to G.Q.G.: 'All means of resistance finished. Troops inside narrow limits and mixed with civilian population, have stopped fighting at many points. Famine now unavoidable. To spare sacrifice of human beings believe conditions such that moment has come to stop fighting, following public statement of six days ago to the whole country. Am ordering such troops as I can still command to lay down their arms at 15.00 hours today (22nd). German authorities warned.'

On the 24th General Bourret released what remained of his staff officers and told them to escape. On the following day he dismissed his motor-cycle escort. He himself, with his chief of staff, his orderly officer and radio officer, marched into Gérardmer and surrendered to the German general, who remarked that for an army commander Bourret had a remarkably small staff.

[3]

The last of the Maginot

While the three centre corps of the German First Army were pursuing the retreating infantry, tentative attacks were made on the *ouvrages* of the Maginot. They were ineffective. A few casemates were taken. On the 19th two blockhouses, Windstein and Matstall, at the eastern end of the Haguenau sector, were captured by the 215th Division aided by dive-bombers. Attempts in the Faulquemont sector to enter the line between Teting and Bambiderstroff from the rear were not successful. At the armistice, all *ouvrages* except Le Haut-Poirier were still in being. Their commanders refused to surrender. Eventually the Germans brought up a French colonel, who went from *ouvrage* to *ouvrage* ordering the garrisons to come out. They did so in the belief that they would be allowed to go free, but the Germans, who like to talk about chivalry, refused to recognize 'the honours of war'.

[4]

In spite of preparing for some nine months to take advantage of the expected German victory, the Italian Army was still unready for the assault. Mussolini had more than once confided to Hitler that Italian equipment was deficient. His ambitions, however, were less in France than in North Africa. Nevertheless, from his point of view, the Italian Army would have to play some part in the European campaign if it was to share the spoils. The declaration of war on 10 June had not been succeeded by any violent activity. The great Italian fort at Mont

Chaberton, north-east of Briançon, opened fire but was reduced to silence in a couple of days by the French guns.

It is to be admitted that the terrain for the battle was formidably difficult, particularly north of Barcelonnette. Mountains and steep valleys, absence of roads, snow and mist, combined to render any attack one of small gains slowly acquired. The Italians had mobilized two armies on the frontier, with a third, of eight divisions, in reserve. In the north facing the Savoy Fortified Sector from the Little St Bernard to beyond the Col de Larche, the Italian Fourth Army, three army corps each of four divisions, moved against the French XIV Corps in the Savoy and Dauphiné sectors, two B infantry divisions, the 66th and 64th Alpine and four Alpine Fortress demi-brigades. In the south, the Italian First Army attacked the French XV Corps holding the Alpes-Maritimes Fortified Sector from Barcelonnette to Menton, two corps each of four divisions against the 65th B Division and the 2nd Colonial, which had already been milked almost dry to reinforce the north-east.

The French defences, however, were really strong, owing to the activities of General Degoutte in 1936. On the main defensive line, great concrete bunkers of various sizes, and garrisons from a small platoon or even a section under a subaltern up to a mixed infantry-artillery body of perhaps the strength of a brigade, equipped with powerful guns. Further, when the active Alpine divisions had been sent northward in October 1939, they had left behind them their trained ski-patrols, who manned the advanced posts along the frontier.

The first three days of Italian operations were spent in gaining contact with the French and issuing numerous orders of the day: 'Everywhere Black Shirts and Army troops share the same ideal and prepare to renew the heroic actions of Africa and Spain.' Mussolini, on the other hand, feared that he might come too late: 'If we merely limit ourselves to watching the French cataclysm, we shall have no pretext to demand our share of the plunder. I tell you that in the state of the French Army at this moment, it is unnecessary to waste so many days in bringing up artillery.' In spite of the Duce's urging, the Italians in the centre made little progress. In the southern sector in front of Menton certain contacts and even progress was made between the days of the 14th and 21st, but much of this was no more than affairs of outposts and patrols. After Pétain's broadcast on the 17th, a number of attempts were made by the Italians to enter into negotiations with the garrisons of the bunkers, without success.

In the north, on the Little St Bernard pass, they had some success, but not as much as they had hoped: the 'Redoute Ruinée', a small fort just across the frontier, defied them. They expected that the French in the Savoy sector and in the Rhône defences would feel at their back the pressure of the German advance down the Rhône. For with the throwing back of Requin's Fourth Army behind the Loire and the destruction of the Second Army between the Upper Meuse and the

Jura, the road to Lyon and Marseille was completely open to Hoeppner's XVI Panzer Korps, which, with two armoured divisions and three motorized divisions attached, was certainly stronger than any French formation in the neighbourhood. Should these turn east they could attack the Army of the Alps from the rear and ease the task of the Italian Alpine Corps.

On the 17th, General Prételat, cut off from the gradually weakening armies of Army Group Two, was ordered by G.Q.G. to do what he could to prevent the Germans moving down the Rhône valley or occupying the country south of the Lake of Geneva. For this he had in the Rhône Defensive Sector the Reconnaissance group of XIV Corps and the 1st Spahi Brigade, which had been sent to this area at the beginning of the month. Otherwise all that was available were seven mixed groups commanded by General Cartier, made up of local troops, of borrowed companies, depot battalions, *gardes républicains*, training centres, pioneers, a single battalion of *chasseurs alpins*, and one of Senegalese. The mounted troops he sent southward to defend the Rhône valley, the Cartier detachments he ordered to face westward and hold the river-line from Bellegarde to St Génix-sur-Guiers and thence in front of the Massif of the Grande-Chartreuse to Voreppe. West of the Rhône, similar fragments were set out on the hills between Tarare and Roanne.

The Germans, however, did not hurry. On the 19th they entered Lyon, declared an open city. On the same day, General Jouffrault's Spahis began detraining at Vienne, a mere twenty-eight kilometres further south. General Jouffrault soon discovered that the citizens of Vienne were much opposed to being defended. The general and the local commander were assailed with supplications, pleas, abuse and threats, by all the local authorities, the deputy, the *maire* and the *sous-préfet*, as well as by all the respectable ladies and gentlemen of the town. It was wholesale abject cowardice, notes the general. During the evening, however, 'the coalition of egotistical interests of the town of Vienne' at length gained the day and governmental intervention. The Spahis were ordered to cross the Rhône and retire some fifty kilometres down-stream. Reinforced by a regional regiment, two 47-mm. anti-tank guns, a battery of 75s and a mountain battery, Jouffrault's command took up a new position at Sarras, across the river from St Vallier. 'At a period when so many of the elected representatives offered so lamentable an example of flight and desertion of those in their charge and of the interests of their city, the attitude of the *maire* of Sarras must be quoted. . . . At the hour of battle, with the curé, who showed proof of the finest courage, the *maire* stayed at the head of his fellow citizens, feeding, tending and helping the Spahis in defiance of shot and shell.' Gradually General Jouffrault's forces were built up into a respectable force. The mountain battery was commanded by what must have been the most junior subaltern in the army; his section officer was still a cadet; the gunners were even younger. The battery was installed high above the river on the steep hill between Annonay and Andance.

On the night of the 21st/22nd, the Germans entered St Vallier across the river, but failed to occupy the telegraph office, which was thus able to relay messages across the river to the Spahis, while the general enlisted the services of the *châtelaine* of the house in which he had placed his headquarters to take the telephone in order to deceive German listeners, 'that they might not suspect that telephone Eclassan 1, the Château des Près, was a battle command-post'. During these days, Jouffrault's command, augmented by whatever detachments could be sent him, stopped the Germans from a further descent of the Rhône valley. Communications were somehow kept up with the towns and villages between Annonay and St Vallier, in spite of their occupation at the last hour. About 11 p.m. on the night of the 24th, the general was informed that the armistice would come into force in an hour and a half. On which he ordered every detachment he could reach to advance as far as they could.[2]

During 22–4 June, on the Corniches sector of XV Corps, the Italians made their big effort against the line from the sea as far as the Bervera stream, by two divisions augmented by some Blackshirt battalions. To the north as far as the Tinée and Vésubie, there were other attacks. The weather throughout was appalling. There was thick mist, and torrential rain which filled the trenches cut out of the rock. North of the Bervera, the Italians had no serious success whatever. It was only on the coast that they advanced, infiltrating between the outposts and the support-posts. During the 22nd, the garrison of the strong-points in front of Menton fired 20,000 rounds, and 200 rifle-grenades, and used 300 bombs. They had four killed and nine missing. They were withdrawn in the late afternoon of that day. The attacking Italians on the other hand suffered severely. They continued to attack on the 23rd and 24th. The French withdrew from two advanced posts, and the Italians were thus enabled to occupy some three quarters of Menton. Elsewhere the extent of the Italian advance was nowhere deeper than a couple of kilometres. Some of the advanced posts had been by-passed. The main line of resistance had nowhere been reached. In the Alpes-Maritimes sector they had some four to five thousand casualties, while the French had eight killed, thirty-six wounded and thirty-three missing.

Meanwhile, further north, in response to an Italian request for help after an abortive attack at the Little St Bernard, General List ordered the 13th Motorized to move eastward towards Annecy, Aix-les-Bains and Grenoble. On the 23rd this division crossed the Rhône north of St Genix-en-Guiers and moved towards Chambéry, while the 3rd Panzer advance guards were in action against a couple of battalions of Senegalese near Moirans and Voreppe. On the 24th, still anxious to swell their claims to a share in the loot, the Italian Chief of Staff asked German Army headquarters to transport by air an Italian battalion and land it behind the Twelfth Army front. 'The whole thing is just the usual kind of fraud,' wrote General Halder indignantly. 'I have made it quite clear that I won't have my name mixed up with this business.'[3]

[5]

The failure to demolish the bridges at Nantes allowed the German armour to pass through to La Roche-sur-Yon and then press inland. O.K.H. ordered von Bock to pursue the French rearguards until he reached the Spanish frontier. XIV Panzer Korps was transferred from the Kleist Group to the Eighteenth Army, and Rommel's 7th Panzer and three Motorized divisions were added. The French III Corps did its best to protect the outer flank of the Army of Paris as it retreated across the Indre, the corps falling back eastward. Once again General de la Laurencie was outraged, this time by the behaviour of the city council of Poitiers, which gave rise to what he refers to as scandalous incidents. Taking advantage of a telegram from G.Q.G. leaving local commanders judges of military dispositions at open towns, he attempted to put Poitiers in a state of defence. But he was outwitted and a telephone message from higher authority gave him specific orders not to defend the city.

In these last five days, the French commanders were instructed to get back as far as they could towards the Dordogne. On the 24th, there was nearly a catastrophe in and near Angoulême, when III Corps got across the line of retreat of X Corps, and the 10th Panzer Division came straight through the city (nearly, it seems, catching the author of *Le Crèvecoeur*) and, coming out on the other side, ran into the 8th Colonial preparing to retreat. In view of its being only a few hours to the end of hostilities, everyone showed the greatest discretion. It is also said that a group of dismounted men from the 3rd Light Armoured, who had been captured, were released at the last moment by a German armoured division.

[6]

On the morning of the 25th, the French armies, such as they were, lay along a rough line from between Libourne and Périgueux towards Brantôme to La Rochefoucauld. The Seventh Army stretched from Chasseneuil to beyond Limoges, the remnants of the Sixth assembled near Eymoutiers. The Fourth occupied Ussel, and over the Monts Dore to Issoire, with the remains of the 53rd Division on the Chaise-Dieu. Beyond, the hills overlooking Andance and St Vallier were held by the Spahis, while the line of the Isère was still defended by Cartier's detachments. Grenoble was still in French hands, but Aix-les-Bains had been lost. In a few places French soldiers still held out; La Redoute Ruinée at the Little St Bernard, the Fort des Ecluses near the Bellegarde tunnel. Except for the loss of the better part of Menton, the line of the Army of the Alps was intact.

On 15 June, Weygand ordered whatever aircraft could make the distance to fly to North Africa. Some 700 machines, including training planes and obsolete models as well as fighters, made the passage. But in Africa there were no spare parts, few bombs and no ground transport.

After Jena in November 1806, Murat reported to the Emperor, 'Sire, the fighting is over. There are no more combatants.' This was very close to the situation of the French Army on 25 June 1940. Except for General Orly's Army of the Alps, three B divisions, the sector garrisons and the much depleted 2nd Colonial, which must remain in position to face the Italians, there was no serious fighting force. In Brittany the Tenth Army had surrendered. The Third, Fifth, Eighth Armies and the débris of the Second, the bulk, that is, of AG Two, were in the hands of the enemy. From the centre armies, Paris, Seventh, Sixth and Fourth, no coherent body could be organized. The 11th Division, the 'Iron Division' of General Arlabosse, was still in fighting trim with some 12,000 men, but the 87th which had fought with it since 5 June was reduced to two small battalions. The 19th and 29th had each two battalions, the 47th and 7th North African three. Other divisions were no more than names. General de Lattre's 14th Division is said to have been reinforced by recruits drawn from depots, but there are no figures. Grandsard's two X Corps divisions had rather less than 3,000 infantry, perhaps the same number of gunners and about eighty guns of various calibres. III Corps of General de la Laurencie, with one infantry division, one cavalry division and two light armoured, consisted of one infantry battalion and two companies, and three groups of 75s. The Light Armoured Division comprised four armoured cars, ten Hotchkiss and six Somua with 300 dragoons. The 3rd Cavalry Division had neither armoured cars nor tanks, but fifteen guns.

Many small groups of infantry were drifting southward, engaging the enemy to the last. Lame, haggard, hungry men limped down roads in the faint hope of escape. Others lay up behind the German outposts until they could get away. On the hills west of the Rhône, General Jouffrault and his Spahis remained in action to the last minute. On the other hand, there is the strange episode of the senior officer in Clermont Ferrand who collected all the French soldiers reaching the town into barracks to be surrendered to the Germans on their arrival, before taking his own departure.

All down the coast from St Nazaire to St Jean-de-Luz, ships, some French but chiefly British, carried off parties, groups and individuals to destinations of which they knew nothing, to Falmouth or Casablanca or Dakar, British, Poles, Czechs, and some indomitable French. Brave trawler skippers took small parties from Breton ports.

General Weygand had become Minister of Defence in the Pétain government. He entrusted General Frère with the task of concealing such anti-aircraft and anti-tank guns as he could collect in the caves of Lozère and Aveyron hills, a duty which would bring that gallant man to a lonely death in Struthof.

On 25 June, there were still in being the greater number of the Maginot Line forts. In fact, only one had been captured. When informed of the armistice, the commanders of the garrisons refused to come out or admit the enemy, until their freedom was guaranteed. They beat off some not very strongly pressed attacks. The Germans eventually called on the French to order the surrender. French headquarters finally dispatched a number of officers, ironically enough members of Gamelin's personal staff, to deal with the problem. The commanders of the forts were told to surrender, but their claim to go free was ignored.

EPILOGUE

BETWEEN 1940 and 1951 a number of public investigations threw a little light, usually oblique and often contradictory, on the reasons for the catastrophe. In 1942, at Riom, the trial of Daladier, Blum, Reynaud, Guy la Chambre, Jacomet and Gamelin occupied six weeks. Gamelin refused to plead, which somewhat hampered proceedings. Some thirty or so army officers gave evidence, much of it controversial; none of it seriously inculpated the defendants. The proceedings took a turn which was not what Pétain had hoped and not at all what Hitler required: a declaration of the aggressiveness of earlier French governments. The cases were adjourned at Easter and the court was never reconvened. There is no official record of the proceedings. The accounts by journalists and lawyers are fragmentary.

There followed the trials of Pétain and Laval in 1945. The reports, though fuller, are inconsecutive and much of what was said is irrelevant to the preparation for war and its conduct.

Later a Commission of Inquiry '*sur les événements survenus en France de 1933 à 1945*', appointed in August 1946, sat from May 1947 to April 1951 and produced more than 2,500 pages of verbal testimony from some sixty witnesses, and another couple of volumes of report and documents. Of the sixty-two witnesses, nearly a third were soldiers of various sorts, including ordnance officers; another dozen or so were politicians. Of the forty-seven members of the committee, twenty-nine were members of the National Assembly. The Commission had not completed its work at the end of the legislature, and the new National Assembly did not renew its mandate. The report produced by Charles Serre, member for Corrèze, who had been an *indépendent de gauche* in 1940, is not very illuminating and to some extent reflects the intention of the commissioners to absolve the politicians. Since Pétain had been tried and imprisoned and was now hopelessly decayed, he was the obvious scapegoat. Of the soldiers, Gamelin, heard early, was glib. Georges had no hesitation in demonstrating Gamelin's avoidance of responsibility. Some members of the committee made considerable efforts to saddle Weygand with the armistice, with the failure to carry on the war from North Africa and even with the conduct of operations. His examination occupied eleven sessions, more than those of Gamelin and Georges together. He withstood the insinuations with restraint and dignity. The most illuminating evidence came from the armament officers and those of the armoured divisions. The most noticeable absence was that of the Air Force Staff. Whereas Guy la Chambre described the obsolete organization of the aircraft industry and his attempts to remedy it, not a single officer appeared from the Air Staff, not Denain, nor Pujo, nor Vuillemin, in spite of La Chambre's acid comments on the interference of the last in production.

Serre's report brought out the catastrophic consequences of the failure to act when the Rhineland was reoccupied in 1936, especially in view of Gamelin's forecast of the German intentions. It did little else. The committee indeed had not asked the right questions. When a witness produced an unwelcome fact, which might inculpate a politician, it was rarely followed up.

[2]

Elsewhere every kind of explanation was offered for the defeat. It was said that the rout was due to bad morale, to pacifist and communist propaganda. The infantry, said Daladier, were not those of 1914–18. In fact, the infantry had fought as stoutly as their fathers. 'There was nothing much wrong with the French Army,' wrote the commander of the British 5th Division, 'if only they had been better led.'

There had, of course, been a number of errors which had eased the task of the Germans: the late arrivals on the Meuse and the failure of the battalion of the 39th Infantry Regiment to cover the stream, the calamitous panic of Movement Control which distributed the Second Armoured over a huge area, and the subsequent blundering of General Keller. There was General Flavigny's no less effective dissolution of the 3rd Armoured. There was the failure of the 4th Armoured to come to grips with Guderian's armour on 17 and 18 May. Singly, these errors might have been remedied. In the circumstances they added up to defeat. There were many mishaps which, given time, might have been repaired, but the pace had been too hot. There was the flight of the civilians, especially the Belgians, who blocked the roads and prevented the movement of reinforcements, ammunition and fuel. The dispersion of the 1st Armoured stemmed almost entirely from the fact that the Belgian government had never considered what might occur, and had made no preparations. Yet though these contretemps hurt those who suffered them, it is obvious that such misadventures were no more than symptoms of a deep-rooted evil, roots that went back to the organization of the army after the ratification of the Versailles treaty.

[3]

What happened between 10 May and 25 June 1940 was the result of twenty years' blindness to the facts of 1914–18. Since the French had borne the major weight of that war on the side of the Allies and had found by far the largest number of divisions, the Allied armies had quite properly been commanded by a French general. *Ergo*, it was believed that a French commander and a French general staff had won the war, and that French military theory must be correct. This was not true. The Allied victory in 1918 had not been won by the military genius of a Foch or a Pétain. The end came through a series of contingencies which persuaded the German general staff to risk all in a series of offensives. Though initially successful, the gamble failed. It so weakened the German Army that it could not resist the counter-strokes. Its failure coincided with the inflow of new men and new materials from America. Anticipating the inevitable defeat, the Germans surrendered.

The German military leaders analysed what had happened, weighed the facts and drew certain conclusions. They realized that the geographical position of Germany meant that in a war with the west they were always subject to blockade. They saw that their early successes had been frustrated and their military superiority worn down by their inability to provide the materials needed to support a long war and that this could not be avoided. Therefore a new war must be short. Speed, with all that speed comprises, was vital. The military clauses of the Versailles treaty allowed them to create the highly skilled nucleus of an army, to train cadres for later expansion and to draft new plans on the *tabula rasa* enforced by the victors. Much obsolete and obsolescent war material had been compulsorily discarded, and the ingenuity and adaptability of German engineers and German scientists could be coupled with the industriousness of German workers to forge the new instrument as soon as German diplomacy had removed the ban on arms manufacture.

The French made no such analysis. They looked at their own land, the appalling destruction, the flaying and stripping of ten departments, the huge death-roll, the failure of the birth-rate to rise after its first recovery, the financial chaos and the 80 per cent devaluation of the currency, at their own industrial lethargy and the peasants' penurious conservatism. They said 'Never again', and imagined that the Germans would flinch from a repetition.

Accepting the assumption that war was unlikely to threaten for a long time, that the League of Nations would in any case intervene effectively, that Germany was outflanked by French allies and even that the Disarmament Conference might succeed, many army officers believed that they would never go into battle again. Senior officers with connections in industry, commerce and banking retired into directorates. Those with no civilian associations remained until they reached the age-limit of their rank. After the ratification of the Versailles treaty, Pétain and his clan brought back the higher age-limits of the pre-war regulations, which had been reduced by Clemenceau. Promotion was blocked. Weygand noted with bitterness that most of the brigade and regimental commanders at the Centre des Hautes Études Militaires looked on their attendance as a mere formality. They lacked the mental qualities required of senior officers; they were not conscious of their ignorance; they had neither curiosity nor freedom of mind. After 1919, a new type of professional appeared, pliant, conformist, unwilling to jeopardize his career by unorthodoxy. 'During the years of crisis, it was these who coloured the army with their own psychological shade, the mental tints of second-grade government servants, devoted, needy and often with a narrow intellectual horizon.'[1]

It could scarcely be otherwise during the régime of the whirligig Painlevé, of the ageing Pétain, who confessed that after 1918 his mind was a closed book, and of the ulcer-troubled Debeney. These men reflected the desire of the citizen to be defended without fighting and to be assured of the invulnerability of the Maginot Line. Officers who criticized the vast sums expended on fortification were frowned on. 'If the liberty of officers to write was recognized, that liberty did not cease to be limited. Studies relating to the last war might be published only with the authorization of the Minister of War's secretariat. A few years later this was extended to everything connected with foreign armies. Consequently, thanks to a disguised censorship, there reigned the most absolute conformism.'[2] There must be no questioning of the Painlevé–Pétain thesis of the defensive army, that self-contradictory chimera. Gamelin expressly forbade the publication of articles discussing mechanization without War Office sanction,[3] and General Héring, when commanding XX Corps, was not permitted to publish an article on mixed tank and artillery columns. There were few rebels. As General Bourret wrote:[4] in the early part of the century, generals, including two Commanders-in-Chief, had resigned over professional questions, but 'not one of our generation has. There has never been any serious question of it. Just a few passing sulks. No resignation was asked for.' No one, except junior officers, read the imaginative doctrines of Liddell Hart: with their career to think of, they were helpless.

[4]

From the point of view of the senior officers, the problem was fundamentally political. The army was the instrument of government policy. Up to the advent of Hitler in January 1933, the leading characters on the political stage were men of the first decade of the century, Poincaré, Briand, Painlevé, Caillaux, Blum, who had known the prolonged convulsions of the Dreyfus case and experienced the various crises of the war. On the one hand, they still regarded the army officer with suspicion. When Reynaud took up de Gaulle's *Vers l'armée de métier*, he was attacked by Blum, not at the professional but at the political level, as if the colonel were a Boulanger *redivivus* preparing to march on the Élysée. Blum was quite unaware of the change since 1905 in the social structure of the army. At the same time, he accepted Pétain wholly uncritically. 'I lived,' he admitted at Pétain's trial, 'under the same illusion as the whole of France.' The 'Saviour of Verdun' could be trusted. Everything was therefore left to the mind that was now only working at intervals and that on the methods of 1916. Blum was to discover the reality when he came to power in June 1936, two months after the reoccupation of the Rhineland.

It was too late to repair the situations The allocation of fourteen billion francs to armaments was made too late. The German lead could not be overtaken. There was no plan except to wait. The modern weapons were few and the heavy tanks were still at the prototype stage. It had not yet been decided whether armoured divisions were desirable, and if they were, what form they should take. The government arsenals had been turned over to non-military work, agricultural instruments, typewriter parts, trucks. The Air Ministry, even less alert than the War Office, was constructing obsolescent planes.

'A nation with responsible parliamentary government is not the victim but the author of its government's blunders; and if it seeks to transfer the responsibility to politicians and a party system, or to some other scapegoat, it is guilty of the lie in the soul.'

There were no congenital idiots. There was a scattering of men who detested social change more than they detested Hitler, but there were few traitors, and no effective traitors. Most Frenchmen were passionately French. Even Laval was a patriot by his own lights, who believed that the war ought to have been avoided.

There was error everywhere. There was hesitation, there was indecision, there was sheer bloody funk at the highest level, among ministers, politicians, generals, civil service chiefs. Among the older officers, there was a shrinking from weapons and methods they did not understand. Worst of all was the general lack of foresight.

Of the French armies of 1870, the Germans said that they were armies made to be beaten. The same preparations were made between 1919 and 1939. Neither politically, nor militarily, nor psychologically, was the French nation in a state to face the war into which, against its deepest will, it was inveigled. None the less, its soldiers fought.

Appendixes

A THE MAKE-UP OF THE FRENCH GROUND FORCES, *10 May-25 June*

Grand-Quartier Général (Forces terrestres)

Commandant-en-chef	10 May	Maurice Gamelin
	19	Maxime Weygand
Major-Général	10 May	J. E. A. Doumenc
Aide-Major-Général		M. L. Koeltz

Grand-Quartier-Général (Nord-Est)

Commandant-en-chef	10 May	A. J. Georges
Major-Général		J. E. A. Doumenc
Aide-Major-Général		G. Roton

G.Q.G. (F.T.) was at Vincennes until 19 May, when Weygand took over and went to Montry. G.Q.G. (N.E.) occupied the Château de Bondon at La Ferté-sous-Jouarre until 8 June. The joint G.Q.G. occupied by Bureaux 1 and 4 with parts of 3, was at Montry from 19 January to 8 June. Bureaux 2 and 3 were at La Ferté. Montry and La Ferté went to Château de Ferrières (A.G. Three) on 8 June, to Briare on 9 June. It left Briare at 5 p.m. on 15 June for Vichy. On 17 June it moved to La Bourboule in the Monts Dore, and on 20 June reached Montauban, where it was at the armistice.

Army Group Commanders

10 May	A.G. One	G. H. G. Billotte	24 May, died
24 May	„ „	J. G. M. Blanchard	1 June, ends
10 May	A.G. Two	A. G. Prételat	18 June
18 June	„ „	C. M. Condé	22 June, p.o.w.
22 May	A.G. Three	A. M. B. Besson	25 June
6 June	A.G. Four	C. L. C. Huntziger	25 June

Army Commanders

10 May	First	J. G. M. Blanchard	24 May to A.G. One
24 May	„	R. J. A. Prioux	29 May p.o.w.
10 May	Second	C. L. C. Huntziger	4 June to A.G. Four
4 June	„	H. Freydenberg	25 June
10 May	Third	C. M. Condé	18 June to A.G. Two.
May	Fourth	E. J. Requin	4 June to 25 June
May	Fifth	V. Bourret	24 June p.o.w.

14 May	Sixth	R. A. Touchon	25 June
10 May	Seventh	H. H. Giraud	18 May to Ninth Army
18 May	Seventh (2)	A. Frère	25 June
10 May	Eighth	J. J. M. Garchery	22 May sick
22 May	„	A. M. E. Laure	23 June p.o.w.
10 May	Ninth	A. G. Corap	15 May Seventh
17 May	„	H. H. Giraud	19 May p.o.w.
30 May	Tenth	M. R. Altmayer	17 June p.o.w.
12 June	Paris	P. Héring	25 June

Army Corps Commanders

10 May	Cavalry	R. J. A. Prioux	24 May First Army
24 May	„	Langlois	25 June
10 May	I	T. M. Sciard	25 June
	II	J. G. Bouffet	16 May k/a
17 May	„	C. S. Molinié	31 May p.o.w.
10 May	III	B. L. Fournel de la Laurencie	25 June
10 May	IV	H. M. J. Aymes	29 May p.o.w.
10 May	V	René Altmayer	31 May to England
10 May	VI	L. Loizeau	22 June p.o.w.
10 May	VII	J. de la Porte du Theil	25 June
10 May	VIII	A. Frère	17 May Seventh Army
17 May	„	M. A. R. A. Desmazes	25 June
10 May	IX	A. M. E. Laure	22 May Eighth Army
22 May	„	M. Ihler	15 June p.o.w.
10 May	X	P. P. J. Grandsard	25 June
10 May	XI	J. R. R. Martin	4 June ends
10 May	XII	H. F. Dentz	2 June to Paris government
2 June	„	P. L. C. Champon	22 June p.o.w.
10 May	XIII	G. H. J. B. Misserey	22 June p.o.w.
10 May	XVI	M. B. A. Fagalde	28 May disbanded
16 June	XVI	M. B. A. Fagalde	19 June p.o.w.
10 May	XVII	O. P. Noel	25 June
10 May	XVIII	P. A. Doyen	25 June
20 May	XX	L. E. Hubert	22 June p.o.w.
10 May	XXI	J. A. Flavigny	24 June p.o.w.
10 May	XXIII	R. A. Touchon	14 May to Sixth Army
14 May	„	G. L. Germain	25 June
10 May	XXIV	F. M. J. Fougère	25 June

8 June	XXV	E. A. Libaud	25 June
10 May	Colonial	H. Freydenberg	4 June to Second Army
4 June	„	E. J. C. Carlès	24 June p.o.w.

ARMY OF THE ALPS

Commander Gen. J. H. Orly   Chief of Staff Col. Mer
Army Corps Commanders
  10 May   XIV   Beynet
  10 May   XV   A..M. J. L. Montagne

Fortified sectors

Alpes-Maritimes (St Pons)	Magnien
Corniches, Sospel, Aution	
Dauphiné (Gap)	Cyvoct
Ubaye, Queyras, Briançonnais	
Savoie (Albertville)	de la Baume
Maurienne, Tarentaise	

Defensive sector

Rhône (Annecy)   Michel

THE FRENCH ARMY (NORTH-EAST) IN MAY AND JUNE 1940

Considerable changes were made in the French Army between September 1939 and May 1940. At the latter date, there were 77 infantry divisions apart from those designated Fortress, five cavalry divisions (Division de cavalerie légère), three light armoured divisions (Division légère mécanisée) and three armoured divisions (Division cuirassée). There were also one cavalry brigade and three brigades of Spahis.

The categories of infantry divisions were as follows:

 7 Active Motorized, 1, 3, 5, 9, 12, 15, 25
10 Active 10, 11, 13, 14, 19, 21, 23, 36, 42, 43
17 A. 2, 4, 6, 7, 8, 16, 18, 20, 22, 24, 26, 32, 35, 41, 44, 45, 47
 5 Alpine, 27, 28, 29, 30, 31
19 B. 51–58, 60–68, 70 and 71   (Nos. 64, 65, 66 were Alpine)
10 North African, 1, 2, 3, 4, 5, 6, 7, 82, 87 and the Moroccan Division
 7 Colonial, 1, 2, 3, 4, 5, 6, 7

Active divisions consisted of the regulars, the conscripts and the first three years of reservists. The A formations came from the next groups up to the age of 32. The B divisions, the oldest reservists, have an average age of about 36.

The Alpine divisions were amalgamations of two active with three A reserve divisions. These had a larger establishment than the other divisions and also a number of specialist ski companies. All five were brought from the Italian frontier during the autumn of 1939, when their mountain artillery was transformed to normal batteries, and one demi-brigade of infantry removed. The three B Alpine divisions remained on the Italian front.

The North African divisions, of which a number were stationed in France in 1939, had been expanded by newly formed units from Morocco, Algeria and Tunisia and included Zouave regiments (i.e. white conscripts) as well as coloured *tirailleurs*. The 14th Zouaves in the 5th North African Division had some 500 recently naturalized Italian volunteers. The 7th North African Division was formed in France and did not join the armies until 18 May. Nos. 82 and 87 were formed and trained in Algeria and came to France in October 1939. 3rd Tirailleurs Marocains were incorporated in the 43rd Division and the 8th in the 13th Division.

The colonial divisions, of which Nos. 1–4 were regulars, not conscript but white volunteers used for overseas duties, had been expanded to six by December 1939, later augmented by No. 7. This was done by the importation of *tirailleurs sénégalais* into 1, 2, 4, 5 and 6. 3rd Colonial Division remained white. 2nd Colonial was mobilized with the Alpine divisions and remained facing the Italians in the Alpes-Maritimes sector.

In addition to the above, there were 42 fortress regiments, some of which were incorporated in static divisions with machine-gun companies of colonial natives from Indo-China and Madagascar (Malgaches). These were numbered 101–5; 101 garrisoned the Maubeuge defences, 102 the Meuse from Pont-à-Bar to the Dames de Meuse, while the other three were in Rhine defences.

Later there became available, as needed, a number of units formed from training centres, regional or labour regiments, and pioneer regiments. There were also battalions from the *Légion étrangère*, regiments of expatriate Austrians and Germans (*Régiments de marche des volontaires étrangers*), two Polish divisions and two Czech legions, some African Light Infantry (i.e. penal battalions).

In the south, on the Spanish frontier, were battalions of *chasseurs pyrénéens*, some of which were later transferred to Alsace.

In March and April 1940 the units withdrawn from the five Alpine divisions now with the North-Eastern armies were used to create new formations. First, 44th Division was made up of two *chasseur* demi-brigades, 2nd and 26th with the 173rd Regiment from Corsica. Then three light infantry divisions each of two demi-brigades were organized for Norway: 1st Light of 5th and 27th Chasseur Demi-Brigades from 28th and 31st Divisions; the 2nd Light of 2nd and 24th Demi-Brigades; the 3rd of 140 and 141 Alpine Infantry Regiments.*

---

* Of these light divisions, only 1st reached Norway. The 2nd Light was stopped at Glasgow, where it remained until June, when it was brought back to Brest with the 5th Demi-Brigade from Norway and the whole formed into the 40th Division and sent to the Tenth Army. The 3rd Light did not get

A number of other formations between 10 May and 25 June: 8th Division composed of four training battalions, one fortress regiment and one regiment of Foreign Volunteers; 17th Division from the remains of the broken 55th and 71st Divisions; 8th Colonial of one Moroccan and one Senegalese regiment; 84th African from Tunisia, a normal division of one Zouave and two *tirailleurs* regiments; 85th African from Constantine, chiefly coloured, three *tirailleur* regiments and one Zouave with a battalion of *tirailleurs*. Seven light divisions, 235–41, from depots and training centres, etc., usually with a reconnaissance group and though not invariably, a skeleton artillery, but in one case no general. 59th Light came from the debris of X Corps divisions, while 53rd Light was the original division less the 239th Regiment destroyed.

Infantry regiments of the A series were supposed to have a proportion of active officers, N.C.O.s and soldiers. The number varied from unit to unit. Probably typical are the figures given by the historian of the 2nd Division, viz. Officers 19, N.C.O.s 76, other ranks 53. Of the B regiments, there were never more than three active officers.

ESTABLISHMENTS

The normal infantry division consisted of three infantry regiments of three battalions or two regiments and one demi-brigade (3 battalions) of *chasseurs*. An infantry regiment should have 81 officers, 432 sergeants and above, and 2,667 other ranks. A North African regiment had 57 French and nine Arab officers, 331 French and 1,995 native other ranks. A regiment ought to have 12 25-mm. anti-tank guns, 48 machine-guns and 36 light machine-guns.

The division had two regiments of field artillery, one of three groups each of three four-gun batteries of 75-mm., the other of two groups of medium field artillery, each of three four-gun batteries, one group being of 105-mm. (or 155-mm.), the second of 155-mm. It should also have a battery of 12 25-mm. anti-tank guns.

It had a reconnaissance group (G.R.D.I.) of one headquarter squadron, one horsed squadron, one motor-cycle squadron and one weapon squadron with 4 25-mm. guns, 10 machine-guns and 24 light machine-guns. These groups were formed in part from disbanded cavalry regiments.

The division had also two companies of engineers, one signal (communication) company, two companies of train, an artillery park and a medical group.

---

beyond Brest. On 17 May it was sent to XXIV Corps (Seventh Army) on the upper Somme. The remainder of the Norwegian Force was made up from 13th Demi-Brigade of the *Légion étrangère* and a brigade of Polish *chasseurs du Nord*. The legion and the 27th Alpine Demi-Brigade under General Béthouart got back to Brest on 13/14 June. Discovering the situation, Béthouart re-embarked his brigade, finally reaching Casablanca. But one battalion, 14th Chasseurs Alpins of 27th Demi-Brigade, seems to have been destroyed covering Brest.

The reconnaissance groups of the seven motorized divisions apart from headquarters and weapon squadrons had one squadron of 44 armoured cars and one of 13 Hotchkiss 35 tanks and two of motor-cyclists.

An army corps had a reconnaissance group of two horsed squadrons, one motor-cycle (75 side-cars) squadron, one weapon squadron (4 25-mm. guns and 8 machine-guns). Three corps groups were motorized. A corps had also two groups of 105-mm. guns of two batteries each and two of 155-mm. It had a communications group, a regiment of pioneers and should, but rarely if ever did, have an observation group of eight planes.

Cavalry and Armour

At the outbreak of war, there were three cavalry divisions each of two horsed brigades, with one regiment of 35 armoured cars (*automitrailleuses de découverte*), one battalion of *dragons portés* (lorry-carried dismounted dragoons),* one regiment of artillery of one group of 75s and one of short 105s, and one battalion of engineers. During the winter and spring these divisions were broken up; only the 1st Cavalry Brigade remained as a cavalry formation, consisting of two horsed regiments without artillery.

Each of the other five horsed brigades were transferred to one of the five new light cavalry divisions. Each of these had two brigades, one the horsed with two regiments (*cuirassiers*, dragoons, *chasseurs* or hussars), and one mechanized. The mechanized brigade had one regiment with a combat group and a reconnaissance group. The combat group had a squadron of Hotchkiss 35 or 39 (but in a number of cases with the 37-mm. gun of 1918) and a motor-cyclist squadron. The *groupe de découverte* had 15 armoured cars and a squadron of motor-cyclists. To these new formations a second battalion of dismounted dragoons was added. Each of these battalions now consisted of three squadrons, one of *automitrailleuses de reconnaissance*, one of riflemen in carriers, one of infantry weapons (25-mm. anti-tank guns, machine-guns and 81-mm. mortars). The artillery had been increased to six groups, three of 75s and three of 105s, i.e. twelve guns of each calibre. There was also an eight-gun battery of 47-mm. anti-tank guns. There was now only one company of engineers.

The conception of these divisions was basically wrong. Every time the division moved, the horsed brigade was left behind. It was vulnerable to air attack, especially as it had no A.-A. guns. At least one further group of artillery was needed and probably another anti-tank battery. As everywhere else, the signal unit was weak.

The *divisions légères mécanisées* (D.L.M., here to be called light armoured divisions as distinct from armoured divisions) were three in number and grouped under the title of the Cavalry Corps. They had

* Dragoons were originally muskets, and the soldiers designated dragoons were mounted infantry.

been one of Weygand's conceptions. Each consisted of a *brigade de combat*, a *brigade de découverte*, a regiment of artillery, a regiment (three battalions) of dismounted dragoons, and a battalion of engineers. The combat brigade had two regiments, each of four squadrons, two of Hotchkiss, two of Somua, 87 tanks of each type. The reconnaissance brigade had (a) a *régiment de découverte* of two groups each of two squadrons, one of 20 armoured cars, one of four pelotons of motor-cyclists, each with two light machine-guns, and (b) one regiment of dismounted dragoons of three battalions. Each battalion had one squadron of *automitrailleuses de reconnaissance* (A.M.R.), one squadron of motor-cyclists, two squadrons of riflemen with a platoon of machine-guns and 60-mm. mortars in Laffly armoured carriers, one squadron of weapons, two machine-gun pelotons, two groups of 25-mm. A.-T. guns and four 81-mm. mortars.*

The artillery regiment had two groups of 75s and one of short 105s (24 75s and 12 105s) and a 9-gun 47-mm. A.-T. battery. There was one battalion of engineers which included a bridging train.

The strength of a light armoured division was about 400 officers and 10,000 other ranks, with 240 A.F.V. and 50 armoured cars. There were 475 tracked and 1,200 wheeled vehicles with 1,500 motor-cycles. The fire-power of the division was:

12 105-mm. gun-howitzers	80 37-mm. guns
24 75-mm. guns	100 25-mm. anti-tank guns
90 47-mm. anti-tank guns	450 machine-guns and light m.g.

The *division cuirassée* (D.C.R., the Armoured Division), did not come into existence until January 1940. Up to that time it had been believed impossible to establish these formations since the number of B tanks (either B.1 or B.1 *bis*) was insufficient to give the fire-power believed necessary. The first two divisions were formed on 16 January, the 3rd Division not until mid-March. 4th Armoured was a scratch formation gradually built up under the command of Colonel de Gaulle between 16 and 28 May without regard to the official establishment.

The Armoured Division consisted of (a) a *brigade de combat* of two demi-brigades: (i) two battalions of B, each of 34 A.F.V. (Each consisted of three companies of 10 A.F.V. each, with one battalion commander's tank. The remaining three were replacements with the 2nd echelon); (ii) two battalions of Hotchkiss 39, each of 45 A.F.V. (Each had three companies of 13 A.F.V. with three command tanks and 3 spares with 2nd echelon. Fighting strength of the division was thus 62 B.1 and 84 H.39.) (b) One battalion of *chasseurs-à-pied* carried in Lorraine armoured carriers, of four companies, three of riflemen and one of weapons (12 25-mm. anti-tank guns and 4 81-mm. mortars) plus one

---

* The A.M.R. was a lightly armoured tracked vehicle manned by two men with one machine-gun. The Laffly armoured carriers accommodated ten men.

platoon of motor-cyclists and one section of five scout cars and motor-machine-guns. (c) One artillery regiment of two groups, each of three batteries of short 105-mm. There was one battery of tractor-drawn 47-mm. anti-tank guns. (d) One company of lorry-borne engineers; one company of signallers, part line, part radio; H.Q. company. There were also transport company, traffic police, etc. One air-squadron was laid down of 12 Potez 63. Only one of these seems to have been allotted (for the 2nd Division), but it never arrived. The strength of a division was 310 officers, 6,200 other ranks, with 1,400 vehicles of which 550 were tracked (240 armoured) and 400 m/c. The transport of the division by rail required 28 trains. The fire-power of an armoured division was

24 105-mm. guns	84 37-mm. (1938) guns
65 75-mm. guns	12 25-mm anti-tank guns
71 47-mm. guns	

The armoured division, apart from the number of A.F.V., which was at least a hundred machines short of what was required, suffered also from the lack of fire power; another (a third) artillery group should have been provided, and the provision of only one infantry battalion was ridiculous. It also needed one or two squadrons of armoured cars.

Unincorporated Armoured Units

The Renault 35 18 regiments were normally attached to armies, but three battalions were sent to 4th Armoured.

The two battalions of F.C.M. were sent to Second Army. One battalion of Hotchkiss 35, the 13th Battalion remained attached to First Army. There were seven battalions of the obsolescent F.T., which were sent to different armies. The 51st Battalion of Estienne's 70-ton experimental tank of 1919, of which six examples were with the Third Army, was caught on the railway in June and smashed.

The 18 Renault, two F.C.M. and one Hotchkiss battalions each had 45 tanks. The battalions of the obsolescent Renault F.T. had 63 machines. None of these units had artillery or infantry. They were used entirely as adjuncts to infantry divisions.

Altogether, excluding 441 obsolete F.T., the 6 C and the spare machines with the 2nd echelons, there appear to have been 2,235 tanks as against 2,683, the figure given by Guderian for the German armour. But the German tanks were organized in ten divisions. Moreover, he stated that each armoured division had 56 armoured cars.

ARTILLERY AND ARMOUR

The famous 75-mm. had been much improved from the 1914 model. Its range had been increased to 10,000 yards. The 105-mm. had also an increased range. The 47-mm. anti-tank gun was reputed the best in Europe, but it was horse-drawn and very conspicuous. On the dreadful morning of 11 May, Lacaille, Chief of Staff of Second Army, reported to the neighbouring Ninth that the gun was proving useless, but this may have been the repetition of a panic rumour. The 37-mm. was badly delayed in production. A number of Hotchkiss tanks had to be armed with the 1918 37-mm. of which the muzzle-velocity was no more than half that of the modern guns. The 25-mm anti-tank gun made by Hotchkiss had a muzzle-velocity of about 2,900 ft per second. There were complaints that it was not powerful enough and not heavy enough. Although there are said to have been 6,000 on 10 May, a number of formations had not received their complement.

FRENCH A.F.V.

Type	Weight (tons)	Speed (k.p.h.)	Armour (thickest mm.)	Crew	Armament
A.M.D. Panhard (Armoured car)	8	30	18	2	1 25-mm. 1 M.G.
D.1	11	40	30	2	1 4·7-cm. 2 M.G.
D.2	22	20	30	3	1 4·7-cm. 2 M.G.
FCM	12	24	40		1 3·7-mm.(1916) 1 M.G.
Renault 35	11	18	12/14	2	1 3·7-cm. (1916) 1 M.G.
Hotchkiss 35 39	12	15 40	15/18	2	1 3·7-cm. or 1 2·5-cm. 1 M.G.
Somua	20	40	40	3	1 4·7-cm. 1 M.G.
B.1	33	40	40/80	4/5	1 7·5-cm. 1 4·7-cm. 2 M.G.

General Martell said the Hotchkiss was slow, rather under-engined. Somua also under-engined. Both suited to mass-production. B.1 had 'an ideal but very complicated steering system. Very expensive and not suited for mass production. Less heavily armed than the British Matilda.'

The original B.1 had an 8 hours' radius, but to give more power a second carburettor was added. Hence the B.1 *bis* had its radius reduced to 5½ hours. It could not let the tank fall below 180 litres (full tank 450). Hotchkiss was also reduced to 5½ hours' radius. This reduced the tasks to be ordered. Also the tank commander began to get anxious after about three hours.

The obsolete F.T. of 1918 weighed 6·5–7 tons. Its maximum speed was 8 k.p.h. It had a crew of two and was armed with either a 3·7 gun or a heavy machine-gun.

B THE GERMAN FORCES

On 10 May, the German attacking armies were in three army groups. Starting from the north, Army Group B of von Bock consisted of Eighteenth Army (Küchler), X and XXVI Korps with one airborne division (22), two S.S. divisions (motorized), one cavalry, one armoured (9 Pz.) and 4 infantry divisions. Von Reichenau's Sixth Army had five Korps, IX, XI, IV, XXVII and Hoeppner's XVI Panzer made up of two armoured divisions and 14 infantry divisions. In group reserve was one Korps with five infantry divisions, one motorized, and one S.S. also motorized.

The boundary between von Bock's group and Army Group A of von Rundstedt ran from Eupen to Cologne.

Army Group A on north had Fourth Army (von Kluge) with three Korps, V, VIII, II, with Hoth's XV Panzer, nine infantry and two two Panzer divisions. Twelfth Army (List) had three Korps, III, VI, XVIII, with ten infantry and one mountain divisions. Sixteenth Army (Busch) had three Korps, VII, XIII, XXIII, with XL in reserve and twelve infantry divisions. In addition, von Rundstedt had the Kleist Group, Guderian's XIX Panzer Korps, 1st, 2nd and 10th Panzer divisions and the Gross-Deutschland Motorized Regiment (four battalions), Reinhardt's XLI Panzer Korps with 6th and 8th Panzer Divisions, and von Wietersheim's XIV Korps with 2, 13 and 29 Motorized Divisions. In Group reserve was the skeleton II Korps and three infantry divisions.

The southern boundary of von Rundstedt's group ran from Koblenz to Trier (Trèves).

Group C, von Leeb, held from the Moselle to the Rhine with the First Army (Witzleben) of four Korps and 11 infantry divisions. On the Rhine to Bâle was Dollmann's Seventh Army, two Korps with four static divisions. There were four active divisions in group reserve.

In German G.H.Q. reserve were the Second and Ninth Armies of Weichs and Blaskowitz with six Korps and two skeleton korps and 41 infantry divisions.

On 10 May, the German forces engaged in the West amounted to 114 infantry divisions, 10 armoured, 4 motorized and 2 SS motorized divisions, 1 cavalry division and 1 parachute division.

On the eve of *Fall Rot*, the armour was reorganized into five Panzer Korps, each of two Pz. divisions and one motorized division. XIX Pz. Korps was dissolved. 1st and 2nd Pz. divisions with the 29th Motorized Division went to XXXIX Korps commanded by Rudolf Schmidt. Wietersheim's XIV Korps was converted to Panzer by the introduction of the former independent 9th Pz. and 10th Pz. from XIX Pz. Korps, and the Gross Deutschland motorized regiment.

XV (Hoth), XVI (Hoeppner) and XLI (Reinhardt) were unchanged except for the addition of 2nd, 13th and 20th motorized divisions. XV Korps became independent under Fourth Army. XIV and XVI remained under Kleist, while XXXIX and XLI were grouped under Guderian in Twelfth Army.

THE PANZER DIVISIONS

Mark	I	II	III	IV		
1. Kirschner	30	100	90	56	276	
2. Veiel	30	100	90	56	276	
3. Stumpff	140	110	50	24	324	
4. Stever	140	110	50	24	324	
5. von Hartlieb	140	110	50	24	324	
6. Kempff	10	40	36	132	218	In these three divi-
7. Rommel	10	40	36	132	218	sions, the Mk IV
8. Kuntzen	10	40	36	132	218	were Czech Skodas
9. Hubicki	100	75	36	18	229	
10. Schaal	30	100	90	56	276	
	640	825	564	654	2683	

The above figures are derived from Commandant Rogé's interview with Guderian (*RHA*, 1947, I, pp. 109-19) and Guderian's *Panzer Leader*. They appear to be establishment numbers. Zimmermann in his history of XVI Korps gives:

3rd Pz. I, 109; II, 122; III–IV, 49. Total 280
4th Pz. I, 160; II, 107; III, 41; IV, 32. Total: 343

Each division had also 56 wheeled armoured cars.

Title	Weight (tons)	Speed (k.p.h.)	Armour (thickest mm.)	Crew	Armament
Pz. Kw. I	5·7	51	14	2	2 L.M.G.
Pz. Kw. II	9	44	15	3	1 H.M.G.
Pz. Kw. III	18–20	44	30	3/4	1 3·7 gun 2 L.M.G.
Pz. Kw. IV	22	49	43	5	1 7·5 gun 2 L.M.G.
Skoda	11·5	35	25	3	1 3·7 gun 2 L.M.G.

All have W/T. Skoda and Panzer Mk IV also have radio.

C THE BRITISH EXPEDITIONARY FORCE

The British Expeditionary Force on 10 May consisted of 1st, 2nd, 3rd, 4th, 42nd, 44th, 48th and 50th infantry divisions of three infantry brigades with artillery and engineers. The 5th Division, which had only two brigades, was at Le Havre, but now started to return to the north. The 51st (Highland), with certain additional troops (yeomanry, artillery, engineers and machine-gun battalions), was in the Maginot defences east of Thionville. The 12th, 23rd (two brigades) and 46th Divisions, which had no artillery, were on labour duties near the base. The 1st Army Tank Brigade of two battalions of infantry tanks was attached to I Corps.

On 22 May and after, the 30th Infantry Brigade landed at Calais with a battalion of tanks and one of motor-cycle infantry, where they were eventually captured.

From 16 May onwards, 2nd Armoured Brigade (three cavalry regiments) and 3rd Armoured Brigade (Cruiser tanks), less the battalion at Calais, began landing at Cherbourg.

BRITISH A.F.V.

Type	Weight (tons)	Speed (k.p.h.)	Armour (mm.)	Crew	Armament
Light	4/5	48	12/14	3	1 M.G. 1 L.M.G.
Cruiser	12/14	40	14/30	4/5	1 2-pr. gun
Infantry	11	13	60	2	1 7·9 M.G.
Infantry heavy	25	24	78	4	1 7·9 M.G. and 1 2-pr. gun.

D THE BELGIAN ARMED FORCES

The Belgian Army consisted of active troops, first and second reserve. When all were called up the army amounted to eighteen divisions, of which Nos. 17 and 18 were second reserve. There were also two special divisions of *chasseurs ardennais* responsible for the covering of the area south of the Meuse between Namur and Liège. These were either on motor-cycles or lorries. They had no artillery. The normal divisions consisted of three infantry regiments, one artillery and one engineer.

Each infantry regiment had three battalions of three companies and one company of 12 machine-guns plus a fourth battalion of machine-guns, mortars and anti-tank guns. Each of the divisions 1–12 had a cyclist squadron, a company of 47-mm. anti-tank guns and 47-mm. tracked guns. Artillery regiments had four groups, except divisions 13 to 18, which had only two.

There were two motorized cavalry divisions and a lorried brigade. There was practically no armour and the air force was obsolescent. Some time in late 1938 or early 1939 the German government offered the Belgians Czech fighters, which were accepted pending the construction of Hurricanes, but these had not been delivered before 10 May.

E RELATIVE AIRCRAFT TYPES

Type	k.p.h.	Ceiling (feet)	Range (miles)	Bomb load (lb.)	Armament
FRENCH					
Potez 63. F.	442	28,600			2 2-cm. 1 m.g.
Breguet 693. B.	461			880	
Lioré 45. B.	496			3,080	
Curtis. F.	496	30,000			4/6 m.g.
Morane 406. F.	488	30,200			1 2-cm. 2 m.g.
Bloch 152. F.	496	30,100			2 2-cm. 2–4 m.g.
Amiot 143. B.	300			1,640	
BRITISH					
Battle. B.	385	23,500	1,050	1,000	2 × 303 m.g.
Blenheim. B.	424	22,600	1,460	1,000	5 × 303
Hurricane. I.F.	504	33,200			8 × 303
Spitfire. I.F.	568	34,000			8 × 303
GERMAN					
Junkers 87. B. (Stuka)	392	23,500	800	1,100	3 × ·79-mm.
Dornier 17. B.	408	21,000	1,440	1,100	7 × ·79-mm. 1 2-cm.
Heinkel 111. B.	388	26,000	1,510	2,200	1 2-cm. 7 79-mm.
Messerschmidt 109. E. F. (single engine)	568	35,000			2 2-cm. 2 79-mm.

F AIR OPERATIONS

Of the operations of the three allied air forces, little concrete evidence is to be found, particularly as to strength and organization, during the period up to 15 June 1940, when General Weygand ordered what remained of the French Air Force to North Africa. Except at Dunkirk, where the evacuation was covered largely by Royal Air Force fighters from southern England, the battlefield was dominated by the German Air Force, in part because the *Wehrmacht* had the initiative in the attack on static objectives, but also because the Germans had organized a combination of army and air forces for war in two elements, whereas the French and British staffs had prepared for war in the air and war on the land.[1] In consequence, the components of the Luftwaffe differed from those of the Allies. The Germans did not waste their fighter pilots' strength in defence, but relied on their excellent anti-aircraft guns, supplemented by those taken from Czechs, Poles and Danes. Their fighters were employed in escorting their bombers. Dorniers and Heinkels were used against permanent targets such as towns, ports, rail clusters and air-fields, but for attacks in the field against troops they employed the Stuka (the Junkers 87B), not a fast machine but workmanlike and expendable, such as neither French nor British had conceived. As Colonel de Lesquen wrote, it could be argued that the efficacy of the Stuka was due rather to the absence of light anti-aircraft guns than to its own value.

Like the army, the French Air Force was planned for defence. Its main arm was the fighter, and since French anti-aircraft artillery was both deficient and ineffective, the burden on the fighter was very heavy. According to the figures given by Guy la Chambre, the fighters *en ligne* on 10 May amounted to 790.[2] One French Air Force writer says that to protect the whole front 120 groups (or 3,120 planes) were needed, whereas usually, out of 26, no more than 18 were available.[3] None of the French fighters available on 10 May had an air-speed approaching that of the German Messerschmidt 109 (or of the British Hurricane and Spitfire) or the ceiling. The Dewoitine 520 and the Bloch 152, introduced during the next weeks, were faster. The standard fighter was the Morane 406, which, though not fast, was easily handled and in which the French pilots had confidence.

On 10 May there were 140 bombers *en ligne*. It is probable that the potential figure was considerably higher since at the moment 16 of the 28 bomber groups were in the process of conversion to recent types. Of these new planes, two were the Glenn-Martin reconnaissance-bomber and the Douglas bomber, both from the United States: the former went into action on 22 May, the Douglas on 31 May. The greater number of sorties were carried out by the Bréguet 691 and the Lioré 45. Of the 1,198 bomber sorties recorded between 10 May and 12 June, 439 were by Bréguets, 314 by Liorés and 352 by Glenn-Martins. They lost, respectively, 44, 44 and 21 machines.[4]

On 10 May the British Air Component, stationed roughly between Lille and the Somme, had four fighter squadrons which were reinforced during 10th–12th by three more, about 110 planes in all, with two squadrons of bombers and two of reconnaissance bombers. The Advanced Air Striking Force established on air-fields between the Aisne and the Marne, east of Reims, had ten bomber squadrons and two fighter, reinforced by a third on 10 May. The whole British force amounted to 416, of which 216 were bombers and 100 fighters. These contingents could, of course, be reinforced from England.

The Belgians had eighteen squadrons, perhaps 200 planes in all, but many of them obsolescent.

Against these, the Germans mustered perhaps 1,200 fighters (Me. 109 and 110), 1,300 bombers (Dornier 17 and Heinkel 111) with 380 Stukas (Ju. 87). They had also 640 reconnaissance/observation planes and a thousand transport aircraft.

The reorganization of the air defence in France had been modified more than once. On 10 May it consisted of three zones: North under General the Baron d'Astier de la Vigerie, whose area stretched from the sea to the Meuse; East beyond the Meuse, in the area of Toul; and South, chiefly south of the Loire, each Army had one reconnaissance group and one fighter. Each corps, and each armoured, light armoured, and cavalry division had one observation group—on paper.

[2]

Soon after daylight on 10 May, the German Air Force attacked, first the railways, especially junctions and entraining points, secondly the airfields. The Belgians suffered badly. By the end of the day, of their 18 squadrons a number had been destroyed on the ground. The British escaped with the extinction of 18 bombers of the A.A.S.F. on one aerodrome. A large number of French aircraft seems to have been destroyed or damaged on the ground at the 47 aerodromes attacked, but it is not certain what proportion of the 240 recorded as destroyed on the ground were in fact destroyed on this day.

Although on 10 May the French Air Force, with the British and Belgian, was not capable of carrying out the tasks required, this was not only due to an overall shortage of aircraft. There was also misdirection. Gamelin asserted that Vuillemin did little to influence operations, and although Gamelin's criticisms may be suspect, there is no doubt that liaison between air and army commands was clumsy and ineffective. During the first days of the battle, Army Group One asked for a concentration of fighters on the left in support of Giraud's rush towards Breda. Hence the number of squadrons available to First, Ninth and

Second Armies was much reduced. On the evening of the 12th, however, the expectation of the attack at Sedan led the command of Northern Air Zone to switch its strength to Second Army. During the morning of the 13th, the fighter groups were continuously employed, including the provision of large escorts for reconnaissance planes. The fighter pilots were worn out with the successive sorties. About midday the crossing of the Meuse at Houx was reported. At first Army Group One said that Ninth Army could deal with it, but later a call from 4th Cavalry led Northern Zone to reinforce the Ninth Army fighter squadrons. Later still, bombers were diverted to the Dinant–Godinne area and the Houx sector. Army Group One therefore cancelled the hitherto imposed air priority for objectives which were within the range of artillery in the Second Army area. Thus when the great air assault on the 55th Divisions' defences began during the afternoon, there were no fighters to protect the infantry, while the anti-aircraft batteries, themselves subject to attack and in consequence moving position, were impotent. It was now that the inadequacy of air-army liaison became hideously clear. 'All the requests for fighter intervention coming from X Corps were at once transmitted by Second Army headquarters to its air headquarters. General Roque, the commander of the army's air groups, even installed himself at Senuc to be in closest touch with Colonel Lacaille and his staff. What this shows is the enormity of the vicious organization of Air Force Command, which deprived army commands of the disposition of their fighters. Requests for fighter action were addressed to Northern Air Zone, which, harassed on every side, were probably unable to satisfy them.' The only attempt at relief seems to have been an attack by 12 Lioré 45 bombers, of which half were badly damaged by flak. That night all French bombers were ordered to attack the Sedan bridgehead. At midday on the 14th, in response to a request from La Ferté, Air Marshal Barratt ordered bombers from every one of the A.A.S.F. squadrons to support the French at Sedan.

As has been seen, the Germans had one pontoon over the river at Gaulier by midnight, and, it seems, two more at Donchery and south-east of Sedan during the next day. The repeated attempts of both French and British bombers to destroy these bridges were costly failures. The British lost 40 out of 71, the French 13 with 35 crippled. All or nearly all were victims of anti-aircraft fire. No air force could allow such losses, and the enemy had not been stopped. Daylight bombing was renounced from the evening of the 14th. By noon on the fifteenth, French Northern Air Zone had lost half its fighters, and Ninth Army air group no longer existed.[5]

These calamities were due not only to shortage of fighters and pilots, but also to the immense length of the chain of command whereby application for support from the ground required the transmission of the message to the head of the chain before it could be passed over the gulf and travel down the other side, causing immeasurable delays.

The air force had its own troubles. By the opening of the battle, the production of aircraft had got into full swing. Now there were not enough pilots, while the airfields of the depots and the schools were being crowded with new deliveries. The commander of the 3rd Air Region reported that there were more than 200 modern fighters at Tours, Bloch 151s. He was refused permission to use them for patrols over the towns on the Loire, although, as he pointed out, it would be excellent training. These machines were unarmed. When the crash came in June, and the chain of command no longer functioned, he sent to the arms depot at Châtellerault from which he got everything he needed to produce fighting patrols.

Furthermore, Ninth Army Air detachment had had all its Potez 63s destroyed on the ground. The whole of its personnel, including its pilots, and all its transport, were sent to the Châtellerault neighbourhood on 15 May. On the same day, 3rd Air Division was instructed to collect all the Potez 63s from the schools, equip them and hold them at the disposition of air headquarters. This was carried out within forty-eight hours. And there they remained. The Ninth Army pilots were not employed and the 30 Potez were eventually sent south by road on airplane transporters.[6]

On the other hand, air group commanders found that when offered the use of squadrons, Army and Army Group Headquarters invariably replied: 'Thank you very much, but we have no use for them.'[7]

In spite of repeated demands on the British for fighter squadrons, it appears that after its initial disaster the French Air Force was recovering all the time. 'We believe that the Commander-in-Chief could reckon available daily, between Dunkirk and Menton, 350–400 modern fighters, a figure which fell to 300 about 10 June. But at the beginning the majority were Morane 406, whereas in June they were Bloch or Dewoitine. The figure of 80 modern bombers rose to 150–180 in mid-June, when the 80 obsolescent were withdrawn.'[8]

Source Notes

SOURCE NOTES

PART I: THE WITHERED LAURELS

Chapter One: The Quavering Hands

1. Mordacq, *Le ministère Clemenceau*, IV, pp. 55ff. and 302ff.
2. See Serrigny, *Trente Ans avec Pétain*, pp. 140, 146, 151, and Fayolle, *Carnets secrets*, pp. 271ff. In spite of his digestion, Debeney lived until 1943 when at the age of seventy-nine he was blown up with his car.

Chapter Two: The Return to the Middle Ages

1. Weygand, *Mémoires*, II, p. 320.

Chapter Three: The Baulking of Weygand

1. The obscure story of Weygand's birth and early career is ventilated in Tournoux's *Pétain et de Gaulle*, pp. 274–6. It is clear that Weygand stood apart from the ordinary career officers, but could not be ignored.
2. Gamelin, *Servir*, II, pp. xxiiiff.
3. Before 1914, it had rejected a machine-gun accepted by the infantry and had then taken eight years to provide one. On the other hand, General Dufieux in *Commission sur Événements 1933–45 (Témoignages)*, IV, p. 884, hereafter referred to as *C/E (T)*, says that the Direction of Infantry affected to be scandalized because he, Dufieux, I.G. Infantry and A.F.V., had General Velpry as his inspector of tanks. Velpry was a gunner! The fact that he had commanded the first French tank battalion in May 1918 and a group of six battalions in the great counter-attack of July 1918, and furthermore had been General Estienne's right-hand man, went for nothing. He was a gunner and the tank was an infantry weapon.
4. *C/E (T)*., V., pp. 1459–78. See also Rinderknech, ibid., pp. 1479ff.

Chapter Four: The Surrender of the Rhineland Outwork

1. Weygand, *Mémoires*, II, pp. 396–7.
2. Weygand, ibid., II, p. 434.
3. The first account was given by General Georges-René Alexandre in *Avec Joffre d'Agadir à Verdun*, 1931, and is supplemented by Gamelin's *Manœuvre et victoire de la Marne*, 1954.
4. Loustaunau-Lacau, *Mémoires d'un français rebelle*, p. 90.
5. *C/E (T)*, III, pp. 762–4.
6. Jean Zay (Under-secretary to the President of the Council), *Souvenirs et solitude*, pp. 65–8.
7. *C/E (T)*, V, pp. 1256–7, General Albord, representing General Héring, G.O.C. Strasbourg (VII and XX Corps).
8. Ibid.
9. Gamelin, *Servir*, II, pp. 193 and 217.
10. *C/E (T)*, III, p. 616.
11. Jordan, *Great Britain, France and the German Problem*, pp. 183–4.
12. Gamelin, *Servir*, II, pp. 127–9.
13. *C/E (T)*, I, p. 131.

Chapter Five: Arms for Defeat

1. *The Economist*, 21 August 1943, p. 244.
2. Jacomet, *L'Armement de France*, p. 50.
3. Ibid., p. 52.
4. *C/E* (*T*), II, pp. 295ff. La Chambre.
5. All this is from the evidence of Guy la Chambre in *C/E* (*T*), II, pp. 295–366.
6. Dufieux in *C/E* (*T*), III, p. 1056 and pp. 1062–3.
7. Jacomet, *L'Armement de France*, pp. 338–95 and Gamelin, *Servir*, II, pp. 367–8.
8. Loustaunau-Lacau, *Mémoires d'un français rebelle*, p. 120.
9. In 1938, de Gaulle published *La France et son armée*. De Gaulle's original preface thanked the Marshal 'who guided with his advice the composition of the first five chapters'. Pétain thought this exaggerated and insisted on its reduction to less exaggerated thanks. De Gaulle appears to have taken this ill, though why is impossible to surmise. See Tournoux, *Pétain et de Gaulle*, pp. 169ff.
10. Reynaud, *Mémoires*, I, p. 439.
11. 'Le chef de guerre' in *R.D.M.*, 1 March 1958, pp. 3ff.
12. Brigadier E. D. H. Tollemache, 'French Military Training for Defeat', in *Quarterly Review*, October 1941.

Chapter Six: The Betrayal of an Ally

1. Gamelin, *Servir*, II, pp. 351–2.
2. Ibid., pp. 344–9.
3. Baudouin, *Neuf Mois au gouvernement*, p. 21.
4. cf. his letter to the Air Minister, Guy la Chambre, in *C/E* (*T*), p. 313, and his remarks to Bonnet.
5. Coulondre, *De Staline à Hitler*, p. 195.

Chapter Seven: On the Brink

1. Coulondre, *De Staline à Hitler*, p. 196–7.
2. Noël, *L'Agression contre la Pologne*, pp. 257–60.
3. *C/E* (*T*), VII, p. 1949.
4. *C/E* (*Rapport*), II, pp. 187–96.
5. Coulondre, *De Staline à Hitler*, p. 198.
6. *Rélations polono-allemandes . . .*, Doc. 61.
7. Kennedy, *The Business of War*, p. 4.
8. Gamelin, *Servir*, II, pp. 415ff.
9. Noël, *L'Agression contre la Pologne*, p. 421.
10. Précis of the negotiations are set out in *Documents on British Foreign Policy* (Third Series), Vol. VII, pp. 566ff.
11. Gamelin, both in *Servir* (I. Ch. II) and to the Commission on Events, makes a great fuss over the meaning of the word 'ready', saying that he did not mean ready for war but merely that mobilization could be carried out at once. Nobody, however, could possibly have thought he meant the first. All the rest of the minutes proclaim the council's lack of confidence in the future.

PART II: DRÔLE DE GUERRE

Chapter One: The Loss of a Second Ally

1. Gontaut-Biron, *Les Dragons au combat*, pp. 28–9.
2. Mordal, 'La garantie polonaise' in *R.D.N.*
3. Bourret, *Tragédie de l'armée française*, p. 65.
4. Prételat, *Destin tragique de la Ligne Maginot*.
5. Gamelin (*Servir*, I, pp. 185–6) admits that in spite of harrying, the armament services had been able to produce little over 500,000 mines by the beginning of May 1940, a totally insufficient number. But he is unable to explain why.

Chapter Two: Illusions and Disillusion

1. Anon, *Les transports pendant la guerre*.
2. Paillart, *Les 40 jours du deuxième G.R.C.A.*, p. 19.
3. Lespès, *Corps-à-corps avec les blindés*, p. 4.
4. Minart, *P.C. Vincennes, Secteur 4*, I, p. 60.
5. La Laurencie, *Les opérations du IIIe corps de l'armée*, pp. 8–9, f.n.
6. Bourret, *Tragédie de l'armée française*, p. 50.
7. Rebattet, *Les Décombres*, p. 256.
8. Vallet in *C/E (T)*, V, p. 1374.
9. *C/E (T)*, VII, p. 1949.
10. Ibid., p. 1953.
11. But 'three days after their incorporation (in the 159th Alpine Regiment) five hundred peasants from the hills have been sent home on a month's agricultural leave which they will spend watching the snow'— Rebattet, *Les Décombres*, p. 265.
12. *C/E (T)*, VII, pp. 1962–3.
13. Ibid., p. 1965.
14. Vidalenc, *L'Exode de mai-juin 1940*, pp. 44–5.

Chapter Three: Deficiencies and Defects

1. Very full accounts for all three divisions were given to the *C/E (T)*, V. Every officer stresses the deficiencies in what they actually received. The 4th Armoured Division of de Gaulle was a mixed body, but eventually became the strongest.
2. Coulondre, *De Staline à Hitler*, p. 200.
3. Prételat, *Destin tragique de la Ligne Maginot*, p. 46.
4. *C/E (R)*, II, pp. 312–13.
5. *C/E (T)*, p. 325.
6. Ibid., p. 312.
7. Vallet in *C/E (T)*, V, p. 1374; Prételat, *Destin tragique de la Ligne Maginot*, pp. 43 and 96ff.; Le Goaster, 'L'Action des forces aériennes.'
8. *C/E (T)*, I, p. 25.

Chapter Four: Forecasts and Plans

1. Gamelin, *Servir*, I, pp. 86ff.; III, pp. 135ff.
2. Kennedy, *The Business of War*, p. 30.
3. Gamelin, *Servir*, I, p. 107.
4. Bryant (ed.), *The Turn of the Tide*, p. 70.

5. Lyet, *La Bataille de France, mai-juin, 1940*, p. 21. Memo. 16 November 1939, Blanchard-Billotte and Roton. Lugand, 'Les Forces en présence au mai 1940', p. 25.

6. Villate, 'L'Entrée des Français en Belgique, etc.' in *Revue d'histoire de la 2ème guerre mondiale*, June 1953, pp. 60–70. Van Overstraeten, *Au service de la Belgique*, pp. 153–60 and pp. 169ff.

7. Telford Taylor, *The March of Conquest*, pp. 62–3 and Ellis, *The War in France and Flanders, 1939–40*, pp. 335–46, for the most lucid exposition of the German plan.

8. Gamelin, *Servir*, II, p. 128.

Chapter Five: The Eleventh Hour

1. Gamelin, *Servir*, III, p. 256.
2. Ibid., I, pp. 44 and 6off.
3. *C/E (T)*, II, pp. 675ff. (Georges).
4. *C/E (T)*, VII, p. 2019. Dautry was replying to a question about the cabinet meeting of 9 May, but he has confused it with this one of 12 April. The account here is confirmed by Baudouin, *Neuf Mois au gouvernement*, pp. 26–34 and Gamelin himself in *Servir*, III, pp. 336–8.

PART III: THE DISASTER

Chapter Three: The Meuse; Dinant

1. Kosak, *Belgique et France*, 1940, p. 15.
2. Ibid., p. 17.
3. Rollet, 'L'Offensive de Sedan: les rapports franco-belges', in *Revue d'histoire de la 2ème guerre mondiale*, No. 38, April 1960.
4. The destruction of the bridges is obscure. Doumenc, for example, in *Histoire de la Neuvième Armée*, p. 55, says that the bridge at Bouvignes, almost opposite Dinant, was destroyed. There was no bridge. See also *The Rommel Papers*: Fox and Ornano, 'La Percée des Ardennes'; Hauteclerc, 'Rommel contre Corap'.
5. Menu, *Lumière sur les ruines*, pp. 59, 67–8.

Chapter Four: The Meuse; Sedan

1. Rollet, 'L'Offensive de Sedan: les rapports franco-belges', in *Revue d'histoire de la 2ème guerre mondiale*, No. 38, April 1960; Wanty, '*La Défense des Ardennes*', in *Revue d'histoire de la 2ème guerre mondiale*, April 1961.
2. Ruby, *Sedan, terre d'épreuve*, p. 81.
3. Vidalenc, *l'Exode de mai-juin, 1940*, pp. 78–9.
4. Roton, *Années cruciales*, pp. 149–50. Véron in *C/E (T)*, V, p. 1289.
5. Grandsard, *Le Xe corps d'armée*, p. 119 f.n.
6. Ibid, pp. 123ff. This gives a lucid exposition of the position and its garrison.
7. Cf. Grandsard, *Le Xe corps d'armée*, pp. 107–8, 114–15.
8. It appears to have extended as far west as Flize. The 2nd Panzer Division had entered the undefended village of Nouvion opposite Flize. The bridge here had been destroyed. A German attempt to cross on rafts, etc., failed. Ornano, 'Après la percée de Sedan', *R.H.A.*, 1950, I, pp. 35ff.

9. Guderian and others say that many of the French shelters were destroyed by the shells of the 88-mm. anti-aircraft guns fired from within 2,000–3,000 yards. On the other hand, Balck, who commanded the 1st Rifle Regiment, claimed (according to Mellenthin, *Panzer Battles*, p. 15) that the assault was made by infantry unsupported by any other guns than their own. Cf. p. 235 on the defence of Abbeville on 30 May.

10. Quoted by Vidalenc, *L'Exode de mai-juin, 1940*, p. 82 (where Tannay is given as Toncy).

11. Grandsard, *Le Xe corps d'armée*, p. 150; Ruby, *Sedan, terre d'épreuve*, pp. 151–3.

Chapter Six: G.Q.G. Action

1. Beaufre, *Le drame de 1940*, pp. 233–4; Roton, *Années cruciales*, pp. 158–9; Lyet, *La Bataille de France, mai-juin, 1940*, p. 56 and f.n. The confirming orders were timed 3.30 p.m. on the 14th, by which time, of course, circumstances were largely transformed.

Chapter Seven: Dismemberment of the Ninth Army

1. *C/E (T)*, V, Bruneau, pp. 1171ff. General Vallet (Ninth Army Operations) says that Corap gave Martin orders to counter-attack—ibid., p. 1379.

2. Menu, *Lumière sur les ruines*, p. 88.

3. Véron in *C/E (T)*, V, pp. 1293–5.

Chapter Eight: The Splitting of the Centre

1. The state of the 3rd Armoured is given in full by General Devaux (in 1940, Lieutenant-Colonel and Chief of Staff to the division) in *C/E (T)*, V, pp. 1325ff.

2. Ruby, *Sedan, terre d'épreuve*, p. 160.

3. Devaux in *C/E (T)*, V, pp. 1325ff. 'This general who seemed to know nothing whatever about the technical exigencies of the machine . . .'

4. Fox and Ornano in 'La Percée des Ardennes' in *Revue d'histoire de la 2ème guerre mondiale* 1953, pp. 77–118.

5. Roton, *Années cruciales*, p. 174.

6. Gamelin, *Servir*, I, pp. 339–41 and III, pp. 399ff.

7. A full account is given by Devaux in *C/E (T)*, V, pp. 1335ff. Flavigny, in a long letter written to the Commission on his death-bed, gave his version (ibid., pp. 1253–5). There are wide differences between the hours at which Flavigny's verbal order was issued. Devaux notes there was no written confirmation. Ruby gives 1.30 p.m., Devaux 3.30, Flavigny 5.30.

8. Huntziger's report on Brocard is quoted by Devaux in *C/E (T)*, V, p. 1341, f.n. 2.

9. Ruby, *Sedan, terre d'épreuve*, pp. 168–70.

Chapter Nine: The Disarming of the 2nd Armoured Division

1. Bruché's lamentable but exciting story is given by him in *C/E (T)*, V.

2. Guderian, *Panzer Leaders*, p. 111, mistakenly believed this to be from de Gaulle's division.

Chapter Ten: The End of the Ninth Army

1. The 2nd Battery of the 54th North African Artillery crossed the Sambre near Berlaimont during the night of the 16th/17th, and marched due south by the road through Avesnes to Etroeungt, through Le Nouvion forest to Etreux, undisturbed (Doumenc, *Neuvième Armée*, p. 199 f.n.). The 5th Chasseurs, the last coherent element of the 1st Armoured, was waiting with its carriers a little north of Solre-le-Château when Rommel and his raiders drove through the town about 10.30 p.m. with 'lights blazing and machine-guns firing tracer' before turning off on the Avesnes road, leaving half a dozen armoured cars at the crossroads. The officer in charge of the French carriers told the drivers not to start the engines until he gave the signal and then give full throttle. The signal was followed by a shattering roar. The German cars fled, and taking up the Chasseurs the convoy set out peacefully for Maubeuge. Later they joined the 1st Light Armoured near Jolimetz. Menu, *Lumière sur les ruines*, p. 125; Doumenc, *Neuvième Armée*, p. 265.

2. *C/E (T)*, V, p. 1300.

3. Liddell Hart, *Rommel Papers*, p. 27.

Chapter Eleven: The Loss of Maubeuge and the Oise

1. Albert-Sorel, *Le Chemin des croix*, p. 90.

Chapter Twelve: Reaction in Paris

1. There is no reason to suspect the general truthfulness of this narrative, given in M. André Guéraud's *The Gravediggers of France* at p. 74. 'Pertinax' can have had it only from Mr Bullitt while he was a refugee in New York. So far as I know, it was not contradicted by Mr Bullitt. It is given by no one else; it scarcely could be. Gamelin's memoirs are singularly empty of the incidents of the 15th/16th. He does not mention the meeting of 3 a.m. on the 16th, though it is recorded by Reynaud, Baudouin (writing of his conversation about it with Reynaud) and Minart, II, pp. 151–4. Gamelin denies his presence at the 3 a.m. meeting and by implication that of Daladier, but offers a telephone conversation with Reynaud, obviously much later in the day (*Servir*, III, pp. 407–8 and p. 408 f.n.). He says that he gave orders on the 15th for the preparation of advanced headquarters at Briare and Gien on the Loire. Then, 'I quickly settled a few personal matters that I might have my mind free and could concentrate all my time to my task. I judged that the fate of my country was going to rest on me.'

2. For this chapter, Baudouin's diary, *Neuf Mois au gouvernement*, has been used extensively. Great efforts were made to discredit Baudouin's notes by the Commission on Events, largely because he became Foreign Minister to Pétain. Nothing serious was proved and it is as valid as any other personal document.

Chapter Thirteen: Stopgaps

1. Its Hotchkiss squadron, which had been severely hammered in Lorraine, had been sent off to refit on 13 May and did not rejoin the division until 9 June, when it had the latest models (Petiet, *R.D.M.*, 15 June 1943).

2. Galimand, *Vive Pétain, Vive de Gaulle*, p. 12.

3. The historian of the 2nd Dragoons gives a terrific account of this affair in which a strong motorized force of German infantry preceded by armoured cars was 'literally pulverized; crushed by the 75s and 47s of the Bs, and the German soldiers, absolutely terrified by the frightful avalanche of steel and fire, had no alternative but to seek safety by plunging into the marshes'. He speaks of a long line of crushed and burned vehicles; it is suspected that the ammunition wagon was the destroyer. (Gontaut-Biron, *Les Dragons au combat*, p. 85.)

4. It was more probably from Commandant Bourgin's detachment from the 2nd Armoured, cf. *C/E (T)*, V, p. 1235.

5. Guderian, *Panzer Leader*, p. 108. The German higher command was nervous of what might be being built up south of the Aisne. Kleist, who commanded the Armoured Group, had ordered a halt until the southern flank was covered by the arrival of infantry. After a fierce quarrel between the generals, Guderian was allowed to send forward light reconnaissance forces. Interpreting this phrase to his own purposes, the XIX Panzer Korps commander took a considerable body of armour forward and was able to cross the Oise at Moy.

6. This account of the fighting round Laon on 17–21 May is derived from a number of sources, viz. (1) the first of General Perré's two articles in *Écrits de Paris*; (2) Commandant Weygand's article on the 3rd Régiment des Automitrailleuses; (3) Gontaut-Biron's *Les Dragons au combat*; (4) *Vive Pétain, Vive de Gaulle*, by Galimand, deputy for a Dieppe constituency and on the staff of the 4th Armoured Division; (5) de Gaulle's memoirs, Vol. I; (6) *Historique des combats de la 4ème Division cuirassée*, printed in Tournoux, *Pétain et de Gaulle*, pp. 412ff., which is not only thoroughly unenlightening (it ignores whatever happened on 18 May and does not mention the attached units from the 3rd Cavalry Division), but also, like de Gaulle's own writing, makes extravagant claims of success. The fullest account of the fighting of the 4th Armoured Division are General J. Perré's articles.

Chapter Fourteen: The End of Gamelin and Arrival of Weygand

1. '. . . who had given the B.E.F. no orders for some eight days, nor had Gort complained to the Cabinet or to me'—*The Ironside Diaries, 1937–40*, p. 321.

2. Gort, *Despatch*, pp. 5914–15.

3. Menu, *Lumière sur les ruines*, p. 337.

4. Roton, *Années cruciales*, p. 202.

5. Minart, *P. C. Vincennes; Secteur 4*, II, pp. 188 and 190–1.

6. Gamelin, *Servir*, III, p. 432.

7. Beaufre, *Le Drame de 1940*, pp. 238–9.

8. Gamelin, *Servir*, III, pp. 427–34. Minart, *P. C. Vincennes; Secteur 4*, II, pp. 194–7. Minart, who later became some kind of a provost-marshal under Vichy, is critical, but not unsympathetic to Gamelin, but the latter obviously considers Minart his enemy.

9. Gamelin, *Servir*, I, pp. 7–8.

10. Baudouin, *Neuf Mois au gouvernement*, pp. 60–1.

11. Gamelin, *Servir*, III, pp. 435–8; Weygand, *Rappelé au service*, p.

87. Baudouin, *Neuf Mois au gouvernement*, p. 61, says 'his takeover was very short. General Gamelin left him after a conversation of ten minutes.'
    12. *C/E (T)*, III, pp. 689–90.

Chapter Fifteen: The British at Arras

1. Gort, *Despatch*, p. 5916; Ironside, *The Ironside Diaries, 1937–40*, pp. 319–23. At the same time, General Dill had gone to La Ferté to tell Georges what was afoot and obtain his agreement. Ironside spoke on the telephone to Weygand to tell him that Billotte ought to be relieved. According to Ironside, Gort said he had had no orders for about eight days. This is an error, either by Gort or by Ironside, since Billotte's order of the 16th had been received.

2. Franklyn says that Billotte was also present when he arrived, but was not introduced, nor did he say anything about the intentions. 'If he only had, I would have rung up Gort and got confirmation for an operation which alone stood even a faint chance'—*The Story of One Green Howard in the Dunkirk Campaign*, p. 15.

3. Prioux, *Souvenirs de guerre, 1934–43*, 19–20 May.

4. Vautrin's report to Blanchard in Reynaud, *Au coeur de la mêlée*, p. 557.

5. Most of the detail is derived from the late General Sir Harold Franklyn's *The Story of One Green Howard in the Dunkirk Campaign*. Not being a politician, the general made no effort to exaggerate the success into a victory. Rommel apparently inflated his report to show that he was faced by superior forces, which he was not.

Chapter Sixteen: The Widening of the Gap

1. No. 102d. 18 May, 23.00 hrs (Roton, *Années cruciales, 1933–40*, p. 202).

2. See the important articles by Commandant Jean Vial, 'Une semaine décisive sur la Somme, 18–25 mai, 1940', in *Revue historique de l'armée*, 1949, IV, pp. 45–58 and 1950, I, pp. 46–60, from which is derived the fully argued account of the arrival of divisions on the Somme.

3. Fagalde, 'L'Odyssée d'une division française' (21st division), *R. mil. suisse*, 1954; Mordal, *La Bataille de Dunkerque*, pp. 131–62; Grandsard, *10 corps d'armée*, pp. 188 ff.; Linklater, *Highland Division*, p. 29.

4. Molinié's account in the *Revue de la défense nationale*, 1948, erroneously says 23rd Division.

5. Vibraye, *Avec mon Groupe de reconnaissance*, 22 May.

Chapter Seventeen: Weygand; Consultations and Orders

1. Van Overstraeten, *Au Service de la Belgique*, p. 286.

2. 'It would have taken at least four days to mount such an attack, and then it would have been too late'—Franklyn, *The Story of One Green Howard in the Dunkirk Campaign*, p. 21.

3. Spears, *Assignment to Catastrophe*, I, p. 166 f.n. The anecdote is from Major Miles Reid, M.C., liaison officer with the First French Army. Spears dates it the 20th. It should be the 22nd. Gort was not at Premesques on the 20th, and anyhow it took place after the Ypres meeting on the 21st.

4. Grandsard, *Le 10ᵉ corps d'armée* ... *1939–40*, p. 189 f.n.
5. Ibid., pp. 190–1.

Chapter Eighteen: Confused Discussion

1. See Jacobsen, *Dokumente zur Westfeldzug, 1940*, pp. 114–46, on the 'Halt-Befehl', and Ellis, *The War in France and Flanders, 1939–40*, Supplement.
2. Jacobsen, *Dokumente zur Westfeldzug, 1940*, p. 69.
3. There were also some fifteen coastal support points manned by naval parties. And for a short time a few British units (cf. Ellis, *The War in France and Flanders, 1939–40*, p. 136), on the 24th and 25th, when they were relieved by the 137th and retired to Bergues. Fagalde speaks of British detachments of all sizes up to a division which suddenly appeared in the area and then, from the 24th onward, disappeared without warning to go and embark. For Fagalde's detailed account of the period 24 May–4 June, see his 'Bataille de Dunkerque' in *Revue militaire suisse*, March–July 1952.
4. The Weygand message is given by Lyet (*La Bataille de France, mai–juin, 1940*, p. 96) without any time of dispatch. As Lyet says, with perhaps a superfluity of caution, 'it corresponds with reality only incompletely'. Ham had not been taken and the troops facing it had been there for some time. The attack on Amiens had failed (cf. Grandsard, *Le 10ᵉ corps d'armée* ... *1939–40*, pp. 193–6). The words *'forces mécaniques'* have no precise meaning; they may be anything from a thirty-ton tank to an infantry battalion on lorries. There is no text of Blanchard's telegram. The words 'own initiative' and 'towards the ports' are obviously hostile by intent. In view of his conversation with General de la Laurencie, they are probably Blanchard's. Cf. note 12 below.
5. Baudouin, *Neuf Mois au gouvernement*, pp. 72–7.
6. Lyet, *La Bataille de France, mai–juin, 1940*, p. 97 and f.n. 45.
7. La Laurencie, *Les Opérations du IIIᵉ corps d'armée, 1939–40*, p. 93.
8. Ibid., pp. 74–6.
9. Bryant (ed.), *The Turn of the Tide*, 24 May, p. 102; Bloch, *L'Étrange Défaite*, pp. 129–30.
10. Gort, *Despatch*, pp. 5920–1. There are great difficulties as to facts about these days. Gort speaks of a conference between Churchill, Reynaud and Weygand in Paris on 24 May. There was none. He asked for Dill. Dill apparently did not come until the morning of the 25th (p. 5923). Nevertheless, after a conference at Premesques at 9 a.m. on the 24th, Gort went to Poperinghe to meet Dill (Bryant ed., *The Turn of the Tide*, p. 102) and left Pownall to deal with Blanchard. The only thing that emerges from most writings is that neither French nor British ever informed the other of what they were intending to do and doing.
11. Franklyn, *The Story of One Green Howard in the Dunkirk Campaign*, p. 28, says that as he was sitting on the side of the road near Douai on the morning of the 24th, waiting for some of his 5th Division to come, he was found by Adam, who told him to attend a conference with the French.
12. The only evidence of the Pownall-Blanchard agreement appears in La Laurencie's notes, *Les Opérations du IIIᵉ corps d'armée, 1939–40*, pp. 98–9.

13. Rundstedt's Army Group reported on the evening of the 24th that German bridgeheads at Amiens, Corbie and Péronne had been reduced, but that the attacks had been repulsed. 'The German Fourth Army line (Kluge): VIII and II Korps, Valenciennes—south of Denain—south of Bouchain—the water-line—Gavrelle—Arras. Hoth Group on Vimy ridge—Béthune—Lillers. Kleist Group has reached Aire—St Omer—Gravelines. Enemy tenacious but not counter-attacking'—Jacobsen, *Dokumente zur Westfeldzug, 1940*, p. 75.

14. Lyet, *La Bataille de France, mai–juin, 1940*, p. 98.

15. Grandsard, *Le 10e corps d'armée . . . 1939–40*, p. 196.

16. This probably refers only to the super-heavy, which had marched up slowly and then marched back again without firing a shot (Menu, *Lumière sur les ruines*, pp. 307–9). Supply through Dunkirk began to be renewed on this or the next day.

17. Spears, *Assignment to Catastrophe*, I, pp. 188–98; Mordal, *La Bataille de Dunkerque*, pp. 100–5; Baudouin, *Neuf Mois au gouvernement*, pp. 78–80.

18. Bryant (ed.), *The Turn of the Tide*, pp. 104–5.

19. Lyet, *La Bataille de France, mai–juin, 1940*, p. 96, penultimate line; no time given and no originator.

20. Ellis, *The War in France and Flanders, 1939–40*, p. 258.

21. Lyet, *La Bataille de France, mai–juin, 1940*, p. 99.

22. Franklyn, *The Story of One Green Howard in the Dunkirk Campaign*, p. 28. Bryant, *The Turn of the Tide*, pp. 106–9.

23. It seems that General Altmayer (V Corps) was aware before nightfall, through British liaison officers, of the end of British participation (Doumenc, *Dunkerque et la campagne de Flandre*, p. 246). He ordered the 2nd North African back to a position covering Attiches.

24. President Lebrun, Reynaud, Pétain, Campinchi (Marine), Laurent-Eynac (Air), Weygand, Rollin (Colonies), General Buhrer (Colonial Troops), Darlan, Vuillemin, and Baudouin. Baudouin's *procès-verbal* is printed in *C/E (T)*, VII, pp. 1711–16. See also *Revue d'histoire de la 2ème guerre mondiale*, 1953, pp. 165–83.

Chapter Nineteen: The Retreat: Lille and Dunkirk

1. Doumenc, *Dunkerque et la campagne de Flandre*, p. 248 and f.n.

2. Fagalde, 'Bataille de Dunkerque', II, p. 179, says that on the 24th, the line Cassel-Watten was not disturbed, but on that day a German car near Watten bridge was hit by an A.-T. gun. A patrol found in it a dead officer whose papers contained an order to XIX and XLI Panzer Korps to attack Dunkirk on the 23rd on the line Gravelines-St Omer.

3. Fagalde, *Bataille de Dunkerque*, II, pp. 210ff.

4. La Laurencie, *Les Operations du IIIe corps d'armée, 1939–40*, p. 79 and f.n.

5. Aymes, *Gembloux*, p. 94.

6. The bridges at Don, railway and road, had not been occupied by the enemy. They were in fact guarded by the 92nd Reconnaissance Group of the 2nd North African (Commandant Mozat), who remained here undisturbed until 6 a.m. on the 28th, although they could see enemy armoured cars in the distance. They then left the bridge and marched to

Sequedin. It is presumed that the 2nd North African had thought it more probable, from the attacks of Strauss's II Korps, that the nearer bridges had already fallen—Ibid., p. 99.

7. Koeltz's evidence, *C/E (T)*, IX, pp. 2801ff. Ellis, *The War in France and Flanders, 1939–40*, pp. 197–9. The warning message from the British Mission at Belgian headquarters went astray. The Belgian emissary reached the Germans at 7.30 and was given the answer: unconditional surrender.

8. Gort, *Despatch*, p. 5927.

9. The Gort-Blanchard conversation is from a record made by General Pownall for Churchill, *The Second World War*, III, Ch. 4. Also Gort, *Despatch*, p. 5927.

10. Lyet, *La Bataille de France, mai–juin*, 1940, p. 111, f.n. 67.

11. Ibid., p. 111, f.n. 67.

12. Galtier, *Le 14e Zouaves . . . de 1939–40*, p. 140.

13. Von Bock, on 31 May, claims that to date, in and round Lille, 20,000 prisoners had been made, chiefly French, with, later, four generals and another 6,000—Jacobsen, *Dokumente zur Westfeldzug*, 1940, p. 102.

14. La Laurencie, *Les Opérations du IIIe corps d'armée, 1939–40*, pp. 83ff.

15. Ellis, *The War in France and Flanders, 1939–40*, pp. 210 and 215.

16. The question of evacuation of French and British *pari passu* was proposed by Churchill this afternoon, at a meeting which began at 2 p.m. in the rue St Dominique. His indication that the British troops should form the rearguard—'as so few French have got out so far, I will not accept further sacrifices'—was in the end reduced to 'the British troops will remain as long as possible'—Spears, *Assignment to Catastrophe*, I, pp. 308–9.

17. This admirably simple and moving account of the conclusion of the evacuation was written by Commander H. R. Troup, who had been directing the evacuation. It is printed in Ellis, *The War in France and Flanders, 1939–40*, p. 245.

18. Mordal, *La Bataille de Dunkerque*, p. 325.

19. Jacobsen, *Dokumente zur Westfeldzug, 1940*, p. 113 (June 4).

20. The account given in the *British Official History*, pp. 239–40, omits the conversation between the French (Abrial, Leclerc, Altmayer and Fagalde) and the British (Alexander, his G.S.O.1, another general, and Captain Tennant, R.N., the Senior Naval Officer) in Bastion 32 in the afternoon of the 31st, an episode of some bitterness, ending when Abrial said: 'I insist on drawing your attention to the fact that the last British troops will only be able to embark because the French troops continue to fight'—Mordal, *La Bataille de Dunkerque*, pp. 96–9. As Mordal says, Gort and Alexander were more realistic than the French, 'who possibly nursed too many illusions'.

The British official account also omits Churchill's statement to the Supreme Command that the British would provide three divisions for the rearguard.

Chapter Twenty: Failure on the Somme

1. Perré, 'De la propagande à l'histoire', in *Écrits de Paris*, 1954.

2. Linklater (*Highland Division*, p. 31) says that the 2nd Seaforth occupied Bienfay and Moyenneville in the early morning of 31 May.

3. De Gaulle, *L'Appel*, p. 38.

4. Galimand, *Vive Pétain, Vive de Gaulle*, p. 17. Galimand continues: 'I regretted his departure. To this man, whom I met daily, I owe my first "mentions" and a number of snubs. He was haughty, sometimes violent, not a little of an actor. . . . He had courage. I saw him at Limecourt walk up to exposed forward positions, drawing along behind him one or two *École de Guerre* officers who did not seem to relish such audacity and who, modern Saint Élois, commended prudence. . . . He did not flinch from danger and his command-post as often as not was within the danger-line. He had great physical endurance and sometimes he himself moved from place to place in order to superintend the execution of his orders. At these times he would adopt the accents of a sergeant-major. But because, with all his disdain, this commander was there in the flesh for officers and men, he won their esteem without gaining their sympathy.'

5. Perré, *loc. cit.*

Chapter Twenty-one: 'Fall Rot'; to the Oise

1. Ellis, *The War in France and Flanders, 1939–40*, p. 271.

2. There is no doubt of the confusion that reigned at various headquarters, and none more chaotic than at the highest. About midnight on 5/6 June, X Corps (Grandsard) was told by Tenth Army that Army Group Three was urging close liaison between 4th Colonial and 7th North African in order to combine an operation which 7th North African had been ordered to carry out. 4th Colonial at length replied that 7th North African reported they had been given no operation to carry out and that the situation was normal—Grandsard, *Le 10e Corps d'armée . . . 1939–40*, p. 217.

3. Ibid., p. 241.

4. Ibid., pp. 251–2, and P. Vasselle, *La Bataille au sud d'Amiens*.

5. Marchand, *Un Régiment de formation au feu*, pp. 68–75.

Chapter Twenty-two: The End of IX Corps

1. Baudouin, *Neuf Mois au gouvernement*, p. 99.

2. Weygand speaks of the counter-attack ordered by Georges on the 'western flank of the German thrust', which can only mean by IX Corps, to which no additional forces had been or could be sent. At the same time he forbade Evans to counter-attack on the other German flank. Cf. Weygand, *Le Général Frère*, pp. 177–81.

3. 'Instead of taking a radical decision . . . which might have saved something, IX Corps . . . issued no order. Faced by this situation our divisional commander [General Chanoine] came to an agreement with our neighbours to maintain as far as possible the direction we had been given before the break-in at Poix, retiring as little as possible'—Lerecouvreux, *L'Armée Giraud en Hollande, 1939–40*, pp. 230–1 (6 June).

4. Liddell Hart, *Rommel Papers*, pp. 55–6.

5. Gontaut-Biron, *Les Dragons au combat*, p. 143

6. Lerecouvreux, *Huit mois d'attente* etc., pp. 238–9.

7. The senior officer of a lethargic and querulous nature caustically described by Lerecouvreux (ibid., p. 262) can be none other than the

commander of IX Corps. He may have done little, but he let loose 'this profound thought: "A war of this kind ought not to be made with men of sixty."' It appears that the average age of French commanders of higher formations (omitting those of Pétain and Weygand) was over sixty. The British average was about fifty-three, the German fifty-seven.

Chapter Twenty-three: Reynaud Reconstructs. Italy Declares War. Paris Evacuated

1. Baudouin, *Neuf Mois au gouvernement*, pp. 96–101 (29 May) and 103. These entries make it clear that Reynaud was the inventor of the Breton 'Redoubt'. Since de Gaulle was still with the 4th Armoured, he was not the author of the idea.
2. Reynaud, *La France a sauvée*, II, p. 185.
3. 'He's vain, ungrateful and embittered,' said Pétain to Baudouin on 7 June (*Neuf Mois au gouvernement*, p. 130).
4. Ibid., p. 132.
5. Serrigny, *Trente Ans avec Pétain*, pp. 173–4. This from the Serrigny papers is dated 11 June, reporting it as happening on 10 June. This date is impossible, since on 10 June Pétain was either at or on his way to the Loire. Nor could it have taken place on the 9th, since Pétain had already spoken about the armistice at the morning conference of the war committee and at the evening session, he was somnolent. (Lebrun, *C/E (T)*, IV, p. 731.) The evening of the 8th appears to be the only possible date.
6. Vidalenc, *L'Exode de mai–juin, 1940*, p. 253.
7. Baudouin, *Neuf Mois au gouvernement*, p. 135.
8. Vidalenc, *L'Exode de mai–juin, 1940*, p. 263.

Chapter Twenty-four: General Prételat and Army Group Two

1. C. Jamet, *Carnets de déroute*, quoted by Vidalenc, *L'Exode de mai–juin, 1940*, p. 129.
2. Prételat, *Destin tragique de la Ligne Maginot*, pp. 165–8.

Chapter Twenty-five: Army Groups Four and Two

1. Villate, *Le Lion de Flandres à la guerre*, p. 174.
2. Ibid., pp. 174–90.
3. Requin, *Combats pour l'honneur, 1939–40*, pp. 97–8.
4. The French bomber history (*C/E (T)*, II, p. 350) says: 'Columns of lorries between Rethel and Neufchâteau [i.e. Neuchâtel] Groupement 6.13 Lioré 45. Because of the low ceiling, 400 metres, ten bombers and the escort fighter about-turned.'
5. Ruby, *Sedan, terre d'épreuve*, p. 236.

Chapter Twenty-six: Army Group Two Isolated

1. Cooper and Freeman, *The Road to Bordeaux*, p. 125.
2. Quoted by Vidalenc, *L'Exode de mai–juin, 1940*, p. 228. The place is Moutier-en-Der.
3. Requin, *Combats pour l'honneur, 1939–40*, p. 142.
4. General Frére quoted by Weygand, *Le Général Frère*, pp. 191–2.

Chapter Twenty-seven: Across the Loire

1. André Chamson, *Le Dernier Village*, pp. 109–11. The division was the 28th Alpine.

2. Spears, *Assignment*, II, pp. 41–3.

3. But neither Pétain nor de Gaulle (*Au Cœur de la mêlée*, p. 741, f.n. 1).

4. Cf. Astier de la Vigerie, *Les Dieux et les hommes*, p. 41. Churchill liked Georges and loathed Weygand, because the latter pressed him to send twenty-five squadrons when he already intended to negotiate the armistice. 'It was Georges who told me the truth. I shall never forget him. If I had given them, I should no doubt have lost the battle and the war.'

Chapter Twenty-eight: Alsace-Lorraine

1. Von Mellenthin, *Panzer Battles, 1939–45*, p. 22, says that the line at Puttelange was easily breached. He appears to think it was Maginot, which it was not, and ignores the fact that it had been partly evacuated by the garrison.

Chapter Twenty-nine: From Seine to Loire

1. Bersaucourt, *Sous la Croix de Lorraine*, pp. 130–3. See also La Laurencie, *Les Opérations du IIIᵉ corps d'armée, 1939–40*, pp. 174–5. There was a superfluity of unarmed soldiers. These were formed into *régiments de marche* which moved on what transport they could pick up, otherwise on foot, and rearmed themselves with discarded weapons.

2. Moussinac, *Le Radeau de la Méduse*, quoted by Vidalenc, *L'Exode de mai–juin, 1940*, p. 287. Pillard, *La bataille de Gien*.

Chapter Thirty: Armistice

1. Freeman and Cooper, *The Road to Bordeaux*, pp. 291–2. The place is Bourges. This extract is quoted by permission of the Cresset Press.

Chapter Thirty-one: The Last of the Maginot. The Italian Farce

1. Missenard, *Combats et retraite en Lorraine*, p. 103.

2. Jouffrault, *Les Spahis au feu*, pp. 159 ff.

3. Jacobsen, *Fall Gelb. Der Kampf um das Deutschen Operations Plan*, p. 240.

Epilogue

1. Girardet, *La France militaire*, p. 318.

2. Carrias, *La Pensée militaire française*, pp. 317–18.

3. Beaufre, *Le Drame de 1940*, p. 67.

4. Bourret, *Tragédie de l'armée française*, p. 130.

Appendix F

1. Liddell Hart, *History of the Royal Tank Corps*, I, says that the air force showed no interest in General Hobart's attempt to procure air-armour co-operation in the thirties.

2. *En ligne* means ready and equipped to take off from an air-field, but it does not mean a 'modern' plane, that is, one built within at least the last two years. The figure is reasonable. On 1 February the Air Ministry

report gave 614 fighters *en ligne*, of which 523 were modern. But of 179 bombers only 37 were modern.

3. Accart, *On s'est battu dans le ciel*.

4. *C/E (T)*, II, pp. 337, 343, 346–51 and *C/E (R)*, II, pp. 312–13.

5. Paquier, *L'Aviation de chasse*, p. 91; Accart, *On s'est battu dans le ciel*, pp. 111ff.; Ruby, *Sedan, terre d'épreuve avec la IIe Armée, mai–juin, 1940*, pp. 127–8; *C/E (T)*, II, p. 346; Ellis, *The War in France and Flanders, 1939–40*, pp. 55–6.

6. *C/E (T)*, II, pp. 354–5.

7. Ibid., p. 353, quoting General Astier de la Vigerie.

8. Colonel de Lesquen in *R.D.N.*, January 1952, p. 80.

Select Bibliography

SELECT BIBLIOGRAPHY

(Unless otherwise stated, the place of publication for French books is Paris, for English, London.)

Accart, Capt., *On s'est battu dans le ciel*. Alger, Arthaud, 1942.

Adrien, P., *15ᵉ Batterie*. Baudinière, 1944.

Albert-Sorel, J., *Le Chemin de croix*. Julliard, 1943.

Altmayer, Gen. Robert, *La Xᵉ Armée sur la Basse-Somme, en Normandie et vers 'le réduit breton'*. Édns Défense de la France. s.d. (1946).

Anon., *6ᵉ Régiment de Cuirassiers. Journal de marche, 1940*. Bergerac: Imp. générale du sud-ouest, 1950.

Anon., *Histoire du 56ᵉ régiment d'infanterie . . . 1939–40*. Mâcon: Anc. Imp. X. Perroux et fils, 1947.

Anon., *60ᵉ Régiment d'infanterie, Historique 1939–40*. (Roneo TS).

Anon., *Historique du 152ᵉ R.I., premier régiment de France*.

Anon., *La Manœuvre pour la bataille: les transports pendant la guerre, 1939–40*. Lavauzelle, 1941.

Aris, G., *The Fifth British Division, 1939–45*, p.p., 1959.

Arlabosse, Gen., *La Division de fer (11ᵉ)*. Lavauzelle, 1946.

Astier de la Vigerie, Gen. F. R. d', *Le Ciel n'était pas vide*. Julliard, 1952.

Astier de la Vigerie, Emmanuel d', *Les Dieux et les hommes*. Julliard, 1952.

Avantaggiato Puppo, Franca, *Gli armistizi francese del 1940*. Milan, Giuffre, 1963.

Aymes, Gen. H. M. J., *Gembloux, succès français*. Berger-Levrault, 1948.

Bardel, Lt. René, *Quelques-uns des chars*. Grenoble, Arthaud, 1945.

Bardies, Col. de, *La Campagne 39–40*. Arthème Fayard, 1947.

Baudouin, *Neuf Mois au gouvernement*. Table Ronde, 1948.

Bauer, Maj. Eddy, *La Guerre des blindés*. Lausanne, Payot, 1947. (Also second edition, 2 vols., 1962.)

Beaufre, Gen. André, *Le Drame de 1940*. Plon, 1965. (*1940: The Fall of France*. Tr. Desmond Flower. Cassell, 1967.)

Beddington, Maj.-Gen. W. R., *A History of the Queen's Bays*. Winchester, Warren, 1954.

Béguier, Lt.-Col., *Les Étapes d'un régiment breton; le 71 R.I. et R.I.A.* Berger-Levrault, 1953.

Benoist-Méchin, J., *Soixante Jours qui ébranlèrent l'Occident, 10 mai–10 juillet 1940*. 3 vols. Albin Michel, 1956.

Bersaucourt, E. S. de, *Sous la Croix de Lorraine en 39–40: le 2ᵉ D.L.M.* p.p. 1949.

Bidou, Henri, *La Bataille de la France*. Genève, Milieu du Monde, 1941.

Bonnet, Georges, *Le Quai d'Orsay sous trois républiques*, Fayard, 1961.

Bourret, Gen. Victor, *La Tragédie de l'armée française*. Table Ronde, 1947.

Bryant, Sir Arthur, (Ed.), *The Turn of the Tide*. (The Alanbrooke War Diaries I). Collins, 1957.

Buffières, Comte P. de, *Les Allemands en Dauphiné, 19–25 juin, 1940*. Romans-sur-l'Isère, Domergue, 1942.

Busser, Jean-Martin, *Juin, 1940*. Colmar, Imp. des 'Dernières-Nouvelles du Haut-Rhin', 1947.

Carrias, E., *La Pensée militaire française*. P.U.F. 1960.

Carron, Lucien, *Fantassins sur l'Aisne, mai–juin, 1940*. Grenoble, Arthaud, 1943.

Chamson, André, *Le Dernier Village*. Mercure de France, 1946.

Charles-Roux, F., *Cinq Mois tragiques aux Affaires Étrangères*. Plon, 1947.

Chautemps, Camille, *Cahiers secrets de l'Armistice, 1939–40*. Plon, 1963.

Clark, Douglas, *Three Days to Catastrophe*. Hammond, 1966.

Coquet, James de, *Le Procès de Riom*. Fayard, 1945.

Coulondre, Robert, *De Staline à Hitler, Souvenirs . . . 1936–39*. Hachette, 1950.

Courage, Maj. G., *History of the 15th/19th King's Royal Hussars*. Aldershot, Gale & Polden, 1949.

Czarnomski, F. B., *They Fight for Poland*. Allen & Unwin, 1941.

Dauvergne, Robert, *La Campagne de 1939–40: quelques témoignages français*. Albin Michel, 1947.

Debeney, Gen. M. E., *La Guerre et les hommes*. Plon, 1937.

— *Sur la Sécurité militaire de la France*. Payot, 1930.

Delater, G., *Avec le 3ᵉ D.L.M. et le Corps de Cavalerie*. Grenoble, Arthaud, 1946.

Devevey, Col., *Historique du 31ᵉ R.I., 1939–40*. Lavauzelle, 1947.

Doumenc, Gen. A., *Dunkerque et la campagne de Flandre*. Grenoble, Arthaud, 1947.

— *Histoire de la neuvième armée, 10–18 mai 1940*. Grenoble, Arthaud, 1945.

Ellis, Maj. L. F., *The War in France and Flanders, 1939–40*. H.M.S.O., 1954.

— *The Welsh Guards at War*. Aldershot, Gale & Polden, 1946.

Evans, Maj.-Gen. R., *The Fifth Inniskilling Dragoon Guards*. Aldershot, Gale & Polden, 1951.

Fayolle, Marshal M. E., *Cahiers secrets de la Grande Guerre*. Plon, 1964.

Ferry, Abel, *Carnets secrets, 1914–18*. Grasset, 1957.

Flandin, P. E., *Politique française, 1919–40*. Édns. Nouvelles, 1947.

France: Ministère de la Guerre, *Annuaire de l'Armée française, 1920–1*.

— *État-major de l'Armée. Instruction provisoire du 6 Octobre, 1921, sur l'emploi tactique des grandes unités*. Lavauzelle, 1924.

— *Annexe. Instruction provisoire sur le service en campagne*. 2 vols.

— *Instruction sur l'emploi tactique des grandes unités 12 août, 1936*. Lavauzelle, 1940.

— *Listes d'ancienneté des officiers de l'armée active*. Imp. nationale, 1935.

— *Unités combattantes des campagnes, 1939–45*. Lavauzelle, 1955.

France: Ministère des Affaires Étrangères, Assemblée, Nationale, *Documents diplomatiques français, 1932–39*. 2ᵉᵐᵉ Série. Vol. I. Imp. Nationale, 1962.

— *Rapport fait par la Commission d'enquête sur les Événements survenus en France de 1933 à 1945* (C/E). *Rapport et documents*, Vols. I–II (R.) *Témoignages*, Vols. I–IX (T). Presses universitaires de France, 1947–50.

Franklyn, Maj.-Gen. Sir H. E., *The Story of One Green Howard in the Dunkirk Campaign*, p.p. 1966.

Galimand, Lucien, *Vive Pétain, Vive de Gaulle*. Édns la Couronne, 1948.

Galtier, Col. G., *Le 14ᵉ Zouaves . . . de 1939–40*. Berger-Levrault, 1949.

Gamelin, Gen. M., *Servir*. 3 vols. Plon, 1946–7.

Gaudy, G., *Combats sans gloire*. Lyon, Lardanchet, 1941.

Gaulle, Gen. C. de, *Le Fil de l'épée*. Berger-Levrault, 1932. (*The Edge of the Sword*. Tr. Gerard Hopkins. Faber and Faber, 1960.)

— *La France et son armée*. Plon, 1938. (*France and the Army*. Tr. F. L. Dash. Hutchinson, 1945.)

— *Mémoires de guerre*. Vol. I., *L'Appel*. Plon, 1954. (*Call to Honour 1940–1942*. Tr. Jonathan Griffin. Collins, 1955.)

— *Vers l'Armée de métier*. Berger-Levrault, 1934. (*The Army of the Future*. Hutchinson, 1940.)

Gontaut-Biron, Comte C. A. de, *Les Dragons au combat. Journal de marche des 2ème Dragons*. Imp. H. Maillet, 1954.

Gort, Lord, *Despatch*. H.M.S.O. Oct. 1941.

Goutard, Gen. A., *1940. La Guerre des occasions perdues*. Hachette, 1956.

Grandsard, Gen. C., *Le 10ᵉ Corps d'armée . . . 1939–40*. Berger-Levrault, 1949.

Guderian, Gen. H., *Panzer Leader*. Tr. C. Fitz Gibbon. Michael Joseph, 1952.

Hytier, Adrienne D., *Two Years of French Foreign Policy*. 1958.

Ironside, F.-M. Lord, *The Ironside Diaries, 1937–40*. Constable, 1962.

Jacobsen, Hans-Adolf, *Fall Gelb. Der Kampf um der Deutschen Operations Plan*. Wiesbaden. Franz Steiner Verlag, 1957.

— *Dokumente zum Westfeldzug, 1940*. Göttingen. Munsterschmidt-Verlag, 1960.

— *Dokumente zur Vorgeschichte des Westfeldzuges, 1939–40*. Göttingen. Munsterschmidt-Verlag, 1956.

— *Dunkirchen*. Neckargemund, Vowinckel, 1958.

Jacomet, J. R., *L'Armement de la France, 1936–39*. Éds. La Jeunesse, 1945.

Jordan, W. M., *Great Britain, France and the German Problem 1918–1939*. O.U.P. 1943.

Jouffrault, Gen. P., *Les Spahis au feu; la 1ère Brigade de Spahis, 1939–40*. Lavauzelle, 1949.

Kennedy, Maj.-Gen. Sir J., *The Business of War*. Hutchinson, 1947.

Kohli, Charles, *Débâcle sur le Doubs, 1940*. Neuchâtel, Delachaux, 1950.

Kosak, G., *Belgique et France*. Grenoble, Arthaud, 1946.

Kuntz, François, *L'Officier français dans la nation*. Lavauzelle, 1960.

Laffargue, Gen. André, *Le Général Dentz*. Les Îles D'Or. s.d.

La Gorce, P. M. de, *La République et son Armée*. Fayard, 1963.

La Laurencie, Gen. F. de, *Les Opérations du IIIᵉ corps d'armée, 1939–40*. Lavauzelle, 1948.

Langeron, Roger, *Paris, juin, 1940*. Flammarion, 1946.

Lerecouvreux, Marcel, *L'Armée Giraud en Hollande, 1939–40*. Nouvelles Édns Latines s.d. (1951).

— *Huit Mois d'attente, un mois de guerre*. Lavauzelle, 1946.

Lespès, H., *Corps à corps avec les blindés*. Plon, 1944.

Liddell Hart, Sir B. H., *The Other Side of the Hill*. Third edition. Cassell, 1951.

Liddell Hart, Sir B. H., *The Rommel Papers*. Collins, 1953.
— *The Tanks*. Vol. II, *1939–45*. Cassell, 1959.
Liss, U., *Westfront, 1939/40*. Neckargemund, Vowinckel, 1959.
Loustaunau-Lacau, G., *Mémoires d'un français rebelle, 1914–48*. Laffont, 1948.
Lucas et Hervé, Lts., *41ᵉ R.I. Journal des opérations 1939–40*. Édns de Montsouris, s.d.
Lyet, Cdt. Pierre, *La Bataille de France, mai–juin, 1940*. Payot, 1947.
Manstein, F.-M. E. von, *Lost Victories*. Tr. A. G. Powell. Methuen, 1958.
Marchand, Col. E., *Un Régiment de formation au feu; le 109 R.I. en 1939–40*. Berger-Levrault.
Martel, Lt.-Gen. Sir G., *An Outspoken Soldier*. Sifton Praed, 1949.
— *Our Armoured Forces*. Faber, 1945.
Mazaud, Ltd.-Col., *Les Diables Bleus du 27ᵉ B.C.A. dans la campagne . . . 1939–40*. Annecy, Hérisson Frères, s.d. (1941).
Maze, P., et Génébrier, R., *Les Grandes Journées du procès de Riom*. Jeune Parque, 1945.
Mellenthin, Maj.-Gen. F. W. von, *Panzer Battles, 1939–45*. Tr. T. H. Betzler. Cassell, 1953.
Meltzer, Walther, *Albert-Kanal und Eben-Emael, Heidelberg*. Vowinckel, 1957.
Menu, Gen. C. L., *Lumière sur les ruines*. Plon, 1953.
Michel, H., *Jean Moulin*. Hachette, 1964.
Michiels, Lt.-Gen. O., *18 Jours de guerre en Belgique*. Berger-Levrault, 1947.
Minart, Col. J., *P. C. Vincennes; Secteur 4*. 2 vols. Berger-Levrault, 1945.
Missenard, André, *Combats et retraite en Lorraine, 1939–40*. Plon, 1946.
Montagne, Gen. A., *La Bataille pour Nice et la Provence*. Nice, Édns. des Arceaux, 1952.
Mordal, Jacques, *La Bataille de Dunkerque*. Self, 1948.
— *La Campagne de Norvège*. Self, 1949.
Noel, Léon, *L'agression contre la Pologne*, Flammarion, 1946.
Overstraeten, Gen. R. van, *Albert I-Leopold III*. Bruges.
— *Au Service de la Belgique*. Vol. I, *Dans l'Étau*. Plon, 1960.
Paillart, Pierre, *Les Quarante Jours du 2ᵉ G.R.C.A. en Hollande, en Belgique, en France, 10 mai–18 juin 1940*. Abbeville, Imp. F. Paillart, 1940.
Paquier, Lt.-Col. Pierre, *L'Aviation de bombardement française en 1939–40*. Berger-Levrault, 1940.
— *L'Aviation de renseignement française en 1939–40*. Berger-Levrault, 1947.
— *Combats de chasse*. Colbert, 1946.
— *Le Groupe de bombardement 11/2*. Berger-Levrault, 1947.
Perré, Jean-Paul, *Les Chars de combat; essai de classification positive*. Berger-Levrault, 1937.
'Pertinax' (André Guéraud), *The Gravediggers of France*. New York, Doubleday, 1944.
Petgès, J. P., *Bataille d'Amiens, 1940*. New York, Maison de France, 1943.

Pillard, Albert, *La Bataille de Gien, 15–19 juin 1940*. Gien, Imp. Jeanne d'Arc, 1949.

Prételat, Gen. Gaston, *Le Destin tragique de la ligne Maginot*. Berger-Levrault, 1950.

Prioux, Gen. R. J. A., *Souvenirs de guerre, 1939–43*. Flammarion, 1947.

Rebattet, Lucien, *Les Décombres*. Denoël, 1942.

Requin, Gen. E., *Combats pour l'honneur, 1939–40*. Lavauzelle, 1946.

— *D'une heure à l'autre, 1919–39*. Lavauzelle, 1949.

Richecourt, *La Guerre de cent heures*. Flammarion, 1944.

Reynaud, Paul, *Au Coeur de la mêlée, 1930–45*. Flammarion, 1951. (*In the Thick of the Fight*. Tr. James D. Lambert. Cassell, 1955.)

— *La France a sauvé l'Europe*. 2 vols. Flammarion, 1947.

— *Mémoires*. 2 vols. Flammarion, 1960, 1963.

Richards, Denis, *The Royal Air Force, 1939–45*. Vol. I. H.M.S.O., 1953.

Rodolphe, Lt.-Col. R., *Combats dans la ligne Maginot*. Pourot, 1949.

Rossi, A., *Les Communistes français pendant la drôle de guerre*. Les Îles d'Or, 1951.

Roton, Gen. G., *Années cruciales, 1933–40*. Lavauzelle, 1947.

Rowe, V., *The Great Wall of France*. Putnam, 1959.

Roy, Jules, *Le Métier d'armes; récit*. Gallimard, 1948.

Ruby, Gen. Edmond, *Sedan, terre d'épreuve*. Flammarion, 1948.

Salesse, *L'Aviation de chasse française en 1939–40*. Berger-Levrault, 1948.

Serrigny, Gen. B., *Trente Ans avec Pétain*. Plon, 1959.

Slessor, Air Vice-Marshal J. C., *The Central Blue*. Cassell, 1956.

Soubiran, André, *J'étais médecin avec les chars*. S.E.G.E.P., 1950.

Spears, Maj.-Gen. Sir Edward, *Assignment to Catastrophe*. 2 vols. Heinemann, 1954.

Stewart, Capt. P. F., *History of the XIIth Royal Lancers*. Oxford, O.U.P., 1950.

Tasse, Lt.-Col., *La Randonnée du 9e Zouaves*. Berger-Levrault, 1943.

Taylor, Telford, *The March of Conquest*. Hulton, 1959.

Templewood, Viscount, *Nine Troubled Years*. Collins, 1954.

Teske, Herman, *Bewegungskrieg*. Heidelberg, Vowinckel, 1955.

Thompson, Lt.-Col. P. W., *Modern Battle*. Washington, D.C. *Infantry Journal*, 1942.

Tisseyre, Pierre, *55 Heures de guerre*. Flammarion, 1943.

Tournoux, J.-R., *Pétain et de Gaulle*. Plon, 1964.

Truchet, A., *L'Armistice de 1940 et l'Afrique du Nord*. P.U.F., 1955.

Vasselle, P., *La Bataille au sud d'Amiens, 20 mai–8 juin 1940*. Abbeville, F. Paillart, 1948.

Vibraye, Comte Tony de, *Avec mon groupe de reconnaissance, août 1939–août 1940*. Les Ordres de la Chevalerie, 1943.

Vidalenc, Jean, *L'Exode de mai–juin, 1940*. P.U.F. 1957.

Villate, Col. R., *Le Lion de Flandres à la guerre. La 2e D.I. pendant 1939–40*. Ch.-Lavauzelle, 1946.

Webster, Sir Charles, and Frankland, Noble, *The Strategic Air Offensive against Germany, 1939–45*. Vol. I. H.M.S.O.

Weygand, Cdt. J., *The Rôle of General Weygand. Conversations with His Son*. Tr. J. McEwen. Eyre & Spottiswoode, 1948.

Weygand, Gen. Maxime, *En lisant les Mémoires du Général de Gaulle.* Flammarion, 1955.
— *Le Général Frère.* Flammarion, 1949.
— *Mémoires.* 3 vols. Flammarion, 1953–57.
Zay, Jean, *Souvenirs et solitude.* Julliard, 1945.
Zimmermann, Herman, *Der Griff ins Ungewisse* (*XVI Pz. A.K.*). Neckargemund, Vowinckel, 1964.

Colonial Divisions. Histories of these divisions are to be found in the *Revue des Troupes colonials,* which changed its name to *Tropiques,* between June 1946 and March 1948.

ARTICLES

R.D.M. = *Revue des Deux Mondes*
R.D.N. = *Revue de la Défense nationale*
R.H.A = *Revue historique de l'Armée*
C/E: see entry in Bibliography under 'France: Ministère des Affaires Etrangères'.
Albert-Sorel, J., 'Carnet d'un officier de liaison'. *R.D.M.,* 1–15 juin 1942.
Albord, Gen. Tony, 'L'Ere crépusculaire de la stratégie'. *R.D.N.,* Octobre 1965.
— Letter to C/E (T), V, p. 1248.
Annales de l'Assemblée nationale. Débats, Vol. 22 (23–31 décembre 1948). *Chambre des Députés. Comités secrets des 9 février, 19 mars et 19 avril 1940.* Paris, Imp. des Journaux officiels, 1949.
Beaufre, Gen. André, 'Liddell Hart and the French Army, 1919–30' in Howard, M., *The Theory and Practice of War,* pp. 129–44. Cassell, 1965.
Beauman, Brig. A. B., 'France: May–June 1940'. *Army Quarterly,* 1943–44.
Bidou, Henri, 'Les Combats et la fin de la 8ème Armée'. *R.D.M.,* 1941, pp. 145ff.
Blot, Camille, 'Les Opérations aériennes britanniques dans la Campagne de France, mai–juin 1940'. *Forces Aériennes Françaises,* No. 99, pp. 53ff.
Bonotaux, 'Avec le 3e D.I.M. à Stonne'. *R.H.A.,* 1950, II, pp. 47ff.
Bruneau, Gen., Evidence 1st Armoured Division. *C/E* (*T*), V, pp. 1153ff.
Cairns, John C., 'Great Britain and the Fall of France'. *Journal of Modern History,* XXVII, December 1955.
Chabanier, Col. J., 'Lorraine, 1939–40'. *R.H.A.,* 1962, III, pp. 131–6.
Cossé-Brissac, Col. de, 'L'Armée allemande dans la campagne de France, 1940'. *Revue d'histoire de la 2e guerre mondiale,* No. 53, janvier, 1964.
Debeney, Gen. M. E., 'La Ligne Maginot'. *R.D.M.,* 15 septembre 1934.
— 'Encore l'Armée de métier'. *R.D.M.,* 15 juillet 1935.
Deischner, F., 'Grandeurs, servitudes et misères militaires'. *R.D.M.,* 1 juin 1954.
Drouot, Henri, 'La Fin de la 8e Région'. *Annales de Bourgogne,* 1950, pp. 151–7 and 236–41.
Evans, Maj.-Gen. R., 'The 1st Armoured Division in France'. *Army Quarterly,* 1942–43.

Fagalde, Gen. M. D. A., 'Bataille de Dunkerque'. *Revue militaire suisse,* mars–juillet et septembre–novembre 1952.

— 'Odyssée d'une division française'. *Revue militaire suisse,* mars et mai 1954.

Fox, Col., and Ornano, Cdt. P. D., 'La percée des Ardennes'. *Revue d'histoire de la 2ᵉ guerre mondiale,* 1953, pp. 77–118.

Gastey, Gen., 'Épopée d'une division de cavalerie', *R.H.A.,* 1945, II 262 ff.

Golaz, A., 'Les chars français à Voncq'. *R.H.A.,* 1962, I, pp. 139–50.

Hauteclerc, Cdt. G., 'Chars belges en 1940'. *L'Armée, la Nation,* avril 1957.

— 'Rommel contre Corap; la bataille de la Meuse, 12–15 mai, 1940'. *Revue générale belge,* novembre 1962.

Henniker, Lt.-Col. M. C. A., 'Prelude to Battle'. *Blackwood's Magazine,* September 1947.

Juin, Maréchal, A. P., 'Le Chef de guerre'. *R.D.M.,* 1 mars 1958.

Le Goaster, Lt.-Col. J., 'L'Action des forces aériennes'. *Revue d'histoire de la 2ᵉ guerre mondiale,* juin 1953, pp. 135–49.

Le Goyet, Lt.-Col., 'Contre-attaques manquées, Sedan, 13–15 mai 1940'. *R.H.A.,* 1962, IV, pp. 110–30.

— 'La Percée de Sedan, 10–15 mai 1940'. *Revue d'histoire de la 2ᵉ guerre mondiale,* juillet 1965, pp. 25–52.

— 'Le XI Corps à la bataille de la Meuse, 10–15 mai 1940'. *R.H.A.,* 1962, I, pp. 125–38; II, pp. 83–96.

Lesquen, Col. M. de, 'L'Armée de l'air française en 1940'. *R.D.N.,* 1952, pp. 74ff.

Lugand, Lt.-Col., 'Les Forces en présence au 10 mai 1940'. *Revue d'histoire de la 2ᵉ guerre mondiale,* juin 1953, pp. 5–48.

Lyet, Lt.-Col. P., 'A propos de Sedan, 1940'. *R.H.A.,* 1962, IV, pp. 89–109.

— 'La Couverture et la prise de position de la 1ère armée française sur la position Dyle par le corps de cavalerie Prioux'. *L'Armée, la Nation,* mai 1955, pp. 28–55.

— 'Documents militaires sur l'Armistice, juin 1940'. *R.H.A.,* 1947, I, pp. 45ff.

Menneer, Maj. K. C., 'Coming Events ? Another View'. *Army Quarterly,* 1942–3.

Mer, Gen., 'La Bataille des Alpes en 1940'. *R.H.A.,* 1946, I; 1947, III; 1948, IV.

Milward, A. S., 'The End of the Blitzkrieg'. *Economic History Review,* April 1964, pp. 791ff.

Molinié, Gen. E., 'La 25ᵉ Division d'infanterie motorisée de Breda à Lille et à Dunkerque'. *R.D.N.,* août–septembre and octobre 1948.

Mordal, J., 'La Garantie polonaise et l'offensive en Sarre de septembre 1939'. *R.D.N.,* avril 1957, pp. 602–22.

Ornano, Cdt. P. d', 'Après la Percée de Sedan; de la Bar à la Vence, 14–15 mai 1940'. *R.H.A.,* 1950, I, pp. 35–45.

— 'XIXᵉ Corps d'armée allemande, 10–13 mai 1940'. *R.H.A.,* 1955, III.

Pakenham-Walsh, Maj.-Gen. R. P., 'The "Pill-Box Row" etc.'. *Royal Engineers Journal,* 1960, pp. 496ff.

Perré, Gen. Jean, 'De la Propagande à l'histoire : quinze jours d'opérations avec de Gaulle en 1940'. *Écrits de Paris*, décembre 1953–janvier 1954.

Pétain, Maréchal P., 'La Sécurité française pendant les années creuses'. *R.D.M.*, 1 mars 1935.

Petiet, Gen. R. M. E., 'La Bataille de la Somme, Journées de 5 et 6 juin, 1940'. *R.D.M.*, 1–15 mars 1943.

— 'La Bataille de la Seine (9, 10, 11 juin 1940)'. *R.D.M.*, 1–15 juin 1943.

— 'Sur le front de Luxembourg (10–14 mai 1940). *R.D.M.*, 1–15 septembre 1943.

Rogé, Cdt., 'La Campagne de France vue par le General Guderian'. *R.H.A.*, 1947, I, pp. 109–19.

— 'Les Aviations allemande, française et anglaise du 10 mai–25 juin 1940'. *R.D.N.*, février 1951, pp. 162ff.

Rolland, Cdt. de, 'Le 29e G.R.D.I. dans la bataille'. *R.H.A.*, 1947, III and IV.

Rollet, Gen., 'L'Offensive de Sedan; les rapports franco-belges'. *Revue d'histoire de la 2e guerre mondiale*, No. 38, avril 1960.

Roux, Cdt. R., 'Les Dix Mille du secteur fortifié de Faulquemont, juin 1940'. *R.H.A.*, 1953, I. pp. 81–98.

Sereau, Ch. d'esc., 'Avec les Chasseurs et les Artilleurs à Blaregnies'. *R.H.A.*, 1950, II, pp. 51–60.

Tollemache, Brig. E. D. H., 'French Military Training for Defeat'. *Quarterly Review*, October 1941.

Vautrin, Cdt., Report to Reynaud, 19–26 May 1940, in *Au Coeur de la mêlée*, pp. 550ff.

Vial, Cdt. J., 'La Division de Paris au feu (10 D.I.)', *R.H.A.*, 1952, I, pp. 88–100.

— 'Une Semaine décisive sur la Somme, 18–25 mai 1940'. *R.H.A.*, 1949, IV; 1950, I.

Villate, Col. Robert, 'L'Entrée des Français en Belgique'. *Revue d'histoire de la 2e guerre mondiale*, juin 1953, pp. 60–76.

Wanty, Gen. Émile, 'Improvisation de la liaison Belge-Britannique du 10 mai au 18 mai 1940'. *Revue d'histoire de la 2e guerre mondiale*, janvier 1964.

— 'La Bataille de la Lys vue dans un cadre élargi'. *L'Armée, la Nation*, mai 1956, pp. 10–21.

— 'La Défense des Ardennes, 1940'. *Revue d'histoire de la 2e guerre mondiale*, avril 1961.

Weygand, Cdt. J., 'Le 3ème Régiment d'Automitrailleuses, 1939–40'. *R.D.M.*, 15 novembre 1942, p. 148.

Indexes

GENERAL INDEX

(*See also* 'Index of French and German Formations.)

Notes

1. Personal names prefixed with 'De', 'La', 'Von', *etc.* are arranged under their substantive surnames; place names are as printed. Thus: Gaulle, Charles de, *and* Porte du Theil, General J. de la; *but* La Ferté *and* Le Creusot.

2. '*bis*', '*ter*' or '*quat*' after a page reference means that the name or topic is mentioned two, three or four times *in separate paragraphs* on the page indicated; '*p*' (*passim*) means 'here and there' (scattered references); '*q.v.*' means 'which see'; '*n*' means 'footnote'.

A.A.S.F., *see* Advance Air Striking Force

A.F.V.'s (armoured fighting vehicles: *chars* (*q.v.*), *blindés*, *panzers* and 'tanks'): 7, 10, 15, 29–30, 35–38, 44, 60, 199 *n*, 283, 343–4, 345, 347, 348; production of, 35; Inspector-General of, *see* Keller, General M. J. P.

Abbeville fiasco, 230–7

Abrial, Admiral ('Amiral Nord'), 191, 192, 196–7, 203, 212, 213, 218 *bis*, 219, 220, 225 *bis*, 227

Abyssinia, 21–4 *passim*, 26, 50

Adam, General Sir Ronald, 197, 206 *bis*, 207, 218 *bis*

Advance Air Striking Force (British), 70, 179, 238–9, 281

African: Light Infantry, 68; Volunteers, 68

Agents militaires, 11

Air Committee (of Chamber of Deputies), 32 *n*, 36

Air Component (of B.E.F.), 70, 179, 186, 238

Air Ministry, French, 11, 16, 33 *bis*, 334

Air operations, 351–4

Air Staff, French, *see* Denain *and* Vuillemin

Air warfare doctrine in 1939, 70

Aircraft: British, 70–1, 350; French, 71, 350; German, 71, 135, 136, 177, 178, 350

Aircraft production, French, 32–4, 32 *n*

Airfields, deficiency of, 71

Aisne, battle of the (9–12 June), 266–80

Alaurent, General, 226, 228

Albert Canal, 94, 95, 99, 100, 103

Albord, General, *quoted*, 24

Alexander, King of Yugoslavia, 20, 47

Alexander, Major-General Hon. Harold, 225 *bis*, 367

Algerian troops, 7, 8, 11, 66 & *n*, *et passim*

Alliance Démocratique, 86

Allied Supreme War Council, 85, 206

Allied victory (1918), reasons for, 331–2

Alpine divisions and troops, 68, 340, *et passim*

Alsace, 3, 12, 57, 65

Alsace-Lorraine (11–16 June), 293–301

Altmayer, General René (V Corps), 103, 106, 153, 167, 169, 184–6 *p*, 192, 193, 194, 197, 198, 201, 206, 207, 225, 306

Altmayer, General Robert (Tenth Army), 198, 240, 251–2, 257, 303, 306–7

'Amiral Nord', *see* Abrial, Admiral

Angers (city), 319

French Army—*cont.*
332–3; unprepared in 1939, 334; in action, *see* Index of French (and German) Formations
French Army (North-East), composition of, 339–41
French: artillery, 344–5; Cabinet (June 1940), 290, 291; cavalry, 7, 67, 342–3, *et passim*; Communist Party, 22, 291; delegates to peace talks, 313–14, 316–17; fleet, 98, 225, 289, 311, 316; General Staff, 38
French ground forces, composition of, 337–45
French infantry, 339–42
French Intelligence, *see* Deuxième Bureau
French military mission to London, 48–9
French military thinking (1919–39), 18–19, 332–3
French Navy, 47 (*see also* French: fleet)
French Order of Battle, 337–9
French political leaders (1918–32), 333
Frère, General Aubert, 174 *ter*, 188, 189 *bis*, 195, 198, 206, 240, 248, 258, 287, 289, 310, 328
Freydenberg, General H., 262, 277, 284 *bis*
Front populaire, le, see Popular Front
Frontier departments, evacuation and manning of, 57–8, 64–5
Frontier regions, defensive, 18, 23, 25, 26–8, 42, 43, 69
Fugitives, civilian, *see* Refugees
Führerheer, ein (in Germany, after Versailles), 13
Fuller, Major-General J. F. C., 29
Fürst, Colonel, 110, 111

G.Q.G. (Grand-Quartier Général, at Vincennes and Briare), 64, 76, 128, 156, 203, 262, 263, 264, 284, 287, 300, 305, 319, 321–7 *p*, 337
G.Q.G. Action (13 May), 127–9
G.Q.G. Reserve, 108

G.Q.G.N.E. (at La Ferté and Montry), 60, 76, 81, 84, 111 *n*, 127, 129, 150, 174, 175, 182, 189 *bis*, 262, 294, 307, 337
Gamelin, General Maurice-Gustave: 10 *n*, 12–25 *p*, 32, 35, 39–43 *p*, 45–8 *p*, 49, 50–3 *p*, 59–61 *p*, 64, 69, 70, 74–81 *p*, 78 *n*, 84–9 *p*, 94–97 *p*, 127, 142, 159, 165, 170–2, 174, 180–3, 188, 261 *bis*, 330 *bis*, 333; personal details, 20–1, 25, 43, 84 *bis*, 181, 182–3; end of, 180–3; *quoted*, 183
Gap, widening of the, 188–94
Garde Républicaine Mobile, 68, 139, 162, 171, 226, 325
Gaulle, Colonel (*later* General) Charles A. de; xiv, 15, 29, 36, 37 *ter*, 86, 129, 175–8 *p*, 189, 199, 231, 234–7, 239, 256, 258, 261 *bis*, 289 & *n*, 291, 292, 307, 312, 333; on the use of armour, 37; at French War Office, 235, 256, 258; criticism of, 235–7; and Breton redoubt, 291, 292, 307; his broadcast from London (18 June 1940), 317; personal details, 236, 256, 258
Gdynia (city & port), 46
Georges, General Alphonse-Joseph, 20, 39, 43, 47 *bis*, 51, 59, 60, 70, 74–6, 78 & *n*, 80 *bis*, 84 *bis*, 85, 94, 101, 127, 128–9, 142, 143, 150, 165, 175, 177, 181–5 *p*, 195, 203, 207, 209, 219, 261, 265, 287–90 *p*, 293, 294 *bis*, 305, 318, 330; personal details, 47–8; *quoted*, 183
Germain, General G. L., 277, 285
German advance postponed (and plans changed), 79
German Air Force (*Luftwaffe*), 21, 60 *bis*, 80, 83, 173, 240, 256, 258, 274 *n*, 281, 350, 351–4
German Army: in 1928, 11, 38; Skoda 'tanks' of, 44 *n*, 347
German fifth column, 93 *bis*
German ground forces: composition of, 346–7; in action, *see* Index of (French and) German Formations

Succession States (Czechoslovakia, *q.v. and* Poland, *q.v.*), 17
Sudeten Germans, 40, 43
Supreme War Council (in London), 88
Surprise (9 May 1940), 93–4
Sweden, iron-ore for Germany from, 85, 87

'Tanks', *see* A.F.V.'s
Tarbe de Saint-Hardouin, M., 93 *bis*
Tardieu, André, 12, 14, 27
Tardu, Colonel, 201, 217
Tarrit, General R. F. J., 156, 159 *ter*, 163, 201
'Ten Year Rule', 49
Terrier, Colonel, 274
Thierry-d'Argenlieu, General, 162
Thionville (steel centre), flight from, 263, 294
Thomas, Albert, 63
Thorez (French communist), 65, 291
Tirailleurs, 8 *n*, 66 *nn*, *et passim*
Tiso, Father (Slovak), 48
Touchon, General R. A., 147–9 *p*, 151, 173–7 *p*, 195, 240, 251, 270, 282 *bis*, 287
Tours, 320 *bis*
Trabila, General, 157, 159
Traditionalism in industry, 31, 33
Training establishments and A.F.V.'s, 38
Trap, the, 94–5
Trials of French leaders, 330 *bis*
Trolley de Prévaux, General, 276 *n*, 286
Tunisian troops, 7, 8, 11, 66 *& n*, *et passim*

U.S.S.R., *see* Russia
United States of America (*see also* Roosevelt): Senate of, 4 *bis*; Curtis aircraft bought from, 32

Vallet, General, 148
Vauthier, General, 124, 146
Vautran, Commandant, 186
Velpry, General G. M., 357

Vernillat, General H. P., 164, 166, 168, 201, 215, 216, 218
Véron, Colonel, 134, 160, 161, 162
Vers l'armée de métier (de Gaulle), 36, 37 *bis*, 333
Versailles, Treaty of (June 1919): 3, 4 *ter*, 13, 23, 42, 331, 332 *bis*; military clauses of, 4, 13; its limitations, 13
Vervins, 159–60
Victor Emmanuel (King of Italy), 49
Vienne (town), 325
Vigerie, Astier de la, 15
Villelume, Colonel de, 170 *bis*, 289
Vincennes (G.H.Q., *q.v.*), 84 *bis*, 94, 95, 127, 165, 182 *ter*, 219, 251, 337
Voroshilov, Marshal, 52 *bis*
Vosges mountains (unfortified), 59, 300
Vuillemin, General (C.A.S.), 34, 43, 47, 51, 53, 59, 71 *bis*, 72, 181 *bis*, 210, 239, 259, 290, 331

Walcheren, 98
War Committee, French, 255, 257, 258 *bis*
War Ministry, French (Rue St Dominique), 4 *& n*, 5, 12–20 *p*, 25, 27, 32–8 *p*, 40, 43, 47, 63, 93, 334
Warning (9/10 May 1940), 93
Warsaw (Varsova), 14, 45, 46, 48, 50, 60
Weapons, production of, 16
Weichs, General von, 267
Weiler, Paul-Louis, 36
Welvert, General M. J., 244
Werner, Colonel, 109 *bis*, 110 *bis*, 130, 136–7
West African troops, 8, 11, *et passim*
Weygand, General Maxime: xiv, 5, 10 *n*, 12, 14–21 *p*, 34, 35, 36, 43, 46, 47, 67, 68, 84, 172 *&n*, 180–3, 188, 195–9, 200, 203–12 *p*, 218–220, 228–9, 236, 239, 250–9 *p*, 261–5 *p*, 277, 289–94 *p*, 298, 300, 302, 305 *bis*, 306, 311, 312, 317

Weygand, General Maxime—*cont.*
bis, 320, 327, 328, 332, 337;
takes over from Gamelin, 180–3;
consultations and orders, 195–9;
and de Gaulle, 258; on the situation (11 June 1940), 289–90;
'examined', 330; personal details,
180, 182–3
Wietersheim (*or* Wittersheim),
General G. von, 143, 190, 242,
285

Wilson, President Woodrow, 4
Witzleben, General, 295, 300

Ybarnégaray, 290
Young Plan (for reparations), 13
bis
Yugoslavia, 41

Zeeland, Paul van, 27
Zouaves, 8 *n*, 66 *n*, *et passim*

INDEX OF FRENCH AND GERMAN FORMATIONS